P9-DFB-724

Dattalun
8/15/94

ADVANCED INTEREST RATE AND CURRENCY SWAPS

State-of-the-Art Products, Strategies & Risk Management Applications

Ravi E. Dattatreya
Kensuke Hotta

PROBUS PUBLISHING COMPANY
Chicago, Illinois
Cambridge, England

© 1994, Ravi E. Dattatreya and Kensuke Hotta

ALL RIGHTS RESERVED. No part of this publication may be reproduced, stored in a retrieval system, or transmitted, in any form or by any means, electronic, mechanical, photocopying, recording, or otherwise, without the prior written permission of the publisher and the author.

This publication is designed to provide accurate and authoritative information in regard to the subject matter covered. It is sold with the understanding that the author and the publisher are not engaged in rendering legal, accounting, or other professional service.

Authorization to photocopy items for internal or personal use, or the internal or personal use of specific clients, is granted by PROBUS PUBLISHING COMPANY, provided that the U.S. $7.00 per page fee is paid directly to Copyright Clearance Center, 222 Rosewood Drive, Danvers, MA 01923, USA; Phone: 1-508-750-8400. For those organizations that have been granted a photocopy license by CCC, a separate system of payment has been arranged. The fee code for users of the Transactional Reporting Service is 1-55738-444-4/94/$00.00 + $7.00.

ISBN 1-55738-444-4

Printed in the United States of America

BB

1 2 3 4 5 6 7 8 9 0

PG

Probus books are available at quantity discounts when purchased for business, educational, or sales promotional use. For more information, please call the Director, Corporate/Institutional Sales at (800) 998-4644, or write:

Director, Corporate/Institutional Sales
Probus Publishing Company
1925 N. Clybourn Avenue
Chicago. IL 60614
PHONE (800) 998-4644   FAX (312) 868-6250

To my wife, Kimiko

Kensuke Hotta

To my daughter, Mallika Lakshmi

Ravi E. Dattatreya

CONTENTS

PART II Corporate and Investor Viewpoint

CONTRIBUTORS

Mark Abbott, *Head of Corporate Finance,*
Bristol & West Building Society (UK)

DiAnne Calabrisotto, *Assistant Vice President, Williams Financial Markets,*
a division of Jefferies & Company

Satyajit Das, *Treasurer, TNT Group*

Ravi E. Dattatreya, *Senior Vice President,*
Sumitomo Bank Capital Markets, Inc.

Bernardo Frydman, *Director General, Banco Finantia (Lisbon, Portugal)*

Jon Frye, *Vice President, Continental Bank*

Laurie S. Goodman, *Senior Vice President, Paine Webber*

Thomas S. Y. Ho, *President, Global Advanced Technology Corporation*

Ming Jiao Hsia, Ph.D., *Vice President, Williams Financial Markets,*
a division of Jefferies & Company

Marcus Huie, *Vice President, Fixed Income Research Department,*
Goldman, Sachs & Co.

Beth A. Kostick, *Portfolio Manager, Amoco Pension Fund*

Edward P. Krawitt, *Director, Treasury Centre, Lawson Mardon Packaging,*
a division of Alusuisse-Lonza Holding AG

Hasan Latif, *Senior Vice President, Williams Financial Markets,*
a division of Jefferies & Company

Afsaneh Mashayekhi-Beschloss, *Senior Manager, Derivatives and Liability Management Division, Financial Operations Department, World Bank*

Thomas A. McAvity, Jr., *Vice President and Director of Quantitative Research, Lincoln National Investment Management Company*

Scott McDermott, *Vice President, Fixed Income Research Department, Goldman, Sachs & Co.*

Azam Mistry, *Vice President, Capital Markets Marketing, Midland Bank, Hongkong and Shanghai Bank Group*

Arun Muralidhar, *Financial Officer, Derivatives and Liability Management Division, Financial Operations Department, World Bank*

Jacob Navon, *Senior Vice President, The Boston Company*

Bjørn Pettersen, *Assistant Vice President, First National Bank of Chicago*

Raj S. Pundarika, *Debt and Derivatives Marketer, Paribas Capital Markets*

Vijay R. Raghavan, *Senior Managing Director, First National Bank of Chicago*

K. Ravindran, *Vice President, Equity Derivatives, RBC Dominion Securities Adjunct Assistant Professor, University of Waterloo*

Ramine Rouhani, *Senior Vice President, CDC Investment Management Company*

Matthew R. Smith, *Senior Portfolio Manager, Amoco Pension Fund*

Melinda M. Twomey, *Senior Vice President, Williams Financial Markets, a division of Jefferies & Company*

Hans Gisbert Ulmke, *Treasurer, Continental Can Europe*

Bruce M. Usher, *Senior Vice President, Williams Financial Markets, a division of Jefferies & Company*

Christopher J. Williams, *Managing Principal, Williams Financial Markets, a division of Jefferies & Company*

PREFACE

The last dozen or so years have been very satisfying from the point of view of corporate treasurers and investment managers, as far as the availability of risk management tools is concerned. We saw the ripening of the treasury and Eurodollar futures markets. Fixed income options started trading in the early 1980s and have achieved their own level. However, the most exciting area has been that of interest rate and currency swaps.

Paradoxically, the swap market is at once mature and still-developing. Its maturity is evidenced by the ease with which it was able to absorb the fall of some major players (e.g., Drexel) and the size and liquidity that it offers demanding customers. At the same time, new structures and applications in new markets (e.g., investments) are being developed almost every day showing the potential for further enormous growth.

To the liability risk manager and the investor alike, the properties of swaps are of paramount interest: price transparency, ease of execution, availability of large sizes, flexibility of structuring, and, most of all, the ability to manage the risk in new ways not previously obtainable.

In the companion book, *Interest Rate and Currency Swaps* (Probus Publishing, Chicago, 1994), our goal was to introduce this influential market to the reader starting from the basics. The emphasis was on understanding how the swap tool can be applied to various real-life situations. In *Advanced Interest Rate and Currency Swaps,* we take this process one step further, introducing advanced topics.

This book is one in what we hope will be a long series of related book projects. Our goal, in each and every one of these projects, has been (and will continue to be) to provide *insight* into the financial markets and instruments, to take them out of the black box in which they are usually packaged. We strongly feel that we, as users, should not accept any strategy or instrument as a black box.

A ROAD MAP

This book is logically divided into two parts. Part I covers analytical techniques, models, and strategies.

In Chapter 1, Jon Frye describes one way credit risk can be modeled. Credit risk has received increased attention recently not only because of the failure of a few counterparties, the shocks from which, fortunately, have been absorbed with little disruption, but also because of the increased exposure to counterparties due to large positions that have been building up over the years. John suggests a portfolio approach that actually decreases the perceived exposure. In this sense, the proposed approach is aggressive. However, as described in the chapter, we can only be (overly) conservative at (often unnecessary) cost.

In Chapter 2, Satyajit Das describes differential swaps. These swaps include cash flows which are denominated in one currency but determined by interest rates in another currency. Differential swaps provide the user with very interesting risk-reward trade-offs and were a very important development of the early 1990s.

The next two chapters (3 and 4), the first by Bjørn Pettersen and Vijay Raghavan and the second by Scott McDermott and Marcus Huie, address indexed amortization swaps and notes (IAS and IAN, respectively).[1] These swaps (or notes) are amortizing. The amortization rate itself is variable, and is indexed to market parameters, e.g., LIBOR. One of the interesting contributions of the derivative markets has been to create acceptable alternatives to mortgage-backed securities. The major advantage of the indexed notes is that they remove an entire layer of uncertainty, represented by a pre-payment model, that haunts investors in mortgage-backed securities.[2] In contrast, the indexed amortizers need no leap of faith[3] in a prepayment model and can be

---

1. We prefer a slightly different, more descriptive terminology for these: IVAR (Indexed Variable Amortization Rate) swaps and notes.
2. The risk in this uncertainty was realized in a painful way by investors during the recent bond market rally when most, if not all, prepayment models failed to anticipate the unprecedented prepayment rates, requiring major rejiggering of these models. One reason for this failure is that the models take into account only the behavior of the borrower, but not that of the lender. During the rally, the lender behavior changed dramatically as they initiated refinancing activity with zero-cost transactions.
    Those investors and traders who did not patch their prepayment models correctly got whipsawed again in early 1994 when rates rose quickly.
3. Prepayment modeling will always be less than scientific as there are too many factors involved with too much slippage between cause and effect.

analyzed completely in any interest rate scenario with a simple spreadsheet. We believe that the concept of indexed amortization, either in its present form or something newer, has a lot of potential.

Chapter 5, by Ravindran, is on exotic options. According to the built-in thesaurus on this word processor, the word "exotic" has several synonyms, including alien, foreign, imported, fascinating, romantic, strange, unusual, and wondrous. In the financial world, however, exotic most often simply means "new."[4] The current crop of exotic options is made possible by the dramatic development of mathematical models that can be used to price and hedge them as well as the level of comfort that traders and users have attained in using these models. In addition to the investment community's need for new and varied risk-reward profiles, exotics also fulfill two hedging needs. They allow for more complete hedging of actual risks in liabilities— for example, insurance contracts. Secondly, they can result in more cost-effective hedges via their ability to select what particular risks are hedged.

In Chapter 6, Chris Williams, Melinda Twomey, and Hasan Latif describe new fixed income securities. These are hybrids, commonly known as *structured notes,* that combine traditional forms of fixed income investment with exotic options and swaps. The reason for their existence is the need for yield enhancement without attendant credit risk,[5] as well as the need for new and unusual risk-return patterns. Structured notes can also be used as hedges in many situations, e.g., the single premium deferred annuity (SPDA) product in the insurance industry.

Azam Mistry offers a fresh approach to corporate exposure management in Chapter 7. Here you will find some guidelines for escaping from what he calls "conventional confusion" and for developing effective corporate risk management policies, which have become a must in light of recent disclosures of derivative-related losses by several corporations.

The next three chapters deal with the important subject of tools and techniques for analyzing derivatives. In Chapter 8, Ravi Dattatreya and Raj Pundarika propose the use of interest rate risk management as an integral part of a comprehensive program. They also recommend the application of the *risk point method* to accomplish the 4 Ms of risk management: measurement, monitoring, modification, and management. The risk point method has other

---

4. The so-called plain vanilla swap was an exotic transaction not too long ago.
5. Mortgage-backed securities also offer higher promised yield with little credit risk. In this context, structured notes are also alternatives to mortgage-backed securities.

related applications in investment management, such as replication of bond indexes and immunization.

In Chapters 9 and 10, Thomas Ho presents additional analytical tools. Securities or portfolios with known, fixed cash flows can be built using single cash flows or zero-coupon bonds. If contingent cash flows are involved, then we need to use Ho's *primitive securities* as building blocks, as discussed in Chapter 9. In Chapter 10, Ho proposes using the linear path space as a way to manage illiquid bonds. However, the techniques presented have much broader application.

Part II of the book presents the viewpoint of the end-user, both corporate and investor. The collection is disparate, covering pension funds, supranationals, multinational corporations, hedge funds, insurance companies, and foreign firms.

In Chapter 11, Laurie Goodman attempts to dispel the myths that the buy-side and the sell-side have about each other. In Chapter 12, Ed Krawitt speaks about how PepsiCo has used swaps for its hedging and funding needs. In Chapter 13, Tom McAvity of the Lincoln National Insurance Company discusses how the insurance industry has liabilities that include option-like features that can be effectively hedged with more structured swaps and other derivative products. In Chapter 14, Jacob Navon of The Boston Company shows how swap-embedded MTNs can be used to add value to a portfolio.

The next two chapters (15 and 16) pertain to funds whose goal is to enhance yield using exotic investments, albeit in totally different environments and applications. Ramine Rouhani of CDC Investment Management Company looks to the indexed amortizing notes for adding value to the company's portfolio. Matthew Smith and Beth Kostick of the Amoco Pension Fund use derivatives for enhancing the return on their equity investment.

Bernardo Frydman (Chapter 17) of the International Finance Corporation (IFC) and Afsaneh Mashayekhi-Beschloss and Arun Muralidhar (Chapter 18) of the World Bank share with us some insight into how derivatives are used in these supranational entities not only for their own use but also for the use of their clients, i.e., developing countries. We believe that these two entities and other development banks hold the key to helping developing countries compete effectively in a global economy by providing access to capital markets products.

Finally, in Chapters 19 and 20, Hans Gisbert Ulmke of VIAG and Mark Abbott of Bristol & West give us a continental flavor. Europe has led the United States in many fields; effective application of derivatives is no exception.

ACKNOWLEDGMENTS

First of all, we thank all of our contributing authors who patiently stayed with us over the extended time period that it took to bring the book to a final form. We also thank several authors who worked on articles that did not make it into the book for various reasons beyond their control.

We also wish to thank Akira Kondoh, Kenji Kita, and John Copenhaver of Sumitomo Bank Capital Markets, Inc., New York, and Atsuo Konishi of SBCM (UK) Ltd., London, for providing assistance and for their encouragement throughout this long project. We acknowledge the help of Joyce Frost, Scott Peng, Timothy Quinn, and Raj S. Pundarika in reading drafts of parts of the book.

Finally, we thank Joan Rosa for managing the entire process so efficiently.

Kensuke Hotta   *Ravi E. Dattatreya*
Tokyo   *Summit, NJ*

ACKNOWLEDGMENTS

PART I

Analysis, Modeling, and New Products

Portfolio Approach to Credit Risk Evaluation

Jon Frye
Vice President, Continental Bank

An interest rate swap is the exchange of a promise for a promise, for example, the promise to pay a fixed rate in return for the promise to be paid a floating rate. If one of the parties to the swap defaults, the other may experience a loss. Default may occur at any time. The amount of the resulting loss depends on the interest rate market at the time of default and cannot be foreseen.

The *credit exposure* calculation attempts to measure the loss that might occur on an interest rate swap. As such, the calculation requires a look into the uncertain future. However, the *effects* of the calculation are far from uncertain. Distorted estimates of credit exposure provoke several problems. Business managers produce inaccurate estimates of their credit-associated costs. Credit, a scarce resource at financial institutions, is allocated inefficiently. Regulators who look to credit exposures require swap dealerships to hold wrong levels of capital.

In its early days, the swaps market ignored these problems as it concentrated on its own growth. The potential for a credit loss was small, compared to the potential for gain in the expanding market. After all, the amount at stake was not notional principal, nor even the interest on notional principal, but only the difference between two rates of interest, say, between a fixed rate and a floating rate. Further, only highly rated institutions participated in the swaps market.

Swap dealers began to care about the potential for credit losses as the market expanded in volume of deals and breadth of participation. Corporate users, the customers of the swaps market, now care as well. Most participants estimate the credit exposure for each swap in turn as some percentage of notional principal; the percentage is greater for longer-term swaps. The credit exposure to a counterparty is then taken to be the sum of the exposures of the swaps in force.

This article presents a portfolio approach to calculating credit exposure. Here, "the bank" is the entity that may lose if "the counterparty" defaults, but the principles apply to the exposure of any participant. The focus is on interest rate swaps, but the approach applies to over-the-counter portfolios of other trades as well. The first section discusses a probabilistic basis for the calculations. The second applies the approach to single deals, finding percentage factors for single deals similar to current market practice. The third applies the approach to all the deals in force with a particular counterparty.

The portfolio approach never results in a higher estimate of credit exposure than the deal-by-deal approach. Both in the "Counterparty ABC" portfolio presented as an example, and in case studies of actual counterparties, the portfolio approach results in materially lower estimates of exposure. The article concludes that the common use of summation to find the credit exposure of a portfolio may overestimate risk by several fold. Thus, the proper calculation of credit exposure reduces both the costs and the perceived risk of the swaps business.

PROBABILISTIC BASIS

The credit loss on an interest rate swap depends on interest rate levels at the time of default. That uncertainty can beget contention within a swap dealership. The deal-making side may stress that marked-to-market (MTM) values are small or change little with wide swings in interest rates. The credit side may emphasize that it is the future that matters. The result is heat rather than light until the sides agree on a framework for calculating exposure. The framework must recognize the inherent uncertainty by adopting a probabilistic basis.

Consider the next payment date on a five-year swap. MTM may be positive or negative, owing to the randomness of interest rates. Exhibit 1 depicts the distribution of MTM. The highest likelihood is that neither side owes the other. Half the time the bank owes the counterparty and half the time the counterparty owes the bank.

Suppose the counterparty defaults (or declares bankruptcy) on this forward date. The transaction ends prematurely. If the bank owes the counterparty, the transaction is marked to market and the value paid to the counterparty or receiver. The MTM loss becomes a realized loss.

Any amount owed the bank is a trading gain that may have been reported as income. Usually there is a matching loss on a hedge position. Thus, if the counterparty defaults, the bank's loss is real and equal to the amount owed. (As with a loan in default, the bank may recover some fraction of the loss as a general creditor in bankruptcy proceedings, or through some other channel.) Exhibit 1 shows a greater likelihood of a small loss and a lesser likelihood of a larger loss. The credit exposure calculation summarizes this uncertainty.

95 Percent Confidence Criterion

Many swap dealerships use a 95 percent confidence criterion for calculating credit exposure: credit exposure is a number larger than MTM with probabili-

EXHIBIT 1   Distribution of MTM on a Forward Date

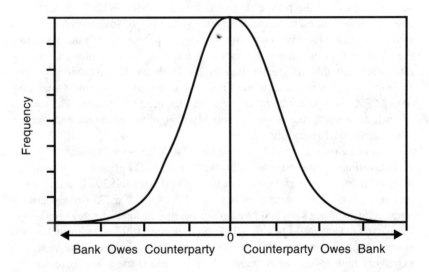

The marked-to-market (MTM) that might come about on a forward date is random in line with the interest rate market. The amount owed is on the horizontal axis. To the left, the bank owes the counterparty. The concern from a credit perspective is to the right, where the counterparty owes the bank. The vertical axis measures likelihood. The most likely outcome is that neither side owes the other. There is a chance, though, that the counterparty may owe the bank a large amount.

ty 95 percent. With only one (remaining) settlement, Exhibit 2 depicts the 95 percent confidence criterion.

The choice of 95 percent confidence, rather than 99 percent or $66^2/_3$ percent confidence, is a practical compromise between opposite goals. Arguing for greater confidence, credit exposure should be larger than the possible loss. In its traditional lending operations, the bank assigns a credit limit to each customer. If the MTM of an interest rate swap exceeds the credit exposure number, there is a chance that default would subject the bank to a greater loss than the counterparty's limit. On the other hand, credit exposure should not be so large that interest rate swaps suffer relative to other products in the bank's credit allocation decision.

It appears, however, that 95 percent is enough confidence for interest rate swaps. Although the amount owed may be greater than calculated using the 95 percent confidence approach, the risk of that excess must be judged in its own context.

Consider the context and consequences of an unusual movement of interest rates from the perspective of December, 1991. With 95 percent frequency in the last eight years, long-term (one year or longer) interest rates move less than 240 basis points in one year. In proportion as rates rise more than 240 basis points in one year some, but not all, long positions in interest rate swaps have MTMs greater than the originally calculated credit exposure. For example, if rates rise 300 basis points in one year, some long swaps may have MTMs as much as 25 percent greater than credit exposures. The context of such an interest rate move is probably a vigorous economic recovery in which credit quality rapidly improves.

In proportion as rates fall more than 240 basis points some, but not all, short positions in interest rate swaps will have MTMs greater than the originally calculated credit exposure. For example, if rates fall 300 basis points in one year, some short swaps may have MTMs as much as 25 percent greater than credit exposures. A 300 basis point decline in interest rates implies the two-year Treasury yield below 3.00 percent by late 1992 and almost surely a severe economic contraction with abysmal credit conditions. There would be extremely high losses on the bank's loan portfolio, and some losses on the interest rate swap portfolio. Some of these losses might exceed calculated credit exposure.

In either case, the bank can accept the risk. If rates rise sharply in an improving credit environment, the bank may willingly raise the limits of many counterparties. If rates fall sharply, the problem of MTM exceeding credit exposure pales before other economic problems. The risk that a MTM may exceed credit exposure is a business risk the bank can accept.

EXHIBIT 2   Distribution of MTM on a Forward Date

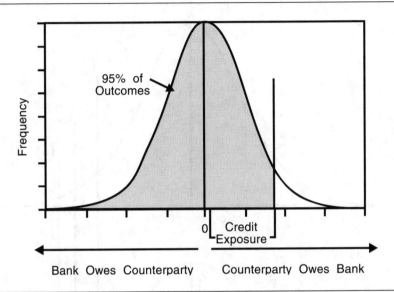

Many swaps market participants take a 95 percent confidence approach to credit exposure. The credit exposure number should be greater than the MTM that comes about, with probability 95 percent.

Three Interpretations

If more than one settlement remains, 95 percent confidence has at least three interpretations. There can be 95 percent confidence that credit exposure is greater than MTM (1) on average over the life of the swap, (2) on any possible default date, or (3) ever.

Exhibit 3 shows that the three interpretations lead to different results. With interpretation (1), the probability that MTM exceeds exposure is greater than 5 percent on some days and less on others, so the average is 5 percent. With (2), the probability is equal to 5 percent on one or more days and less than 5 percent on all others. With (3), the probability is equal to 5 percent on all dates put together, so the probability on each date is less than 5 percent. (Exhibit 3 simplifies somewhat, because it overlooks the dependence of the outcomes on the two dates.) The result of (2) is greater than (1), and (3) is greater than (2). The choice among the three, like the choice of 95 percent

EXHIBIT 3   Three Interpretations of 95 Percent Confidence

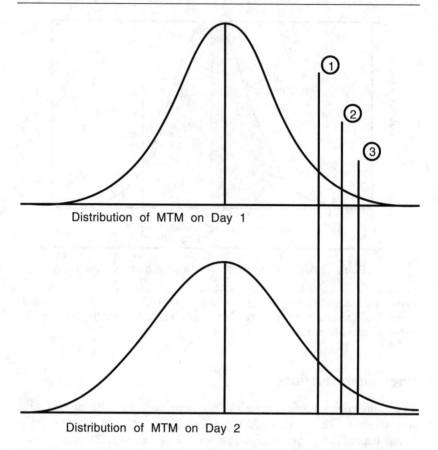

Distribution of MTM on Day 1

Distribution of MTM on Day 2

1. The probability MTM exceeds credit exposure number is 4 percent on Day One and 6 percent on Day Two. Average probability is 5 percent.
2. The probability MTM exceeds credit exposure number is 3 percent on Day One and 5 percent on Day Two. Maximum probability is 5 percent.
3. The probability MTM exceeds credit exposure number is 1 percent on Day One and 4 percent on Day Two. Total probability is 5 percent.

confidence rather some other level of confidence, depends on practical rather than theoretical considerations.

This article uses (2) because it allows the easiest calculation: each date is separate. Either of the others requires analyzing jointly all dates. It is especially difficult to implement (3), as it requires either the joint distribution of MTM on various dates or a Monte Carlo analysis.

ESTIMATING CREDIT EXPOSURE ON A DEAL

Applying the 95 percent confidence criterion to an interest rate swap is a four-step process. The method looks forward from today to find the 95th percentile outcome for each date; it then takes the greatest among these to be credit exposure. More specifically:

For each possible default date:

1. A probability model projects the 95th percentile interest rate if the bank is long the swap, or the 5th percentile interest rate if short;

2. The settlements from that date forward are marked to the interest rate found in (1);

3. The result is the *potential exposure* for that date.

Then:

4. *Credit exposure* is the maximum among the potential exposures for all dates.

(1) The probability model can be simple or elaborate. Single factor interest rate models allow the yield curve to shift either up or down. Two factor models allow the curve to twist steeper or flatter, as well as shift. More complicated models are possible. (A related matter is how realistically the interest rate model represents the current yield curve.) To focus attention, this article uses a simple interest rate model: a single factor shifts a flat yield curve. Exhibit 4 shows the current level of interest rates and the 5th and 95th percentiles for several years hence.

(2 and 3) Consider a long position in an in-the-money five-year interest rate swap. Exhibit 4 shows the MTM. Long the swap, the bank pays the fixed side and receives the higher current rate. The bank expects to receive this same positive spread for the life of the swap, because the yield curve is flat. Undiscounted MTM corresponds to the shaded rectangle in Exhibit 4.

EXHIBIT 4   Interest Rate Model
Flat Yield Curve, Single Factor

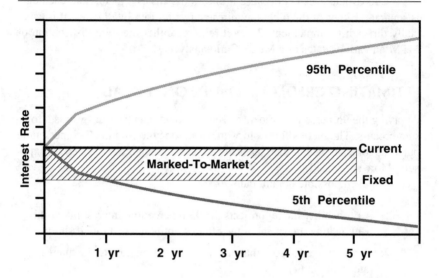

The current level of interest rates—for simplicity, the yield curve is assumed to be flat—is indicated on the vertical axis. Time forward from today is on the horizontal axis. A statistical model projects the 5th and 95th percentiles for interest rates for the next several years. The 95th percentile rises into the future, though at an ever slower rate. The diagram also shows the (undiscounted) MTM of an in-the-money five-year swap, which is equal to the spread earned (difference between the current rate and the fixed rate) times the five-year term.

Exhibit 5 looks forward to the prospects one year from today. The interest rate model projects the 95th percentile interest rate one year forward. Suppose that in one year this rate comes about, and the counterparty defaults. Potential MTM is the 95th percentile rate less the fixed side, times the four years remaining on the swap. This *potential exposure* at year one corresponds to the shaded rectangle in Exhibit 5. One year from now the potential in-the-money amount will be greater than in Exhibit 4, but only four years will remain to maturity.

Exhibit 6 displays the two factors affecting potential exposure. The *potential in-the-money amount*, which is the 95th percentile interest rate less the fixed rate, increases over time. The rate of increase is rapid at first but

EXHIBIT 5   Potential Exposure on Five-Year Swap at Year 1

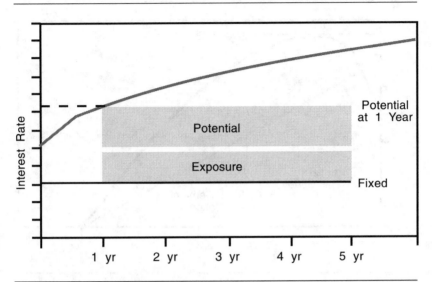

The interest rate model projects the 95th percentile one year from now. The *fixed* rate is for the in-the-money five-year swap. If the counterparty defaults in one year and interest rates are at the projected level, MTM would be equal to *potential exposure:* the spread between the projected rate and the fixed rate, times the four years then remaining.

declines. *Total remaining notional* is the notional amount times the number of payments remaining. It declines linearly if notional principal is constant.

Exhibit 6 also shows *potential exposure*, the 95th percentile of the distribution of MTM. Potential exposure is the product of the potential in-the-money amount and total remaining notional. If default occurs today, the credit loss equals MTM because interest rates have had no time to depart from current levels. Potential exposure rises at first, because the latitude for rising rates dominates the decline in total remaining notional. At some point—one year forward for this swap—the decline in total remaining notional begins to dominate and potential exposure turns down. Finally, potential exposure is zero because the swap has matured.

(4) Credit exposure is the maximum potential exposure. Therefore, credit exposure is equal to potential exposure at one time, the *time of greatest risk*, and greater than potential exposure at all other times. The time of greatest

EXHIBIT 6   Credit Exposure Is Maximum Potential Exposure

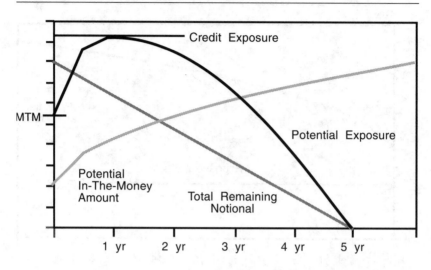

Two factors affect potential exposure. The *potential in-the-money amount* is the 95th percentile interest rate less the fixed rate and increases over time. *Total remaining notional* is the notional amount times the number of payments remaining. *Potential exposure* is the product of these two. Today, potential exposure is equal to MTM. In the near future, potential exposure rises because the potential for interest rates to rise dominates the decline in total remaining notional. Eventually, the decline in total remaining notional dominates, establishing maximum potential exposure. Credit exposure is equal to this maximum potential exposure.

risk is one year for this deal. In one year the probability is 95 percent that MTM will be below credit exposure. At all other times, the probability is greater than 95 percent that MTM will be below credit exposure. Put another way, if interest rates rise beyond the 95th percentile at the one-year horizon, MTM will be greater than credit exposure for this deal. If interest rates rise beyond the 95th percentile at some other time, MTM may or may not exceed credit exposure.

Exhibit 7 shows credit exposure for a five-year at-the-money swap. The potential exposure line begins at zero, since the MTM of an at-the-money swap is zero. Potential exposure peaks two years forward. This is later than, and at a lower level than, the in-the-money case.

EXHIBIT 7   Credit Exposure of At-the-Money Five-Year Swap

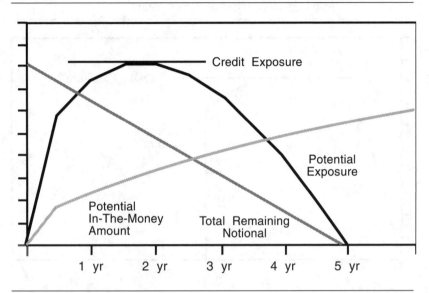

Analysis of an at-the-money swap proceeds identically. Current potential in-the-money amount and MTM are zero for the at-the-money swap.

CREDIT EXPOSURE ON MORE SOPHISTICATED SWAPS

The method as outlined above can handle a variety of more sophisticated swaps. Exhibit 8 shows the potential exposure curve for an at-the-money five-year swap that is to be marked to market and terminated with a cash settlement in three years. Marking to market affects the timing of exposure to the counterparty, but leaves unaffected the maximum potential exposure facing the bank.

If long a swaption, the bank can enter a swap. Exhibit 9 shows the situation for a one-year option on a four-year swap. Compared to a spot-starting five-year swap, this structure lacks contractual settlements at six months and one year, so potential exposures are slightly less at these times. Potential exposures beyond one year are the same as the spot-starting five-year swap, so maximum potential exposure is also the same. If the swaption is cash settled, maximum potential exposure is only slightly lower than that for the five-year swap. The difference between a long cash-settled option on a swap and a

EXHIBIT 8   Credit Exposure of Five-Year Swap Marked-to-Market at Three Years

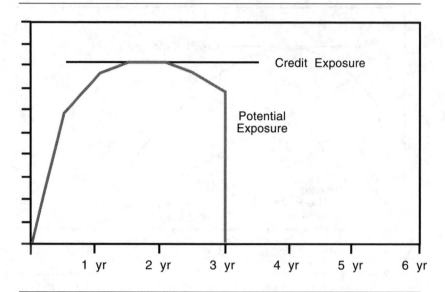

The analysis can be extended to more sophisticated deals. One example is a five-year swap that is agreed to be terminated at the end of three years. Although it controls the timing of exposure to the counterparty, this mark-to-market feature has no effect on maximum potential exposure.

spot-starting swap of the same final maturity is material only if the term of the option is short and the term of the swap is long.

Exhibit 10 illustrates an amortizing swap that begins with higher notional amounts than the level-pay case and ends with lower notional amounts. The total remaining notional line begins at the same intercept as in Exhibit 7, but declines faster. Potential exposure peaks earlier and lower than in the level-pay case for Exhibit 7.

If the bank pays more often and earlier than it receives, those payments increase potential exposure. For example, the bank might pay the floating commercial paper rate each month and receive LIBOR twice a year. Exhibit 11 shows the bank paying the fixed rate for six months before the possible default at one year. This same payment is part of potential exposure at each possible date of default and maximum potential exposure is commensurately greater.

**EXHIBIT 9   Credit Exposure of Long One-Year Option
                on Five-Year Swap**

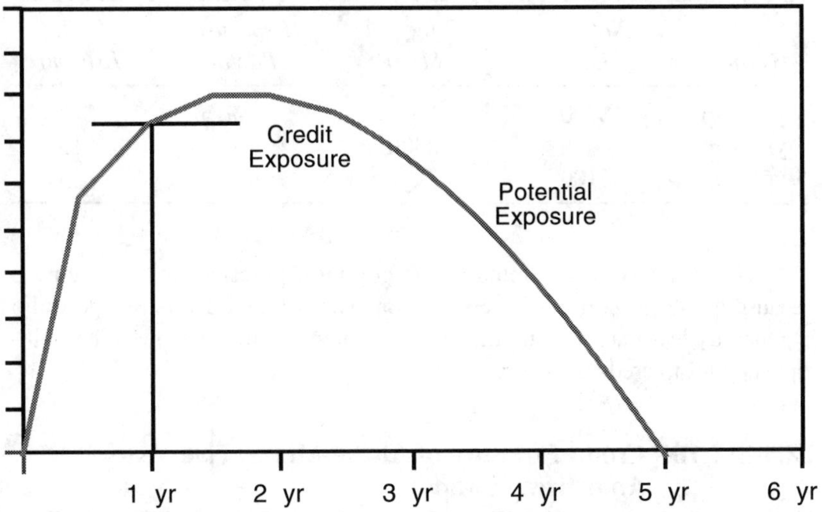

Options on swaps have potential exposure profiles similar to conventional
swaps. Even if the option is cash-settled, there is little impact on maximum
potential exposure unless the option period is short and the swap period is long.

THE PORTFOLIO APPROACH

Using the method discussed above it is easy to calculate the bank's credit
exposure to a single interest rate swap. The next step is to calculate the exposure to a counterparty that has several swaps in force. Common practice is
simply to add the exposures to arrive at a total. Two alternative portfolio
methods are presented; the choice between them depends on the defaulting
party's legal options.

    Consider the portfolio of a hypothetical counterparty ABC. The bank is
long a one-year swap and a five-year swap with ABC, and short a three-year
swap. All swaps are at-the-money. The notional amounts, conventional credit
exposure factors, and dollar exposure amounts are shown in the following
table. Most swap market participants add the dollar exposure amounts, resulting in estimated $30,000,000 credit exposure.

Bank Position with Counterparty ABC
Interest Rate Swap Portfolio
Dollar Amounts in Millions

Term	Notional Long	Principal Short	Exposure Factor	Dollar Exposure
1-yr Swap	$700		1%	$ 7
3-yr Swap		$300	5%	$15
5-yr Swap	$100		8%	$ 8

Although simple summation is common practice, it is inaccurate because it ignores portfolio diversification. The risk of a diversified portfolio is generally less than the sum of the risks of items in the portfolio. That principle applies to credit exposure.

EXHIBIT 10 Credit Exposure of At-the-Money Five-Year Amortizing Swap

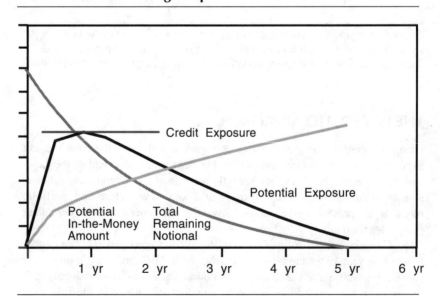

Potential exposure for an amortizing at-the-money swap reaches its maximum earlier than, and at a lower level than, the level-pay case.

EXHIBIT 11 **Credit Exposure of Five-Year Swap with Adverse Payment Frequency**

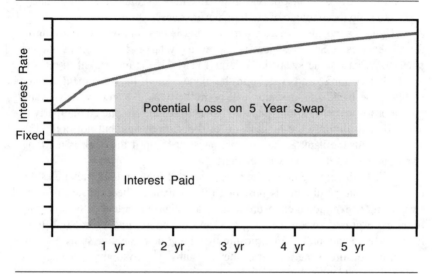

There is an additional component of credit risk if the bank pays more frequently than it is paid. Here, the bank has paid the gross fixed side each month for six months before receiving the semi-annual floating payment. The worst case for the bank is that the counterparty defaults at the time the floating payment is due.

The counterparty's legal options in default complicate the situation. The most common situation within the U.S. is that (1) all interest rate swaps tie to an ISDA master agreement, and (2) legal action would proceed under U.S. law, including the Financial Institutions Reform, Recovery, and Enforcement Act of 1989 (FIRREA), with respect to default by an insured bank, or the U.S. Bankruptcy Code, with respect to U.S. corporations other than banks and insurance companies. In each case, a default on any swap is a default on all swaps. All positions are marked to market to arrive at a net closeout amount. If the counterparty defaults and owes the net amount to the bank, the bank becomes a general creditor for that amount (unless the exposure is secured).

The special provisions of the Bankruptcy Code basically prohibit the trustee for a counterparty from forcing performance on deals favorable to him and defaulting on others. Thus, the bank may be "cherry picked" only by certain non-U.S. counterparties, or by counterparties with nonstandard or deficient documentation. If cherry picking is possible, the resulting credit loss will be at least as great as in the legal closeout case. If there is doubt about the counterparty's legal options, the bank may assume it will be cherry picked to keep the estimate of credit exposure conservative.

Consider the case where cherry picking is possible before returning to the closeout case. Suppose there is an unusually large rise or fall in interest rates, so at least some swaps have large MTMs. If the movement in rates is up, the bank's long swaps will be in-the-money, and if the movement in rates is down, the bank's short swaps will be in-the-money. Rarely will the bank have a profit on both its long and short swaps.[1] Therefore, the counterparty is apt to default on only the long swaps or the short swaps, but not both. The worst case for the bank is that interest rates move up if the bank is net long swaps, and down if the bank is net short.

The following method, called the greater-of-long-and-short, handles the case where cherry picking is possible. First, calculate the exposure of each swap using conventional exposure factors, as in current practice. Second, partition exposures between the long side and the short side. Third, find total long exposure and total short exposure by taking the respective sums. Fourth, portfolio exposure is the greater of the two sums. The following table applies this method to Counterparty ABC.

Bank Position with Counterparty ABC
Interest Rate Swap Portfolio
Dollar Amounts in Millions

Term	Notional Long	Principal Short	Exposure Factor	Long Exposure	Short Exposure
1-yr Swap	$700		1%	$ 7	
3-yr Swap		$300	5%		$15
5-yr Swap	$100		8%	$ 8	
				$15	$15

---

1. The exception requires an unbalanced position and a severe twist in the yield curve. For example, the bank could have a long position in long-term swaps and a short position in short-term swaps. To produce MTM greater than the exposure calculated by greater-of-long-and-short, there must be an unusually large rise in long-term rates and a twist in the yield curve severe enough that short-term rates fall. In post-WWII U.S. history, yield curve twists of this severity have occurred rarely, with most episodes surrounding the imposition and removal of credit controls in 1980.

If the counterparty defaults on either the long or short positions, the loss should be less than $15,000,000. In an extreme movement of interest rates, it is unlikely that the counterparty would default on both. Exposure by the method of greater-of-long-and-short is therefore $15,000,000.

Portfolio Approach with Closeout

If the legal agreements require closeout on default, two features of the portfolio influence the credit exposure calculation. First is the *diversification effect* that allows the rational offset of the risk of long positions with the risk of short positions. If interest rates rise, for example, the bank is apt to have a positive MTM on its long swaps with ABC, and negative MTM on its short swaps. The closeout settlement is the net of these amounts. Second is the *portfolio effect* that recognizes all swaps terminate at default. Thus, if ABC defaults while the one-year swap is still in force, there is little time for MTM to build on the five-year swap. The time of maximum risk on a five-year swap is about two years.

A three-step process calculates credit exposure for a portfolio with closeout.

For each interest rate scenario:

1. Calculate the potential exposure profile of each swap as in the single-swap case;

2. Add the potential exposures of all swaps in the portfolio, date by date, to arrive at the potential exposure profile of the portfolio.

Then:

3. Credit exposure is the maximum value in any interest rate scenario.

Exhibit 12 applies step (1) to each swap in the counterparty ABC portfolio. If rates rise, the long swaps will have positive MTM, and the short swaps will have negative MTM. Exhibit 13 shows total portfolio potential at each date, which is the sum of the potential exposures at that date.

Exhibit 13 shows that the portfolio has little current sensitivity to market rates. Even if interest rates rise to the 95th percentile, portfolio MTM will move little in the next six months or so. This currently unresponsive portfolio has significant credit exposure, however; its nature changes later. Around the one-year horizon, the short $300,000,000 three-year swap dominates the long $100,000,000 five-year swap, so bank MTM is negative in this interest rate

EXHIBIT 12   Counterparty ABC Portfolio Potential Exposures If Rates Rise

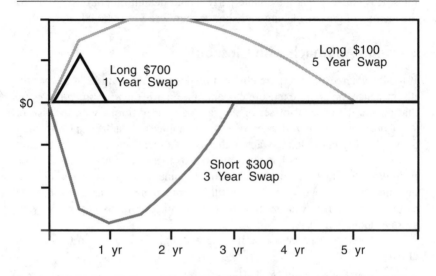

The bank has three swaps in force with counterparty ABC: Long $700,000,000 one-year swap, short $300,000,000 three-year swap, and long $100,000,000 five-year swap. Exhibit 12 shows the potential exposure profile of each of these swaps, contingent on the scenario of rising rates.

scenario. Beyond two years, MTM turns positive. It reaches its maximum when the three-year swap matures. This maximum potential exposure is less than the maximum of the $100,000,000 five-year swap taken in isolation. The short three-year swap hedges part of the risk of the long five-year swap during the latter's time of maximum risk.

For a portfolio that contains both long and short positions, two interest rate scenarios matter: rates up and rates down. (A two-factor interest rate model would require checking scenarios that allow the yield curve to steepen and flatten as well as shift up or down.) For a portfolio containing only at-the-money interest rate swaps valued against a flat yield curve, the potential exposure profile in the rates-down scenario is the mirror image of the rates-up profile. Exhibit 14 shows both scenarios.

**EXHIBIT 13 Counterparty ABC Portfolio Exposure
If Rates Rise**

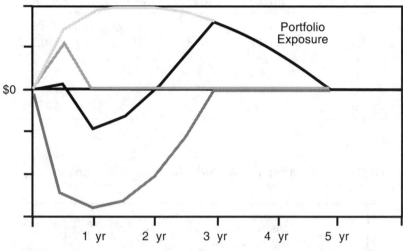

If interest rates rise to the 95th percentile at each forward date, the value of the counterparty ABC portfolio is equal to the sum of the three potential exposures. The *portfolio exposure* profile is the sum of the profiles of the three swaps.

Portfolio potential exposure is the upper envelope of all scenario-dependent profiles. Exhibit 14 shows that at the one-year horizon the exposure stems from the rates-down scenario. After two years, the risk is of rising rates.

Maximum potential exposure comes from the rates-up scenario, at the three-year horizon. That maximum, $8,500,000, is credit exposure.

This example shows that the simple summation approach—by far the most common approach to estimating credit exposure—can overstate portfolio exposure by a large factor. The same is true of actual interest rate swap portfolios. The following table reports, for twelve Continental Bank counterparties, the sum-of-the-exposures estimate as a fraction of portfolio exposure.

Credit Exposure Using Simple Summation as a Fraction of Portfolio Exposure

Customer	Fraction	Customer	Fraction
A	170%	G	970%
B	1150%	H	310%
C	120%	I	520%
D	360%	J	210%
E	140%	K	780%
F	350%	L	340%

EXHIBIT 14   Customer ABC Portfolio Potential Exposure

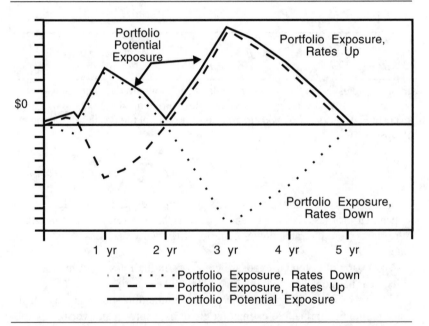

If rates fall to the fifth percentile, the portfolio exposure is the mirror image of the previous figure. (This is not always the case, except for at-the-money swaps valued against a flat yield curve.) *Portfolio potential exposure* is the upper bound of all portfolio exposure profiles. It represents the greatest MTM the bank can face at a point in time under any examined scenario.

The table shows that simple summation can overestimate exposure by tenfold, as for customers B and G. On the other hand, the degree of overestimation varies enormously from counterparty to counterparty. Simple summation is tolerably close for counterparties C and E.

The degree of difference between the two estimates, portfolio with closeout and simple summation, stems from the nature of the portfolio. Counterparties B and G are swap dealerships. Their portfolios are large and well diversified between long and short positions. Further, these portfolios are well balanced between long and short swaps of every maturity. Counterparties C and E, by contrast, have one-sided portfolios with high MTMs. The latter establishes a high floor for any credit exposure calculation, and so reduces the percentage overstatement of the faulty method.

The overstatement of risk of the simple summation method is important for the swaps business. Dollar-weighted, the simple sum is four times as great as portfolio exposure for the twelve highlighted counterparties. If the twelve are representative, the credit-associated risks and costs of the swaps business are being seriously overestimated. That causes swap dealers to hold fewer than the optimal number of swaps and reduces profits.

CONCLUSION

This article has presented a portfolio approach to calculating credit exposure. Any estimate of credit exposure must face the uncertainty of the future value of the swap. A conservative approach is that the estimate should be greater than MTM with 95 percent confidence. This approach is easy to apply to plain-vanilla swaps and more sophisticated variants. It is nearly as easy to apply to an entire portfolio of interest rate deals. The resulting estimate is no greater than the simple sum of exposures. The common use of summation to find the credit exposure of a portfolio may overestimate risk by several hundred percent. Thus, the improper calculation of credit exposure increases both the costs and the perceived risk of the swaps business.

Differential Swaps

Satyajit Das
Treasurer, TNT Group

INTRODUCTION

The late 1980s and early 1990s have been characterized by exponential growth in derivative markets. The volatility of prices for financial instruments combined with the necessity for asset or liability managers to perform competitively in dealing with this volatility has been a key factor in the development of "new" derivative products. The differential swap is one such development. The differential swap, which is also known as the index differential swap, cross rate swap, or cross index basis swap, is a particularly interesting product designed to allow financial managers to take positions in respect of interest differentials between various currency sectors without incurring currency exposures.

DIFFERENTIAL SWAPS—STRUCTURE

Definition and General Description

As noted above, the differential swap structure is designed to allow financial managers to capture existing and expected differentials in floating or money

---

The author would like to thank Matt Levins (Bankers Trust Australia Limited) and Bernd Luedecke (Mitsubishi Bank of Australia) for their assistance with the preparation of this paper.

© Copyright 1992 Satyajit Das

---

market rates between alternative currencies without incurring any foreign exchange exposure. In a typical differential swap, the party entering into the transaction will:

- Agree to receive payment in a particular currency on a specific principal amount for a specified term at the prevailing floating money market rate in that currency.

- In exchange, it will make payments on the same principal amount, in the same currency, for the same term, and make payment based on the prevailing floating money market rate in an alternative or different currency.

The major features of this arrangement include:

- Both payments and receipts (which are based on the same notional principal amount) are on a floating rate basis, with the rate being reset at specified intervals (usually, quarterly or semi-annually).

- All payments under the transaction are made in the counterparty's nominated currency thereby eliminating any foreign exchange exposure.

- Consistent with its status as a single currency transaction, no exchange of principal amounts are required to be exchanged.

Example

The following numerical example illustrates the concept utilizing a transaction whereby a borrower elects to enter into a Deutschemark ("DEM")/US dollars ("USD") differential swap seeking to benefit from the fact that floating money market rates in the USD sector are currency well below equivalent floating money market rates in the DEM sector.

Exhibit 1 sets out the structure of this differential swap. The counterparty enters into a differential swap for a term of three years in which it agrees to pay interest in DEM, which will be calculated by applying the nominal six-month USD LIBOR rate to a notional principal amount of DEM160.0m (based on an exchange rate of 1.60, equivalent to USD100.0m). The Counterparty will receive interest in DEM which will be calculated by applying the nominal six-month DEM LIBOR rate to DEM160.0m.

EXHIBIT 1 Differential Swap—Structure

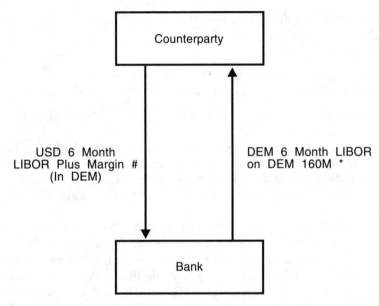

* Assumed Exchange Range USD 1 = DEM 1.60
# Margin Agreed Between Bank and Counterparty

The Counterparty will pay interest under this transaction at a rate equivalent to the six-month USD LIBOR rate plus a margin (assumed to be 2.15 percent or 215 basis points (bps) in DEM). The margin represents, primarily, the differential between interest rates of the relevant maturity (three years) in USD and DEM markets as well as the hedging costs to the Bank. The derivation of this margin is discussed below in the section on pricing and hedging.

The cash flows under this differential swap transaction from the perspective of the Counterparty is summarized in Exhibit 2.

At the end of each interest period (semi-annually), the Counterparty makes payments on DEM160.0m at the six-month USD LIBOR rate (plus the differential swap margin) and receives payment on DEM160.0m at the six-month DEM LIBOR rate. The net settlement amount calculation is as follows:

27

Settlement Calculation—1 September 1992
Counterparty:

Pays DEM160,000,000 @ USD 6-month LIBOR plus Margin (4.25% + 2.15% = 6.40%) × 184/360 days:	DEM (5,237,033)
Receives DEM 160,000,000 @ DEM 6-month LIBOR (9.50%) × 184/360 days:	DEM 7,768,889
Net Receipt	DEM 2,531,856

Based on these assumed rates, as at the first settlement date, the Bank would pay to the Counterparty the net settlement sum of DEM2,531,856.

Exhibit 2 sets out the settlement sums for each of the remaining interest periods over the life of the swap based on assumed USD and DEM LIBOR rates.

Under the terms of this differential swap, the Counterparty will receive a net settlement amount that equates to the net differential between DEM and USD LIBOR rates adjusted for the margin. If the USD LIBOR rate inclusive of the margin is below the DEM six-month LIBOR rate, then the Counterparty receives a net settlement payment. Conversely, if the six-month USD LIBOR rate plus the margin rises to a level above the then prevailing DEM six-month LIBOR rate on any particular rate setting date, the Counterparty will pay to the Bank the difference in the two nominal interest rates in DEM.

It is evident from this example, all payments are made in the nominated base currency (DEM) on a net settlement basis.

From the viewpoint of the Counterparty (assumed to be a DEM borrower) the transaction results in the following:

- The borrower has created a DEM liability with USD nominal six-month LIBOR rate as the interest benchmark. This means that it benefits where USD six-month LIBOR rates are below DEM six-month LIBOR rates by more than the margin.

- From a mechanical perspective, this reduction in interest cost is achieved by the net settlement amounts under the swap that reduce the borrower's interest payments under its underlying DEM borrowing.

- The borrower has achieved a conversion of its DEM based liability to a USD based liability without incurring any foreign exchange exposure, as all its payments continue to be in DEM.

EXHIBIT 2

Assumptions

Structure:	PAY	USD LIBOR					
	REC	DEM LIBOR					
FX Currency:	USD	100,000,000					
Base Currency:	DEM	160,000,000					
Exchange Rate:		1.6000					
Term (Years):		3					
Start Date:		01-Mar-92					
Maturity Date:		01-Mar-95					

Interest Rates:

Term Swap	USD	7.20%					
	DEM	8.70%					

Floating Rates

Period		1	2	3	4	5	6
6 Month LIBOR	USD	4.25%	4.38%	4.13%	4.75%	5.13%	5.50%
6 Month LIBOR	DEM	9.50%	9.35%	9.62%	9.00%	8.63%	8.25%
Differential		5.25%	4.98%	5.50%	4.25%	3.50%	2.75%
Pricing Margin (BPS):	+	215	215	215	215	215	215
USD LIBOR + Margin:		6.40%	6.53%	6.28%	6.90%	7.28%	7.65%

Cash Flows

Period	Days	Counterparty Payments USD LIBOR (DEM)	Counterparty Receipts DEM LIBOR (DEM)	Net Receipt Payment (−) (DEM)
01-Mar-92				
01-Sep-92	184	5,237,033	7,768,889	2,531,856
01-Mar-93	181	5,252,202	7,521,556	2,269,353
01-Sep-93	184	5,134,811	7,867,022	2,732,211
01-Mar-94	181	5,553,869	7,240,000	1,686,131
01-Sep-94	184	5,952,589	7,053,333	1,100,745
01-Mar-95	181	6,157,202	6,636,667	479,464

EXHIBIT 3   Differential Swap—Alternative Structure for Investor

```
                    ┌─────────────────────────┐
                    │      Counterparty        │
                    └─────────────────────────┘
                         │               ▲
                         │               │
    USD  6  Month        │               │   DEM  6  Month
    LIBOR  on            │               │   LIBOR  Minus  Margin
    USD  100M            │               │   on  USD  100M
                         │               │   (In  USD)
                         ▼               │
                    ┌─────────────────────────┐
                    │          Bank            │
                    └─────────────────────────┘
```

   An identical transaction could be utilized by an asset manager to convert an underlying USD asset yielding a floating rate of return linked to USD
LIBOR into a USD asset yielding a return linked to DEM six-month LIBOR.
   Under this transaction structure, the base currency would be restructured to be USD 100.0m (equating to DEM160.0m at the assumed exchange
rate). The investor would pay USD six-month LIBOR on USD 100.0m and
receive DEM six-month LIBOR *less* a specified margin on USD 100.0m in
USD. Under the terms of this transaction, all payments would be in USD to
insulate the investor from any foreign exchange risk. Such a transaction
would allow the investor to benefit from the positive differential between
DEM floating rate assets and USD floating rate assets while maintaining its
underlying USD investment position.
   Exhibit 3 summarizes the structure of this differential swap from an
investor perspective.

PRICING AND HEDGING CONSIDERATIONS

The pricing of a differential swap transaction is integral to and is derived
from the techniques utilized by the Bank to hedge its own exposures as a
result of entering into a transaction with its Counterparty.

The essential structure of the hedge for a differential swap entails two discrete steps:

- Entry by the Bank into two separate interest rate swap transactions to generate the cash-flow stream of a differential swap.
- Management of a complex series of foreign exchange exposures that are created in structuring the hedge.

Each of these two steps is considered in detail below. The analysis of pricing and hedging considerations is based on the numerical example of the DEM/USD differential swap (for a liability management application) discussed above.

Hedging Structure

In order to hedge its underlying positions (see Exhibit 1), the Bank would enter into two three-year interest rate swaps to replicate the cash flows of the differential swap. These swaps to be entered into by the Bank would be as follows:

- A three-year DEM160.0m interest rate swap under which the Bank:
  (i) pays 8.7 percent on DEM160.0m (payable semi-annually on an actual/365 basis); and
  (ii) receives DEM six-month LIBOR on DEM160.0m
- A three-year USD100.0m interest rate swap in which the Bank:
  (i) pays USD six-month LIBOR; and
  (ii) receives 7.2 percent (payable semi-annually on an actual/365 basis).

The fixed rate on the USD and DEM swaps are the prevailing market swap rates. The currency parities between the USD and DEM interest rate swaps is established by the assumed USD/DEM exchange of USD1:DEM1.60 (the market rate at the time the transaction is entered into).

The overall hedging structure is illustrated in Exhibit 4.

For analytical purposes, the structure of the hedge can be simplified in two steps:

- In order to assist in deriving the spread over USD LIBOR payable by the Counterparty, the USD interest rate swap is restructured to an

EXHIBIT 4 Differential Swap—Hedging Structure (1)

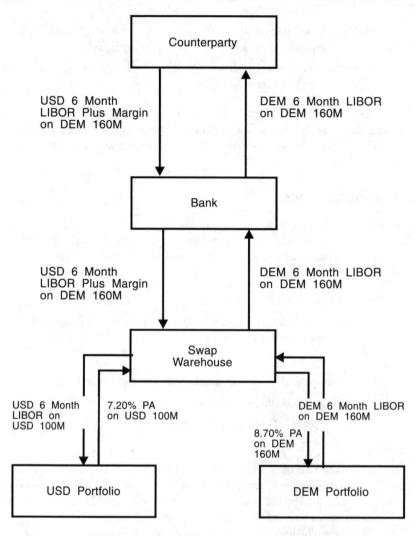

off-market rate basis with the fixed rate under the USD swap being restructured to match the fixed coupon of 8.7 percent payable under the corresponding DEM interest rate swap.

- This necessitates the Bank paying the present valued equivalent of 1.5 percent at the commencement of the swap. The up-front payment

EXHIBIT 5

Period	Days	USD Payments @ Market 7.20% (USD)	USD Payments @ Off Market 8.70% (USD)	Payment Difference (USD)	PV of Payment Difference (USD)
01-Mar-92					(3,845,463)
01-Sep-92	184	3,629,589	4,385,753	(756,164)	
01-Mar-93	181	3,570,411	4,314,247	(743,836)	
01-Sep-93	184	3,629,589	4,385,753	(756,164)	
01-Mar-94	181	3,570,411	4,314,247	(743,836)	
01-Sep-94	184	3,629,589	4,385,753	(756,164)	
01-Mar-95	181	3,570,411	4,314,247	(743,836)	

required to restructure the swap is USD3,845,463 (equivalent DEM6,152,741). Exhibit 5 sets out the derivation of this up-front payment.

Please note that for convenience the swap rate has been utilized to present value the cash flow differences as between the 8.7 percent fixed rate payments required and the market rate of 7.2 percent. In practice, zero coupon rates would be utilized, adjusted for the fact that the USD swap portfolio is essentially accepting a deposit over the life of the transaction. The "deposit" is repaid in the form of annuity by way of the higher coupon under the USD interest rate swap requiring assumption of a re-investment risk on these cash flows.

Exhibit 6 sets out the cash-flow structure of the hedge following the restructure of the USD interest rate swap flows.

A review of Exhibit 6 illustrates that two sets of cash flows completely offset each other in the hedge. The DEM six-month LIBOR received on DEM160.0m by the swap warehouse is exactly matched by the corresponding payments required to be made to the Counterparty. These cash flows cancel or offset each other and can be ignored for the purposes of the hedge and are eliminated. Exhibit 7 sets out the remaining cashflows.

Currency Risk Management

Exhibit 7 clearly identifies the foreign exchange exposures inherent in the hedge structure. The Bank, under the terms of the differential swap, has a

EXHIBIT 6   Differential Swap—Hedging Structure (2)

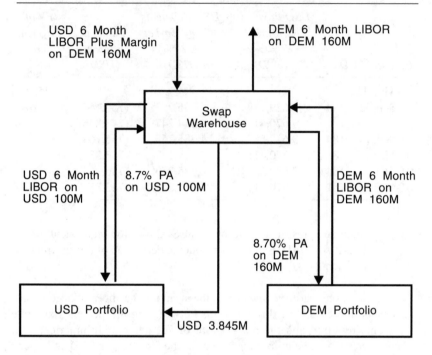

complex foreign exchange exposure to movements in the USD/DEM interest rates reflecting the fact that the Bank has a series of USD and DEM cash flows to manage.

The unique aspect of this currency risk management position is that:

- The Bank's USD and DEM net cash flow as of each settlement date is determined by an exogenous factor—USD six-month LIBOR (which is not known until the rate is set at the commencement of the relevant interest period).
- The nature of the exposure to the USD/DEM rate *changes* depending upon the nominal level of six-month USD LIBOR.

Exhibit 8 details the analysis of the net cash-flow exposures experienced by the Bank (within its swap portfolio) as of the first settlement. Please note that while this discussion focuses on the first settlement date only, a sim-

EXHIBIT 7   Differential Swap—Hedging Structure (3)

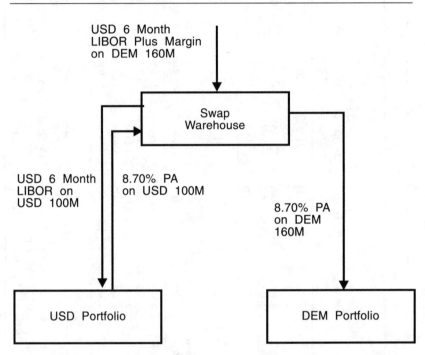

ilar problem exists in respect of each of the remaining five interest periods and settlement dates.

As is evident from a review of Exhibit 8, if USD six-month LIBOR is less than 8.7 percent (the fixed rate payable under the DEM swap), then the Bank will have a net receipt of USD, which will be needed to fund a net DEM outflow. Conversely, if USD six-month LIBOR exceeds 8.7 percent, then the Bank has a net DEM inflow, which is required to fund a net USD outflow.

Consequently, the Bank's swap portfolio, in hedging its exposure under the differential swap, is required to make a number of payments in one currency (either DEM or USD) while receiving the equivalent cash flow in the other currency. This complex foreign exchange exposure must be managed by the Bank.

In analyzing the complex foreign exchange exposures generated by the hedge structure, any exposure in regard to the *margin* over USD six-month LIBOR payable by the Counterparty in DEM is ignored. In practice, part of

EXHIBIT 8

FX HEDGE MANAGEMENT ANALYSIS (FIRST SETTLEMENT)

Case 1: USD 6-Month LIBOR Less Than 8.70%

USD LIBOR (%)	Receipts (DEM)	Payments (DEM)	Payments (USD)	Receipts (USD)	Net DEM Flow (DEM)	Net USD Flow (USD)	FX Rate	Net Cash Flow (DEM)
4.25%	3,475,556	(7,017,205)	(2,172,222)	4,385,753	(3,541,650)	2,213,531	1.6000	0
4.25%	3,475,556	(7,017,205)	(2,172,222)	4,385,753	(3,541,650)	2,213,531	2.0000	442,706
4.25%	3,475,556	(7,017,205)	(2,172,222)	4,385,753	(3,541,650)	2,213,531	1.8000	245,948
4.25%	3,475,556	(7,017,205)	(2,172,222)	4,385,753	(3,541,650)	2,213,531	1.4000	(316,219)
4.25%	3,475,556	(7,017,205)	(2,172,222)	4,385,753	(3,541,650)	2,213,531	1.2000	(737,844)

Case 2: USD 6-Month LIBOR Greater Than 8.70%

USD LIBOR (%)	Receipts (DEM)	Payments (DEM)	Payments (USD)	Receipts (USD)	Net DEM Flow (DEM)	Net USD Flow (USD)	FX Rate	Net Cash Flow (DEM)
10.50%	8,586,667	(7,017,205)	(5,366,667)	4,385,753	1,569,461	(980,913)	1.6000	0
10.50%	8,586,667	(7,017,205)	(5,366,667)	4,385,753	1,569,461	(980,913)	2.0000	(196,183)
10.50%	8,586,667	(7,017,205)	(5,366,667)	4,385,753	1,569,461	(980,913)	1.8000	(108,990)
10.50%	8,586,667	(7,017,205)	(5,366,667)	4,385,753	1,569,461	(980,913)	1.4000	140,130
10.50%	8,586,667	(7,017,205)	(5,366,667)	4,385,753	1,569,461	(980,913)	1.2000	326,971

FX HEDGE POSITION ANALYSIS

USD LIBOR Rate	4.250%	4.250%	6.250%	7.250%	8.250%	9.250%	10.250%	10.500%
USD Cash Flows	2,213,531	1,702,420	1,191,309	680,198	169,087	(342,024)	(853,135)	(980,913)
DEM Cash Flows	(3,541,650)	(2,723,872)	(1,906,094)	(1,088,317)	(270,539)	547,239	1,365,017	1,569,461
B/Even Exchange Rate	1.6000	1.6000	1.6000	1.6000	1.6000	1.6000	1.6000	1.6000

the margin (see below) will represent an annuity designed to recover the up-front USD payment made as part of restructuring the cash flows of the USD interest rate swap to equate the fixed rate payable under the DEM interest rate swap. In practice, this exposure can be eliminated quite simply by the following strategies:

- The swap structure could have been realigned by *reducing* the DEM coupon to equate to the USD interest rate swap coupon of 7.2 percent.

- Alternatively, the DEM equivalent of the USD payment to the USD swap portfolio could have been "borrowed" from the DEM swap portfolio with the borrowing being repaid by the margin payable by the Counterparty (in DEM).

This exposure is ignored for the remainder of this analysis.

As is evident from Exhibit 8, if USD six-month LIBOR is less than 8.7 percent, then the Bank has a net positive USD cash flow, which is utilized to fund a net DEM cash outflow. If USD six-month LIBOR (for the first settlement) is set at 4.25 percent, then the Bank has a net USD inflow of USD 2,213,531 and a net DEM outflow of DEM 3,541,650. If the USD/DEM exchange rate remains at USD1:DEM1.6000 (the rate of the commencement of the transaction), then the Bank's net cash-flow position is zero; that is, the DEM equivalent of the net USD inflow exactly matches the Bank's DEM shortfall. However, the Bank has a currency gain if the DEM depreciates against the USD and has a currency loss if the DEM appreciates against the USD. The cash flows realized by the Bank under alternative currency rate is summarized in Exhibit 8.

The Bank's exposure to an appreciating DEM is *reversed* where USD six-month LIBOR is greater than 8.7 percent. As set out in Exhibit 8, where USD six-month LIBOR is greater than 8.7 percent, the Bank has a net USD outflow, which must be funded from a net DEM cash surplus. As a consequence, the Bank's exposure is to a depreciating DEM relative to the USD.

The difficulty in managing this exposure is the inherent linkage between the nature of the underlying currency exposure to the USD six-month LIBOR rate for any interest period during the life of the differential swap (see Exhibit 8).

In practice, this exposure is treated as one that is similar to those incurred under currency options and hedged through the use of foreign exchange option techniques.

To structure the currency option hedge it is necessary to make assumptions regarding the anticipated maximum and minimum future level of the six-month USD LIBOR rate over the life of the differential swap transaction. This is because the exact quantum of the cash flows to be hedged is generated by the actual level of USD six-month LIBOR as at any rate set date.

For the purpose of illustration, assume that it is anticipated that USD six-month LIBOR will never be set below 4.25 percent or above 10.5 percent over the three-year term of the differential swap. Utilizing this assumption, to fully hedge against losses, the Bank would need to purchase the following options:

1. Purchase of DEM call/USD put option:

    The Bank would purchase a series of six DEM call options (with maturities corresponding with the payment date under the differential swap structure) at a strike price equal to the prevailing spot rate of USD1:DEM1.6000.

    The Bank would purchase the DEM call on approximately 2.21 percent of the USD100.0m notional principal amount. The amount of DEM calls required is calculated by taking the difference between the assumed minimum LIBOR rate and the break-even USD six-month LIBOR rate (which equates to the USD swap rate payable under the swap) to generate the USD cash inflow.

2. Purchase of DEM Put/USD call:

    To hedge its exposure where USD six-month LIBOR is greater than 8.70 percent, the Bank would purchase a series of six DEM put options with strike price of USD1:DEM1.6000. The Bank would purchase DEM puts on approximately 0.98 percent of the USD100.0m notional principal amount of the transaction.

As is evident, the structure of this currency hedge is far from efficient. In particular, the effectiveness of the hedge depends on the forecasting accuracy of the minimum and maximum USD six-month LIBOR rates over the life of the differential swap. For example, even if the Bank is accurate in prescribing the minimum and maximum levels of USD six-month LIBOR over the swap, there will be certain circumstances in which the hedge will not be accurate.

In periods in which USD six-month LIBOR is between the minimum level assumed (4.25 percent) and the break-even rate (8.7 percent), if the DEM strengthens against the USD, the DEM call/USD put option purchased by the Bank will generate a higher gain than the actual cash-flow loss incurred by the Bank under the swap. Similarly, the Bank will be over-hedged where USD six-month LIBOR is between 8.7 percent and the assumed maximum of 10.5 percent and the USD strengthens.

A common approach to avoid over-hedging is for the amount of the options required to be calculated on the maximum and minimum rates that USD six-month LIBOR is expected to *average* over the life of the transaction, rather than the lowest and highest possible USD six-month LIBOR rate over the term of the transaction.

A problem in structuring the hedge that lowers hedge efficiency is the inherent assumption that movement in the USD six-month LIBOR rate is *not* correlated to movement in the USD/DEM exchange rate. In practice, there will be some correlation between movement in the USD six-month LIBOR rate and the USD/DEM rate, which will necessarily influence the *actual* exposure under the differential swap.

A number of institutions utilize proprietary hedging techniques designed to improve the efficiency of the currency hedge necessitated by the differential swap. Improving the efficiency of the currency risk management process necessarily minimizes the cost of implementing and maintaining the hedge.

For example, if it is assumed that increases in USD LIBOR are likely to coincide with a stronger USD, the hedge structure could be adjusted to lower the effective level of protection against a depreciation of the USD against the DEM. This could entail the Bank purchasing a lower face value amount of DEM call/USD put option (in the extreme case, this exposure could be left unhedged).

The correlation concepts underlying the derivation of the option value are common to a whole class of emerging derivative instruments usually referred to as *quanto options*. The central feature of these instruments is the uncertainty underlying the *value* or *amount of cash-flow* required to be hedged.

An example other than differential swaps of this class of instrument is currency hedged equity warrants. Under this type of transaction, the warrant purchaser receives the value of any appreciation (in the case of a call option or warrant) in a nominated foreign equity market index in its base currency, *that is, without currency risk.*

This type of transaction is equivalent to a purchase of a relevant option on the foreign equity market index and the simultaneous entry into a derivative transaction to hedge the return on the warrant into its base currency, usually at rates prevailing at the commencement of the transaction. Given the uncertainty in the value of the foreign equity market and therefore the maturity value of the option, the currency hedge must be structured to allow for the uncertainty of the value to be hedged. In effect, the hedge needs to recognize the correlation between the change in value of the foreign equity market index and the movements in the currency relativities. The problem is similar to that in the case of the index linked to the interest rate relativities as between the currencies.

Mathematical pricing models for valuing quanto options or derivatives of this type have been developed. Reiner (March 1992) and Rubinstein (May 1991) outline two valuation approaches. Increasingly, the approach to pricing quanto options is to utilize the correlation between the relevant variables as a parameter in the pricing of the option. For example, in the context of the currency hedged warrant structures, the relevant correlation is that between the returns on the relevant currency values and the return on the foreign market index in the currency *of the index*. In the case of index differential swaps, the relevant correlation is that between the relevant currencies and the interest rate *differential* between interest rates in the relevant currencies. A problem underlying this approach to pricing is the need to assume stationarity of the relationship between the variables.

An alternative approach would be for the Bank to hedge its currency exposure by purchasing *options on the relevant currency options*. Where options of whatever type are utilized, the Bank may choose not to actually purchase the identified options but utilize dynamic hedging techniques to synthetically create the requisite option position.

In practice, quanto option pricing approaches are utilized by major financial institutions active as differential swap market-makers.

Margin Determination

The actual margin payable under the differential swap requires the amortization over the life of the transaction of the following items:

- The up-front payment required to be made by the Bank to rewrite one of the interest rate swap coupons.

- The cost of purchasing or creating the options designed to hedge the foreign exchange exposure.

In the above example, the total cost that must be amortized over the life of the transaction is as follows:

Up-front payment in respect of USD interest rate swap:	USD3,845,463
Option premiums:	USD1,029,348

This total cost of USD4,874,811 (DEM7,799,698) is amortized over the six payments (three years of semi-annual payments) and equates to 2.15 percent or 1.08 percent semi-annually (refer to Exhibit 9).

Based on these calculations, the pricing of the differential swap requires the Counterparty to pay USD six-month LIBOR plus 2.15 percent on a notional principal amount of DEM160.0m in return for receiving DEM six-month LIBOR on DEM160.0m. Accordingly, the Counterparty would benefit from the transaction as long as USD six-month LIBOR was, at least, 2.15 percent below DEM six-month LIBOR over the term of this transaction.

In general, pricing of a differential swap will closely approximate the net difference in swap rates in the relevant currencies for the maturities relevant to the desired term of the differential swap plus the cost of hedging the currency risk entailed for the Bank in the transaction.

The margin component relating to the net difference in the swap rates will, typically, be similar for most institutions. However, the cost of management of the currency risk position may vary between institutions.

The actual imputed price for management of the currency risk will depend, initially, on the approach of the institution—that is, whether the institution will accept the currency risk or seek to neutralize the risk. In the event that the institution seeks to neutralize the risk, the premium charged to cover the cost of hedging will depend upon a variety of factors including: the assumptions regarding the future path of the relevant floating rate index and the exact structure of the currency hedge (particularly, the level of protection through currency options—irrespective of whether they are outright purchases or synthetically created) utilized in the structure.

The cost of hedging the currency risk, will, generally, depend on the shape of the yield curve of the two relevant currencies. The wider the interest differential between the two currencies over the life of the transaction, the higher the hedging costs (or benefits). The importance of this factor relates to the fact that the strike price of the relevant options will be set at the prevailing spot rate at the commencement of the transaction but the prevailing forward rate (determined by interest differential) will dictate whether the options are in or out-of-the-money and, therefore, their relative cost.

For example, in the above example, because of the positive interest rate differential in favor of the DEM, forward rates for the purchase of DEM against sales of the USD will be above the prevailing swap rate of USD1:DEM1.60. This means that DEM call/USD puts with the strike price of DEM1.60 required to be purchased will be out-of-the-money options, thereby, reducing the cost of the option. Conversely, the DEM put/USD calls required to

41

EXHIBIT 9

DIFFERENTIAL SWAP MARGIN ADJUSTMENT

(1) Option Cost

	Face Value (USD)	Premium (USD)	Period (% of FV)	1	2	3	4	5	6
USD Put/DEM Call	2,123,531	533,006		2.60%	3.30%	3.80%	4.40%	5.50%	5.50%
USD Call/DEM Put	980,913	496,342		5.00%	7.30%	8.70%	9.50%	10.00%	10.10%
TOTAL		1,029,348							

		(USD)	(DEM)
PV Amount		3,845,463	6,152,741
Hedging Costs		1,029,348	1,646,957
TOTAL		4,874,811	7,799,698
Amortized Equivalent	USD (SA)	1,029,038	1,723,185
	BPS (SA)	1.03%	1.08%
	BPS (A)	2.06%	2.15%

hedge the Bank's cash-flow mismatch where USD six-month LIBOR is greater than 8.7 percent will be in-the-money commensurately increasing the cost.

Consequently, the pricing of the differential swap in terms of the margin components will be most favorable where the net difference in swap rates between the two respective currencies for the relevant maturities is low and the shape of the yield curve for the two currencies means that the cost of hedging the currency risks is minimal.

APPLICATIONS

Potential applications of differential swaps reflect swaps' capacity to be utilized to capitalize on existing expected differences in short-term interest rates between currency sectors without incurring any currency exposure. The differential structure also allows a counterparty to engineer yield curve positions whereby it assumes an exposure to future short-term interest rate differentials as against long-term interest differentials in the relevant currencies.

Both liability and asset managers can utilize differential swaps to manage underlying liability and asset portfolios.

A central aspect of differential swaps is that entry into these types of transactions is predicated on the counterparty assuming an interest rate risk position across currencies. The transaction is inherently not free of risk, as changes in interest rate differentials will increase the cost of borrowing or reduce the return to investors utilizing such transactions.

Differential swaps can be utilized to trade the shape of the yield curve as between two currencies. For example, an existing differential swap position can be traded and unwound to lock in gains where the change in the yield differential (in the long-term interest rates in the relevant currencies that determine the differential swap margin) alter in favor of the counterparty. An issue in trading differential swaps is the relatively higher bid/offer spread, which may increase the cost of such trading in these instruments.

Liability Management

Differential swaps are primarily utilized by liability managers to assume short-term interest rate positions (without incurring currency risk) designed to reduce the interest cost on borrowings.

In the example outlined above, the Counterparty has effectively converted a three-year DEM160.0m floating rate liability into a DEM liability on which it pays interest rates calculated as USD six-month LIBOR plus 2.15 percent.

For example, as at the first settlement date, assuming DEM six-month USD LIBOR is set at 9.5 percent and USD six-month LIBOR set at 4.25 percent, the Counterparty locks in a positive margin of 3.10 percent (the LIBOR differential of 5.25 percent adjusted for the differential swap margin of 2.15 percent). This has the impact of reducing its borrowing cost by 3.10 percent to 6.40 percent (in DEM) as opposed to a borrowing cost of 9.5 percent if it had not entered into the differential swap. Exhibit 10 illustrates this transaction.

The Counterparty benefits from transacting this differential swap against underlying DEM borrowing as long as USD six-month LIBOR is, at least, 2.15 percent below DEM six-month LIBOR.

In a number of high short-term interest currencies (primarily, DEM, Pound Sterling ["GBP"], Japanese Yen ["JPY"] and Canadian Dollars ["CAD"]), the benefit of the differential swap has been incorporated in the underlying loan transaction. Such loans (referred to as cross-rate loans) entail a borrowing in a high short-term interest rate currency (such as JPY, DEM,

EXHIBIT 10   Liability-Based Differential Swap Structure

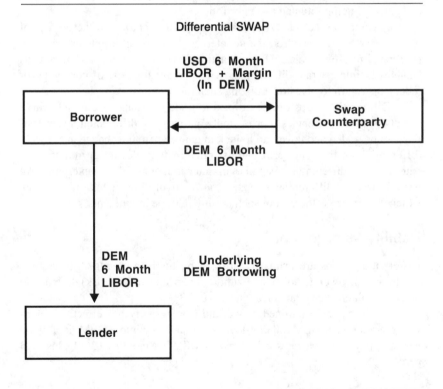

CAD, or GBP) on which the interest payable is calculated with reference to a lower interest rate currency such as USD plus a cross-rate spread.

Exhibit 11 illustrates the structure of such cross-rate loan financings. The structure essentially entails the funding bank entering into a differential swap to restructure the normal single currency loan flows to create the cross-rate loan.

EXHIBIT 11   Cross-Rate Loan Transaction

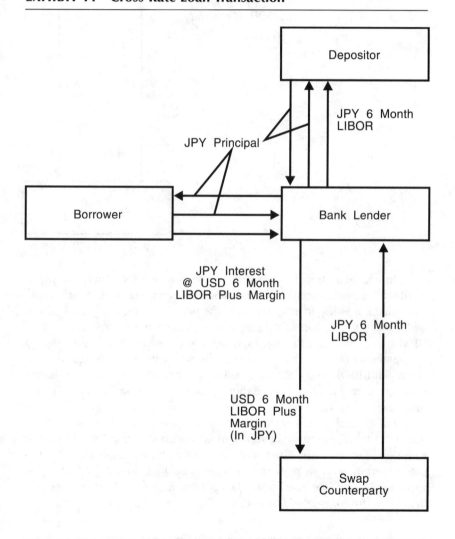

EXHIBIT 12   Differential Swap Embedded Security (1)

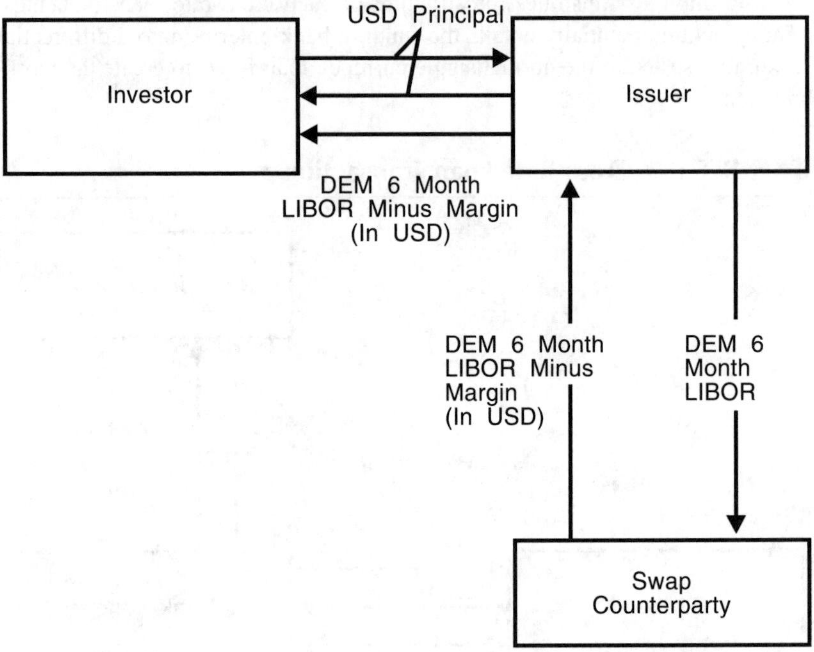

In a similar structure arrangement, the number of security issues (primarily private placements) have been undertaken with embedded differential swap characteristics. In a typical issue, the borrower issues securities (say in USD) that carry a interest coupon in a high short-term rate currency (say DEM six-month LIBOR minus a spread). The borrower, in turn, enters into a differential swap with a bank to convert its payments stream linked to DEM six-month LIBOR to a USD six-month LIBOR related payment at a margin below its normal funding costs. Exhibit 12 sets out an example of this type of structure.

Differential swap transactions are also embedded in Reverse Floating Rate Note ("FRN") issues. In such a transaction, the investor would receive an interest rate on its investment of, say, 18.00 percent minus USD LIBOR plus a margin, with all payments being in Australian dollars ("AUD"). The issuer of the AUD Reverse FRN would convert its borrowing onto a conventional basis by entering into two swaps:

- A differential swap under which it pays USD LIBOR plus a margin and receives AUD LIBOR (all payments in AUD).
- A conventional AUD interest rate swap on *double the total amount of the face value of the Reverse FRN* whereby it receives a fixed AUD rate (say, 2×9.50 percent = 19.00 percent) and pays AUD LIBOR ($2 \times$ AUD LIBOR).

The result of these swaps would be to leverage the issuer with a borrowing (equivalent to the face value of the FRN) at a margin under AUD LIBOR (in this example, 1.00 percent). Exhibit 13 sets out an example of this structure.

An interesting potential application of differential swaps relates to existing interest rate swaps. For example, where corporations have entered into an interest rate swap, say in USD, to hedge underlying borrowings, the shape of the yield curve in that currency, currently, results in the borrower incurring substantial cost. This cost is represented by the differential between short-term USD six-month LIBOR rate and medium- to long-term swap rates payable in USD (a differential of approximately 3 percent to 4 percent). The yield curve cost under such USD interest swap transactions can be managed using differential swaps as follows:

- The borrower enters into a USD interest rate swap where it pays a fixed rate and receives a floating rate (USD six-month LIBOR);
- Simultaneously, the borrower enters into a differential swap for the same USD notional principal amount whereby the borrower agrees to pay USD six-month LIBOR and receive DEM six-month LIBOR less a margin (in USD).

The result of this transaction is to increase the floating rate receipts under the USD interest rate swap as long as DEM six-month LIBOR adjusted for the differential swap margin exceeds USD six-month LIBOR. This has the impact of lowering the effective fixed rate cost to the borrower. Exhibit 14 sets out this particular application.

Asset Management

A significant impetus for differential swaps derives from investors seeking to increase returns on money market interest related investment assets. Asset managers, willing to take positions in interest rate differentials between cur-

EXHIBIT 13   Differential Swap Embedded Security (2)

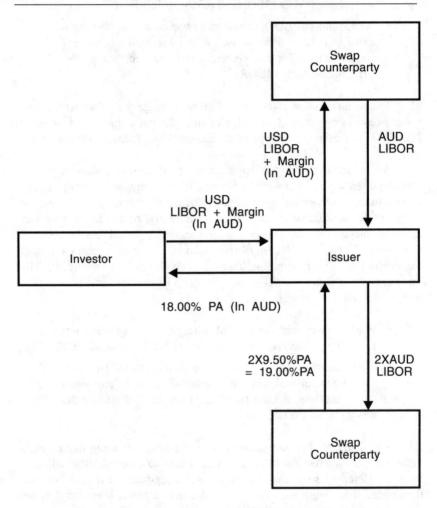

rencies, have utilized differential swaps to enhance returns on investment assets in currencies where money market rates have dropped to relatively low levels, such as USD short-term investments.

Asset managers in this case would enter into a differential swap whereby they would receive DEM six-month LIBOR minus differential swap spread (in USD) and pay USD six-month LIBOR.

EXHIBIT 14   Differential Swap Transacted Against Existing Interest Rate Swap

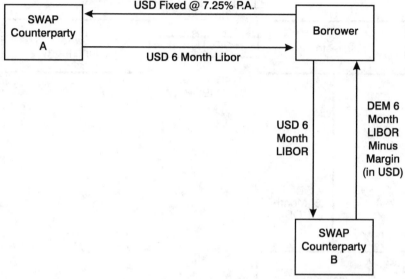

Under this structure, the USD six-month LIBOR flows would be matched by the return accruing to the investor from its underlying USD investment asset. The overall return to the investor would be based on DEM six-month LIBOR rates. Accordingly, the investor would benefit from utilizing the differential swaps where DEM six-month LIBOR minus the differential swap margin exceeded USD six-month LIBOR over the life of the transaction.

Exhibit 15 sets out an example of a differential swap structure that can be utilized by an asset manager.

As an alternative to entering into the differential swap, investors can benefit from the structural advantages of this type of transaction by purchasing securities where the differential swap cash flow profile is embedded into the bond to provide the anticipated interest rate differential benefit. Exhibits 12 and 13 outline the structures of such securities.

An additional advantage for asset managers of differential swap structures is that they allow investors to take positions in interest rate differentials *between any two currencies* without incurring currency exposures. For exam-

EXHIBIT 15   Asset-Based Differential Swap Structure

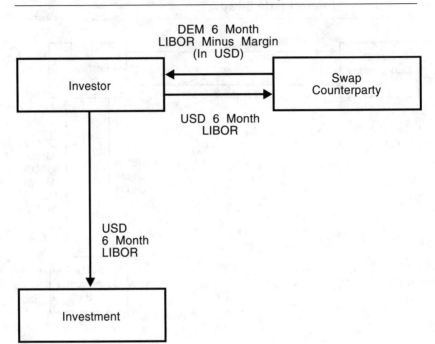

ple, an investment manager with a predominant USD investment portfolio could seek to take advantage of anticipated movements in the differential between DEM and JPY interest rates by entering into a DEM/JPY differential swap (where all payments are in USD) to create the required exposure to DEM/JPY interest differentials.

MARKET FOR DIFFERENTIAL SWAPS

The market for differential swaps is of recent origin. The first differential swap was undertaken in late 1990/early 1991. The differential swap has increased in popularity with a significant number of transactions being completed in the latter half of 1991 and early 1992.

The major impetus to the market has been the prevailing structure of global interest rates. In the present environment, the difference in short-term interest rates between a number of currencies is significantly different from the differential in long-term rates in these currencies. In addition, the prevalence of flat or inverted yield curves in a number of currencies (primarily European currencies) and the corresponding incidence of sharply positively sloped yield curves in some currencies (for example, USD) has assisted in creating differential swap opportunities.

The incidence of this type of interest rate environment has allowed differential swaps to be structured for two main types of capital market participants.

A major group of participants has been asset managers seeking to enhance returns on relatively low yielding USD denominated investment assets yielding USD money market related rates of return. These investors have entered into differential swaps where they pay USD LIBOR and receive in USD DEM, CHF, GBP and (until recently) JPY LIBOR minus the differential swap margin. Asset managers have sought to benefit from differential swap structure either directly by entering into such transactions or, indirectly, through purchasing securities in which the differential swap structure is embedded.

Another major class of participant in the differential swap market has been borrowers in currencies in which short-term money market rates have been relatively high. These borrowers have entered into differential swaps where they receive, for example, DEM, CHF, or GBP six-month LIBOR and pay USD six-month LIBOR plus the differential swap margin. These transactions are designed to reduce the borrowers' interest cost by seeking to capitalize on the interest differential as between the relevant currencies.

One group of borrowers that has been active in utilizing the differential swap structure has been smaller Japanese companies that have restructured their liabilities to carry interest rates that are related to USD floating rates seeking to capitalize on the favorable interest differential between USD and JPY.

The development of a market in differential swaps is still in its early stages. The technology necessary to hedge and manage the currency exposures entailed by such transactions is confined to a relatively small group of financial institutions. Major providers of differential swaps include Bankers Trust, CS Financial Products, Merrill Lynch, JP Morgan, and Morgan Stanley.

However, as transaction volumes grow and the hedging technology, inevitably, proliferates, other institutions are likely to enter the market with a resultant drop in bid-offer spreads thereby decreasing the cost for participants in transacting differential swaps.

SUMMARY

Differential swaps are a hybrid swap structure designed to enable the parties entering into such transactions to take positions in interest rate differentials across currencies without incurring any currency exposure.

Such transactions belong to an increasingly rapidly growing class of transactions (often referred to as "quantos") designed to allow the participant to benefit from anticipated movements in a price index of some financial asset while insulating it from any potential currency exposure related to the index itself; that is, a structural separation of currency and interest rate derived value characteristics.

Differential swap transactions are an interesting addition to the swap market with potentially wide-ranging applications for asset and liability managers alike.

REFERENCES

Cookson, Richard, "Cross Wise Companies," *Risk,* Vol. 4 No. 8 (September 1991): 4.

Cooper, Martin, "Exploring Differential Swaps," *Treasury Management*, Euromoney Publications 15 December 1991.

Das, Satyajit, "Differential Strip Down," *Risk,* Vol. 5 No 6 (June 1992): 65, 66, 68, 72.

Das, Satyajit, "Differential Operators," *Risk,* Vol. 5 No 7 (July–August 1992): 51–53.

Frank, David, "Index Swaps Trade High Rates for Low Ones," *Global Finance* (January 1992): 18–20.

Reiner, Eric, "Quanto Mechanics," *Risk,* Vol. 5 No 3 (March 1992): 59–63.

Robinson, Danielle, "Diff Swaps Tempt the Wary," *Euromoney* (October 1991): 10–11.

Rubinstein, Mark, "Two Into One," *Risk,* Vol. 4 No 5 (May 1991): 49.

Walker, Andrew and Warner, Eric, "A Strategy for High Deustchemark Interest Rates," *Corporate Finance,* Euromoney Publications (June 1992): 43–44.

3

Indexed Amortizing Swaps

Bjørn Pettersen
Assistant Vice President, First National Bank of Chicago

Vijay R. Raghavan
Senior Managing Director, First National Bank of Chicago

INTRODUCTION

An Indexed Amortizing Swap (IAS) or Note (IAN) is a synthetic mortgage product whose amortization characteristics are based primarily on the evolution of a specific interest rate index. The swap counterparty/investor typically receives a fixed rate on a varying notional amount. The latter is indexed to changes in the level of LIBOR or the yields of any of the Constant Maturity Treasuries (CMTs). In return, on the outstanding notional amount, a floating rate is paid in the case of a swap. In the case of a note, the present value of the uncertain cash flows is paid as its initial price.

As a result, both indexed amortizing notes and swaps have return characteristics that replicate mortgage-backed securities (MBSs) such as collateralized mortgage obligations (CMOs). However a note is an on-balance sheet transaction that has credit exposure to the issuer, while a swap is an off-balance sheet transaction with credit exposure to the swap counterparty. To avoid confusion, the remainder of the chapter focuses on IASs.

The first indexed amortizing structures were created in the late 1980s to compete with CMOs as alternative assets, held off balance sheet. The off-balance sheet swaps gained popularity among banks as alternative assets to

We would like to thank Mary Baumann and Joseph Williams for their invaluable editorial suggestions and Sandy Matthews and Kelly Ferrell for their excellent computational assistance.

cash mortgage products. Since then, the use of indexed amortizing swaps and notes has increased dramatically. The size of the market is presently estimated to be more than $200 billion in notional value. Other users interested in the product, either in the swap or note format, would primarily include investors in the mortgage market, such as insurance companies, mutual and hedge fund managers, and pension fund managers.

CHARACTERIZING AN INDEXED AMORTIZING SWAP

Before continuing further, four IAS-specific parameters, namely lockout period, base rate, amortization schedule, and clean-up call, are discussed.

The lockout period is the time interval during which there is no amortization. The lockout guarantees the counterparty a minimum duration. The lockout date must be less than the final maturity of the instrument. The choice of the lockout period affects the duration (or expected average life), but not the final maturity. Typically, an increase in the lockout period leads to an increase in the duration in a standard IAS structure.

The base rate is the specific value of the index that is chosen as a reference, which, in turn, determines the extent of the principal reduction at each reset date. The base rate has all the characteristics of a "strike" price in the terminology of options. The base rate in combination with the amortization schedule determines the expected amortization speed (or average life) at inception as well as the actual amortization during the life of the instrument, due to the evolution of the index. Typically, the actual rate of the index is compared to the base rate on a reset date. This difference (actual rate – base rate) determines the extent of the principal reduction, through the pre-specified amortization schedule. If the difference is a large negative number, the paydown is high, and if the difference is a large positive number, the paydown is usually zero.

Changing the base rate will change the characteristics of the indexed amortizing swap. In a plain indexed amortizing structure, a high base rate is usually associated with a greater amortization speed and a short duration. Usually the investor sets a base rate based on his view of future interest rates. The usual choice of indices for the base rate are LIBOR and CMTs. The former has largely evolved out of the convenience it has offered swap dealers in hedging their portfolios on the supply side, and the latter have evolved from the demand side as they are the common benchmarks for fixed income portfolio managers.

As mentioned above, the amortization schedule combined with the set base rate determines how the product will amortize in the future. The prepayment schedule for an IAS is derived from the amortization table that is agreed upon prior to the trade. The table maps the deviations of the index from the base rate to the extent of principal reduction, on any of the reset dates. Typically large positive differences of the actual index value over the base rate at a reset date result in no paydown and large negative differences result in high paydown.

The paydown fractions on a reset date can be based on either remaining notional or original notional. An IAS based on remaining notional will amortize at a slower speed. The first IAS transactions done were based on original notional. As the market for these transactions has mushroomed, and with the intent of closely mimicking mortgage transactions, paydowns based on remaining notional have emerged as the dominant format.

It is the amortization schedule that gives the security shortening and extension risk. The shortening risk is reduced by the lockout period, which protects the user against prepayment. All extension risk occurs between the lockout and the final maturity. The amortization schedule is chosen prior to the trade execution by the end user to satisfy his specific return or hedging needs. Usually the schedule is based on the investor's view of the level of interest rates in the futures. As an example, if the index is three-month LIBOR, the investor will pick an amortization schedule (in combination with the base rate) that fits his view of expected forward LIBOR rates. The current forward LIBOR curve can be observed in the Eurodollar futures market as traded on different futures exchanges worldwide (MERC, SIMEX, LIFFE).

It is common to include a clean-up call in the structure, to avoid the nuisance of the notional amount decreasing to levels too low to administer. This feature will assure that the IAS will amortize to zero when the remaining notional is less than or equal to a pre-specified percentage of original notional. It is common to have clean-up calls up to 20 percent. However, on occasion one may see them as high as 80 percent (embedded in some of the more recent "mega clean-up" call structures).

IAS's have return characteristics that are similar to MBSs such as CMOs. Typically the weighted average life of the structure (average maturity) shortens when the index rate drops and extends when the index rate rises relative to the base rate. The fixed rate receiver is short volatility or convexity. Convexity is the change in the duration of the security due to a change in its yield. Duration is the weighted average term to maturity of a security's cash flow, and relates the change in the price of the security to a change in its yield. An option-free fixed income coupon security usually has positive convexity. Because of the negative convexity of the indexed amortizing swap, the investor will receive an above market coupon. The convexity of the IAS depends on the choice of the index and the amortization schedule. Under stable rate scenarios, the premiums inherent in negatively convex securities are realized as higher total returns to other comparable-duration assets.

The differences between IASs and CMOs have also to be noted. While IASs are inherently tied to the LIBOR and swap market rates and volatilities, CMOs trade relative to mortgage rates and volatilities. In addition, the amortization schedules in CMOs are dependent on interest rate movements as well as a host of other special demographic and idiosyncratic factors inherent in specific mortgage pools. Conversely, IAS paydowns are purely determined by interest rate movements, in reference to the chosen base rate. CMOs have uncertain maturities tied to unanticipated amortization. IASs, on the other hand, have relatively well-defined maturities. Most of the outstanding transactions at the present time were structured to have final maturities of under five years at inception. In addition, the advantageous lockout features in IASs mitigate prepayment risk by preserving the outstanding notional amounts with certainty up until the lockout date. As a result, the maturity uncertainty on IASs is confined to a range between the lockout and final maturity dates.

INDEXED AMORTIZING SWAP STRUCTURE

The main advantage of an IAS is its flexibility in customization; it allows the users to design structures to meet their specific return needs and risk appetite. As an example, the term sheet for a typical IAS structure is shown in Exhibit 1.

IASs are usually traded with notional upwards of $25 million. Our example illustrates a spot settlement, but it is not uncommon to structure forward-starting IASs. The swap has a lockout period of two years and a final maturity of five years. The fixed coupon the investor receives is 6.25 percent semi-bond and in return he will pay three-month LIBOR (floating). The IAS has quarterly resets, meaning that the floating payment is reset to LIBOR every three months. The amortization frequency decides how often the index is to be polled to set the current outstanding notional. The base rate is set at cash three-month LIBOR. The amortization schedule, in conjunction with the base rate, decides the expected amortization speed of the transaction and the actual amortization at each reset date in the future. To illustrate, if LIBOR is at or below 3.875 percent on March 9, 1996 (at the end of the lockout period), the notional will amortize by 100 percent and the IAS will mature. How-

EXHIBIT 1   Indexed Amortizing Swap

Indicative Terms & Conditions

Principal Amount:	$100 million
Settlement Date:	March 11, 1994
Final Maturity:	Five-year final maturity, two-year lockout period subject to amortization schedule, and a 15% clean-up call.
Coupon Rate:	6.25%
Index Reset:	Quarterly
Payment Frequency:	Quarterly
Amortization Frequency:	Quarterly
Base Rate (BR):	3.875% (3-month LIBOR)
Amortization Schedule:	At the conclusion of the lockout period, the Principal Amount shall amortize quarterly based on the level of three-month USD LIBOR. The amortization for each period shall equal the Notional Percentage Reduction (NPR) and will be linearly interpolated between the points displayed in the table.

3M LIBOR	3M LIBOR – BR	Average Life	NPR
3.875%	+0 bp	2.00 year	100.00%
4.875%	+100 bp	3.00 year	17.28%
5.875%	+200 bp	4.00 year	6.42%
6.875%	+300 bp	5.00 year	0.00%

ever, if LIBOR sets at 6.875 percent or higher there will be no amortization of notional. For any LIBOR setting after the two-year lockout period where three-month LIBOR falls between the discrete rate points in the table, the swap will amortize based on the schedule using linear interpolation between the points. Changing any of the above parameters will change the duration and convexity features of the IAS, and hence could lead to a change in the fixed coupon to be paid on the swap.

For the example discussed above, the structure gives a yield of 135 bp, 95 bp, and 45 bp over two-, three- and five-year Treasuries respectively. On a comparable three-year PAC the concurrent yield was about 60 bp over three-year Treasuries. It is therefore evident that the swap market may at times (depending on the existing volatility and rate structures) be able to give superior returns on synthetic securities over comparable securities in the mortgage market. At other times, when mortgage spreads and volatilities widen relative to the swap market, cash-based mortgage swaps may turn out to have potentially more attractive relative return characteristics.

THE NOTIONAL PERCENTAGE REDUCTION SCHEDULE

Let us take a closer look at how one can design an amortization schedule based on the desired average life characteristics under specifically chosen rate scenarios. Average life represents the weighted-average (by notional outstanding) maturity (not to be confused with duration) on a particular rate path. Converting from average life to a Notional Percentage Reduction Schedule (NPR) is a fairly straightforward calculation. In the following example, the investor is interested in a two-year lockout, five-year final IAS, with quarterly amortization frequency. We want to match the following average life schedule to an appropriate NPR schedule for the following instantaneous LIBOR shifts. Assume that there is a 15 percent clean-up call.

3M LIBOR – Base Rate	Desired Average Life
0bp	2.0 year
+100bp	3.0 year

Consider first the case of (3-month LIBOR – Base Rate) at 0 bp. The desired average life is 2.0 years. Assume that NPR = 100%. The transaction will have to amortize to zero at the two-year lockout date to result in an average life of two years as desired in this scenario.

3M LIBOR – Base Rate	Average Life	NPR
0	2.0 year	100%

Consider now the case of (3-month LIBOR – Base Rate) at +100 bp. The desired average life is 3.0 years.

We illustrate with a trial and error routine how to find the correct NPR that gives a 3.0 year average life. Try an NPR = 17.28%. The first column lists the time nodes and the second column shows the product of the following three items: Notional Remaining (i) * NPR(i) * Time Period (i). The net result is a time period weighted paydown in the second column.

Period i	Time Period Weighted Paydown
2.00 year node	1.00*.1728*2.00* = .345600
2.25 year node	.8272*.1728*2.25 = .321615
2.50 year node	.684260*.1728*2.50 = .295600
2.75 year node	.566020*.1728*2.75 = .268973
3.00 year node	.468212*.1728*3.00 = .242721
3.25 year node	.387305*.1728*3.25 = .217510
3.50 year node	.320378*.1728*3.50 = .193765
3.75 year node	.265017*.1728*3.75 = .171731
4.00 year node	.219222*.1728*4.0 = .151526
4.25 year node	.181340*.1728*4.25 = .133176
4.50 year node	.150005*4.50 = .675022
4.75 year node	zero
5.00 year node	zero

Note that the 15 percent clean-up call terminates the deal at the 4.5 year node.

The sum of all the numbers in the second column gives an average life of approximately three years.

3M LIBOR – Base Rate	Average Life	NPR
0	2.0 year	100%
+100bp	3.0 year	17.28%

Therefore, by selecting an NPR of 17.28 percent we get an average life of 3.0 years for +100bp as desired.

We can also calculate NPRs for 4.0 year average life (6.42 percent) and 5.0 year average life (0 percent) in the same way. The end result is an NPR schedule that matches the desired average life schedule the investor prefers for various assumed instantaneous movements of the chosen index.

PERFORMANCE CHARACTERISTICS OF INDEXED AMORTIZING SWAPS

In this section we examine the performance characteristics of the example discussed above under three assumed future rate scenarios. We assume that rates evolve (1) at levels slower than the forward rates indicate (labeled S1), (2) as indicated by the forward rate structure as of the transaction date (S2), and (3) at levels higher than those indicated by forward rates (S3). These assumptions are shown in Exhibit 2. Exhibit 2 also indicates the levels of

EXHIBIT 2   Interest Rate Scenarios
Implied Three-Month LIBOR   Forward Rates

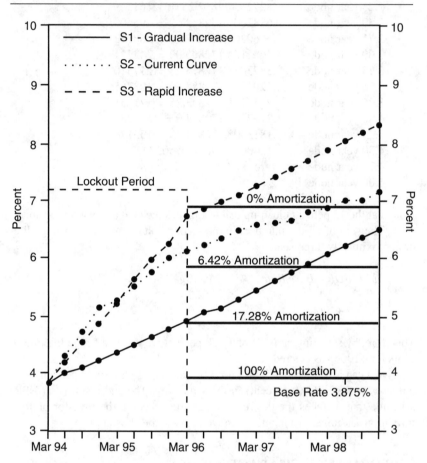

amortization expected at various LIBOR rate levels. Note that the higher the LIBOR realization, the lower the rate of amortization. The assumed rate paths for the three scenarios enter into decreasing levels of amortizations with time. From the term sheet, the base rate was set at 3.875 percent. The amortization schedule is marked on the graph with horizontal lines. We assume straight line interpolation between the amortization nodes.

If LIBOR follows the forward path as of today (S2), the structure will amortize by 4.815 percent at the lockout (two years from the start date) with a LIBOR set at that time at 6.125 percent. However, if LIBOR follows the slower rate increase path (S1), and sets at 4.875 percent, 17.28 percent of the notional will amortize.

For each of these scenarios we track the profits or losses (P&L) accumulated by the fixed rate receiver. The accumulation is done by compounding the positions at the assumed LIBOR rates on a given path. The sensitivity of the swap P&L performance to various assumed based rates was also computed. Note, however, that the break-even fixed rates paid may vary slightly for these different base rates, and hence the P&L numbers may not be strictly comparable. Nevertheless, it is useful to study the behavior of these swaps under the different rate scenarios. The same set of data was also complied for a five-year final, three-year lockout structure (with a break-even fixed rate of 6.15 percent), in order to study the effect of extending the lockout date. These results are shown in Exhibit 3. Exhibit 4 shows the average life variation with different base rates for the two structures under the different scenarios.

EXHIBIT 3 Comparative P&L Performance Details

| | Slower than Forward | | Forward Curve | | Faster than Forward | |
| | Average | | Average | | Average | |
Base Rate	Life	Gain	Life	Gain	Life	Gain
5/2 Structure						
5.375	2.00	3.7MM	2.54	2.3MM	3.70	–1.3MM
4.875	2.00	3.9MM	3.52	2.1MM	4.23	–0.4MM
4.375	2.16	4.3MM	4.04	2.0MM	4.67	–0.8MM
4.125	2.74	5.4MM	4.31	2.2MM	4.84	–1.0MM
3.875	3.35	5.9MM	4.54	1.7MM	4.95	–1.2MM
3.625	3.58	6.1MM	4.76	1.5MM	5.00	–1.3MM
3.375	3.84	6.1MM	4.91	1.3MM	5.00	–1.4MM
5/3 Structure						
5.375	3.00	4.8MM	4.12	1.5MM	4.39	–1.1MM
4.875	3.15	5.2MM	4.19	1.4MM	4.39	–1.6MM
4.375	3.88	6.1MM	4.51	1.2MM	4.98	–1.9MM
4.125	3.88	6.1MM	4.70	1.1MM	5.00	–1.9MM
3.875	4.11	6.1MM	4.88	0.9MM	5.00	–1.9MM
3.625	4.26	6.1MM	4.98	0.7MM	5.00	–2.0MM
3.375	4.42	6.1MM	5.00	0.7MM	5.00	–2.0MM

EXHIBIT 4 Base Rate vs. Average Life

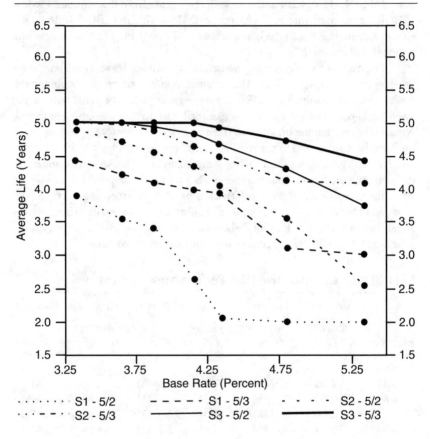

From Exhibit 4 the following observations can be made about average lives:

1. Increasing base rates decrease average lives because of increased amortization speeds;
2. Average lives tend to be higher for higher rate increases compared to lower rate increases, as should be expected;
3. Average lives increase with higher lockout periods.

Going back to Exhibit 3, the variation of the P&L over the different structures, scenarios, and base rates could now be easily explained through the linkage to average life behavior. As can be seen, profits tend to be higher with lower base rates (higher average lives) in scenarios with relatively slower rate increases. On the other hand, extension risk also contributes to higher losses in bearish scenarios with higher than expected rate increases. To summarize, if amortization is accelerated by either altering the amortization schedule or increasing the base rate, the average life and the break-even fixed rate decrease. The user will increase his yield pickup by increasing the option value embedded in the swap. This can be accomplished by an optimal choice of the base rate and by increasing the time period from lockout to final maturity (increasing duration risk). The optionality manifests itself in increased uncertainty of the duration of the swap.

PRICING AND HEDGING INDEXED AMORTIZING SWAPS

As described earlier, the indexed amortizing swap can be viewed as a callable swap, with the call structure predefined only to rate movements. Note, however, that while the exercise of the call (the notional paydown) is indexed to the short rate, the value of the paydown on a given interest rate path depends upon the swap yield to the remaining term to maturity. The pricing of an IAS is, therefore, dependent on the entire yield curve movement over time. The models that are used to price IASs vary in the degree of the trade-offs between simplicity on the one hand and capturing the realities of term structure movements on the other.

In the former class, a variety of one-factor models have been developed, which assume that all yields along the term structure are completely correlated. These models have computational simplicity but may not be accurate in pricing the IASs because of the complete correlation assumption. Introducing a second factor in term structure models helps overcome this inaccuracy by incorporating an extra degree of freedom in term structure movements. However, utilization of the second factor is critically dependent upon having a source of liquid market pricing to calibrate the correlation between different parts of the yield curve. As the liquidity in the markets for instruments such as yield curve swaps, for example, is very low, calibrations to market are relatively meaningless. Often historical data are used to calibrate correlation parameters. It is well known that historical correlation data tend to be unstable and the noise introduced by inaccurate calibration may outweigh the advantages of incorporating a second factor. This is particularly true for the IAS market as it stands today, as it is dominated by short average life structures (between two and three years) where the additional degree of freedom is of relatively low significance. On the other hand, if longer-dated structures become more popular, the need for a two-factor model becomes more imperative.

Regardless of the model used, the basic valuation principles dictate calibrating the model to the following observed market yields and volatilities:

a. The swap yield curve;
b. At-the-money cap volatilities;
c. At-the-money swaption volatilities.

Calibration to the above ensures that the model used is arbitrage-free in terms of observed market data. In general, because the IAS is a path-dependent option (the payoffs depend on the path of rate movements, rather than on ending rate values as in a simple option such as a cap) Monte-Carlo simulation procedures are used for pricing and hedging. Clean-up calls and IASs based on original notionals, in particular, make it difficult for simpler lattice-based transformations to be employed. The Monte-Carlo procedure involves generating arbitrage-free rate paths consistent with given yield and volatility structures as mentioned above. Cash flows generated on these paths for a specified IAS structure are discounted backwards both on the fixed and floating rate payments. Pricing involves identifying the fixed rate that equates the present value of the floating rate payments.

The same procedures can also be used for hedging purposes. Perturbations of each of the individual rate and volatility inputs, holding everything else constant, alters the price of the structure. The same perturbations applied to the hedge instruments identify their respective sensitivities to the inputs. The objective is to find a set of hedge instruments at a given point in time (hence known as "dynamic" hedging) that match the sensitivities of the IAS to all of the input variables. It is also important to keep in mind that the relative stability of the hedges (for large perturbations) determines the level of transactions costs, especially in volatile conditions. The hedges are rebalanced on a dynamic basis. As the model is calibrated to the variables that are implicit in Eurodollar futures (or FRAs), swaps, at-the-money caps (and/or floors), and swaptions, these comprise the relevant hedge instrument universe.

VARIATIONS ON INDEXED AMORTIZING SWAPS AND USES

Alternative Indices

In the discussion above, it was assumed that the indexing rate is three-month LIBOR. This index has the advantage of a high volatility and hence can be translated to higher coupons on the fixed side in lieu of the options sold. However, given that the market for IASs is intended to be an alternative to that for MBSs, it may be more pertinent to structure IASs that are tied to comparable indices such as the five- or 10-year CMT rates.

The market has thus far been entirely one-sided in that the end users achieve yield enhancement on the fixed rate they receive in exchange for the underlying call options sold. It is, however, conceivable that with the yield curve bouncing upwards and flattening considerably, the demand for IASs from end users may switch from using them as instruments for yield enhancement to hedges for their existing MBS portfolios. In other words, they may prefer to pay fixed (equivalent of shorting MBSs) rather than receive fixed. The hedges are likely to be more accurate if the index is the 10-year CMT rate. In addition, as the 10-year CMT rate is less volatile than three-month LIBOR, the cost of the options they purchase is likely to be lower. The Constant Maturity Swap (CMS) rate is a likely alternative for a CMT rate.

The index could also be specified to be the difference between a long rate and a short rate, in which case the swap can be structured as a yield curve indexed amortizing swap. Alternatively, the index could be an exchange rate, with the swap enabling the sale of exchange rate volatility to enhance yields. It is obvious that the enormous flexibility available in the choice of the index could give rise to a variety of interesting structured products. However, the pricing and risk management of these swaps may be complicated by the additional correlation variable.

Alternative Amortizing Schedules

In the example discussed, the paydown schedule was constructed in such a way that the swap amortized when rates went down. Alternatively, if the swap accretes when rates fall, and stays level when rates move upwards, the convexity of the IAS becomes completely positive. Such an instrument can provide a good prepayment hedge for the negative convexity of an existing MBS portfolio when rates fall. Note that the investor buys call options on the swap in such a case. Alternatively, if the hedge is to be constructed for a rising rate scenario, the swap can pay down with rising rates and stay level under falling rates. Again, this accentuates the positive convexity of a regular swap, and the investor is buying put options.

Alternative Payoff Streams

In the examples above, the idea of path-dependent amortization was applied to structure a swap. The same idea could be applied to the purchase of options such as caps and floors. For example, a corporation may be interested in limiting the costs of its floating-rate liabilities with the purchase of a cap. However, the cost of an outright purchase of an at-the-money cap may be perceived as too high. This cost can be lowered by purchasing caps at higher strike prices, out-of-the-money, but the protection may be ineffective, particularly if rates hovered just below the strike level. Alternatively, we can think of buying down the price of an at-the-money cap by reducing the notional protected as rates fall. Such structures can be viewed as partial knockouts. The advantage of this structure is that the investor gets the protection when he needs it most. Similarly floors can be subsidized by amortizing the notional as rates head upwards. Such path-dependent caps and floors can be further customized in strike levels and amortizing schedules to suit the risk profiles needed in protection.

THE FUTURE FOR THE INDEXED AMORTIZING SWAP MARKET

The growth of the IAS market has largely evolved over a low interest rate, steep yield curve environment. As short-term LIBOR remained relatively stable over a fairly long period of time, investors gained substantially on their swaps. However, we are currently in a situation where the economy seems to be picking up steam and rates are headed upwards. Further, as the expectation is that of a series of further Fed tightenings in the near future, the yield curve is likely to flatten as long as the inflation numbers remain fairly low. Investors extending out in maturity are likely to see a smaller carry in holding IASs, as assets, due to the yield curve component. The other factor that contributes to the yield pickup is volatility. As volatilities have been relatively low over the last year, the expectation is that they are likely to trend upwards. Hence, this component is likely to contribute to a higher yield pickup over time. As mortgage originations and refinancings diminish, the supply in the mortgage market is likely to be constrained, making mortgage assets richer relative to IASs. On balance, IASs still have the potential for outperforming CMOs as alternative assets under the assumed scenarios.

However, in a bearish rate environment, the potential of IASs as hedge instruments for existing MBSs in portfolio has to receive greater emphasis. Investors could pay fixed on indexed amortizing swaps to utilize them as hedges in their portfolios. Alternatively, they could structure positively convex IASs to mitigate the effect of an increase in rates on the overall portfolio. Finally, as discussed in an earlier section, the path-dependent cap as an alternative to other option products remains eminently attractive.

4

Index Amortization Swaps and Notes
How They Work and How They Compare to CMOs

Scott McDermott
Marcus Huie
Vice Presidents, Fixed Income Research Department,
Goldman, Sachs & Co.

Since their introduction more than three years ago, index amortization swaps and notes have competed with more traditional mortgage derivative products, mainly collateralized mortgage obligations (CMOs), for the attention of investors. This report both describes the characteristics of the index amortization swap and note market and presents a side-by-side comparison of CMOs and index amortization swaps and notes using a traditional mortgage valuation tool, option-adjusted spread (OAS) analysis. Broadly speaking, we conclude that index amortization swaps and notes and CMOs are comparable products, but there are times when the index amortization swap and note market offers better value than do CMOs, and vice versa. This paper will examine some of the considerations that investors should find useful in trying to find that value.

This study was originally presented in a series of Goldman Sachs seminars entitled *Fixed Income Portfolio Strategy for 1993* and published in the Goldman Sachs Fixed Income Research series. We are grateful to Peter Niculescu, Scott Pinkus, and Larry Weiss for their helpful comments; to Chip Carver, Bill Grathwohl, Tom Montag, and Bruce Petersen of the Derivative Products Group and Sam Collins of the Fixed Income Research Department for their insights into the index amortization swaps & notes market; and to Lynn Edens, Brad Tuthill, and Adam Wizon of the Mortgage Securities Research Group for their assistance in executing the option-adjusted spread analysis.

Copyright © 1993 by Goldman, Sachs & Co.

KEY FEATURES

An investor entering into an *index amortization swap* receives the fixed rate side of an interest rate swap, paying a floating rate; an investor purchasing an *index amortization note*, purchases a corporate medium-term note. Most significantly, the notional principal balance of the swap and the principal balance of the note amortize over time based on changes in interest rates. The swap's notional balance declines and the note's principal balance is prepaid when interest rates are low. As in the case of a mortgage, the swap's notional balance and note's principal balance may decline, but the notional and principal balances can never increase.

Index amortization swaps and notes are a relatively new product, and like most new derivative products, they originally were created to satisfy the needs of a narrow group of investors. Developed in 1989, index amortization swaps were offered to banks as an off-balance-sheet alternative to mortgage products when new bank capital requirements made off-balance-sheet investments attractive. At first, the notional principal balance of these swaps amortized based upon the actual prepayment experience of a pool of mortgage pass-through securities. Later, the amortization was based upon an interest rate index, such as three-month LIBOR, with a schedule specifying faster amortization (faster prepayment) as interest rates fell and slower amortization (slower prepayment) as interest rates rose.

This latter innovation—amortization based upon a LIBOR index—was crucial to the development of the index amortization swap and note market. The new structure eliminated uncertainty regarding the relationship between interest rate levels and mortgage prepayments. What is more important, a LIBOR index opened the market up to participation by interest rate swap dealers, a community already accustomed to making markets in and hedging LIBOR-based instruments. This permitted narrower bid/offered spreads and increased the market's liquidity. Today, index amortization swaps and notes are mature products used not only by banks but by a broad range of mortgage portfolio managers, including pension fund managers, insurance company asset managers, and corporate cash managers.

Index amortization swaps and notes compete directly with the CMO market for investors' attention. Exhibit 1 compares the characteristics of these two products. Broadly speaking, these markets are similar, with the principal difference being the way the amortization occurs. Index amortization swaps and notes amortize based upon LIBOR, while the amortization that CMOs experience is ultimately linked, through the prepayment function, to mortgage refinancing rates.

EXHIBIT 1 Product Characteristics

	Index Amortization Swaps and Notes	*CMOs*
Interest rate amortization risk exposure	LIBOR	Mortgage refinancing rates
Amortization based solely on interest rate	Yes	No—there are other considerations that also affect prepayment rates
Guaranteed initial lockout and final maturity	Yes	No—there is risk of early call or delayed maturity under unusual prepayment scenarios
Investor sells options to increase yield	Yes—put and call options	Yes—prepayment options

Example: A 2/5 Index Amortization Note

When an investor selects an index amortization swap or note, three characteristics are important: the lockout period, the final maturity, and the reference interest rate index. To see why, examine Exhibit 2, which describes the characteristics of a two-year lockout/five-year final maturity index amortization note. By two-year lockout period, we mean that for the first two years, or first seven quarters (since the swaps and notes amortize quarterly), the note's principal balance remains unchanged at 100 percent of the original balance. By five-year final maturity, we mean an absolute final maturity such that at the end of five years, whatever principal balance remains in the note is returned to the investor. Between years two through five (at the end of the eighth through 19th quarters), the note's principal balance amortizes according to the schedule shown in Exhibit 2. The amortization schedule makes it easy to see why index amortization swaps and notes are similar to mortgage securities.

The amortization is based upon changes in interest rates, so we use a reference interest rate index (a "reference rate") to determine whether interest rates are low (below the reference rate) or high (above the reference rate). The reference rate is determined when the note is issued or the swap becomes effective, and like the maturity date, it does not change thereafter. In this

EXHIBIT 2   Two-Year Lockout/Five-Year Final Maturity Index Amortization Note

First seven quarters:	No amortization (lockout period).
Quarters 8 to 19:	Amortization according to the schedule shown below. Reference rate = 3.50% (three-month LIBOR interest rate index). Use linear interpolation for interest rate changes not explicitly shown.
Last quarter (20):	100% of remaining balance amortized (maturity).

Three-Month LIBOR Less Reference Rate	Amortization of Remaining Balance[a]	Average Life
Unchanged or below	100.00%	2.0 years
100 bp increase	11.26%	3.5 years
200 bp increase	2.84%	4.5 years
300 bp increase or more	0.00%	5.0 years

a. In the example shown here, the schedule specifies amortization as a percentage of the note's remaining balance. Other amortization swaps and notes may specify amortization as a percentage of the swap's or note's original balance. Read the term sheet and prospectus carefully.

example, the reference rate is 3.5 percent three-month LIBOR.[1] During the two- through five-year amortization period and on any of the quarterly amortization dates, if three-month LIBOR is unchanged or has fallen, or with a 3.5 percent reference rate if three-month LIBOR is 3.5 percent or less, then 100 percent of the note's outstanding balance will amortize in that quarter.[2] At the other extreme, if three-month LIBOR has risen by 300 basis points or more, or with a 3.5 percent reference rate if three-month LIBOR is 6.5 percent or above, then none of the note's outstanding balance will amortize.

The amortization schedule also specifies the amortization for interest rate changes between these two extremes. For interest rate changes that are not explicitly shown in Exhibit 2, we use a linear interpolation. For example, if during the two- through five-year amortization period interest rates had increased by 50 basis points on any of the quarterly amortization dates, or

---

1. While LIBOR is the most common interest rate reference index, other index amortization swaps and notes may use constant maturity Treasury (CMT) yields as the interest rate reference index. Read the term sheet and prospectus carefully.
2. In practice, three-month LIBOR is usually measured two or more business days prior to the date of the actual cash payment of principal and interest.

with a 3.5 percent reference rate if three-month LIBOR is 4.0 percent, then 55.63 percent of the note's outstanding balance would amortize [55.63% = 1/2 × (100% + 11.26%)]. For convenience, there is usually a clause in the prospectus called the "clean-up provision" that obliges the issuer to call the note at par if the outstanding balance falls below a minimum level, usually 15 percent of the original balance.

Finally, Exhibit 2 also shows the note's average life, calculated according to standard mortgage market convention. For example, if three-month LIBOR rates are constant at 100 basis points above the reference rate throughout the amortization period, the note's average life is 3.5 years.

FORWARD RATES AND EXPECTED AMORTIZATION

While the amortization schedule specifies how the index amortization note will behave in any given interest rate environment, it tells us little about investors' principal concerns: how index amortization notes are priced and how they are expected to behave in a portfolio context. The answers to these questions are complex, since the note's amortization depends upon the uncertain level of future interest rates. We can gain some insight by studying forward interest rates.

The solid line in Exhibit 3 shows forward three-month LIBOR, implied by the shape of the yield curve, for each quarter over the next five years. (All market prices, interest rates, and forward rates quoted in this report are based on market conditions as of December 18, 1992.) Note that three-month LIBOR rises rapidly, consistent with the upward sloping yield curve in the U.S. Treasury market.[3] In practice, we would be surprised if interest rates in the future followed these forward rates exactly; interest rates are volatile. To provide an idea of the range of possible forward three-month LIBOR, we use the dotted lines to show three-month LIBOR one standard deviation above and below the forward values, based on a 15 percent short rate volatility. In

---

3. Forward rates are future short-term interest rates that would be required to make the returns from a series of short-term investments equal to today's long-term investment return. For example, a three-month investment at 3.5 percent reinvested in a subsequent three-month investment at 3.72 percent is economically equivalent to a six-month investment at 3.625 percent. If today's three-month LIBOR is 3.5 percent and today's six-month LIBOR is 3.625 percent, we say that 3.72 percent is the forward three-month LIBOR beginning three months hence.

EXHIBIT 3 A 2/5 Index Amortization Note, 3.5% Reference Rate

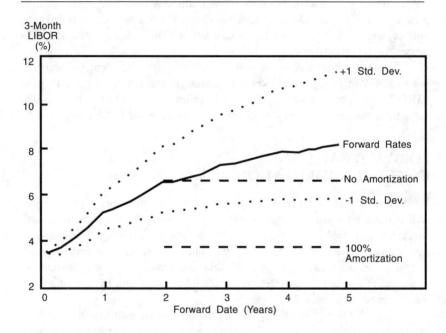

other words, if future interest rates stayed within ± one standard deviation of forward rates, then three-month LIBOR would follow a path somewhere between the two dotted lines.

To indicate how the two-year lockout/five-year final maturity index amortization note would behave in this interest rate environment, we show as dashed lines in Exhibit 3 the extremes of the amortization schedule. We draw the dashed lines only between years two and five because the amortization occurs only in this interval. With a 3.5 percent reference rate, 100 percent of the note's remaining balance would amortize if three-month LIBOR was 3.5 percent or less on any quarterly amortization date; none of the note's remaining balance would amortize if three-month LIBOR was 6.5 percent or above. By comparing the dashed lines in the chart with the solid line, we see that if interest rates follow forward rates, then very little, or none, of the note's balance would amortize, and the note's average life should be just below five years. In fact, to get 100 percent amortization in any quarter, interest rates would have to fall by two or more standard deviations below their forward

EXHIBIT 4   A 2/5 Index Amortization Note, 6.5% Reference Rate

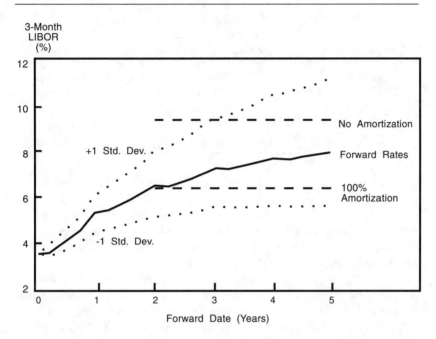

values. This index amortization note—a two-year lockout/five-year final maturity with a 3.5 percent reference rate—would be expected to behave in an investor's portfolio like a five-year note against which the investor has sold out-of-the-money call options (i.e., takes on prepayment risk) expiring in years two through five. The investor would receive the premium from these options in the form of additional coupon income.

It is also useful to consider what would happen had we chosen a 6.5 percent reference rate instead of a 3.5 percent reference rate. After all, we may choose any reference rate that we wish, although, as we shall see, our choice will influence the coupon rate of the security as well as (obviously) its return profile. Our choice of reference rate will not change the amortization schedule shown in Exhibit 2 but will determine the interest rate levels at which amortization occurs.

Exhibit 4 shows the effect of choosing a 6.5 percent reference rate. The forward three-month LIBOR is unchanged and the ± one standard deviation range remains the same, but the amortization schedule now reflects a 6.5 per-

EXHIBIT 5   A 2/5 Index Amortization Note: Effect of Reference Rate

Reference Rate	Fixed Rate Coupon (Yield Spread to Two-Year Treasury Note)	Average Life
3.5%	167 bp	4.67 years
4.0%	170 bp	4.42 years
4.5%	171 bp	4.12 years
5.5%	160 bp	3.34 years
6.5%	123 bp	2.70 years

cent reference rate. With a 6.5 percent reference rate, 100 percent of the note's remaining balance would amortize if three-month LIBOR was 6.5 percent or less on any quarterly amortization date, and none of the note's remaining balance would amortize if three-month LIBOR was 9.5 percent or above. Choosing a higher reference rate has the effect of moving the amortization schedule up on the graph.

Now, by comparing the dashed lines in Exhibit 4 with the solid line, we see that if interest rates followed forward rates, then the note's principal balance would amortize very rapidly after the two-year lockout period, and the note's average life should be just larger than two years. In fact, to get no amortization in any quarter, interest rates would have to rise by one or more standard deviations from their forward values. This index amortization note—same two-year lockout/five year final maturity but with a 6.5 percent reference rate—would be expected to behave in an investor's portfolio like an approximately 2 1/2-year maturity note against which the investor has sold out-of-the-money put options (i.e., takes on extension risk) expiring in years two through five.[4] Again, the investor would receive the premium from these options in the form of additional coupon income.

Exhibit 5 shows the effect of choosing different reference rates on the coupon rate and average life of the two-year lockout/five-year final maturity index amortization note. In this table, the average life is calculated from a probability-weighted Monte Carlo simulation of future interest rate scenarios.

---

4. It is also correct to think of this index amortization note as a five-year note against which the investor has sold deep-in-the-money call options expiring in years two through five.

As the reference rate increases from 3.5 percent to 6.5 percent, the average life falls smoothly from 4.67 to 2.70 years. As Exhibit 5 indicates, the highest coupon rates are achieved when the amortization schedule is centered about forward rates.

Normally, as the note's average life decreases—and since the yield curve is steeply upward sloping—we might have expected the coupon rate of the index amortization note to fall uniformly. But that is not what the table shows. In practice, as the reference rate increases from 3.5 percent to 4.5 percent, the average life falls from 4.67 years to 4.12 years, but the coupon rate actually *increases* slightly—to 171 basis points above the two-year Treasury note yield from 167 basis points above. We can explain this increase in the coupon rate by the types of options we are selling at each choice of reference rate. By using a 3.5 percent reference rate, we are choosing a long average life security against which we have sold call options (prepayment risk). By using a 6.5 percent reference rate, we are choosing a short average life security against which we have sold put options (extension risk). The choice of a 4.5 percent reference rate represents an intermediate average life security with both prepayment risk and extension risk, where, in option terms, we have sold an at-the-money straddle. For selling these at-the-money options—for assuming both prepayment and extension risk—we are compensated by a higher coupon rate on the security.

COMPARABILITY TO CMOs

Exhibit 6 on the next page shows the results of a direct comparison between index amortization notes and CMOs. We used market prices for a collection of FNMA CMOs—vanillas, supports, but mainly PACs—and market prices for two-year lockout/five-year final maturity index amortization notes. We studied the OASs of these securities using Goldman Sachs' mortgage prepayment and interest rate models. For the two-year lockout/five-year final maturity index amortization notes, we obtained market prices for notes with a 3.5 percent, 4.0 percent, 4.5 percent, . . . , 6.5 percent reference interest rate index. We concluded that, broadly speaking, these two markets are comparable. Depending upon the choice of lockout period, final maturity, and reference interest rate index, investors may find significantly more value in the index amortization note market than in the CMO market, or vice versa.

In making the comparison shown in Exhibit 6, we used market prices for index amortization notes issued by a LIBOR-flat credit, namely an A-rated industrial or financial credit that would otherwise issue floating rate

EXHIBIT 6   Option Adjusted Spreads of CMOs and 2/5 Index Amortization Notes

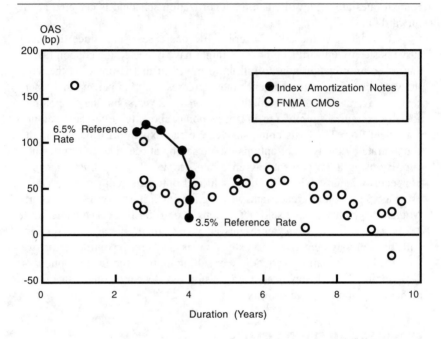

securities at LIBOR. With this choice, the chart also compares index amortization swaps against CMOs, since the swaps are based on a LIBOR floating rate index. Unfortunately, this choice of a LIBOR credit misrepresents the credit risk in the comparison, since FNMA is a government agency credit. On a comparable scale, FNMA's credit would lie at LIBOR less 25 to 45 basis points. To fully adjust for the credit difference, therefore, we should reduce the OASs of the index amortization notes by 25 to 45 basis points. Yet even with this adjustment, our conclusion remains unchanged: Broadly speaking, the index amortization swap and note market is comparable to the CMO market. In the course of a rigorous security selection decision, and depending upon market conditions, investors may find that an index amortization swap or note is cheaper and provides better value than an alternative CMO issue or vice versa. Investors are always better off for having this choice.

Finally, readers should be aware of one additional simplification. The OASs shown in Exhibit 6 represent the expected spread over Treasury forward rates, assuming a 12 percent short rate volatility. The assumption of 12 percent short rate volatility is a commonly used assumption in mortgage market analysis, but it may understate the actual short rate volatility priced into the market for short-duration securities. Increasing the short rate volatility above our 12 percent assumption would reduce the OAS for both CMOs and index amortization notes. It may be appropriate to use a higher short rate volatility for index amortization swaps and notes, whose amortization is LIBOR-based, than for CMOs, whose amortization is ultimately linked to mortgage refinancing rates.

SECURITY SELECTION

As with the CMO market, finding value in the index amortization swap and note market requires a thorough and careful security selection process. Investors should pay particular attention to credit risk. As we have seen, there may be up to a 45 basis point difference between the coupon rate of an agency-issued index amortization note and the same note issued by an A-rated credit, even though the lockout period, maturity, reference interest rate index, and amortization schedule are identical. In some cases, investors can use the swap market to create a high coupon synthetic index amortization note by purchasing a AAA-rated floating rate note and entering into an index amortization swap. Strategies of this nature can help portfolio managers add value.

While we have described a two-year lockout/five-year final maturity index amortization note in this report, many alternatives are possible—from $1^1/_4$-year lockout/$3^1/_4$-year final maturity to five-year lockout/nine-year final maturity structures—with a wide variety of amortization schedules and a correspondingly wide variety of average lives, prepayment risks, and extension risks. Investors considering these securities should pay careful attention to their term sheets and prospectuses.

5

Exotic Options

K. Ravindran
Vice President, Equity Derivatives, RBC Dominion Securities
Adjunct Assistant Professor, University of Waterloo

0. INTRODUCTION

Since the early 1970s, options have been the most widely used hedging and
investment vehicles in many financial markets. Due to the increasing level of
sophistication in the financial markets, the vanilla type options, also known
as the first-generation options, have led to a steady development of two further generations of options (known as the exotic options).

Starting with a brief description of vanilla options, the first section of this
chapter goes on to describe the limitations of such options and how the exotic
options better address the complexity of current risk exposure. Various exotic
options and their uses are described in the second section. The final section surveys the pricing technology available for the exotics, and details the use of the
binomial method as a generic pricing tool for these products.

1. VANILLA OPTIONS AND THEIR LIMITATIONS

Vanilla options refer to the basic European and American style call and put
options. More precisely, a buyer of a European call (put) currency option
pays a premium at the inception of an option contract for the right to buy
(sell) the currency at a specified rate (also known as the strike rate) at the
time of the option expiration. Letting T, X and S_T denote the life of the option,
the strike rate of the currency option and the value of the spot rate at time T
respectively, the buyer of a European style call (put) option can only exercise
his option at time T if $S_T > X$ ($S_T < X$); where throughout this article, the spot
exchange rate is taken to represent the number of units of foreign currency

EXHIBIT 1 Payoffs of the Vanilla Option

Type of Vanilla Option	Payoff at Expiry Time T
$C_E\,(X,0,T,S)$	$\max\,[-P_T^{\,*},S_T - X - P_T^{\,*}]$
$P_E\,(X,0,T,S)$	$\max\,[-P_T^{\,*},X - S_T - P_T^{\,*}]$

where $P_T^{\,*}$ represents the premium of the option paid at the inception of the contract that is future valued to the expiry date of the option, max $[a,b]$ represents the maximum value of a and b, and both $C_E(X,0,T,S)$ and $P_E(X,0,T,S)$ represent the vanilla European call and put option respectively when the strike rate is X, the current time is 0, the option maturity time is T, and the current spot rate is S.

EXHIBIT 2

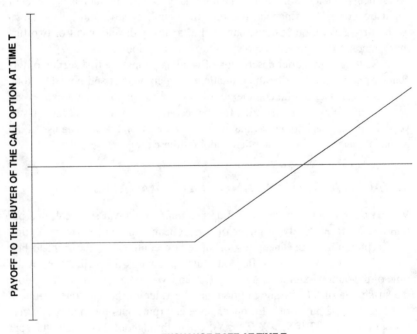

EXCHANGE RATE AT TIME T

for one U.S. dollar. The payoff to the buyer of the currency option at time T is given by Exhibit 1. See Exhibits 2 and 3 for the graphs of these payoffs.

Unlike the buyer of an option who can choose to walk away from the contract, the seller of the option is always obligated to perform his end of the contract. See Hull (1993) for an excellent introduction to the fundamentals of options and Ravindran (1993) for a recreational approach to option pricing.

Besides having all the properties of a European option, the American option also allows the buyer of the option to exercise at any time during the life of the option. Since the European option has only one decision node at time T and the American option has infinite decision nodes in the time interval 0 to T, we would expect the value of an American option to be at least as large as that of a European option. The payoff to the buyer of the American style currency option is given by Exhibit 4.

Note that the value of a European call stock option is the same as that of its American counterpart only for a non-dividend paying stock. An intuitive reason for this feature is that by exercising an American call option early, the buyer of the option has to pay a strike value of X for a stock that does not pay any dividend. Due to the accrued interest on the strike that is foregone if the

EXHIBIT 3

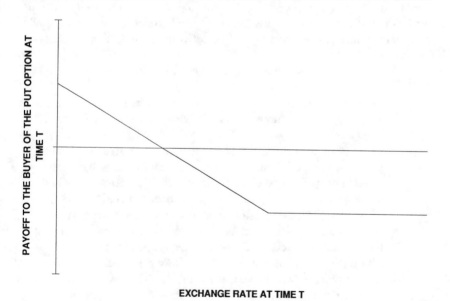

PAYOFF TO THE BUYER OF THE PUT OPTION AT TIME T

EXCHANGE RATE AT TIME T

EXHIBIT 4   Payoffs of the American Style Option

Type of Option	Payoff at Time t	Payoff at Expiry Time T
$C_A(X,0,T,S)$	$\max [S_t - X - P_t^*, C_{A,t} - P_t^*]$	$\max [-P_T^*, S_T - X - P_T^*]$
$P_A(X,0,T,S)$	$\max [X - S_t - P_t^*, P_{A,t} - P_t^*]$	$\max [-P_T^*, X - S_T - P_T^*]$

where $C_A(X,0,T,S)$ and $P_A(X,0,T,S)$ represent the American call and put options respectively when X is the strike rate, the current time is 0, the life of the option is T, the current spot rate is S, t lies in the time interval $[0,T]$, P_t^* represents the premium of the option paid at the inception of the contract that is future valued to time t, and both $C_{A,t}$ and $P_{A,t}$ represent the value of the American call and put options respectively at time t when the strike rate is X, the current time is t, the option expiry time is T, and the current stock price is S_t.

option is exercised before time T, it is optimal for the buyer of the option to delay his/her exercise capability as much as possible.

The pricing and the assumptions underlying the pricing of vanilla currency options will be discussed in the third section. Although we have only discussed vanilla currency options, offering vanilla options on other types of underlying (e.g., equities, interest rates, and commodities) is also possible. Despite the type of insurance or market view taking opportunities the vanilla options provide, clients more often than not need products that manage their risk or monetize their market view more effectively and, if possible, at a lower cost.

As examples, consider the three following scenarios:

a. An investor has bought a new issue of a five-year semi-annual bond with a 10 percent coupon that is callable by its issuer at par three years after its issue on any of its coupon dates. To hedge against the issuer's call, the investor could buy five European style bond options each of which expires at every one of the callable dates and is exercisable into a par value synthetic bond with 10 percent coupon and maturing at the same date as the callable bond's maturity.

Alternatively, the investor could buy a Quasi-American style bond option with both the option and the synthetic bond maturing in five years; the exercise of the option on any one of the coupon dates after three years allows the investor to pay a par value for the 10 percent coupon synthetic bond. Clearly, the second alternative provides a cheaper and more effective means of insurance. This alternative insurance is also known as a Mid-Atlantic/Bermudian option. See Section 2J for a complete description.

b. An importer of Canadian goods would have to make payments for the goods in Canadian dollars on pre-specified dates out in the future. The importer could either lock himself into a sequence of forward contracts on the Cad/U.S. exchange rate or convert his U.S. dollars into Canadian ones on the dates when the payments have to be made. If the U.S dollar currently appears to be weaker than what the exchange rate has historically been, the latter alternative would seem the better choice. The only risk encountered in the latter alternative is when the U.S. dollar gets even weaker. Here, the buying of put options on the U.S. dollar appears to be good insurance because the put options would finish in-the-money when the U.S. dollar weakens. However, buying a series of put options for various option maturities may get expensive. A method of cheapening this cost would be to embed within the put options an extinguishing feature such that if the U.S. dollar strengthens during the life of the option reaching a certain point (called a barrier), the put option is extinguished. This type of insurance is known as the knock-out option and is described in Section 2B.

c. Based on the current shape of the yield curve, an asset manager believes that the spread between the five-year bond yield and the three-year bond yield would widen in three months (i.e., yield curve would get steeper). Instead of buying the underlying bonds and then unwinding the position in three months, which would involve huge cash positions and a large possible downside, he could alternatively buy a European option that pays off the maximum of the difference of the two bond yields (i.e., five-year bond yield less three-year bond yield) and zero at the end of the three months. To enter into such an option, the asset manager only needs to pay an up-front premium to monetize his view. This option, also known as the spread option, is discussed in Section 2O.

The above examples describe just three of the numerous single and multivariate path dependent risks that investors and risk managers may wish to hedge or speculate upon. In each one of the instances, the vanilla European and American options are totally ineffective, thus clearly demonstrating the need for the use of exotic options. In the next section, we will see the detailed uses for the various types of exotic options.

2. EXAMPLES AND USES OF EXOTICS

This section describes the features of the exotic options that are present in the financial markets today. In addition, the section will describe the way these instruments are used in the market place either as yield enhancements or disaster insurance. Although each of the products has been presented in alphabetical order as a separate topic, it is easy to marry the products and arrive at hybrid instruments that combine and possibly contain the risk characteristics of the individual components.

A. Averaging Options

A Canadian company that is exporting to the United States is exposed to the exchange rate risk between the Canadian and U.S. dollar every week. The treasurer of the company is preparing a quarterly budget and has to forecast the cash inflows and outflows from the existing contracts of the company and state the company's expected net profit or loss for the coming quarter in Canadian funds. To do the conversion to Canadian funds, the treasurer picks an average exchange rate of 1.29 Cad/U.S. as a conversion factor. Clearly, the treasurer does not have to worry about anything if the U.S. dollar gets stronger and the average of the weekly Cad/U.S. exchange rates over the next quarter exceeds the 1.29 Cad/U.S. mark. It is only when the Canadian dollar gets stronger over the next quarter that he will not be able to meet his budget. In order to hedge, he would therefore need a currency put option based on weekly averaging of the exchange rates for the next quarter on the U.S. dollar and with a strike price at 1.29 Cad/U.S. More precisely, he needs an averaging put option.

An averaging put option, also known as the Asian put option, is a derivative security that gives the buyer a value at the maturity date of the option that is the greater of zero and the difference between the strike rate and the average value of the exchange rates realized during the averaging period. The following example better illustrates the sequence of events depicting the nature of the transaction:

Time 0 mths: The Canadian dollar is currently trading at 1.33 Cad/U.S. A treasurer who has just submitted his quarterly budget is worried about the Canadian dollar strengthening and pays a premium to buy an averaging put option that is struck at 1.29 Cad/U.S. and matures in four months time. To do the averaging, starting from today's current rate of 1.33

Cad/U.S., the exchange rates are monitored once every week (also called a weekly sampling period) at noon until and inclusive of the exchange rate at the expiry date of the option. An arithmetic average is calculated for all these observed rates and then compared with the strike rate of 1.29 Cad/U.S.

Time 4 mths: *Case 1*
The Canadian dollar is currently trading at 1.30 Cad/U.S. The arithmetic average of the observed exchange rates (inclusive of the exchange rate at the option maturity date) turns out to be 1.2850 Cad/U.S. The option finishes in-the-money and the payoff to the treasurer is $(1.29 - 1.2850 - P_{4\,mths}^{*})$ Cad/U.S., where $P_{4\,mths}^{*}$ represents the premium of the averaging option future valued to a time of four months.

Case 2
Currency is trading at 1.30 Cad/U.S. The arithmetic average of the observed exchange rates turns out to be 1.2950 Cad/U.S. The option goes out-of-the-money, and the treasurer has lost the premium of $P_{4\,mths}^{*}$.

There are a few important observations that should be made from the above example. First, the type of averaging discussed in the above example is of the arithmetic type (i.e., the arithmetic average of the numbers 2, 3, 4 is $(2 + 3 + 4)/3 = 3$). The treasurer could have bought a geometrically averaging put option where the payoff on the maturity date of the option is the geometric average of the observed rates compared against the strike rate, where the geometric average of the numbers 2, 3, 4 is $(2 \times 3 \times 4)^{1/3} = 2.88$. Furthermore, if the notional size of the currency exposure encountered varies over the weekly observed periods, an appropriate hedge instrument would be an averaging option with weighted averaging.

Second, instead of observing the exchange rates weekly, because of daily currency exposure the treasurer could have bought an averaging option that involves daily averaging or averaging over varying intervals (e.g., observing the daily exchange rates for the first month and then observing the exchange rates bi-weekly over the next three months).

Third, although the sampling period for computing the averaging started at the inception of the option contract and ended at the maturity date of the option in the above example, it is easy to buy an averaging option where the sampling period is not a subset of the life of the option.

Letting S_i be the spot rate at time t_i (for $i = 1,2,...,n$), where the time intervals between the observation periods may not be the same (e.g., $t_n - t_{n-1}$ may not be necessarily equal to $t_{n-1} - t_{n-2}$) and w_i be the weight associated with spot rate S_i, where $\Sigma w_i = w_1 + w_2 + ... + w_n = 1$, the payoffs of the averaging option can be more generally written as detailed in Exhibit 5.

EXHIBIT 5   Payoffs of the Averaging Option

Type of Averaging Option	Payoff at Expiry Time T	
$C_{E,A}(X,0,T,S)$	$-P_T^*$	if $\sum_{i=1}^{n} w_i S_{t_i} < X$
	$\sum_{i=1}^{n} w_i S_{t_i} - X - P_T^*$	if $\sum_{i=1}^{n} w_i S_{t_i} > X$
$P_{E,A}(X,0,T,S)$	$-P_T^*$	if $\sum_{i=1}^{n} w_i S_{t_i} > X$
	$X - \sum_{i=1}^{n} w_i S_{t_i} - P_T^*$	if $\sum_{i=1}^{n} w_i S_{t_i} < X$
$C_{E,G}(X,0,T,S)$	$-P_T^*$	if $\prod_{i=1}^{n} S_{t_i}^{w_i} < X$
	$\prod_{i=1}^{n} S_{t_i}^{w_i} - X - P_T^*$	if $\prod_{i=1}^{n} S_{t_i}^{w_i} > X$
$P_{E,G}(X,0,T,S)$	$-P_T^*$	if $\prod_{i=1}^{n} S_{t_i}^{w_i} > X$
	$X - \prod_{i=1}^{n} S_{t_i}^{w_i} - P_T^*$	if $\prod_{i=1}^{n} S_{t_i}^{w_i} < X$

where P_T^* represents the premium of the averaging option future valued to time T, $\prod_{i=1}^{n} S_{t_i}^{w_i} = S_{t_1}^{w_1} S_{t_2}^{w_2}...S_{t_n}^{w_n}$, $C_{EA}(X,0,T,S)$ and $P_{EA}(X,0,T,S)$ represent the arithmetic weighted averaging European call and put options respectively, $C_{EG}(X,0,T,S)$ and $P_{EG}(X,0,T,S)$ represent the geometric weighted averaging European call and put options respectively when the strike rate is X, the current time is 0, the option maturity time is T, and current spot rate is S. Note that when the weights $w_i = 1/n$ and the time intervals $t_{i+1} - t_i$ are the same (for $i = 1,...,n - 1$), the above payoffs simplify to that of an averaging and a geometric option.

The pricing formulae for the arithmetic and geometric averaging options are given in Levy (1992) and Kemna and Vorst (1990), respectively.

By the nature of the arithmetic and geometric averaging options, the contribution of a spot rate toward the averaging of the sampled points decreases as the option maturity date draws close. As such, the risk characteristics of an averaging and a geometric option diminish as the option decays in time, and the delta hedging technique can be easily used to manage these options. Despite the averaging nature (whether be it an arithmetic or a geometric type), it is not necessarily true that the greater the sampling frequency, the cheaper the options. These type of options are, however, cheaper than vanilla options expiring at the same time. Exhibit 6 shows the premium differences between an arithmetic averaging call option and a vanilla call option for varying sampling frequencies when the strike rates and times of maturity of the options are identical.

Although the discussion has so far been based on a currency transaction, averaging options can also be easily used by treasurers to cap their total annual borrowing costs. Averaging options also lend themselves naturally to the commodity markets where the underlying price of a commodity trades as an average index (or price).

B. Barrier Options

Although vanilla options serve as good disaster insurance, current market conditions sometimes make the insurance costly. A way to reduce such cost

EXHIBIT 6

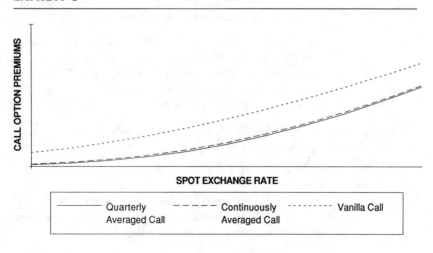

would be to use barrier options. Barrier options, alternatively known as knock-in or knock-out options, are options that serve as conditional insurance which may come into effect (or cease to exist) upon the triggering of an event. Although the investor pays for an option today, the option may only come into existence (or cease to exist) depending on whether a pre-specified barrier (or level) is triggered during the life of the option. The following example better illustrates the use of a barrier option in practice:

Time 0 mth: The Canadian dollar is currently trading at 1.33 Cad/U.S. Because of the currency exposure in a month, the client is worried about the U.S. dollar weakening below the 1.31 Cad/U.S. mark. Buying a one month put option on the U.S. dollar with a strike rate of 1.31 Cad/U.S. would be the ideal solution. Based on the current market conditions, however, the client is apprehensive about the cost of this insurance. To overcome this problem, this put option could be bought with the added feature that if the exchange rate during the life of the option exceeded the 1.36 Cad/U.S. mark (or barrier) the put option would cease to exist. The reason for having the extinguishing feature set at this level is the view that if the U.S. dollar strengthens to the level of 1.36 Cad/U.S. it is unlikely to then weaken past the level of 1.31 Cad/U.S. at the time the option expires. This type of option, also called the up-and-out option (where the term up refers to the current spot level being less than the barrier level and the term out refers to the option being extinguished upon hitting the barrier), has a smaller premium than the vanilla option.

N.B.: It is important to note that the further the barrier is from the current exchange rate level, the more expensive the up-and-out option is going to be. This is due to the fact that the probability of the option extinguishing diminishes as the level of the barrier is raised.

Case 1: Barrier is not breached during the one month period
Because the exchange rate has not exceeded or gone beyond the 1.36 barrier level, the put option is still alive. Thus,

Time 1 mth: *Case 1a*
Currency is now trading at a level of 1.32 Cad/U.S. The option finishes out-of-the-money, and the client has lost the premium that was paid at the inception of the contract.

Case 1b
The U.S. dollar has now weakened to a level of 1.29 Cad/U.S. The option finishes in-the-money, and the payoff to the client is $(1.31 - 1.29 - P_{1\,mth}{}^*)$ Cad/U.S., where $P_{1\,mth}{}^*$ is the premium of the option future valued to 1 month.

Case 2: Barrier is breached during the one month period
Because the U.S. dollar has strengthened to a level that is past 1.36 Cad/U.S. mark (i.e., breached the barrier of 1.36) at some time during the one month period, the put option gets extinguished and the client walks away having lost the premium.

Although the example above illustrates the use of an up-and-out put option, it is not difficult to construct examples of the up-and-in, down-and-out, and down-and-in call and put options. Letting $C_{E,In}(X,H,0,T,S)$ represent the European style knock-in call option, $C_{E,Out}(X,H,0,T,S)$ represent the European style knock-out call option, $P_{E,In}(X,H,0,T,S)$ represent the European style knock-in put option, $P_{E,Out}(X,H,0,T,S)$ represent the European style knock-out put option, where the strike rate is X, the barrier level is H, the current time is 0, the life of the option is T, and the current spot rate is S, the payoffs of the barrier options can be written as detailed in Exhibit 7.

Note that each of the above four payoffs can be decomposed further into the up and down options as according to whether $S < H$. Assuming a 24-hour continuous trading market, the pricing of the barrier options for the above payoffs is given by Rubinstein and Reiner (1991). If a barrier option is bought on an underlying index that is trading in an illiquid market, the exact times of monitoring the breaching of the barrier by the index is pre-specified

EXHIBIT 7 Payoffs of the Barrier Option

Type of Barrier Option	Payoff at Time T if Barrier Is Breached	Payoff at Time T if Barrier Is Not Breached
$C_{E,In}(X,H,0,T,S)$	$\max[-P_T{}^*,S_T-X-P_T{}^*]$	$-P_T{}^*$
$C_{E,Out}(X,H,0,T,S)$	$-P_T{}^*$	$\max[-P_T{}^*,S_T-X-P_T{}^*]$
$P_{E,In}(X,H,0,T,S)$	$\max[-P_T{}^*,X-S_T-P_T{}^*]$	$-P_T{}^*$
$P_{E,Out}(X,H,0,T,S)$	$-P_T{}^*$	$\max[-P_T{}^*,X-S_T-P_T{}^*]$

where $P_T{}^*$ is the option premium future valued to time T and the terms knock-in and knock-out options describe the coming alive and the death respectively of an option upon breaching the barrier.

in advance in the contract. Furthermore, when the monitoring of the index is done at discrete times, no analytical expressions exist for the pricing of the barrier options, and as such the prices can only be evaluated numerically. It can, however, be shown that the premium for a continuously monitored knock-out barrier option cannot be greater than the premium for a discretely monitored knock-out barrier option. The reverse is true for the knock-in barrier options. Although the barrier options are usually hedged using the classical delta-hedging methodology, the effect of gamma is eminent in these options. It should be noted that with the above payoff structures, going long a vanilla call option is equivalent to going long an up-and-in and an up-and-out call option if $S < H$ or going long a down-and-in and a down-and-out call option if $S > H$ regardless of the level of the barrier, where we have implicitly assumed that all the options are struck at the same level and have the same time to maturity. As such, we can conclude that the premium of a barrier option can never be greater than that of a corresponding vanilla option. See Exhibit 8.

An alternative solution that would address the client's expensive premium problem is to have the knockout feature set only on the expiry date. Instead of monitoring the breaching of the barrier during the life of the option, one can instead monitor this breaching only on the option expiry date. Unlike the example discussed above, if we set a barrier level of 1.36 Cad/U.S. at the expiry date, there is no cheapening effect from the use of a barrier. To have a cheapening effect, we have to set a barrier level that is less than 1.31 Cad/U.S., the strike rate of the option. For example, we could set a barrier of 1.10 Cad/U.S. at the expiry date such that if the exchange rate at the end of one month was above 1.31 Cad/U.S. or less than 1.10 Cad/U.S., the client gets a zero payoff. In the range 1.10 Cad/U.S. to 1.31 Cad/U.S., the

EXHIBIT 8

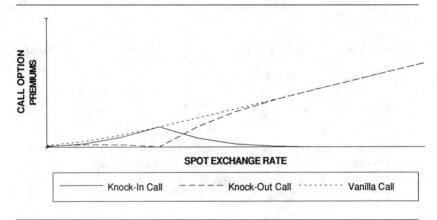

client's payoff will be the difference between the strike rate and the exchange rate at maturity. It is important to note that this type of one-point barrier strategy amounts to the client giving up part of the upside by using the view that the U.S. dollar will never weaken past the 1.10 Cad/U.S. level. One can similarly create an example where the client could buy the vanilla call option and give away part of the upside.

The one-point barrier option is also seen in the issues of the convertible/callable bonds or stock warrants where the issuer is forced to call (or convert) the bond (or warrant) if the price of the underlying trades beyond a prespecified level on a certain date.

C. Binary Options

Based on current market conditions, an asset manager feels that three-month LIBOR is at its lowest level. She feels that the index will increase in a week's time after the announcement of the government budget but does not have a feel for the magnitude of increase. Using a vanilla call option is clearly not going to be useful. Any instrument that reflects strictly the direction of the market would be the most suitable. Binary options, also known as bet, digital, or all-or-nothing options, are instruments that allow the buyer to target the movement of the market. If the buyer of the instrument has a view that the market will not be trading below a certain level in a week's time and wants to receive a prespecified dollar amount if she is right, she could buy a binary option that would help monetize this view. The following sequence of events helps better illustrate the nature of the product:

Time 0 wks: Three-month LIBOR is currently trading at 3.5 percent. Despite the steepness of the yield curve on the short end, the investor feels that given the current economic environment, LIBOR will never go beyond the 4.5 percent mark over the next two weeks. To monetize her view, she pays a premium to buy a binary option that would give a payoff of $1 million if LIBOR trades below the 4.5 percent mark at the end of two weeks. If the view turns out to be wrong, she gets no payoff from the option.

Time 2 wks: *Case 1*
Three-month LIBOR is now trading at 3.8 percent. The option finishes in-the-money. The investor gets a net payoff of $1 million $- P_{2\,wks}{}^*$, where $P_{2\,wks}{}^*$ represents bet option premium future valued to two weeks.

N.B.: Regardless of how much in-the-money the option finishes, the investor always gets a payoff of $1 million $- P_{2\,wks}{}^{*}$.

Case 2

Three-month LIBOR is now trading at 4.8 percent. The option finishes out-of-the-money, and the investor has lost the premium.

If S_T represents the value of the index (e.g., LIBOR or exchange rate) at time T, X represents the strike value, B represents the dollar payoff the buyer of the option receives if she is right, and $P_T{}^{*}$ the premium of the option future valued to time T, the payoffs of a binary option can be rewritten as detailed in Exhibit 9.

Because the binary option has a payoff that is in nature a bet, it is easy to price this product. The premium of the option is equal to the present value of the product of the bet payoff and probability that the option finishes in-the-money. Exhibit 10 compares the difference in premiums between a binary call option and a vanilla call option when the strike levels and time to maturity of the options are identical. Unlike the pricing, the hedging of this product is not that easy. In practice, the binary option is usually hedged by buying call options at a lower strike rate and selling a different amount of call options at a higher strike rate. These hedge amounts can then be rebalanced frequently during the life of the option. It is important to note that because of the discontinuous nature of the payoff, the above-mentioned hedge strategy can be either used to under-hedge or over-hedge the risk.

Binary options have been also very commonly used in note structures. For example, an investor who thinks that the three-month LIBOR at the end of six months will be trading above the region of 4.25 percent could purchase

EXHIBIT 9 Payoffs of the Binary Option

Type of Binary Option	Payoff at Expiry Time T	
$C_E(X,0,T,S)$	$-P_T{}^{*}$	if $S_T < X$
	$B - P_T{}^{*}$	if $S_T > X$
$P_E(X,0,T,S)$	$-P_T{}^{*}$	if $S_T > X$
	$B - P_T{}^{*}$	if $S_T < X$

where $C_E(X,0,T,S)$ and $P_E(X,0,T,S)$ represent the European call and put binary options respectively when the strike value is X, the current time is 0, the option maturity is at time T, and the current value of the index is S.

a six-month note that pays off a coupon of 6.5 percent if he was right and no coupon if he was wrong. An alternative structure that would protect the investor against a last-minute spike in LIBOR would be a payoff that is a fraction of a coupon of 5 percent, where this fraction represents the proportion of the business days where the three-month LIBOR exceeds the 4.25 percent barrier. See Ravindran (1993) for examples of such structures.

Investors can also easily use the notion of a bet on spread options. More precisely, suppose that the difference between the current 10-year and the two-year bond yields is about 160 basis points. The investor feels almost certain that based on the current market conditions this difference in bond yields will widen further in a month's time. He does not have a good feel for how much the widening is going to be and as such is only interested in betting that the spread between the 10-year and the two-year U.S. Treasury bond yields in one month's time will surpass the 160 basis point mark. To monetize his views, he could buy a binary spread option that would pay him $1 million if his view was right and nothing if he was wrong.

Binary options also lend themselves naturally to liability management in the form of contingent premium options. See the topic on contingent premium options in this section.

D. Chooser Options

It is common for someone with a view about how a major event (e.g., election results, outbreak of a war, etc.) could impact a financial market to buy an

EXHIBIT 10

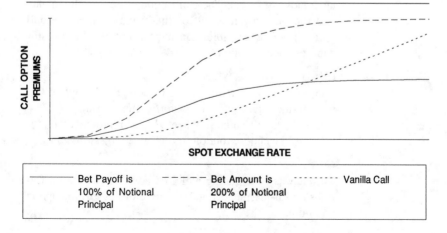

option (e.g., a vanilla call option) that will help monetize this view. Come the event date, it is also common for the same person to realize that the view had been totally wrong and wish that they had instead bought the opposite option, such as a vanilla put option. For such a person, an option that gives the opportunity to choose between a vanilla call option and a vanilla put option on the event date would serve as a useful and valuable instrument. The chooser option, also known as the pay-now-choose-later option, is an option that allows the buyer to choose between a vanilla call option and a vanilla put option at a pre-specified time in the future. More precisely, the investor pays an up-front premium to make a choice between a call and a put option of the same pre-specified strike and maturity date at some pre-specified time in the future. The following sequence of events will better illustrate the mechanics involved with the purchase of a chooser option:

Time 0 mths: The current Canada/U.S. exchange rate is trading at 1.32 Cad/U.S. The federal election is in three months time. An investor who has no view about impact of the election results wants the ability to buy an instrument that will enable him to make a choice between a call and a put option at the end of three months. The investor pays a premium to buy a European style chooser option (i.e., an option to choose three months from now between a European call and a European put option on U.S. dollars with both the options being struck at 1.32 Cad/U.S. and expiring three months after the choice date).

Time 3 mths: Currency is now trading at 1.35 Cad/U.S. (i.e., the U.S. dollar is now stronger). The call option is now in-the-money and the put option is out-of-the-money. Since the call option is more valuable than the put option, the investor chooses the call option.

Time 6 mths: *Case 1*
The dollar is now trading at 1.34 Cad/U.S. The option finishes in-the-money, and the payoff to the investor is $(1.34 - 1.32 - P_{6\,mths}{}^{*})$ Cad/U.S., where $P_{6\,mths}{}^{*}$ represents the premium of the chooser option future valued to six months.

Case 2
Currency is now trading at 1.29 Cad/U.S. The option finishes out-of-the-money, and the investor has lost his option premium.

96

It is important to first note from the above example that the investor upon choosing the call option at the end of the three month period could have alternatively turned around and sold the chosen option in the market instead of holding it for another three months.

Secondly, the type of chooser option mentioned in the above example is known as a simple chooser option. The investor could have alternatively bought a complex chooser option that would have allowed him a choice between a European call option with strike X_1 and time to maturity T_1 and a European put option with strike X_2 and time to maturity T_2. Letting $C_E(X,t,T,S_t)$ and $P_E(X,t,T,S_t)$ represent the European style vanilla call and put option respectively when the strike rate is X, the current (choice) time is t, the option maturity time is T, and the current spot rate is S_t, the payoff to the buyer of a European style chooser option who wishes to choose at time t can be written as detailed in Exhibit 11, where P_T^* represents the premium of the option future valued to time T.

Thirdly, if the choice date in the above example was set to six months, which is the maturity date of the option, the investor has effectively bought himself a straddle (i.e., a call and a put both struck at 1.32 Cad/U.S. and expiring in six months). Because of the ability to choose at the end of six months the investor will always get a positive payoff. Thus, the closer the choice date gets to the option maturity date, the more expensive the chooser

EXHIBIT 11 Payoffs of the Chooser Option

Type of Chooser Option	SIMPLE	COMPLEX
Payoff at Time t	$\max[C_E(X,t,T,S_t),P_E(X,t,T,S_t)]$	$\max[C_E(X_1,t,T_1,S_t),P_E(X_2,t,T_2,S_t)]$
	i) If call is chosen at time t	i) If call is chosen at time t
Payoff at Expiry Date	$\max[-P_T^*,S_T-X-P_T^*]$	$\max[-P_T^*,S_{T_1}-X_1-P_T^*]$
	ii) If put is chosen at time t	ii) If put is chosen at time t
Payoff at Expiry Date	$\max[-P_T^*,X-S_T-P_T^*]$	$\max[-P_T^*,X_2-S_{T_2}-P_T^*]$

EXHIBIT 12

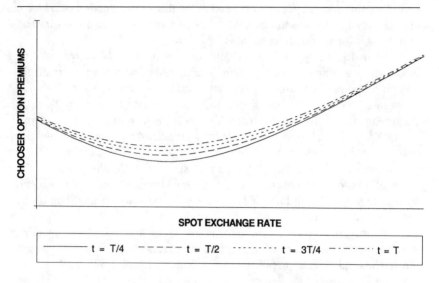

CHOOSER OPTION PREMIUMS

SPOT EXCHANGE RATE

——— t = T/4   – – – – t = T/2   ·········· t = 3T/4   –·–·– t = T

option becomes. Exhibit 12 shows the effect of varying the choice time t for a simple chooser option. The reason for this increase in premium is the fact that there is less uncertainty about the chosen option finishing in-the-money.

Fourthly, although the above example illustrated choosing between a European call and put, we could have just as well offered the investor a choice between an American call and put. It is important to note that the added twist of offering the investor the ability to make a choice at any moment from the inception of the contract till the final choice time t has no value. This is because market information increases as time decays, and as such it is always beneficial for the investor to delay his decision of choice.

A chooser option is usually bought by someone who does not want to be affected by the uncertainty toward the run-up to a major event (e.g., elections, referendum, war, etc.). Buyers who want to avoid paying for the volatility caused by the event and are uncertain about the direction of the market should buy a chooser option with the choice date set about one day after the event. Furthermore, when buying a chooser option, the buyer should also be careful about the short end volatility spiking up, which in turn would cause the straddle to be cheaper than a chooser option. This is due to the fact that, as the event date draws closer and the outcome of the event becomes more uncertain (or equally split), the volatility of the market to the event date increases. Furthermore, since the outcome of the event will be realized on the event date, the volatility of the market out to a day past the event date becomes lesser, hence making a straddle cheaper.

The pricing of the chooser options, both simple and complex, are given in Rubinstein (1991). Hedging of these exotic options can be done using the delta hedging technique.

E. Compound Options

A manufacturer is bidding for a contract to manufacture a certain set of goods. If he gets awarded the bid (e.g., a month after the bid was submitted), he is required to manufacture the goods at the contracted price. If he waits until the date of award and then buys the raw materials, he will lose money on the contract if the cost of the raw materials is higher than when he had submitted the bid. He is exposed to the rising cost of the materials used in the manufacturing process. To hedge himself, he would need a call option on the materials with the strike being set at the level submitted in his bid. However, he would only need this option if he is awarded the contract. Due to the hedging difficulties, it is usually difficult for an investment house to sell an option that is contingent on the buyer winning a contract. As such, the manufacturer can only resort to buying an option that would allow him to buy a call option at the award date for an extra premium. Such an option is called a compound option. More precisely, a compound option, also known as an option on an option, is a derivative security that allows the buyer to pay an initial up-front premium for an option that he may need later. The buyer then pays an additional premium only if he decides that he needs this option. The mechanics associated with a compound option transaction is best illustrated with the following example:

Time 0 mth: The Canadian dollar is currently trading at 1.34 Cad/U.S. The client has bid for a contract based on today's exchange rate and will only know the outcome of the bidding one month from now. If the outcome is successful, he would be faced with a currency exposure six months after the results of the bidding. He is afraid that if the U.S. dollar weakens seven months from now, he is bound to lose money on the contract for which he used the exchange rate of 1.34 Cad/U.S. Thus, he needs a protection against a falling U.S. dollar seven months from now. In addition, he would only need the protection if he is awarded the contract. He would

99

need a put option on the U.S. dollar starting one month from now, having a strike rate of 1.34 Cad/U.S. and a life of six months only if he is awarded the contract. To hedge himself, he wants to buy a call option (so that he can receive his put option by paying an additional premium of 0.050 Cad/U.S. that is lesser than the amount that is prescribed by the market if the call option goes in-the-money) on the put option.

More precisely, he would pay a small initial premium today to buy a call option with a strike rate of 0.050 Cad/U.S. and a life of one month, which exercises into a put option (with strike rate 1.34 Cad/U.S. and a life of six months) upon the payment of an additional premium of 0.050 Cad/U.S. that is pre-specified. Obviously, the client would not mind paying a smaller initial premium and a higher second premium when he wins the contract.

Case 1: The client is awarded the contract

Time 1 mth: The contract is now awarded to the client. He needs a put option on the U.S. dollar with a life of six months and a strike of 1.34 Cad/U.S. He compares the second premium of 0.050 Cad/U.S. that was pre-specified at the inception of the contract to the premium required to buy the put option from the market. If the size of his second additional premium is smaller, he exercises the compound option. However, if it is cheaper for him to buy this option from the market, he does not exercise his compound option and forgoes his initial premium paid at the inception of the contract.

Time 7 mth: *Assuming that the compound option is exercised*

Case 1a
Currency is now trading at 1.35 Cad/U.S. The put option acquired by the client is out-of-the-money, and as such he loses both of his premiums.

Case 1b
The U.S. dollar is weaker and the exchange rate is now at a level of 1.32 Cad/U.S. The put option finishes in-the-money, and the payoff to the client is (1.34 − 1.32 − initial premium − second additional premium) Cad/U.S., where the premiums are future valued to a time of seven months.

Case 2: The client is not awarded the contract

Time 1 mth: He does not receive the contract. He has no use for the put option, so he does not exercise the compound option and forgoes his initial premium.

It is important to note that even if the client does not get awarded the contract, it may still be optimal for him to exercise his compound option if the second additional premium is lower than the premium obtained by selling the put option in the market.

Although the above example illustrates the use of a call option on a put option, one can just as well find the justification for the use of a put option on a put option, call option on a call option, and a put option on a call option. Letting $C_E C_E(X_t, X_T, 0, t, T, S)$ represent a European call option on a European call option, $P_E C_E(X_t, X_T, 0, t, T, S)$ represent a European put option on a European call option, $C_E P_E(X_t, X_T, 0, t, T, S)$ represent a European call option on a European put option, and $P_E P_E(X_t, X_T, 0, t, T, S)$ represent a European put option on a European put option, where X_t is the strike premium (i.e., second additional premium) at time t, X_T is the strike rate at time T, 0 is the current time, t is the time that the first option expires, T is the time that the second option expires, and S is the current spot rate, the payoffs for the various compound options can be written as detailed in Exhibit 13.

Although compound options can be priced using the binomial method, Geske (1979) and Rubinstein (1991) have provided analytical expressions for

EXHIBIT 13   Payoffs of the Compound Option

Type of Compound Option	Payoff at Time t	If Compound Option Is Exercised at Time t Payoff at Expiry Time T
$C_E C_E(X_t, X_T, 0, t, T, S)$	max $[C_{E,t} - X_t - P_t^*, -P_t^*]$	max $[-P_T^*, S_T - X_T - P_T^*]$
$P_E C_E(X_t, X_T, 0, t, T, S)$	max $[X_t - C_{E,t} - P_t^*, -P_t^*]$	max $[-P_T^*, S_T - X_T - P_T^*]$
$C_E P_E(X_t, X_T, 0, t, T, S)$	max $[P_{E,t} - X_t - P_t^*, -P_t^*]$	max $[-P_T^*, X_T - S_T - P_T^*]$
$P_E P_E(X_t, X_T, 0, t, T, S)$	max $[X_t - P_{E,t} - P_t^*, -P_t^*]$	max $[-P_T^*, X_T - S_T - P_T^*]$

where $C_{E,t}$ and $P_{E,t}$ represent the European call and the put premiums respectively when the current time is t, option maturity time is T, the strike rate of the option is X_T and the current spot rate is S_t. P_t^* represents the initial premium future valued to time t and P_T^* represents the sum of the initial and the second additional premium (X_t) that is future valued to time T.

the pricing of the European style options. The concept of a compound option can be easily adapted to embed an option on an exotic option or vice versa (i.e., an exotic option exercising into a vanilla option) depending on the type of risk the client is trying to manage.

F. Contingent Premium Options

After buying insurance, how many times have we wondered whether the purchase of the insurance is actually worth it? More often than not, we think that it would be wonderful if we could purchase an insurance and then pay a premium only if we needed it. Although we expect this premium to be higher than the usual insurance premium, the thought of not paying a single penny for an insurance we do not use is very appealing. Insurance products that allow us to do this are called contingent premium options. Contingent premium options, also known as pay later options, are options that do not require the buyer to pay any up-front premium but require payment of the premium only if the option finishes in-the-money. To understand the mechanics associated with the pay later option, we will look at the following example:

Time 0 mth: The Canadian dollar is currently trading at 1.32 Cad/U.S. The client who has a currency exposure one month from now feels that the U.S. dollar will weaken in a month's time. At the same time, she is afraid that the U.S. dollar might strengthen against her, in which case she would need a protection and is willing to pay for it only then. To monetize this view, she buys a contingent premium call option on the U.S. funds that is struck at 1.32 Cad/U.S. and expires exactly one month from now. She only pays the pre-specified premium if the option finishes in-the-money one month later.

Time 1 mth: *Case 1*
Currency is now trading at 1.3150 Cad/U.S. The client's view turns out to be correct, and the option finishes out-of-the-money. No premium is paid for the whole transaction, and the client walks away without losing a penny.

Case 2
Currency is now trading at 1.3250 Cad/U.S. The client's view turns out to be wrong, and the option finishes in-the-money. The client pays her premium and receives a payoff of (1.3250 – 1.32) Cad/U.S.

N.B.: It is important to note that the client ends up paying the full premium for the protection as long as the option finishes in-the-money.

More generally, letting S_T be the exchange rate at time T, X be the strike rate of the option, and B be the conditional premium paid at time T if the option went in-the-money, the payoffs of a contingent premium option can be written as detailed in Exhibit 14.

By rewriting the payoff of a contingent premium option, we can decompose the buying of a contingent premium option into buying a vanilla European option with exactly the same strike and maturity and selling a binary option with the same strike and maturity that pays off a bet that is equal in size to the conditional premium of a contingent premium option if the option finishes in-the-money. Although we could use this decomposition to price a contingent premium option (i.e., find the conditional premium that needs to be paid if the option finishes in-the-money), it is easier to price the contingent premium option directly. By the nature of the payoff for this option, the premium paid for the protection when the contingent premium option finishes in-the-money is higher than the premium paid at the inception of the contract for a structurally similar vanilla option. Although the pay later option can be hedged by buying call options at a lower strike and selling a different amount of call options at a higher strike, the hedge is not perfect, and as such has to be monitored frequently like the binary option.

Although not paying a premium until the option finishes in-the-money may look attractive, the requirement that this conditional premium must be paid even if the option finishes in-the-money by a quarter of a basis point makes it unattractive. An alternative solution that overcomes this unattrac-

EXHIBIT 14   Payoffs of the Contingent Premium Option

Type of Pay Later Option	Payoff at Expiry Time T	
$C_E(X,0,T,S)$	0	if $S_T < X$
	$S_T - X - B$	if $S_T > X$
$P_E(X,0,T,S)$	0	if $S_T > X$
	$X - S_T - B$	if $S_T < X$

where $C_E(X,0,T,S)$ and $P_E(X,0,T,S)$ represent the call and put pay later options respectively when the strike rate of the option is X, the current time is 0, the maturity of the option is T, and the current spot rate is S.

tiveness is an option that, in addition to requiring a conditional premium to be paid when the option finishes in-the-money, has the feature that the amount of the conditional premium paid will depend on the amount of "in-the-moneyness" of the option until a pre-specified maximum level. Exhibit 15 illustrates the difference in payoffs between the contingent call option and the alternate solution.

Although the above discussion was based on paying a conditional premium on a vanilla option, this concept could just as well be applied to other types of option (e.g., spread option, average option, etc.).

G. Forward Start Options

Forward start options are paid for today but start in the future with the strike rate of the option set equal to the value of the spot rate at the time the option

EXHIBIT 15

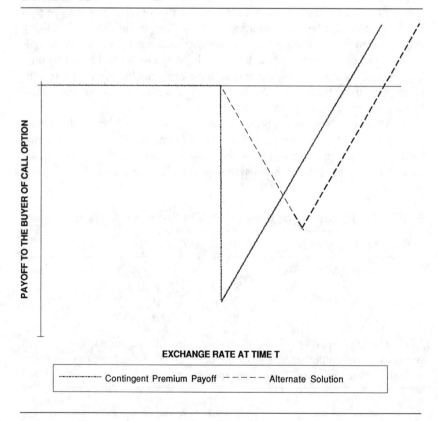

PAYOFF TO THE BUYER OF CALL OPTION

EXCHANGE RATE AT TIME T

·············· Contingent Premium Payoff ⎯ ⎯ ⎯ ⎯ ⎯ Alternate Solution

starts. Thus, the strike rate of a forward start option is not known at the inception of the contract. Variations of the forward start options commonly exist in the interest rate market in the form of periodic caps and floors. Instead of buying vanilla caps (where the strike rate of each caplet is pre-specified in advance and may be different from one another), which could prove expensive during rapidly rising interest rates or a steeply upward sloping yield curve environment, liability managers could buy periodic caps where the strike rate of each caplet is set at a certain spread above the previous LIBOR setting. The following example better illustrates the mechanics behind the transaction of a periodic cap:

Time 0 mths: The client pays a premium to buy a one-year periodic cap where there are three caplets expiring at the three-month, six-month, and nine-month time periods. The strike rate of each caplet will be set equal to the sum of the previous three-month LIBOR setting and 50 basis points. The current three-month LIBOR is 3.5 percent. The strike rate of the first caplet expiring at the three-month period is (3.5% + 50 basis points) = 4%.

Time 3 mths: LIBOR is 3.75 percent. The first caplet finishes out-of-the-money, and the strike rate for the next caplet is set at (3.75% + 50 basis points) = 4.25%.

Time 6 mths: LIBOR is currently at 4.3 percent. The second caplet finishes in-the-money by five basis points, and the strike rate for the third caplet is set at (4.3% + 50 basis points) = 4.8%.

Time 9 mths: LIBOR is at 4 percent. The third caplet finishes out-of-the-money.

Forward start options can be used by investors to bet on reset LIBOR values. Suppose that the current yield curve environment tells the investor that the 3 × 6 FRA (Forward Rate Agreement) is higher than the 6 × 9 FRA and the investor feels that this inversion in the yield curve is only temporary. He could then buy a forward start option with the strike rate set equal to the three-month LIBOR in three months time, following which the vanilla option on the three-month LIBOR expires three months later. Furthermore, given the current inversion in this part of the yield curve, this option does not cost too much.

The forward start option described above can also be thought of as a spread option with the variables being the three-month LIBOR six months from now and the three-month LIBOR three months from now. Unlike a typical spread option, where the correlation coefficient can only be historically calculated, the correlation here can be implicitly calculated most of the time. This possibility is due to the fact that we are actually monitoring a single variable at two different points in time instead of two variables at the same time.

H. Ladder Options

A U.S. manufacturer receives his raw materials from Canada. Upon the receipt of his bills, he has until the end of the month to settle his accounts. He knows the total currency risk he is exposed to at the end of every month and wants to protect himself against a weakening U.S. dollar. As such, he wants to buy a one month put option on the U.S. dollar and at the same time be able to lock in a better rate if the Canadian dollar strengthens during the life of the option. Currently, the Canadian dollar is trading at 1.34 Cad/U.S. He also strongly feels that because of future economic events over the next month, the Canadian dollar will definitely strengthen past the 1.30 Cad/U.S. mark. Furthermore, he feels that he will not be too surprised if the Canadian dollar strengthens even more and goes past the 1.29 Cad/U.S. mark. To be able to monetize his view and satisfy his needs, the manufacturer needs a ladder option. The ladder put option would pay the manufacturer at the expiry date of the option the maximum of zero and the difference between the spot rate at the maturity of the option and the minimum of the spot rate at the option maturity date and the ladder levels (if the levels are breached during the life of the option). The following example better illustrates the mechanics associated with the ladder option.

Time 0 mth:	The Canadian dollar is currently trading at 1.34 Cad/U.S. A manufacturer wants to pay an up-front premium for a European style one month ladder put option with ladder levels at 1.29 Cad/U.S. and 1.30 Cad/U.S. The spot rates used in the calculation of the option payoff are observed at noon on each business day.
Time 1 mth:	*Case 1* The Canadian dollar is trading at 1.32 Cad/U.S. The weakest value attained by the U.S. dollar during the one month period is at the maturity date of the option. The option expires worthless, and the manufacturer has lost his premium paid out at the inception of the contract. *Case 2* The Canadian dollar is trading at 1.32 Cad/U.S. The lowest value attained by the U.S. dollar during the one month

period was a level of 1.295 Cad/U.S., in the process breaching a ladder level of 1.30. The payoff to the buyer is $(1.32 - \min[1.32, 1.30] - P_{1\,mth}^{*})$Cad/U.S. $= (1.32 - 1.30 - P_{1\,mth}^{*})$Cad/U.S., where $P_{1\,mth}^{*}$ represents the premium of the ladder option future valued to one month, 1.32 represents the spot rate at the maturity of the option, and 1.30 represents the ladder level that was breached during the life of the option.

Case 3
The Canadian dollar is trading at 1.32 Cad/U.S. The lowest value attained by the U.S. dollar during the one month period was a level of 1.285 Cad/U.S., in the process breaching the ladder levels of 1.30 and 1.29. The payoff to the buyer is $(1.32 - \min[1.32, 1.30, 1.29] - P_{1\,mth}^{*})$Cad/U.S. $= (1.32 - 1.29 - P_{1\,mth}^{*})$Cad/U.S., where 1.32 represents the spot rate at the maturity of the option, and both 1.30 and 1.29 represent the ladder levels that were breached during the life of the option.

It is first important to note that the ladder put option discussed above is not really an option. If none of the ladder levels is breached during the life of the option, the minimum of the ladder levels and the spot rate at the maturity date is simply the spot rate at the maturity date. Thus, the difference between the spot rate at the maturity of the option and the minimum of the ladder levels and the spot rate at maturity is never negative.

Secondly, although in the above example we had a variable strike rate (i.e., a strike rate that is not known at the inception of the contract), we can just as easily create an option where the strike rate is specified in advance. More precisely, the payoff to the buyer of a European style ladder put option is the maximum of zero and the difference between the pre-specified strike rate and the minimum of the breached ladder levels and the spot rate at the option maturity date. We will call options of these type modified ladder options. Unlike the ladder option, the difference between the pre-specified strike rate and the minimum of the ladder levels and the spot rate at the option maturity date can be negative.

Thirdly, the premium of a ladder option is directly proportional to the number of ladders. Thus, the bigger the number of ladders, the more expensive the ladder option becomes. When there are an infinite number of ladders and the spot rates are monitored continuously, the premium of a ladder option will be the same as that of a lookback option with continuous time sampling. See the section on lookback options. Exhibit 16 illustrates the difference in

EXHIBIT 16

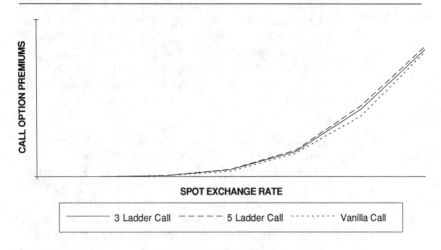

premiums between a modified ladder call option and a vanilla call option when the strikes and the times to maturity of the options are identical.

The payoffs for the various above-mentioned European style ladder options can be written as detailed in Exhibit 17.

Although the discussion above has been restricted to European style options, it is not difficult to offer the ladder and modified ladder options with the American style exercise features and price both the American and the European style ladder and modified ladder options using the binomial method. By rewriting the payoff of a ladder option in terms of a European option payoff and a barrier option payoff, Street (1993) provides a method of pricing and hedging the European style ladder options.

I. Lookback Options

Consider the manufacturer's plight addressed in the section on ladder options, where the manufacturer wanted a protection against a weakening dollar. As before, the manufacturer wants to be able to lock in at the best possible rate the Canadian dollar is going to show during the life of the option. Unlike earlier, however, the manufacturer has no view on the currency market. To address his concerns, he wants to buy a European style lookback put option.

A lookback option is a derivative security that allows the buyer to pay an initial up-front premium for an option that provides maximum protection. The mechanics associated with a lookback option are best illustrated with the following example:

EXHIBIT 17   Payoffs of the Ladder Option

Type of Ladder Option	Payoff at Expiry Time T	
$C_{E,F}(0,T,S)$	$-P_T^*$	if $S_T < \min [L_i,S_T]$
	$S_T - \min [L_i,S_T] - P_T^*$	if $S_T > \min [L_i,S_T]$
$P_{E,F}(0,T,S)$	$-P_T^*$	if $S_T > \max [L_i,S_T]$
	$\max [L_i,S_T] - S_T - P_T^*$	if $S_T < \max [L_i,S_T]$
$C_{E,M}(X,0,T,S)$	$-P_T^*$	if $X > \max [L_i,S_T]$
	$\max [L_i,S_T] - X - P_T^*$	if $X < \max [L_i,S_T]$
$P_{E,M}(X,0,T,S)$	$-P_T^*$	if $X < \min [L_i,S_T]$
	$X - \min [L_i,S_T] - P_T^*$	if $X > \min [L_i,S_T]$

where $C_{E,F}(0,T,S)$, $P_{E,F}(0,T,S)$, $C_{E,M}(X,0,T,S)$, and $P_{E,M}(X,0,T,S)$ represent the European style ladder call option, ladder put option, modified ladder call option, and modified ladder put option respectively when the current time is 0, the option maturity time is T, the current spot rate is S, the strike rate of the modified ladder option is X, P_T^* represents the premium of the ladder option future valued to time T, the ladder levels are L_i (for $i = 1,...,n$), min $[L_i,S_T]$ represents the smallest value of the spot rate at option maturity date, and the ladder levels that are breached during the life of the option and max $[L_i,S_T]$ represents the largest value of the spot rate at the maturity date and the ladder levels that are breached during the life of the option. If no ladder is breached during the life of the option, the min$[L_i,S_T]$ and max$[L_i,S_T]$ both collapse to S_T.

Time 0 mth: The Canadian dollar is currently trading at 1.34 Cad/U.S. A manufacturer who is faced with currency exposure in a month's time is worried about the U.S. weakening. At the same time, he wants to be able to lock at the highest possible level the Canadian dollar may strengthen to during this one month period. As such, he wants to pay an up-front premium for a European style lookback put option that pays off in one month's time the maximum of zero and the difference between the spot rate on the option maturity date and the lowest value the dollar reaches during the life of the option (inclusive of the spot rates at both the inception of the contract and the maturity of the option). The spot rates are observed at noon on each business day.

Time 1 mth: *Case 1*
The Canadian dollar is trading at 1.32 Cad/U.S. The weakest value attained by the U.S. dollar during the one month

period is at the maturity date of the option. The option therefore expires worthless, and the manufacturer has lost his premium paid out at the inception of the contract.

Case 2
The Canadian dollar is trading at 1.33 Cad/U.S. The lowest value attained by the U.S. dollar during the one month period was a level of 1.28 Cad/U.S. The option finishes in-the-money, and the payoff to the manufacturer is $(1.33 - 1.28 - P_{1\,mth}^{*})$ Cad/U.S., where $P_{1\,mth}^{*}$ represents the premium of the lookback option future valued to one month.

It is first important to note from the above example that, like a ladder option, the lookback option is not really an option. This follows from the observation that the sampling period that contains the exchange rates encountered during the life of the option also includes as its points the spot rate at the option maturity date, and as such one cannot do any worse than the spot rate at the option maturity date.

Secondly, although the above option had a variable strike, we could have created an option that paid the buyer at the option maturity date a maximum of zero and the difference between a pre-specified strike rate and the lowest exchange rate realized during the life of the option. Options of these type are called modified lookback options. Unlike the comment made earlier, here it is possible for this difference to be negative.

Thirdly, because this product provides a high level of insurance, one can expect it to be costly. The cost of a lookback option is directly proportional to the frequency of sampling. Thus, the greater the frequency of sampling (or bigger the sampling period), the more expensive the option. Exhibit 18 shows the difference in premiums between a modified lookback call option and a vanilla call option when the strikes and times to maturity of the options are identical. If the manufacturer has a strong view that the Canadian dollar over the next three weeks is never going to get any stronger than the exchange rate at inception, he could use his view to lower the cost by purchasing a partial lookback option, where the sampling period for the lookback feature commences in three weeks and ends on the option maturity date.

Finally, it is important to note that while the sampling procedure in a lookback option is driven by the partitioning of the time axis, the sampling procedure in a ladder option is directly done on the spot rate axis.

The payoffs for the various above-mentioned European style lookback options can be more generally written as detailed in Exhibit 19.

EXHIBIT 18

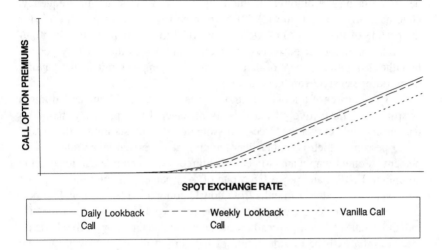

EXHIBIT 19 Payoffs of the Lookback Option

Type of Lookback Option	Payoff at Expiry Time T	
$C_{E,F}(0,T,S)$	$-P_T{}^*$	if $S_T < \min S_{t_i}$
	$S_T - \min S_{t_i} - P_T{}^*$	if $S_T > \min S_{t_i}$
$P_{E,F}(0,T,S)$	$-P_T{}^*$	if $S_T > \max S_{t_i}$
	$\max S_{t_i} - S_T - P_T{}^*$	if $S_T < \max S_{t_i}$
$C_{E,M}(X,0,T,S)$	$-P_T{}^*$	if $X > \max S_{t_i}$
	$\max S_{t_i} - X - P_T{}^*$	if $X < \max S_{t_i}$
$P_{E,M}(X,0,T,S)$	$-P_T{}^*$	if $X < \min S_{t_i}$
	$X - \min S_{t_i} - P_T{}^*$	if $X > \min S_{t_i}$

where $C_{E,F}(0,T,S)$, $P_{E,F}(0,T,S)$, $C_{E,M}(X,0,T,S)$, and $P_{E,M}(X,0,T,S)$ represent the European style full lookback call option, full lookback put option, modified lookback call option, and modified lookback put option, respectively, when the current time is 0, option maturity time is T, current spot rate is S, strike rate of the modified full lookback option is X, $P_T{}^*$ represents the premium of the lookback option future valued to time T, the spot rate used for the sampling of the observations are S_{t_i} when the sampled times are t_i (where $i = 1,...,n$; $t_0 = 0$ and $t_n = T$), min S_{t_i} represents the smallest value of all the spot rates sampled, and max S_{t_i} represents the largest value of all the spot rates sampled. For the partial lookback options and the modified partial lookback options, the payoffs are essentially the same as above with the size of the sampling points being reduced.

Although both the European and American style lookback options can be priced using the binomial method regardless of the sampling frequency, Goldman, Sosin, and Gatto (1979) have provided closed form solutions for the pricing of the European style options when the assumption of a continuous time sampling period is used. Lookback options could be easily hedged by either using the concept of delta-hedging or trying to replicate the payoffs using European style vanilla options.

The concept of a lookback strategy can also be easily embedded into a swap and used effectively by a liability manager. More precisely, based on the current yield curve, the three-year swap rate starting six months from now is 5.5 percent, which is higher than the current three-year swap rate of 4.73 percent. A client who wants to get into a three-year swap rate can receive the six-month LIBOR and pay a fixed rate of 4.73 percent. If she thinks that the three-year swap rate six months from now is going to be lesser than 4.73 percent, she could enter a swap whereby she receives a floating rate of the six-month LIBOR plus some spread on each coupon date and pays a fixed rate on the swap that will be the maximum of the current three-year swap rate and the three-year swap rate in six months time.

J. Mid-Atlantic Options

A European style vanilla option is an option that can be exercised only at the maturity date of the option, and an American style vanilla option is an option that can be exercised at any time during the life of the option. An option that is an intermediary between these two options is called the Mid-Atlantic option. The Mid-Atlantic option, also called the Quasi-American style option, limited exercise option, and the Bermudian option is an option that can be exercised only at discrete points during the life of the option. Thus, at the inception of the contract, in addition to specifying the usual parameters of a vanilla European style option, the buyer of a Mid-Atlantic option must also specify the times of exercise.

Mid-Atlantic options lend themselves naturally as hedge instruments in the interest rate market. The following example better illustrates the mechanics underlying the use of this type of option:

Time 0 yrs: An investor has just bought a large amount of semi-annual 8 percent coupon callable bonds that were issued by a corporate at $100. The issued bond has a five-year life and can be recalled by the issuer for $102 at any one of the coupon dates during the last year of the bond. More precisely, the bond can be recalled by the issuer on the eighth or ninth coupon date at $102. To hedge, the investor pays an up-front premium to buy a Mid-Atlantic option on a synthetic bond with a 8 percent semi-annual coupon that has the same exercise dates as the issue and matures on the same day as the callable bond for $102.

Case 1: Bond is called at the end of four years

Time 4 yrs: The bond is trading at $105, and the issuer pays the investor a coupon of $4 and recalls the bond at $102. The investor then pays $102 to exercise the Mid-Atlantic option into a one-year synthetic bond with a semi-annual coupon of 8 percent.

Case 2: Bond is called at the end of $4^{1}/_{2}$ years

Time 4 yrs: The bond is trading at $99.50. The investor receives a coupon of $4. The issuer does not recall the bond, and hence the investor does not exercise the option.

Time $4^{1}/_{2}$ yrs: The bond is trading at $103. The issuer pays the investor a coupon of $4 and recalls the bond for $102. The investor exercises the Mid-Atlantic option into a six-month synthetic bond with a semi-annual coupon of 8 percent by paying $102.

Case 3: Bond is not called

Time 4 yrs: The bond is trading at $99.50. A coupon of $4 is paid to the investor. The issuer does not recall the bond, and hence the investor does not exercise the option.

Time $4^{1}/_{2}$ yrs: The bond is trading at $101. The issuer does not recall the bond for $102. The investor gets a coupon of $4 and does not exercise the option.

Time 5 yrs: The bond matures at par. In addition to the face value, the investor also receives the $4 coupon. The investor has also lost the premium paid for the Mid-Atlantic option.

It is important to note that although the above example illustrates a scenario where the issuer recalls the bonds only when they are in-the-money, due to accounting or tax reasons it is not uncommon for the issuer to recall bonds even when they are out-of-the-money.

Since the number of exercise points in a Mid-Atlantic option can never exceed that of an American style option and never be lesser than that of a

European style option, it is intuitively reasonable to expect the premium of a Mid-Atlantic option to be no lesser than that of a European style option and no greater than that of an American style option. Mid-Atlantic options can be easily priced using the binomial method, and the concept of discretizing the times of exercise can be easily implemented into the other types of exotic options and underlying.

K. Non-Linear Payoff Options

A vanilla option has a linear payoff if the derivative security finishes in-the-money. More precisely, if S_T and X represent the exchange rate at the maturity of the option and the strike rate respectively, neglecting the cost of the option premium, the European style vanilla call option would have a payoff of $S_T - X$ if the option goes in-the-money and zero otherwise. Note that the in-the-money payoff is a linear function of the exchange rate at maturity. By the same token, a European style non-linear payoff option has an in-the-money payoff that is a non-linear function of the exchange rate at maturity. Examples of these in-the-money payoffs at the maturity date are $e^{S_T} - X$, $S_T^2 - X$, $S_T^{0.5} - X$. See Exhibit 20. Non-linear payoff options that have payoffs where S_T appears as a base rather than a power (e.g., $S_T^2 - X$ and $S_T^{0.5} - X$) are called power options. The following example, although applied to a power option, can be easily modified for any non-linear payoff option.

Time 0 wks: The Canadian dollar is currently trading at 1.30 Cad/U.S. The investor feels that one week from now, the Canadian dollar is going to be much weaker. Because of the investor's certainty, he wants his payoff function at the expiry date to be $S_T^2 - 1.31$ if the option finishes in-the-money (i.e., if the U.S. dollar strengthens and goes past the 1.31 mark). He pays a premium to buy the power option that is struck at 1.31 Cad/U.S. and has a life of one week.

Time 1 wk: *Case 1*
               Currency is now trading at 1.30 Cad/U.S. The option finishes out-of-the-money, and the investor loses his option premium.

               Case 2
               Currency is now trading at 1.34 Cad/U.S. The option finishes in-the-money, and the payoff to the client is $(1.34^2 - 1.31 - P_{1\,wk}^*)$ Cad/U.S., where $P_{1\,wk}^*$ represents the premium of the power option future valued to time 1 week.

EXHIBIT 20

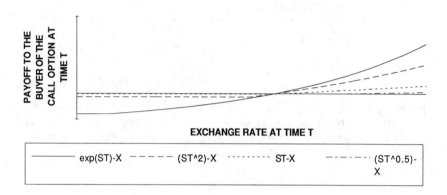

It is first important to note that, neglecting the premiums paid out for the options at the inception of the contract, if the investor had bought a vanilla call option instead, the payoff to the client would have been $(1.34 - 1.31)$ Cad/U.S. This is about one-sixteenth the payoff value obtained from the purchase of the power option above. The payoff to the investor can be further increased by increasing the index (or the power) of S_T in the above example from two to four.

Secondly, due to the high leveraging effect in the payoff function, we can expect the premium of the power option to be higher than that of a vanilla option.

Letting $f(S_T)$ represent any non-linear function of S_T, and X be the strike rate of the option, the payoff to the investor can be more generally written as detailed in Exhibit 21.

As always, the binomial method can be easily used to price both the European and American style power options. Although a power option can be hedged using the concept of delta hedging, due to the amount of leveraging involved, hedging the sale of a power option can be pretty expensive because of the high gamma characteristic possessed by the option. This hedging cost can be reduced by alternatively hedging a power option using a sequence of varying notional amounts of vanilla options struck at varying levels.

Non-linear payoff options can also be easily used for liability or risk management. More precisely, a client could have a non-linear risk profile for the various interest rate levels because of his total borrowing costs. A perfect hedge for the client would be to buy a non-linear payoff option that replicates

EXHIBIT 21   Payoffs of the Non-Linear Payoff Option

Type of Non-Linear Payoff Option	Payoff at Expiry Time T	
$C_E(X,0,T,S)$	$-P_T^*$	if $f(S_T) < X$
	$f(S_T) - X - P_T^*$	if $f(S_T) > X$
$P_E(X,0,T,S)$	$-P_T^*$	if $f(S_T) > X$
	$X - f(S_T) - P_T^*$	if $f(S_T) < X$

where $C_E(X,0,T,S)$ and $P_E(X,0,T,S)$ represent the European call and put non-linear payoff options when the strike rate is X, the current time is 0, the option maturity time is T, the current spot rate is S, and P_T^* represents the premium of the option that is future valued to time T.

his non-linear risk profile. This transaction can then be most easily hedged by the dealer by breaking this non-linear payoff down to linear payoff pieces so as to replicate each linear piece with vanilla options.

L. Quanto Options

A Canadian investor observes the current five-year Canadian and U.S. government bond yields to be 5.53 percent and 5.10 percent respectively. Based on the historical numbers, the investor notices that the current spread between these yields is relatively small compared to the historical values of this difference. She also feels that based on the economic numbers coming out in one week's time, this spread is bound to widen. She wants to buy an instrument that allows her to monetize her view. Furthermore, she does not want to be exposed to the currency risk. She wants the payoff to be strictly the product of the notional amount of the contract and the difference in the bond yields if she is right. The instrument that she actually needs is called a quanto spread option. Before defining a quanto spread option, we will first define a plain (single variable) quanto option. A plain quanto option is a derivative security that allows the buyer to pay an initial up-front premium in domestic currency for an option that trades in a foreign country at a guaranteed exchange rate. The mechanics associated with a quanto option transaction are best illustrated with the following example:

Time 0 wks: The current five-year U.S. government bond yield is currently trading at 5.10 percent. A Canadian investor has a view that this five-year treasury yield is going to be higher in a week's time when the economic numbers are released. To monetize her view, she wants to buy an option that will pay the difference between the five-year bond yield in a week's time and 5.10 percent if she is right. She, however, wants to pay the premium and receive her payoff, if she is in-the-money, in Canadian funds. She does not want to be exposed to the currency risk.

Time 1 wks: *Case 1*
The five-year treasury is trading at a yield of 5.15 percent. The option finishes in-the-money, and the payoff to the buyer in Canadian dollars is the [Notional Principal*(5.15 – 5.10)%] – $P_{1\,wk}{}^*$, where $P_{1\,wk}{}^*$ represents the premium in Canadian dollars of the quanto option future valued to one week.

Case 2
The five-year U.S. bond is trading at 5.05 percent. The option finishes out-of-the-money, and the investor has lost her premium paid out at the inception of the contract.

It is important to note from the above example that although the investor did not have to undergo any currency exposure, it is just as easy to structure an instrument where the investor receives her payoff, if she is in-the-money, at other guaranteed exchange rates or at the exchange rate realized on the option maturity date.

Quanto options are usually priced like their vanilla counterparts with an adjustment made to the drift term. As in the spread options, there is the element of correlation, which in this case is between the bond yield and the exchange rate, that is present in the expression that enables us to price a quanto option. However, the effect of the correlation in the price of a quanto option is smaller than the contribution of the correlation component to the price of a spread option. Although both the European and the American style quanto options can be priced using the binomial method, Reiner (1992) has provided analytical expressions for the pricing of the European style quanto options.

As discussed at the beginning of this topic, quanto spread options can be easily used by asset managers to help monetize views on relative movements between the two environments without undertaking the currency risks. Liability managers can also easily use the concept of quantos in swaps. Because of the nature of their assets and liabilities in the two different environments, liability managers can exploit the cheap borrowing cost in one environment (for example in Canada) to fund the activities in the other environment (for example U.S.) by using a differential swap to swap from a BA to a LIBOR plus some spread without undergoing any currency risk and any exchange of principal.

Quanto structures can also be easily embedded into binary options and presented as structured notes. For example, a Canadian investor could buy a six-month note that paid off a coupon that is a fraction of 5 percent, where this fraction represents the proportion of business days in the six-month period during which the three-month LIBOR exceeds a level of 3.5 percent, where all the transactions are carried out in Canadian funds. One can similarly and easily structure such a binary note where the fraction now depends on the proportion of business days in the life of the note during which the three-month BA exceeds the three-month LIBOR by 50 basis points.

M. Rainbow Options

A U.S. investor observes that the Canadian dollar and the Japanese yen are currently trading at 1.32 Cad/U.S. and 111 Yen/U.S. respectively. Based on the current levels and historical data, the investor feels that the U.S. dollar should get strong enough over the next week so that the maximum of the Yen/U.S. and (85*Cad/U.S.) exchange rates should easily exceed a level of 113 in a week. Furthermore, the investor wants to pay the premium for this yield enhancement vehicle and receive his payoff in U.S. funds if his view turns out to be right. The instrument that he actually needs is called a rainbow option. A rainbow option is an instrument that allows the buyer to pay an initial up-front premium for an option that provides a maximum of zero and the difference between the maximum of the two underlying variables and the strike rate, in the case of a call option. The mechanics associated with a rainbow option transaction are best illustrated with the following example:

Time 0 wks: The Canadian dollar and the Japanese yen are currently trading at 1.32 Cad/U.S. and 111 Yen/U.S. respectively. The investor pays a premium for a rainbow call option that is struck at a level of 113 and expires in a week. If his view is right, ignoring the premium of the option, he would receive a payoff of the difference between the maximum of the Yen/U.S. and (85*Cad/U.S.) exchange rates one week from now and a strike level of 113. Furthermore, the premium and the payoff are done in U.S. funds.

Time 1 wk: *Case 1*
              The Canadian dollar and the Japanese yen are trading at a
              level of 1.35 Cad/U.S. and 112.5 Yen/U.S. respectively.
              The maximum value of the Yen/U.S. and (85*Cad/U.S.)
              exchange rate is max[112.5, (85*1.35)] = max[112.5,
              114.75] = 114.75. The option finishes in-the-money, and
              the payoff to the buyer in U.S. funds is the (114.75 – 113) –
              $P_{1\,wk}{}^*$, where $P_{1\,wk}{}^*$ represents the premium of the rainbow
              option future valued to one week.

              Case 2
              The Canadian dollar and the Japanese yen are trading at a
              level of 1.32 Cad/U.S. and 111.5 Yen/U.S. respectively. The
              maximum value of the Yen/U.S. and (85*Cad/U.S.)
              exchange rate is max[111.5, (85*1.32)] = max[111.5,112.2]
              = 112.5. The option finishes out-of-the-money, and the
              buyer has lost his premium.

Rainbow options can be easily priced like their vanilla counterparts
with an adjustment made to the drift term. Furthermore, both European and
American style rainbow options can be priced using the binomial method.
Stulz (1982) and Rubinstein (1991) provide analytical expressions to price
European style rainbow options. Although the discussion has been based on
the use of an option on the maximum of two variables, we can extend the
concept to entertain the possibility of having an option based on a basket of
indices. See Boyle and Tse (1990) for a detailed discussion pertaining the
pricing of the maximum or the minimum of *n* assets.

Rainbow structures can also be easily embedded into binary quanto
options in the structuring of notes. More precisely, a Canadian investor could
buy a one-month note that pays off a coupon that is a fraction of 5 percent,
where this fraction represents the proportion of business days in the six-
month period during which the maximum of three-month BA and
(1.15*three-month LIBOR) exceeds a level of 4 percent, where all the transactions are carried out in Canadian funds. One can similarly and easily structure such a binary note where the payoff is done in U.S. funds.

N. Shout Options

A shout option is a hybrid of a ladder option and a lookback option. To
understand how a shout option works, it is useful to first revisit the payoffs of

a European style vanilla option, lookback option, modified lookback option, ladder option, and modified ladder option.

A European style vanilla call option on a currency gives the buyer of the contract, on the expiry date of the option, an exchange rate payoff that is the maximum of zero and the difference between the spot exchange rate at the expiry date and the strike rate. The buyer of a European style lookback call option has a payoff on the option expiry date that is the higher of zero and the difference between the spot rate at the option maturity date and the lowest exchange rate achieved by the currency during the life of the option. The buyer of a European style modified lookback call option has a payoff on the expiry date of the option that is the higher of zero and the difference between the highest exchange rate achieved by the currency during the life of the option and a pre-defined strike rate. A ladder call option gives on the expiry of the option a payoff that is the higher of zero and the difference between the spot rate at the maturity date and the minimum of both the spot rate at expiry date and the predetermined ladder levels that have been breached during the life of the option. A modified ladder call option gives on the expiry of the option a payoff that is the higher of zero and the difference between the maximum of both the spot rate at expiry date and the predetermined ladder levels that have been breached during the life of the option and the strike rate. The payoffs corresponding to the five types of European call currency options are detailed in Exhibit 22.

Unlike the above options, the shout option gives the buyer a payoff at maturity date that is the maximum of zero and the difference between the

EXHIBIT 22   Payoffs of the European Call Option

Type of European Call Option	Payoff at Expiry Time T
vanilla	$\max [-P_T{}^*, S_T - X - P_T{}^*]$
lookback	$\max [-P_T{}^*, S_T - \min S_{t_i} - P_T{}^*]$
modified lookback	$\max [-P_T{}^*, \max S_{t_i} - X - P_T{}^*]$
ladder	$\max [-P_T{}^*, S_T - \min (L_1,...,L_n, S_T) - P_T{}^*]$
modified ladder	$\max [-P_T{}^*, \max (L_1,...,L_n, S_T) - X - P_T{}^*]$

where $P_T{}^*$ represents the premium of the option future valued to time T, T denotes the expiry time of the option, X denotes the strike rate of the currency option, S_{t_i} denotes the spot rate at time t_i, and L_i denotes the level of the ith ladder, which is an exchange rate that is pre-specified in advance and breached during the life of the option (where $i = 1,2,...,n$; $t_0 = 0$, $t_n = T$).

spot rate at the maturity date and the minimum of the spot rate at both the expiry date and the time of shout.

The nature of this payoff is best exemplified by the following sequence of events:

Time 0 wks: The currency is currently trading at 1.35 Cad/U.S. Because of the currency risk exposure in a month, the client wants to be protected against the weakening U.S. dollar. At the same time, the client wants to be able to lock in at the best rate the Canadian dollar will probably show during the life of the option. The premium involved in buying a lookback option is quite high. The client feels that because he is very good at calling the markets, he is not prepared to pay for the option that guarantees him a maximum payoff. The client, however, would not mind paying a lesser premium to buy a European style shout put option on U.S. currency that matures in one month with which he could possibly achieve the same payoff as the lookback option.

Time 1 wk: Currency is now trading at 1.30 Cad/U.S. This has been the weakest U.S. level in the past one week. The option owner feels that it is very unlikely that the U.S. dollar will weaken any further and as such phones up the seller of the option to shout at the level of 1.30 Cad/U.S.

Time 1 mth: *Case 1*
                Currency is now trading at 1.34 Cad/U.S. Since min[1.34,1.30] Cad/U.S. = 1.30 Cad/U.S., the option finishes in-the-money and the payoff to the buyer of the option is the $(1.34 - 1.30 - P_{1\,mth}{}^{*})$ Cad/U.S., where $P_{1\,mth}{}^{*}$ represents premium of the option future valued to time of one month, and the numbers 1.34 and 1.30 represent the spot rate at maturity and the shout rate respectively.

                Case 2
                Currency is now trading at 1.28 Cad/U.S. Since min[1.28,1.30] Cad/U.S. = 1.28 Cad/U.S., the option finishes out-of-the-money. The client loses his option premium.

From the example above, it should be first noted that in illustrating the payoffs at option maturity (i.e., one month) it was assumed that there was an opportunity for the owner of the option to shout. If the buyer had shouted at a level that was the strongest showing by the Canadian dollar during the life of the option, the payoff to the buyer will be similar to that of a lookback option. On the other hand, if the shout had been made at a level that turns out to be equal to or lesser than the spot rate at maturity, the payoff will be equal to zero. Because the shout level can be either greater than or lesser than the spot rate at maturity, it readily follows that the premium of a shout option should be no larger than that of a lookback option.

Secondly, like the ladder and lookback option, the shout option is not an option because of the non-negative nature of the payoff. By pre-specifying the strike rate, however, the non-negativity is removed and the modified shout option behaves like an option, where the premium of a modified shout option is no lesser than a premium of a vanilla option that is struck at the same level and no greater than a premium of a modified lookback option that is also struck at the same level.

To the buyer of a European style shout option, the payoff at the maturity date of the option can be written as detailed in Exhibit 23.

Although the buyer of a shout option can theoretically shout at any level the exchange rate realizes during the life of the option, it is rational for the buyer to only consider shouting if the intrinsic value of the option is greater than zero. More precisely, it is rational for the buyer to shout at any one time during the life of the option if the value (premium) of the option by shouting is greater than the value (premium) of the option without shouting. The shout option can be most easily valued using the binomial method. See Thomas (1993) for the use of a binomial method to value a shout option.

EXHIBIT 23 Payoffs of the Shout Option

Type of Shout Option	Payoff at Expiry Time T
$C_{E,F}(0,T,S)$	$\max\,[-P_T^{\,*},\, S_T - \min\,[S^*,S_T] - P_T^{\,*}]$
$P_{E,F}(0,T,S)$	$\max\,[-P_T^{\,*},\, \max\,[S^*,S_T] - S_T - P_T^{\,*}]$
$C_{E,M}(X,0,T,S)$	$\max\,[-P_T^{\,*},\, \max\,[S^*,S_T] - X - P_T^{\,*}]$
$P_{E,M}(X,0,T,S)$	$\max\,[-P_T^{\,*},\, X - \min\,[S^*,S_T] - P_T^{\,*}]$

where S^* represents the exchange rate at which the buyer of the option shouted, $P_T^{\,*}$ is the premium of the shout option future valued to time T, $C_{E,F}(0,T,S)$, $P_{E,F}(0,T,S)$, $C_{E,M}(X,0,T,S)$, and $P_{E,M}(X,0,T,S)$ represent the European style call shout option, put shout option, modified call shout option, and modified put shout option respectively when X is the strike rate of the option, 0 is the current time, T is the time of option maturity, and S is the current spot rate.

Unlike the lookback option, which tends to be expensive, the shout option is cheaper and has the ability to give the buyer (typically an asset manager who is paid for market calling abilities) the same payoff if the market is called correctly. Thus, it serves as a great and cheap yield enhancement tool with a limited downside for someone who is good at calling markets. Exhibit 24 illustrates the difference in premiums between a vanilla call option and the modified versions of lookback, ladder, and shout call options when the strikes and option maturity times are identical.

Because of its cheapness, the shout option can also be used effectively in interest rate liability management by managers who are good at calling markets. For example, a liability manager could pay a fix rate on a five-year swap and receive a six-month LIBOR. If his view is that over the next two months the five-year swap rate cannot get any higher, he could buy a shout option from his counterparty and end up with the following transaction:

The liability manager pays a fix rate on a five-year swap with the fixed rate being determined at the end of two months by setting it to the min[five-year swap rate at time of shout, five-year swap rate at the end of two months] if he decides to shout. If no shout has been made, the counterparty receives a fixed rate given by the five-year swap rate at the end of two months. For this, he receives a floating rate of (six-month LIBOR – spread) on every reset date.

Other variations of the uses of the shout options for liability management are also possible.

EXHIBIT 24

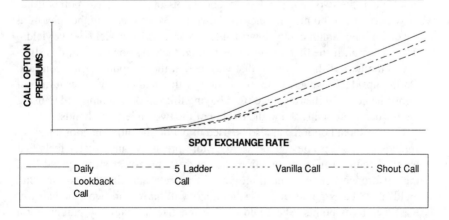

Another interesting feature of this product is the following:

Suppose at some moment during the life of the option, the buyer of a call shout option calls up the dealer to shout at an exchange rate level. The dealer suspects that the buyer wants to lock in a minimum payoff level and as such decides to quote the buyer a higher rate than what it is actually trading at. The impact of this "misquote" to the buyer is that the minimum payoff level that can be locked into is no longer as high as what the buyer of the option initially thought he could get. However, the buyer could seize the opportunity of the over-quoted spot rate and sell currency at that rate and buy off at a lower rate realizing instantaneous risk-free profit. Thus, it would not pay for the dealer to "misquote" his spot rate at the time of shout.

O. Spread Options

Spread options are options that can be used to monetize a view on the relative movement between any two indices in the same economy. Suppose that a fund manager feels that the current yield differential of 100 basis points between the 10-year government bond and the two-year bond is too narrow based on historical data and that this difference in yield will widen in a month. To monetize her view, as her first strategy, she could purchase the underlying bonds by going long and short the appropriate notional amount of the bonds. With this strategy, if she is wrong in a month, she could possibly take huge losses when liquidating this position. Thus, the downside of replicating the spread using the underlying bonds can be costly and sometimes disastrous.

An alternative way to monetize her view would be to buy a spread option that pays at the end of one month the difference between the 10-year bond yield, the two-year bond yield, and an offset of 100 basis points if her view is right and nothing if her view is wrong. More precisely, her payoff at the end of one month could be written as the $\max[0, \text{10-yr yield} - \text{2-yr yield} - 0.01]$. Clearly, if the market view was wrong, the only downside of this strategy is the loss of the premium that was paid at the inception of the contract. On the upside, however, if her prediction of the market movement turns out right, she gets a higher leverage from buying this option as compared to using the former strategy involving the trading of the two underlying bonds.

The spread option can also be used to bet on the movement of the swap spreads (i.e., swap rate – bond yield). More precisely, an investor feels that based on current market conditions, the current three-year swap spread (i.e., the difference between the three-year swap rate and the three-year bond yield) is 28 basis points and this she thinks will narrow in two months by at least five basis points. She could easily monetize her view by purchasing a spread option on the three-year swap spread with an offset of 23 basis points that expires in two months time. At the maturity of the option, the investor gets a payoff that is the max[0,0.0023 − (3-year swap rate − 3-year bond yield)]. The following sequence of events helps illustrate this example better.

Time 0 mths: The current swap spread is 28 basis points. The investor feels that in two months the swap spread will narrow by at least five basis points. So the investor pays a premium for a spread option on a $100 million notional amount with an offset of 23 basis points that allows her to monetize this view.

Time 2 mths: *Case 1*
The current swap spread is 18 basis points. The option finishes in-the-money, and the payoff to the buyer of the option is $100 million*(0.0023 − 0.0018) − $P_{2\,mth}^{*}$, where $P_{2\,mth}^{*}$ represents the premium of the spread option future valued to a time of two months.

Case 2
The current swap spread is 35 basis points. The option finishes out-of-the money. Hence, the investor loses her premium.

It is important to note that although the above two examples illustrate the use of European style spread options, we can just as well structure an American style spread option where the buyer of the option is allowed to exercise at any time during the life of the option. Like the above two examples, the spread option can be very easily and naturally used to monetize a leveraged view on any part of the same yield curve. More precisely, one could write the payoff function of a spread option in a very generic form as max[0,(a*Yield$_1$) + (b*Yield$_2$) + c], where a, b, and c are any three real numbers and Yield$_1$ and Yield$_2$ represent the two variables describing the option. These two variables can represent the two different swap rates or bond yields or one of each on the same yield curve environment.

Although closed form solutions do exist when c (called the offset in the spread option) is zero, the spread option has to be generally evaluated numerically. See Ravindran (1993) for an intuitive approach to spread option pricing. Besides the volatilities of both the variables, which have to be input to arrive at an option premium for the spread option, the effect of correlation between these variables is also an extremely important input to the price. Unlike volatilities, which can be easily traded, there is no market for correlation trading. Thus, the only means of getting a good estimate for the correlation number would be to use the historical data. Hence, correlation estimation is very crucial to the pricing of a spread option. Like a vanilla option, the spread option can also be easily hedged using the delta-hedging technique on both the variables.

When the offset c is zero, the spread option is also known as an exchange option. See Margrabe (1978) and Rubinstein (1991) for a discussion on the pricing of exchange options. The use of an exchange option is best illustrated by the following example:

A portfolio manager may currently have in her portfolio a big collection of two-year and three-year bonds. Her view on the market is that the yield curve, which is currently flat between the two-year point and the three-year point, is going to steepen over the next two weeks. If that happens, the two-year (three-year) bond's yield is going to decrease (increase), which in turn increases (reduces) the value of the portfolio. To enhance the value of the portfolio, the manager wants to buy a two-week option that would allow her to exchange the three-year bonds for the two-year bonds during any day of the two weeks. Clearly, the exchange will only take place if the yield on the three-year bond is higher than that of the two-year bond. As such the payoff to the buyer of the option is the max[0,(3-year bond yield – 2-year bond yield)], which is essentially a spread option with a zero offset.

Liability managers can also use spread options in periodic caps (see the section on forward start options).

3. AN INTUITIVE APPROACH TO THE PRICING OF THE EXOTIC OPTIONS

Black and Scholes in their celebrated 1973 paper developed analytical expressions that helped in the pricing of European style vanilla stock options. Six years later, Cox-Ross-Rubinstein developed a simple, powerful, and intuitively appealing binomial method, which we will describe in detail in this section, to price both the European and American style vanilla stock options. The other methods of option pricing that are currently used in the industry will also be overviewed in this section. Because of the lack of subjectivity in the modeling of an exchange rate process as compared to an interest rate process, much of this section will focus on the pricing of vanilla and exotic currency options. Furthermore, whenever an interest rate process is mentioned, we will assume that the futures (or the forward rate) pricing model due to Black (1976) is used. See Hull (1992).

A. The Pricing of Vanilla Options
Using the Binomial Method

The Cox-Ross-Rubinstein method says that given the current value of the exchange rate, there are only two possible states (i.e., an up state and a down state) the exchange rate process can occupy at time T in the future, where T could be any arbitrary value. Using this assumption, an exchange rate tree is first generated for the entire option period by partitioning the life of the option into small time intervals. This tree is then used to generate a corresponding tree of option prices, which is used to value any American or European style option.

To value a currency option that expires at time T, we first divide the time T into n equal sub time intervals of length T/n. If the current exchange rate level is denoted by S, then the exchange rate at time T/n later either moves up to a level of Su with a probability p or down to a level of Sd with the complimentary probability $1 - p$, where u and p represent the magnitude and the probability of an upward jump respectively and d and $1 - p$ represent the magnitude and the probability of the downward jump respectively. Assuming that the current time is 0, Exhibit 25 shows the generation of the exchange rate tree at times T/n, $2(T/n)$, and $3(T/n)$.

EXHIBIT 25 Binomial Tree Time Line

Time: 0 yr	T/n yr	2(T/n) yr	3(T/n) yr

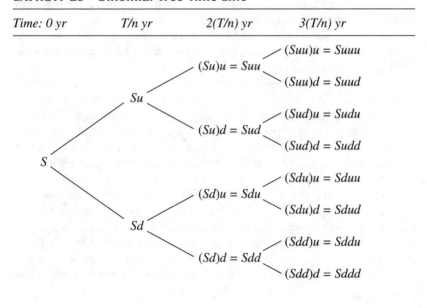

EXHIBIT 26   Recombining Exchange Rate Tree

Time: 0 yr   T/n yr   2(T/n) yr   3(T/n) yr

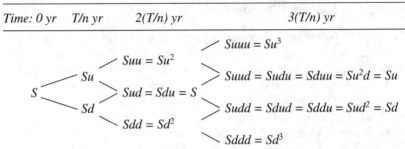

From Exhibit 25, it can be seen that every exchange rate node in the tree generates an upward node and a downward node at time T/n later. As such, if we partitioned the life of the option into n sub time intervals, we would end up with exactly 2^n nodes at time T. Since an accurate value of the option can only be obtained by fine-tuning the length of the sub time interval (or equivalently increasing the value of n), in the pursuit of accuracy we can potentially end up with a massive and messy tree (if n is large, 2^n will be very large). By assuming that the nodes of the tree recombine (i.e., an upward move in the exchange rate followed by a downward one is the same as a downward move in the exchange rate followed by an upward one), we can reduce the number of nodes at time T from 2^n to $n + 1$. The mathematical relationship that allows for this reduction in the number of nodes is the equation $u = 1/d$. Exhibit 26 illustrates this recombining exchange rate tree for the times 0, T/n, $2(T/n)$, and $3(T/n)$.

Although we may have reduced the size of the tree using the relationship $u = 1/d$, it still remains for us to find the value of u and p. To do this, we will assume that given the current exchange rate, the natural logarithm of the future exchange rate is normally distributed and use the concept of risk-neutral valuation, which simply says that investors have no risk preferences and are risk neutral. Here, the natural logarithm of the number 5, for example, is the value of x that satisfies the equation $e^x = 5$, where $e = 2.718....$

Let r_d, r_f and σ represent the annualized continuously compounded domestic risk-free rate, annualized continuously compounded foreign risk-free rate, and volatility respectively. Given that the current time and exchange rate are 0 and S respectively, our assumptions allow us to state that at time T/n in the future the $\ln(S_{T/n})$ has a normal distribution with mean $\ln S + [r_d - r_f - (\sigma^2/2)](T/n)$ and variance $\sigma^2(T/n)$. Here $r_d - r_f$ is known as the drift rate of this

EXHIBIT 27   One-Step Tree

Time: 0 yr   T/n yr

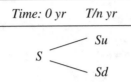

exchange rate process. To obtain the values of u and p, we assume that T/n is small (see Hull (1992) for the limitations of this assumption) and then find the mean and the variance of the $S_{T/n}$ using the properties of a lognormal distribution. We then equate these parameters to the mean and variance of the movement in future exchange rate using the one-step tree shown in Exhibit 27.

This will then give us the following expressions for u, d and p:

$$u = e^{\sigma\sqrt{T/n}}, \ d = \frac{1}{u} \text{ and } p = \frac{e^{(r_d - r_f)(T/n)} - d}{u - d}$$

See Hull (1992) for the details of this concept. Using these expressions, we can now generate an exchange rate tree that would allow us to price both the European and American vanilla currency options. As an example, we will show the use of the binomial method to price European and American currency options.

Example 1

The Canadian dollar is currently trading at 1.30 Cad/U.S. An investor wants to buy a six-month call option on the U.S. funds that is struck at 1.30 Cad/U.S. The current risk-free rates of return in U.S. and Canada are 3 percent and 4 percent respectively. Using a volatility of 5 percent and dividing the six months into four equal sub-intervals of length 0.125 years,

    i) Generate an exchange rate tree for the entire option period using four sub time intervals.

    ii) Price an American style option using this four-step tree.

    iii) Price a European style option using this four-step tree.

Solution:
From the example, we can conclude that $S = 1.30$, $X = 1.30$, $\sigma = 0.05$, $T = 0.5$, $r_d = 0.04$, $r_f = 0.03$, and $n = 4$ (i.e., four sub time intervals).

From the above parameters,

$$\frac{T}{n} = \frac{0.5}{4} = 0.125$$

$$u = e^{s\sqrt{T/n}} \qquad = e^{0.05\sqrt{0.125}} \qquad\qquad = 1.0178$$

$$d = \frac{1}{u} \qquad = \frac{1}{1.0178} \qquad\qquad = 0.9825$$

$$p = \frac{e^{(r_d - r_f)(T/n)} - d}{u - d} = \frac{e^{(0.04 - 0.03)(0.125)} - 0.9825}{1.0178 - 0.9825} = 0.5310$$

i) Using the above parameters, we can generate the exchange tree shown in Exhibit 28.

ii) To find the value of an American style call option on the U.S. dollar, we would have to create an option payoff tree that corresponds to the exchange rate tree generated in Exhibit 28 using the notion of backward induction or dynamic programming. The notion of dynamic programming simply states that in order to value an option today, we should first start with the payoff of the option at its expiry date as if it were a European style option and then work backwards in time incorporating the exercise feature (if any). Ignoring the loss in the future value of the option premium, starting with the maturity time of the option we will write down the payoff of the call option at time 0.5 yr. For the five nodes in the exchange rate tree in Exhibit 28 corresponding to a time of 0.5 yr, the corresponding option payoffs are

$$\max(1.3(1.0178)^4 - 1.3,0) = 0.09525$$
$$\max(1.3(1.0178)^2 - 1.3,0) = 0.04678$$
$$\max(1.3 - 1.3 \qquad ,0) = 0$$
$$\max(1.3(0.9825)^2 - 1.3,0) = 0$$
$$\max(1.3(0.9825)^4 - 1.3,0) = 0$$

To generate the option payoffs that correspond to the exchange rate tree at time 0.375 yr., we have to use both the value of the call option obtained by stopping at that state and the continuing value of the option if we decide not to stop at that state. To see this, we will consider the node in Exhibit 28 at time 0.375 yr that corresponds to an exchange rate of $1.3(1.0178)^3$. At this node, the value obtained by exercising the call option is $1.3(1.0178)^3 - 1.3 = 0.0707$. If we decide to continue from this node, we can only do so to the exchange rate

EXHIBIT 28 Exchange Tree

Time: 0 yr	0.125 yr	0.250 yr	0.375 yr	0.5 yr

$$1.3(1.0178)^4$$

$$1.3(1.0178)^3$$

$$1.3(1.0178)^2 \qquad 1.3(1.0178)^2$$

$$1.3(1.0178) \qquad 1.3(1.0178)$$

$$1.3 \qquad 1.3 \qquad 1.3$$

$$1.3(0.9825) \qquad 1.3(0.9825)$$

$$1.3(0.9825)^2 \qquad 1.3(0.9825)^2$$

$$1.3(0.9825)^3$$

$$1.3(0.9825)^4$$

nodes $1.3(1.0178)^4$ and $1.3(1.0178)^2$ at time 0.5 yr. Therefore, from the present node, the option value can either move up to 0.09525 (the option value corresponding to the exchange rate $1.3(1.0178)^4$) with probability 0.5310 or move down to 0.04678 (the option value corresponding to an exchange rate of $1.3(1.0178)^2$) with probability 0.4690. Hence, if we decide to continue from the present node, we can expect a value $(0.09525*0.5310) + (0.04678*0.4690)$ at time 0.5 yr or a present value of $[(0.09525*0.5310) + (0.04678*0.4690)]e^{-0.04(0.125)} = 0.0722$, where the term $e^{-0.04(0.125)}$ represents the discount factor for a period of 0.125 years. Thus, the value of the option corresponding to an exchange rate node of $1.3(1.0178)^3$ at time 0.375 yr is $\max(0.0707, 0.0722) = 0.0722$. We can similarly compute the option payoffs for the other nodes corresponding to various other exchange rates at time 0.375 yr. The three corresponding option payoffs at 0.375 yr can then be seen to be

$$\max(1.3(1.0178) - 1.3, [(0.04678*0.5310)+(0*0.4690)]e^{-0.04(0.125)})$$
$$= 0.0247$$

$$\max(1.3(0.9825) - 1.3, [(0*0.5310)+(0*0.4690)]e^{-0.04(0.125)}) = 0$$

$$\max(1.3(0.9825)^3 - 1.3, [(0*0.5310)+(0*0.4690)]e^{-0.04(0.125)}) = 0$$

The option payoffs corresponding to the exchange rate nodes at time 0.25 yr in Exhibit 28 are given by

$$\max(1.3(1.0178)^2 - 1.3,$$
$$[(0.0722*0.5310)+(0.0247*0.4690)]e^{-0.04(0.125)}) = 0.0497$$

$$\max(1.3 - 1.3, [(0.0247*0.5310)+(0*0.4690)]e^{-0.04(0.125)}) = 0.0131$$

$$\max(1.3(0.9825)^2 - 1.3, [(0*0.5310)+(0*0.4690)]e^{-0.04(0.125)}) = 0$$

The option payoffs corresponding to the stock price nodes at time 0.125 yr in Exhibit 28 are given by

$$\max(1.3(1.0178) - 1.3,[(0.0497*0.5310)+(0.0131*0.4690)]e^{-0.04(0.125)})$$
$$= 0.0323$$
$$\max(1.3(0.9825) - 1.3, [(0.0131*0.5310)+(0*0.4690)]e^{-0.04(0.125)})$$
$$= 0.0069$$

The value of the option at time of inception (i.e., 0 yr.) is simply $[(0.0323*0.5310)+(0.0069*0.4690)]e^{-0.04(0.125)} = 0.02030$. The following tree in Exhibit 29 summarizes the call option tree generated using the exchange rate tree in Exhibit 28.

We can obtain an accurate value for the option by partitioning the life of the option into finer sub-intervals, e.g., $n = 100$.

iii) To price a European call option, we will have to go through the same routine with one major exception. Only the nodes of option values at time 0.5 yr will still remain the same as in Exhibit 29. At any earlier time, since the European option does not allow for any early exercise, the value of exercise at any one node is zero. As such, the option value nodes at time 0.375 yr are given by

$$\max(0, [(0.0095*0.5310) + (0.0468*0.4690)]e^{-0.04(0.125)}) = 0.0722$$
$$\max(0, [(0.0468*0.5310) + (0*0.4690)]e^{-0.04(0.125)}) = 0.0247$$
$$\max(0, [(0*0.5310)+(0*0.4690)]e^{-0.04(0.125)}) = 0$$
$$\max(0, [(0*0.5310)+(0*0.4690)]e^{-0.04(0.125)}) = 0$$

where the 0 on the left-hand-side in the max expression denotes an exercisable value of 0 or forced continuation.

EXHIBIT 29 Call Option Tree Summary

Time: 0 yr   0.125 yr   0.250 yr   0.375 yr   0.5 yr

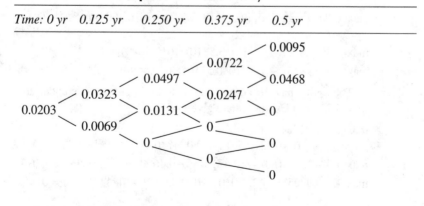

By similarly setting all the stopping values to 0 at all other earlier time nodes, we can arrive at the following option tree, which gives the value of an European call option. See Exhibit 29. In this example, it turns out that the European option value is the same as that of the American option value.

It is important to note that in order to value a European option, one can alternatively compute the option payoffs corresponding to the above exchange rate tree at the option maturity time. The total number of possible paths that can lead to a particular payoff and the probability of getting such a payoff using exactly one of the possible paths is calculated. This total is multiplied by its corresponding probability and payoff following which the weighted payoffs are then summed and present valued to current time.

In our example above, the total number of possible paths in the tree can be calculated to be $2^4 = 16$, where 2 represents the two-state nature of a binary tree and 4 represents the number of sub time intervals. At the time of the option maturity, the option values of (0.0095, 0.04678, 0, 0, 0) can be easily read from Exhibit 29. The number of paths leading to each of the option values can be counted to be (1, 4, 6, 4, 1) respectively. Since each of the option values would have a corresponding probability of $((0.5310)^4, (0.5310)^3(0.4690)^1, (0.5310)^2(0.4690)^2, (0.5310)^1(0.4690)^3, (0.4690)^4)$, the total weighted payoff is then given by $[(1\ (0.5310)^4(0.09525)) + (4(0.5310)^3(0.4690)^1(0.04678)) + (6(0.5310)^2(0.4690)^2\ (0)) + (4(0.5310)^1(0.4690)^3(0)) + (1(0.4690)^4(0))] = 0.02071$. This total weighted payoff of 0.02071 can then be present valued by multiplying it with the discount factor of $e^{-0.04(0.5)}$ and the result can then be computed to be 0.0203, which agrees with our previous method.

The above alternative method, though easier to implement, is only useful when computing European style options that have no early exercise features.

As before, by increasing the value of n, we can arrive at an accurate European call value.

B. The Pricing of Exotic Options Using the Binomial Method

Throughout this section, we will describe how the binomial method, which was discussed in the earlier subsection, can be used to price the exotic structures that were described in Section 2. These exotic options will be addressed in the same order as Section 2. All through this discussion, unless otherwise specified, we will use Example 1 and assume that we are pricing a European style path-dependent call option on the U.S. dollar where $S = 1.30$, $X = 1.30$, $\sigma = 0.05$, $T = 0.5$, $r_d = 0.04$, and $r_f = 0.03$, and $n = 4$ (hence $T/n = 0.125$). We will also ignore the loss of the option premium paid by the buyer at the inception of the contract (if any) throughout this section when computing the option payoffs.

With this set of parameters, we showed in Example 1 that $u = 1.0178$, $d = 0.9825$, and $p = 0.5310$ and then generated an exchange rate tree shown in Exhibit 28. Due to the nature of the path dependent properties possessed by many of the exotic options, for the sake of clarity we will reproduce Exhibit 28 in a "non-recombining" fashion. See Exhibit 30.

a. Averaging Options

Assumption: Sampling is done once every 0.125 years

Payoff at time 0.5 years:

$$\max\left[\frac{S_0 + S_{0.125} + S_{0.25} + S_{0.375} + S_{0.5}}{5} - 1.30, 0\right]$$

To generate the option tree, we will start at the end of the option life at 0.5 years. At 0.5 years, to calculate the option value corresponding to the exchange rate level of 1.3953, we first have to calculate the average value of the exchange rates realized in the path taken to arrive at 1.3953. From Exhibit 30, we can see that to reach an exchange rate value of 1.3953, we have to go through the path (1.3, 1.3232, 1.3468, 1.3708, 1.3953). The average value of this path is 1.3472, which is given by the first ordinate of the node in Exhibit 31. The value of the option, which is given by the second ordinate at this node, is max[1.3472 − 1.30,0] = 0.0472. One can similarly calculate the option payoffs for the other exchange rate nodes at the 0.5 year mark. Like the vanilla options, at any time prior to the 0.5 years, one can similarly calculate the value of the option from both exercising and continuing and then work backwards through time to compute the final option value. Because we are valuing a European style option, there is no value from exercising the option prior to the option maturity date. Calculating the option payoffs that correspond to the exchange rate tree in Exhibit 30, we can arrive at the option tree for the averaging option that is shown in Exhibit 31. The option value turns out to be 0.0118. As before, to obtain a more accurate option premium, the sub time interval has to be finer.

b. Barrier Options

Assumption: Sampling is done once every 0.125 years

Payoff at time 0.5 years:

$\max[S_{0.5} - 1.30,0]$ if the barrier level of 1.33 is not breached

0   otherwise

The option that we will discuss in this example is also known as the up-and-out option. Here, the option that starts to exist at the inception of the con-

EXHIBIT 30   Non-Recombining Tree

Time: 0 yr   0.125 yr   0.250 yr   0.375 yr   0.5 yr

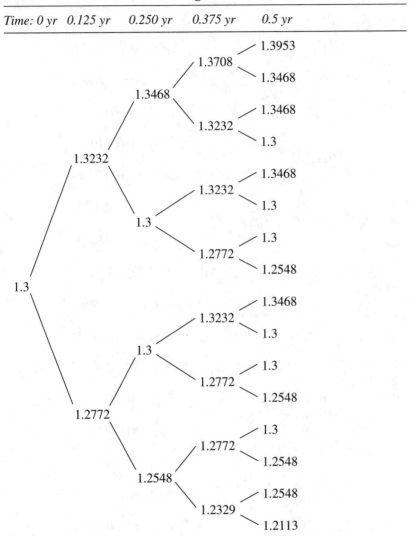

tract will be extinguished only if the barrier level of 1.33 has been breached during the life of the option. Since the vanilla call option would extinguish once the level of 1.33 is breached, a value of zero (denoted by 0* in Exhibit 32) is assigned as an option payoff to the nodes that lie on the path at and after the breaching of the barrier. To assign option values to the other nodes, we

EXHIBIT 31   Averaging Option Tree

Time: 0 yr   0.125 yr   0.250 yr   0.375 yr   0.5 yr

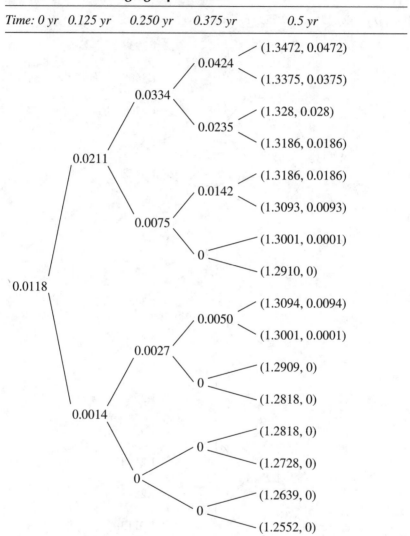

will as before start at the end of the option life at time 0.5 years and calculate the option values corresponding to the exchange rates where the barrier is not breached. This will be similar to finding the values of a vanilla option. Working backwards through time to compute the final option value, we can arrive at

EXHIBIT 32 Barrier Option Tree

Time: 0 yr   0.125 yr   0.250 yr   0.375 yr   0.5 yr

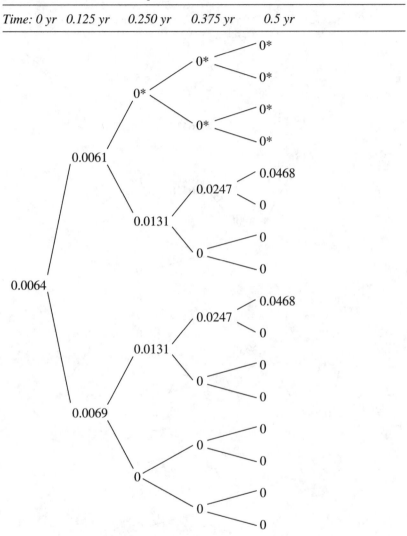

the option tree for the up-and-out option that is shown in Exhibit 32. The option value turns out to be 0.0064. It is important to note that the same premium will be obtained as long as the barrier straddles the interval 1.3232 and 1.3468. More precisely, because the breaching of the barrier is done discretely,

EXHIBIT 33   Binary Option Tree

Time: 0 yr   0.125 yr   0.250 yr   0.375 yr   0.5 yr

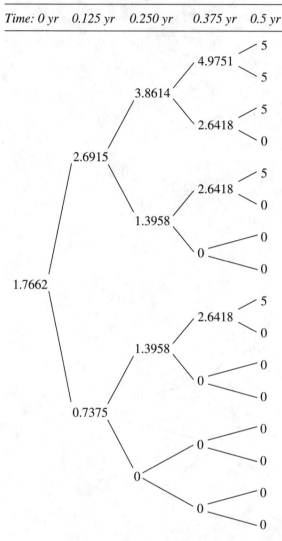

the option premium will be insensitive to the changes in barrier levels when the level of the barrier lies between the nodes. Thus, although fine-tuning the sub time interval increases the accuracy of the premium, the premium may not necessarily converge as the level of partitioning increases.

c. Binary Options

Payoff at time 0.5 years:

5	if $S_{0.5} > 1.30$
0	otherwise

The binary option that we will discuss in this example pays off a bet amount of 5 Cad/U.S. if the option finishes in-the-money.

To find the value of this option using a binomial method, we will as before start at the end of the option life at time 0.5 years and calculate the option value corresponding to the exchange rates. At time 0.5 years, since the option is in-the-money when the exchange rate is 1.3953, the value of the option corresponding to this exchange rate is 5. Similarly, we can go through all the other exchange rate nodes at the 0.5 year time mark and check if the option is in- or out-of-the-money, where the former has an option value of 5 and the latter has no option value. Working backwards through time to compute the final option value, we can arrive at the option tree for the binary option that is shown in Exhibit 33 using the same methodology that was used for a vanilla option. The option value turns out to be 1.7662. The value of the option could easily be made more precise by fine-tuning the length of the sub time intervals.

d. Chooser Options

Assumption: A choice between a vanilla call and a vanilla put both struck at 1.3 Cad/U.S. and expiring in 0.5 years from now is allowed at time 0.25 years.

Payoff at time 0.5 years:

$S_{0.5} - 1.3$	if a call option was chosen at time 0.25 years and $S_{0.5} > 1.30$
$1.3 - S_{0.5}$	if a put option was chosen at time 0.25 years and $S_{0.5} < 1.30$
0	otherwise

To find the value of this simple chooser option using the binomial method, we will as before start at the end of the option life at time 0.5 years and calculate the vanilla option values (both call and put) corresponding to the exchange rates. In Exhibit 34, the first and the second ordinate of each node from times 0.25 year to 0.5 year corresponds to the vanilla call and put option values respectively. Furthermore, at time 0.25 years, the third ordinate of each node represents the choice value corresponding to the maximum value between the vanilla call and put options. At time 0.25 years when the vanilla call and put option values are 0.0497 and 0 respectively, the value of

EXHIBIT 34   Chooser Option Tree

Time: 0 yr   0.125 yr   0.250 yr   0.375 yr   0.5 yr

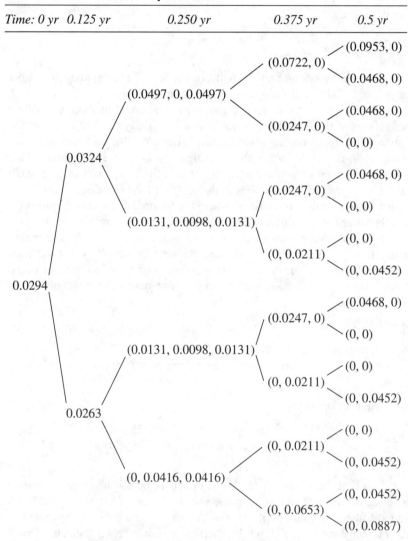

the chooser which is given by the third ordinate in that node is simply the value of max[0.0497,0] = 0.0497.

For times prior to the 0.25 year mark, the usual option valuation technique is applied to the choice values. For example, at the 0.125 year mark, the value of the chooser option at the node corresponding to the exchange rate of 1.3232 is 0 when exercised (as no early exercise is allowed). If the option is not exercised, it can with probability 0.531 move upwards to a chooser option value of 0.0497 and with probability 0.469 move downwards to a chooser option value of 0.0131. Thus, the value of the chooser option at this node is

$$\max[0, [(0.0497*0.5310)+(0.0131*0.4690)]e^{-0.04(0.125)}] = 0.0324$$

Performing this sort of computation for the earlier nodes, one can arrive at a chooser option value of 0.0294.

As before, the value of this option could easily be made more precise by fine-tuning the length of the sub time intervals.

e. Compound Options

Assumption: The first call option is struck at 0.03 Cad/U.S. and expires in 0.25 years. If exercised, the second call option, which is struck at 1.3 Cad/U.S. and expires 0.5 years from now, comes into existence.

Payoff at time 0.5 years:

$S_{0.5} - 1.3$ if the first call option was exercised at time 0.25 years and $S_{0.5} > 1.30$

0   if the first call option was exercised at time 0.25 years and $S_{0.5} < 1.30$

To find the value of this compound (i.e., call on a call) option using the binomial method, we will as before start at the end of the option life at time 0.5 years and calculate the vanilla call option value corresponding to the exchange rates. In Exhibit 35, the number of each node from times 0.375 year to 0.5 year corresponds to the vanilla call value. At time 0.25 years, the first and second ordinate of each node represents the vanilla call and the compound option values respectively. More precisely, at time 0.25 years, when the vanilla call option value is 0.0497, the first option of the compound option is in-the-money and the value to the buyer of the compound option is given by the second number in that node and is simply the value of $\max[0.0497 - 0.03, 0] = 0.0197$, where 0.03 represents the first strike rate. We can apply the same technique to the other three nodes in this time.

For times prior to the 0.25 year mark, the usual option valuation technique is applied to the compound option values. For example, at the 0.125 year mark, the value of the compound option at the node corresponding to the exchange rate of 1.3232 is 0 when exercised (as no early exercise is allowed). If the option is not exercised, it can with probability 0.531 move upwards to a compound option value of 0.0197 and with probability 0.469 move down-

EXHIBIT 35   Compound Option Tree

Time: 0 yr   0.125 yr   0.250 yr   0.375 yr   0.5 yr

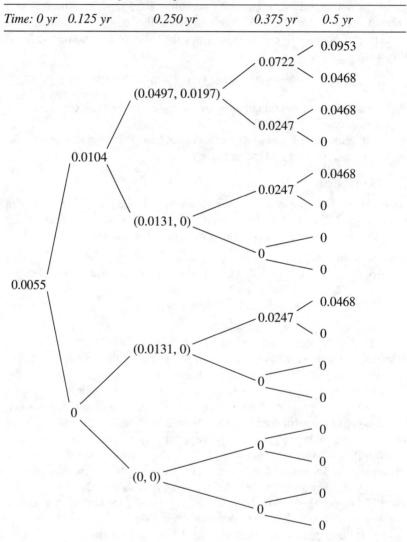

wards to a compound option value of 0. Thus, the value of the compound option at this node is

$$\max[0,[(0.0197*0.5310)+(0*0.4690)]e^{-0.04(0.125)}] = 0.0104$$

Performing this sort of computation for the earlier nodes, one can arrive at a compound option value of 0.0055.

As before, the value of this option could easily be made more precise by fine-tuning the length of the sub time intervals.

f. Contingent Premium Options

Assumption: B is the conditional premium that is paid if the option finishes in-the-money and no premium is paid up-front at the inception of the contract.

Payoff at time 0.5 years:

$S_{0.5} - 1.3 - B$ if $S_{0.5} > 1.30$
0   otherwise

Since no premium for a contingent premium option is paid at the inception of the contract, valuing such an option implies finding the value of the conditional premium B, if the option finishes in-the-money.

To find the value of B using a binomial method, we will first let $B = 0.07$ and start at the end of the option life at time 0.5 years and calculate the option values corresponding to the exchange rates. At time 0.5 years, since the option is in-the-money when the exchange rate is 1.3953, the value of the option corresponding to this exchange rate is $1.3953 - 1.3 - 0.07 = 0.0253$. Similarly, when the exchange rates are 1.3468 and 1.2113, the values of the options corresponding to these exchange rates are $1.3468 - 1.3 - 0.07 = -0.0232$ (since the option finishes in-the-money) and 0 (since the option finishes out-of-the-money) respectively. After calculating the option values for the other nodes at the 0.5 year time zone, we can then work backwards through time to compute the final option value to be -0.0044, as shown in Exhibit 36.

Since by the nature of the product, the premium of the option at the inception of the contract has to be zero, we will have to guess at another value for B and then use this value to check if the resulting inception premium is zero. We keep repeating this process until we converge to a value of B, which in this case is 0.0575, such that the premium of the option at the inception of the contract is zero. See Exhibit 37.

This value of B can be made more precise by fine-tuning the length of the sub time intervals.

EXHIBIT 36   Contingent Premium Option

When B = 0.07
Time: 0 yr   0.125 yr   0.250 yr   0.375 yr   0.5 yr

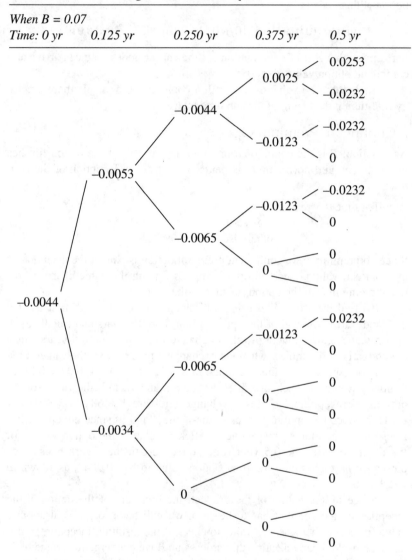

EXHIBIT 37   Contingent Premium Option

When B = 0.0575
Time: 0 yr   0.125 yr   0.250 yr   0.375 yr   0.5 yr

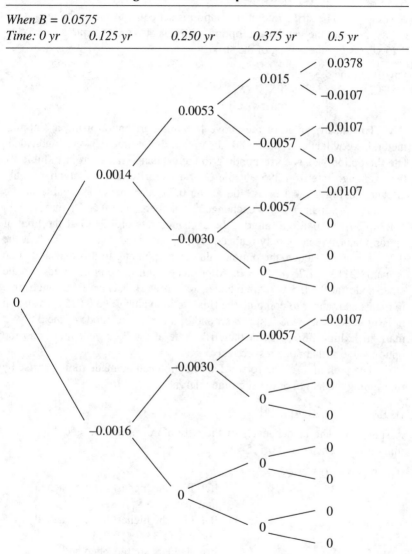

g. Forward Start Options

Assumption: The strike rate of the option is set equal to the exchange rate in 0.25 years, and the vanilla call option with this strike rate expires in another 0.25 years after the setting of the strike.

Payoff at time 0.5 years:

$$S_{0.5} - S_{0.25} \quad \text{if } S_{0.5} > S_{0.25}$$
$$0 \quad \text{otherwise}$$

To find the value of the above forward start option using a binomial method, we will start at the end of the option life at time 0.5 years and calculate the option values corresponding to the exchange rates. From Exhibit 30, the exchange rate of 1.3953 at the option maturity date was realized only after achieving a level of 1.3468 at the 0.25 year mark. The value of the option corresponding to this exchange rate is therefore given by max[1.3953 − 1.3468,0] = 0.0485. Similarly, the exchange rate of 1.2113 at the time of option maturity date is only realized after being at the level of 1.2548 at the 0.25 year mark. Hence, the option value corresponding to this exchange rate is max[1.2113 − 1.2548, 0] = 0. After calculating the option values for the other nodes at the 0.5 year time zone, we can work backwards through time in the usual manner to compute the final option value to be 0.0129, as shown in Exhibit 38, where the first and second ordinate at each node of the 0.5 year mark in Exhibit 38 represent the strike rate at the 0.25 year mark and the option value at that node respectively.

The premium for the forward start option can be made more precise by fine-tuning the length of the sub time intervals.

h. Ladder Options

Assumption: The ladder levels of the option are set at 1.33 and 1.35. Sampling is done once every 0.125 years.

Payoff at time 0.5 years:

$\max(1.35, S_{0.5}) - 1.3$	if 1.35 is the highest level breached and $\max(1.35, S_{0.5}) > 1.3$
$\max(1.33, S_{0.5}) - 1.3$	if 1.33 is the highest level breached and $\max(1.33, S_{0.5}) > 1.3$
$S_{0.5} - 1.3$	if no ladders are breached and $S_{0.5} > 1.3$
0	otherwise

To find the value of the modified ladder option using a binomial method, we start at the end of the option life at time 0.5 years and calculate the option

EXHIBIT 38   Forward Start Option

Time: 0 yr	*0.125 yr*	*0.250 yr*	*0.375 yr*	*0.5 yr*

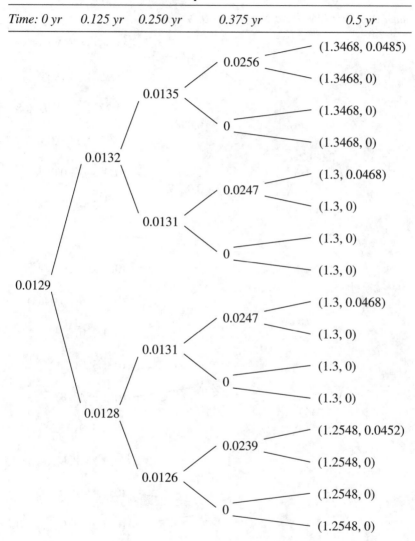

values corresponding to the exchange rates. From Exhibit 30, when the exchange rate is 1.3953 at the option maturity date, the path taken by the exchange rate to achieve this value breaches both the ladder levels of 1.33 and 1.35. The value of the option corresponding to this exchange rate is therefore given by max[max(1.33, 1.35,1.3953) − 1.3,0] = max[1.3953 − 1.3, 0] = 0.0953.

EXHIBIT 39   Ladder Option Tree

Time: 0 yr	0.125 yr	0.250 yr	0.375 yr	0.5 yr

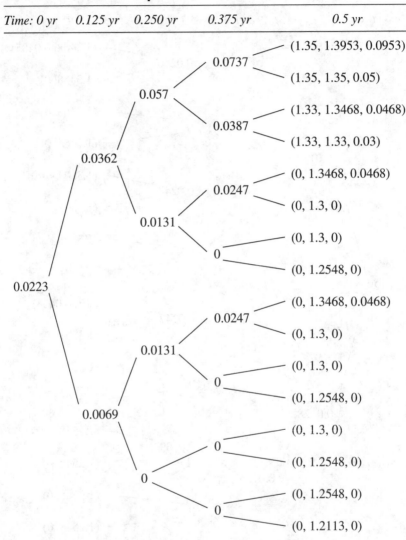

Similarly, since the path taken to reach the exchange rate of 1.2113 at the time of option maturity date did not breach any of the ladders, the option value corresponding to this exchange rate is max[1.2113 − 1.3, 0] = 0. After calculating the option values for the other nodes at the 0.5 year time zone, we can then work backwards through time in the usual manner to compute the final option value to be 0.0223, as shown in Exhibit 39, where the first, second, and third ordinate at each node of the 0.5 year mark in Exhibit 39 represent the highest ladder level breached during the life of the option, the max[highest ladder breached, exchange rate at option maturity], and the option value at the node, respectively. Note that if no ladder was breached during the life of the option, a value of zero is used to represent the level of the highest ladder breached.

Although the premium for the ladder option can be made more precise by fine-tuning the length of the sub time intervals, like the barrier option, the premium may not necessarily converge.

i. Lookback Options

Assumption: Sampling is done once every 0.125 years.

Payoff at time 0.5 years:

$\max[S_0, S_{0.125}, S_{0.25}, S_{0.375}, S_{0.5}] - 1.30$ if $\max[S_0, S_{0.125}, S_{0.25}, S_{0.375}, S_{0.5}] > 1.3$
0 otherwise

To find the value of the modified lookback option using a binomial method, we start at the end of the option life at time 0.5 years and calculate the option values corresponding to the exchange rates. From Exhibit 30, when the exchange rate is 1.3953 at the option maturity date, the path taken by this exchange rate is (1.3, 1.3232, 1.3468, 1.3708, 1.3953). The maximum value encountered during this path is 1.3953. The value of the option corresponding to this exchange rate is therefore given by $\max[1.3953 - 1.3, 0] = 0.0953$. Similarly, since the path taken to reach the exchange rate of 1.2113 at the time of option maturity date is (1.3, 1.2772, 1.2548, 1.2329, 1.2113), the maximum value of this path is 1.3. The value of the option corresponding to this path is $\max[1.3 - 1.3, 0] = 0$. After calculating the option values for the other nodes at the 0.5 year time zone, we can then work backwards through time in the usual manner to compute the final option value to be 0.0303, as shown in Exhibit 40, where the first and second ordinate at each node of the 0.5 year mark in Exhibit 40 represent the maximum value of the path reached during the life of the option and the option value at the node respectively.

The premium for the modified lookback option can be made more precise by fine-tuning the length of the sub time intervals.

j. Mid-Atlantic Options

Assumption: The option can only be exercised at times 0.375 and 0.5 years.

If not exercised earlier, payoff at time 0.5 years:

$S_{0.5} - 1.3$ if $S_{0.5} > 1.3$
0 otherwise

149

EXHIBIT 40   Lookback Option Tree

Time: 0 yr	0.125 yr	0.250 yr	0.375 yr	0.5 yr

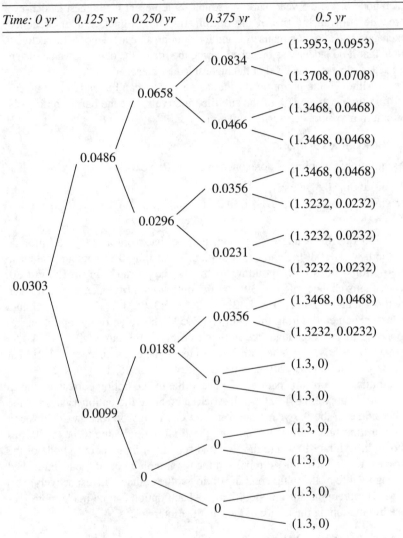

If exercised earlier, payoff at time 0.375 years:

$S_{0.375} - 1.3$ if $S_{0.375} > 1.3$

To value a Mid-Atlantic option using a binomial method, we start at the end of the option life at time 0.5 years, incorporate the exercise features only at the exercisable times, and then calculate the option values corresponding to the exchange rates. The methodology used is no different from the valuation of the American/European vanilla options. See Exhibit 41. This gives us an option premium of 0.0203, which is the same as that of the European and the American option given in Section 3A.

The premium for the Mid-Atlantic option can be made more precise by fine-tuning the length of the sub time intervals.

k. Non-Linear Payoff Options

Assumption: The power option, which is struck at a level of 1.8 Cad/U.S., can only be exercised in 0.5 years.

Payoff at time 0.5 years:

$S^2_{0.5} - 1.8$ if $S^2_{0.5} > 1.8$
0   otherwise

Except for the payoff at the maturity date, a power option is valued like a vanilla option using a binomial method. We again start at the end of the option life at 0.5 years and then calculate the option values corresponding to the exchange rates. When the exchange rate is 1.3953 at the maturity date, the value of the option corresponding this exchange rate is $\max[1.3953^2 - 1.8, 0] = \max[1.9469 - 1.8, 0] = 0.1469$. Similarly, the value of the option corresponding to an exchange rate of 1.2113 is $\max[1.2113^2 - 1.8, 0] = \max[1.467 - 1.8, 0] = 0$. Filling up the option values in the other nodes and applying backward induction, we can arrive at an option value of 0.0154 as shown in Exhibit 42.

The premium for the power option can be made more precise by fine-tuning the length of the sub time intervals.

l. Quanto Options

Due to the nature of a quanto option, we will change our example to illustrate the use of a binomial method to price this instrument.

Example 2

The current three-month LIBOR and the 6 × 9 forward rate agreement (FRA) are currently trading at 3.125 percent and 3.83 percent respectively. The FRA also has a volatility of 17 percent. A Canadian investor wants to buy a notion-

EXHIBIT 41   Mid-Atlantic Option Tree

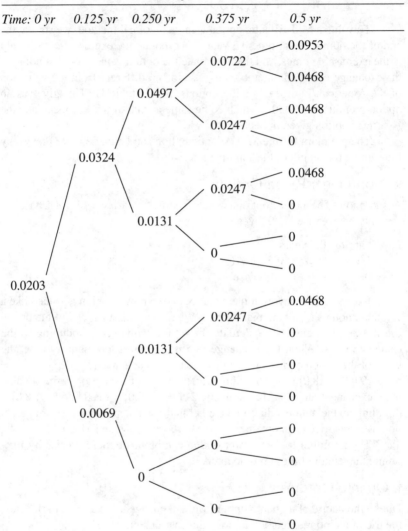

Time: 0 yr   0.125 yr   0.250 yr   0.375 yr   0.5 yr

al amount of Cad$1,000,000 worth of call option on the three-month LIBOR that is struck at 3.2 percent and has a life of 0.5 years. Furthermore, she does not want to be exposed to the currency risk. If the value of the three-month LIBOR in six months is 3.3 percent, she wants the payoff to be Cad$1,000,000*(0.033 − 0.032) = Cad$1000. Thus, she wants the payoff to

EXHIBIT 42   Non-Linear Payoff Option Tree

Time: 0 yr	0.125 yr	0.250 yr	0.375 yr	0.5 yr

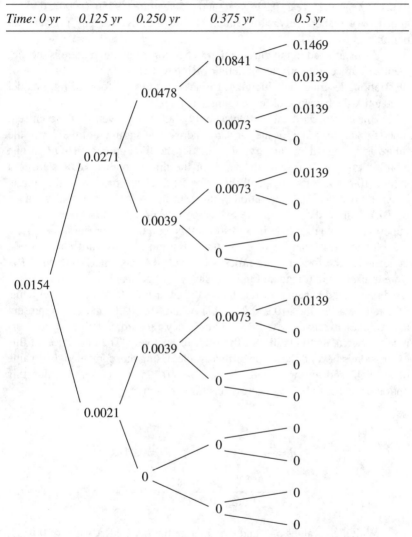

be exactly the same as an American investor purchasing the same option with the added twist that she wants to transact only in Canadian funds with no exposure to the currency risk. The Canadian dollar forward, which is currently trading at 1.3057 Cad/U.S., has a volatility of 6 percent. Furthermore, the historical correlation between the FRA and the currency is calculated to be

0.9. The discount factors obtained from the Canadian yield curve at the times of 0.125 year, 0.25 year, 0.375 year, and 0.5 year are 0.9956, 0.9908, 0.9863, and 0.9814 respectively. How much should the investor pay for such an option?

As mentioned in the introduction to Section 3, although there is the element of subjectivity in the modeling of interest rates, we will, for ease of illustration, describe the widely used Black's futures (or forward rate) model to quantify the behavior of forward interest rates.

Black's forward rate model simply states that given that the current time is 0 and the value of the forward interest rate starting at time T/n in the future is F (e.g., if we are trying to model the three-month LIBOR in one month's time, F represents the value of the three-month LIBOR starting a month from now or equivalently the 1×4 FRA), at time T/n in the future, $\ln(F_{T/n})$ has a normal distribution with mean $\ln F - (\sigma^2/2)(T/n)$ and variance $\sigma^2(T/n)$. Unlike the drift of the exchange rate process in Section 3A, it is important to note that there is no drift for this forward rate process.

To an American investor, by the definition of a forward rate process, the drift for the forward rate process for the FRA has value 0. If this FRA were transacted in Canadian funds, in the eyes of a Canadian investor the forward rate would have a drift rate that is different from 0. More precisely, this drift rate is given by $-(0.9*0.06*0.17)$, where 0.9, 0.06, and 0.17 represent the correlation between the FRA and currency forward, volatility of the currency forward, and volatility of the FRA respectively. The derivation of this expression is beyond the scope of this article. Using this computed drift value of -0.0092 and letting $\sigma = 0.17$ and $T/n = 0.125$, we can now value this option using the following expressions for u, d, and p:

$$u = e^{0.17\sqrt{0.125}} \qquad\qquad = 1.062$$

$$d = \frac{1}{u} \qquad\qquad = 0.9417$$

$$p = \frac{e^{-0.0092(0.125)} - 0.9417}{1.062 - 0.9417} = 0.4754$$

With these values of u and d and the initial 6×9 FRA value of 0.0383, we can first generate the forward rate tree as in Exhibit 43.

Using the forward rate tree in Exhibit 43, we can now value the six-month option that is struck at 3.2 percent using the four sub time intervals. The value of the option from Exhibit 44 is Cad\$1,000,000*0.0062 = Cad\$6,200 where we have used the fact that the discount factors from the times 0 to 0.125

EXHIBIT 43   Forward Rate Tree

Time: 0 yr	0.125 yr	0.250 yr	0.375 yr	0.5 yr

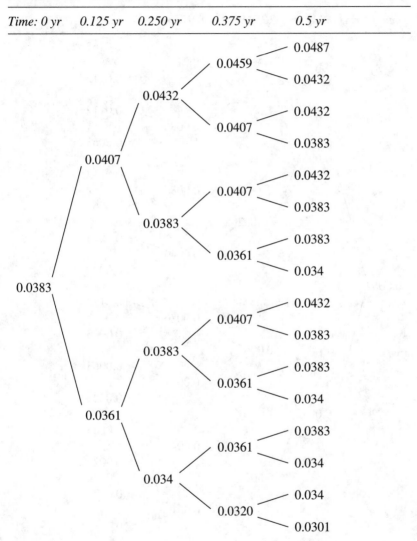

EXHIBIT 44 Quanto Option Tree

Time: 0 yr   0.125 yr   0.250 yr   0.375 yr   0.5 yr

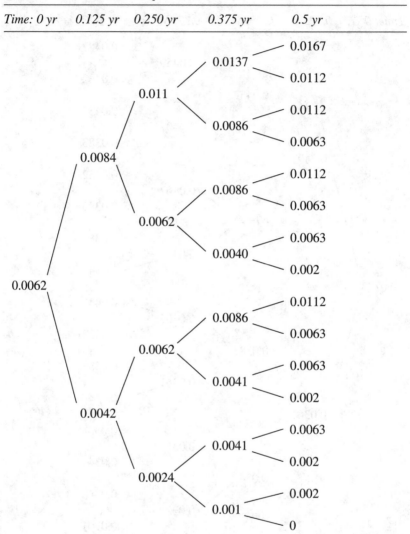

year, 0.125 year to 0.25 year, 0.25 year to 0.375 year, and 0.375 year to 0.5 year are given by 0.9956, 0.9908/0.9956 = 0.9952, 0.9863/0.9908 = 0.9955, and 0.9814/0.9863 = 0.9950, respectively.

m. Rainbow Options

The use of a binomial method to price a rainbow option is best illustrated with the following Canadian interest rate example.

Example 3

The 6×9 Canadian FRA and the 6×10 Canadian FRA are currently trading at 4.06 percent and 4.10 percent respectively. The volatilities of the 6×9 and 6×10 FRAs are 21 percent and 20 percent respectively. A Canadian investor wants to buy a notional amount of Cad\$1,000,000 worth of option on the max[6×9 FRA, 0.99*(6×10 FRA)] that is struck at a level of 4.10 percent and has a life of 0.5 years. More precisely, if the values of the three-month LIBOR and four-month LIBOR in six months time are 4 percent and 4.15 percent respectively, the payoff to the investor is Cad\$1,000,000*max[[max(0.04, 0.99*0.0415) – 0.0410], 0] = Cad\$1,000,000*max[0.0411 – 0.0410, 0] = Cad\$100. The historical correlation between the two FRAs was computed to be 0.9. The discount factors obtained from the yield curve are 0.9908 and 0.9814 for the 0.25 years and 0.5 years respectively. What should the investor pay for this option?

Since the option payoff depends on the realized values of two variables, to use the binomial method to arrive at the option premium, we will first have to model both variables. To do this we will assume that if the current forward rates are F_1 and F_2, letting p_1, p_2, p_3, and p_4 represent the probabilities that F_1 and F_2 move simultaneously to a level $u_1F_1u_2F_2$, $u_1F_1d_2F_2$, $d_1F_1u_2F_2$, and $d_1F_1d_2F_2$ respectively, the forward rates at time T/n in the future can modeled as shown in Exhibit 45.

EXHIBIT 45   Forward Rates

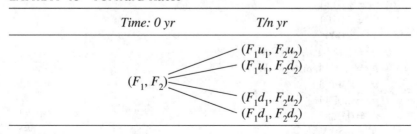

This would then give us the following expressions for u_1, u_2, d_1, d_2, p_1, p_2, p_3, and p_4:

$$A = e^{\sigma_1^2(T/n)}$$

$$B = e^{\sigma_2^2(T/n)}$$

$$C = e^{\rho\sigma_1\sigma_2(T/n)}$$

$$u_1 = \frac{1 + A + \sqrt{(1+A)^2 - 4}}{2}, \quad d_1 = \frac{1}{u_1}$$

$$u_2 = \frac{1 + B + \sqrt{(1+B)^2 - 4}}{2}, \quad d_2 = \frac{1}{u_2}$$

$$p_1 = \frac{C - d_1 d_2 - \dfrac{\left(d_1 u_2 - d_1 d_2\right)\left(1 - d_2\right)}{u_2 - d_2} - \dfrac{\left(u_1 d_2 - d_1 d_2\right)\left(1 - d_1\right)}{u_1 - d_1}}{u_1 u_2 - u_1 d_2 + d_1 d_2 - d_1 u_2}$$

$$p_2 = \frac{1 - d_1}{u_1 - d_1} - p_1$$

$$p_3 = \frac{1 - d_2}{u_2 - d_2} - p_1$$

$$p_4 = 1 - p_1 - p_2 - p_3$$

As in the single variable binomial case, in order to arrive at the above expressions for u_1, u_2, d_1, d_2, p_1, p_2, p_3, and p_4 we had to equate the means, variances and covariance of the movements in the forward rates from the binomial tree to the corresponding means, variances, and covariances of the bivariate lognormal distribution of $F_{1,T/n}$ and $F_{2,T/n}$.

In our example, since $F_1 = 0.0406$, $F_2 = 0.0410$, $\sigma_1 = 0.21$, $\sigma_2 = 0.2$, $\rho = 0.9$ and letting $T/n = 0.25$, it readily follows that

$A = 1.0111$
$B = 1.0101$
$C = 1.0095$
$u_1 = 1.1110$, $d_1 = 0.9001$
$u_2 = 1.1054$, $d_2 = 0.9046$
$p_1 = 0.4493$
$p_2 = 0.0244$
$p_3 = 0.0257$
$p_4 = 0.5006$

From the values of u_1, u_2, d_1, and d_2 we can generate the forward rate trees for the 6 × 9 FRA and the 6 × 10 FRA as given in Exhibits 46 and 47 respectively.

The forward rate trees can now be combined and presented as a four-state process of the two variables as shown in Exhibit 48. In this figure, the first and second ordinate of each node represents the forward rates corresponding to the 6 × 9 FRA and the 6 × 10 FRA respectively.

Using Exhibit 48, we can now easily compute the max[3-month LIBOR, 0.99*4-month LIBOR] for each node at the 0.5 year mark. This is given by the first ordinate of each node in Exhibit 49 when the time is 0.5 years. The second ordinate of each node at the same time represents the option value when the underlying variable of the option is max[3-month LIBOR, 0.99*4-month LIBOR] for each node and the option is struck at a level of 4.10 percent. More precisely, it calculates the max[max[3-month LIBOR, 0.99*4-month LIBOR] − 0.0410, 0].

EXHIBIT 46   6 x 9 FRA

Time: 0 yr	0.250 yr	0.500 yr

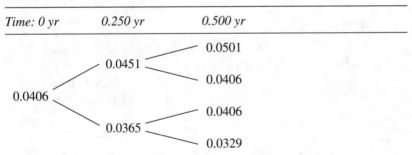

		0.0501
	0.0451	
		0.0406
0.0406		
		0.0406
	0.0365	
		0.0329

EXHIBIT 47   6 x 10 FRA

Time: 0 yr	0.250 yr	0.500 yr

		0.0501
	0.0453	
		0.041
0.041		
		0.041
	0.0371	
		0.0336

EXHIBIT 48   Four-State Process, Two Variables

Time: 0 yr	*0.250 yr*	*0.500 yr*

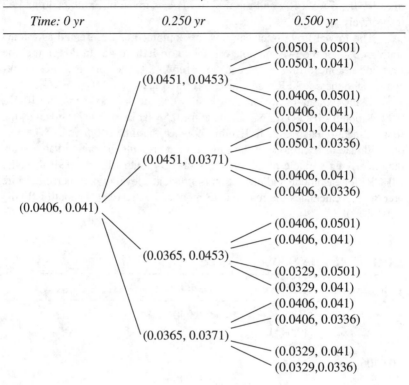

    Since the value of early exercise is 0, at any other time before the 0.5 year mark, a node in the figure would represent the option value that can be obtained by optimally carrying on to the next four states at a later time. More precisely, the option value corresponding to a forward rate coordinate of (0.0451, 0.0453) at the 0.25 year mark in Exhibit 48 can be obtained by calculating the present value of continuing with probabilities 0.4493, 0.0244, 0.0257, and 0.5006 to option states 0.0091, 0.0091, 0.0086, and 0 respectively, at the 0.5 year mark. This present value is given by [(0.4493*0.0091) + (0.0244*0.0091) + (0.0257*0.0086) + (0.5006*0)]0.9905 = 0.0045, where 0.9905 represents the discount factor from 0.25 years to 0.5 years and is given by the quotient 0.9814/0.9908. One can similarly go through the other nodes and arrive at an option value of Cad$1,000,000*0.0022 = Cad$2,200 as shown in Exhibit 49.

EXHIBIT 49   Rainbow Option Tree

Time: 0 yr	0.250 yr	0.500 yr

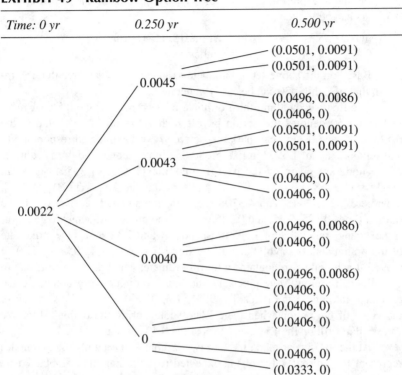

A more precise option value can be obtained using finer partitions of sub time intervals.

n. Shout Options

Before pricing a shout option, we will restate Example 1.

Example 4

An investor wants to buy a European style shout call option on the U.S. dollar that is struck at a level of 1.3 Cad/U.S. and has a life of 0.5 years. Assuming the volatility of the exchange rate is 0.05, the U.S. and Canadian risk-free rates of interest are 3 percent and 4 percent respectively and $n = 4$, find the premium of the option.

Letting S^* represent the value the investor shouted at, the payoff at time 0.5 years can be written as:

$$\max(S_{0.5}, S^*) - 1.3 \qquad \text{if } \max(S_{0.5}, S^*) > 1.3$$
$$0 \qquad\qquad\qquad\qquad \text{otherwise}$$

Based on the above set of parameters, an exchange rate tree that is similar to that of Exhibit 30 can be easily generated.

The first, second, and third ordinate of each node at the 0.5 year mark in Exhibit 50 denotes the option payoff if the investor had shouted at the 0.125, 0.25, and 0.375 year mark respectively. For the node corresponding to an exchange rate of 1.3953 in Exhibit 30, the first, second, and third ordinates of the node are given by the payoffs $\max[\max(1.3232, 1.3953) - 1.3, 0]$, $\max[\max(1.3468, 1.3953) - 1.3, 0]$, and $\max[\max(1.3708, 1.3953) - 1.3, 0]$, where 1.3232, 1.3468, and 1.3708 represent the shouted level of exchange rates at times 0.125, 0.25, and 0.375 years in the process of achieving a maturity exchange rate value of 1.3953 respectively and 1.3 denotes the strike rate of the option. These payoffs can all be simplified to $\max[1.3953 - 1.3, 0] =$ 0.0953. Each node also contains a fourth ordinate, which is the payoff due to a vanilla call option. More precisely, the fourth ordinate corresponding to an exchange rate of 1.3953 is $\max[1.3953 - 1.3, 0] = 0.0953$. This is of course the value of the option when there is no shout during the option's life. We can similarly fill up the 15 other nodes at the 0.5 year mark.

At the 0.375 year mark, the first two ordinates in each of the eight nodes represent the present value of the expected payoffs that can be obtained by moving into their respective future states at 0.5 years. More precisely, the first two ordinates of the 0.375 year node that correspond to an exchange rate of 1.3708 are $[(0.5310*0.0953) + (0.469*0.0468)]e^{-0.04(0.125)}$ and $[(0.5310*0.0953) + (0.469*0.0468)]e^{-0.04(0.125)}$ respectively, where 0.04 represents the domestic rate of interest, 0.0953 and 0.0468 represent both the future upward and downward movement respectively in the first and second ordinates of the option values at time 0.5 years, and 0.5310 and 0.4690 represent the probability of an upward and a downward movement respectively. Both these ordinates simplify to a value of 0.0722. The third ordinate of the node represents the max[present value of the expected payoff of the third value at time 0.5 years, present value of the expected payoff of the fourth value at time 0.5 years], where the first and second expression under the maximum sign represent the option value attained by shouting at time 0.375 years and the option value attained by not shouting at this time. It is important to note that we would expect the investor to shout at this time only if the first expression has a higher value than the second. Carrying on with our example, the third ordinate of the node at time 0.375 years that

EXHIBIT 50   Shout Option Tree

Time:

0 yr	0.125 yr	0.250 yr	0.375 yr	0.5 yr

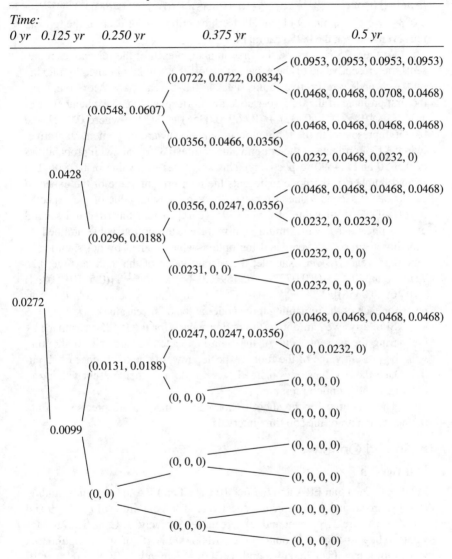

				(0.0953, 0.0953, 0.0953, 0.0953)
			(0.0722, 0.0722, 0.0834)	
				(0.0468, 0.0468, 0.0708, 0.0468)
	(0.0548, 0.0607)			
				(0.0468, 0.0468, 0.0468, 0.0468)
			(0.0356, 0.0466, 0.0356)	
				(0.0232, 0.0468, 0.0232, 0)
0.0428				
				(0.0468, 0.0468, 0.0468, 0.0468)
			(0.0356, 0.0247, 0.0356)	
				(0.0232, 0, 0.0232, 0)
	(0.0296, 0.0188)			
				(0.0232, 0, 0, 0)
			(0.0231, 0, 0)	
				(0.0232, 0, 0, 0)
0.0272				
				(0.0468, 0.0468, 0.0468, 0.0468)
			(0.0247, 0.0247, 0.0356)	
				(0, 0, 0.0232, 0)
	(0.0131, 0.0188)			
				(0, 0, 0, 0)
			(0, 0, 0)	
				(0, 0, 0, 0)
0.0099				
				(0, 0, 0, 0)
			(0, 0, 0)	
				(0, 0, 0, 0)
	(0, 0)			
				(0, 0, 0, 0)
			(0, 0, 0)	
				(0, 0, 0, 0)

corresponds to an exchange rate of 1.3708 is max[[(0.5310*0.0953) + (0.469*0.0708)]$e^{-0.04(0.125)}$, [(0.5310*0.0953) + (0.469*0.0468)]$e^{-0.04(0.125)}$] = 0.0834. We can similarly obtain all the three ordinates for each of the remaining seven nodes at the 0.25 year mark.

At the 0.25 year mark, the first number in each of the four nodes represents the present value of the expected payoff that can be obtained by moving into each node's respective future states at 0.375 year mark. More precisely, the first ordinate of the 0.25 year node that corresponds to an exchange rate of 1.3468 is [(0.5310*0.0722) + (0.469*0.0356)]$e^{-0.04(0.125)}$ where 0.0722 and 0.0356 represent both the future upward and downward movement respectively in the first ordinate of the option value at time 0.375 years with probabilities of 0.5310 and 0.4690 respectively. This simplifies to a value of 0.0548. The second number of the node represents the max[present value of the expected payoff of the second value at time 0.375 years, present value of the expected payoff of the third value at time 0.375 years], where the first and second expression under the maximum sign represent the option value attained by shouting at time 0.25 years and the option value attained by not shouting at time 0.25 years. In our example, the second value of the node at time 0.25 years is max[[(0.5310*0.0722) + (0.469*0.0466)]$e^{-0.04(0.125)}$, [(0.5310*0.0834) + (0.469*0.0356)]$e^{-0.04(0.125)}$] = 0.0607. We can similarly obtain both the ordinates for each of the remaining three nodes at the 0.25 year mark.

Similarly, we can obtain the option values for the 0.125 year mark by comparing the present value of the future expected reward due to shouting with the present value of the future expected reward due to absence of shouting. Once these values are obtained, we can do a further present valuing to obtain the shout option premium.

The premium for the shout option can be made more precise by fine-tuning the length of the sub time intervals.

n. Spread Options

Example 5

The 6 × 9 Canadian FRA and the 6 × 10 Canadian FRA are currently trading at 4.06 percent and 4.10 percent respectively. The volatilities of the 6 × 9 and 6 × 10 FRAs are 21 percent and 20 percent respectively. A Canadian investor wants to buy a notional amount of Cad$1,000,000 worth of spread option that gives him a payoff of max[4-month LIBOR – 3-month LIBOR – 0.0010, 0] and has a life of 0.5 years. If the values of the three-month LIBOR and four-month LIBOR in six months time are 4 percent and 4.15 percent respectively, the payoff to the investor is Cad$1,000,000*max[0.0415 – 0.04 – 0.0010, 0] = Cad$500. The historical correlation between the two FRAs were computed to be 0.9. The discount factors obtained from the Canadian yield curve are 0.9908 and 0.9814 for 0.25 years and 0.5 years respectively. What should the investor pay for such an option?

To use the binomial method to arrive at the option premium, as in the rainbow option, we will first have to model both the variables.

In our example, since $F_1 = 0.0406$, $F_2 = 0.0410$, $\sigma_1 = 0.21$, $\sigma_2 = 0.2$, $\rho = 0.9$ and letting $T/n = 0.25$, it readily follows from Example 3 that

$$u_1 = 1.1110, d_1 = 0.9001$$
$$u_2 = 1.1054, d_2 = 0.9046$$
$$p_1 = 0.4493$$
$$p_2 = 0.0244$$
$$p_3 = 0.0257$$
$$p_4 = 0.5006$$

From the above values of u_1, u_2, d_1, and d_2, we can generate the forward rate trees for the 6×9 FRA and the 6×10 FRA, which can be combined and presented as a four-state process of the two variables as shown in Exhibit 48. As before, the first and second number of each node in the figure represent the forward rates corresponding to the 6×9 FRA and the 6×10 FRA respectively.

Using Exhibit 48, we can now easily compute the 6×10 FRA $- 6 \times 9$ FRA for each node at the 0.5 year mark. This is given by the first ordinate of each node in Exhibit 51 when the time is 0.5 years. The second ordinate of each node at the same time represents the option value when the underlying variable of the option is max[6×10 FRA $- 6 \times 9$ FRA $- 0.0010$, 0] for each node.

Since the value of early exercise is 0, at any other time before the 0.5 year mark, a node in the figure would represent the option value that can be obtained by optimally carrying on the next four states at a later time. More precisely, the option value corresponding to a forward rate coordinate of (0.0451, 0.0453) at the 0.25 year mark in Exhibit 48 can be obtained by calculating the present value of continuing with probabilities 0.4493, 0.0244, 0.0257, and 0.5006 to option states 0, 0, 0.0085, 0 at time 0.5 years respectively. This present value is given by $[(0.4493*0) + (0.0244*0) + (0.0257*0.0085) + (0.5006*0)]0.9905 = 0.0002$, where 0.9905 represents the discount factor from 0.25 years to 0.5 years and is given by the quotient 0.9814/0.9908. One can similarly go through the other nodes and arrive at an option value of Cad\$1,000,000*0.0004 = Cad\$400 as shown in Exhibit 51.

A more precise option value can be obtained using finer partitions of sub time intervals.

EXHIBIT 51   Spread Option Tree

Time: 0 yr	*0.250 yr*	*0.500 yr*

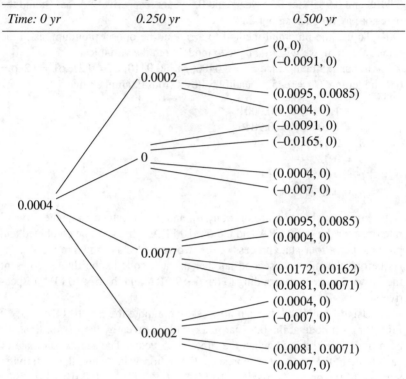

C. Other Methods Used in the Pricing of Exotic Options

Although the binomial method was discussed in detail earlier in this section, practitioners sometimes use other methods, either because of the ease in implementation or increase in efficiency. These methods vary widely according to the different types of products. In this subsection, we categorize and provide a quick overview of these approaches.

I. Trinomial Methods

Although the binomial method is intuitive and easy to implement, more often than not, the size of the sub time intervals has to be made very small before an accurate value of the premium can be obtained. This lack of efficiency can be drastically reduced if we used a trinomial or a three-state process instead. Given the current exchange rate level S, the exchange rate levels at time T/n in the future can either move upwards to a level of Su with probability p_1, remain unchanged at level of S with probability p_2 or move downwards to a level of Sd with probability of p_3. For a further discussion on this topic, see Boyle (1988). Like the binomial method, this method can be easily used to price the American style type of exotic options. Grouped together with this method is the use of numerical methods to solve the partial differential (or diffusion) equations with the appropriate boundary conditions. See Hull (1992).

II. Monte Carlo Methods

Monte Carlo methods have been very widely used in the valuation of both vanilla and path dependent European style options. For example, in order to value a European style vanilla option on currency, we first simulate a path of exchange rates that commences at the time of inception of the contract and ends at the maturity date of the option. We record this value of the exchange rate at the maturity date and compute the payoff associated with this path. More precisely, if we are trying to value a vanilla call option on the U.S. dollar that is struck at a level of 1.3 Cad/U.S. and the value of the simulated exchange rate path at the maturity date is 1.34, the payoff associated with this path is $1.34 - 1.3 = 0.04$. However, if this value at the maturity date is 1.29 Cad/U.S., the value of the option associated with this path is 0. Performing this simulation of paths about 10,000 times, we would be able to collect 10,000 option payoffs that are associated with each individual path. The value of the European style vanilla option is then obtained by present valuing the average of these 10,000 option payoffs.

European style path dependent options can be also easily valued by using the 10,000 simulated paths and incorporating the path dependent conditions associated with each of the paths. As before, averaging these 10,000 option payoffs and present valuing the result yields the option premium for a path dependent European style option. See Hull (1992) and Boyle (1977) for a detailed description of this method. The use of a Monte Carlo simulation to value an American style option has been discussed by Tilley (1993).

Although widely used, the only setback about this method is the length of the computer time required to simulate 10,000 paths.

III. Closed Form Expressions

This method of approach, if feasible, offers the best possible solution to valuing options in terms of implementation and efficiency. The problem with this approach is the inability to find closed form expressions that would allow us to value the options. Despite the fact that this approach does not work for American style options, it works frequently for European style vanilla and path dependent options.

4. CONCLUSION

In this chapter, in addition to providing reasons for the use of various currency/interest rate exotic derivatives that currently exist in the marketplace, we have provided an intuitively simple way to price them. We hope that this would help educate a greater number of asset and liability managers, which in turn would bring them into the exotic option marketplace. Although these exotics currently form a band of products that can be easily classified as leading edge instruments, they can quickly become outdated due to the increasing complexity of the market risk and the dynamic nature of the financial industry. Despite the level of complication, we feel that the binomial method can still be easily tailored to price any type of option.

REFERENCES

Black, F. and Scholes, M. (1973). "The Pricing of Options and Corporate Liabilities." *Journal of Political Economy,* 81, 637–659.

Black, F. (1976). "The Pricing of Commodity Contracts." *Journal of Financial Economics,* 3, 167–179.

Boyle, P.P. (1977). "Options: A Monte Carlo Approach." *Journal of Financial Economics,* 4, 323–338.

Boyle P.P. (1988). "A Lattice Framework for Option Pricing with Two State Variables." *Journal of Financial and Quantitative Analysis,* 23, 1–12.

Boyle, P.P. and Tse, Y.K. (1990). "An Algorithm for Computing Values of Options on the Maximum or Minimum of Several Assets." *Journal of Financial Analysis and Quantitative Analysis,* 25, 231–227.

Cox, J.C., Ross, S.A. and Rubinstein, M. (1979). "Option Pricing: A Simplified Approach." *Journal of Financial Economics,* 7, 229–263.

Geske, R. (1979). "The Valuation of Compound Options." *Journal of Financial Economics,* 7, 63–81.

Goldman, M.B., Sosin, H.B. and Gatto, M.A. (1979). "Path Dependent Options: Buy at the Low and Sell at the High." *Journal of Finance,* XXXIV, 1111–1127.

Hull, J. C. (1993). *Options, Futures, and Other Derivative Securities.* Prentice Hall, (2nd Edition).

Kemna, A. and Vorst, A. (1990). "A Pricing Method for Options Based on Average Asset Values." *Journal of Banking and Finance,* 14, 113–129.

Levy, E. (1992). "Pricing European Average Rate Currency Options." *Journal of International Money and Finance,* 11, 474–491.

Margrabe, W. (1978). "The Value of an Option to Exchange One Asset for Another." *Journal of Finance,* XXXIII, 177–186.

Ravindran, K. (1993). "Option Pricing: An Offspring of the Secretary Problem?" *Mathematicae Japonica,* 38, 905-912.

Ravindran, K. (1993). "Low-Fat Spreads." *RISK,* October.

Ravindran, K. (1993). "LIBOR Binary Notes." *Derivatives Week,* December 6.

Reiner, E. (1992). "Quanto Mechanics." *RISK,* March.

Rubinstein, M. (1991). "Options for the Undecided." *RISK,* April.

Rubinstein, M. (1991). "One for Another." *RISK,* July–August.

Rubinstein, M. and Reiner, E. (1991). "Breaking Down the Barriers." *RISK,* September.

Rubinstein, M. (1991). "Somewhere Over the Rainbow." *RISK,* November.

Rubinstein, M. (1991). "Double Trouble." *RISK,* December.

Street, A. (1992). "Stuck Up a Ladder." *RISK.*

Stulz, R.M. (1982). "Options on the Minimum or the Maximum of Two Risky Assets." *Journal of Financial Economics,* 10, 161–185.

Thomas, B. (1993). "Something to Shout About." *RISK,* May.

Tilley, J. A. (1993). "Valuing American Options in a Path Simulation Model." Preprint.

6

Fixed-Income Hybrid and Synthetic Securities

Christopher J. Williams
Managing Principal
Melinda M. Twomey
Senior Vice President
Hasan Latif
Senior Vice President
Bruce M. Usher
Senior Vice President
Ming Jiao Hsia, Ph.D.
Vice President
DiAnne Calabrisotto
Assistant Vice President

Williams Financial Markets, a division of Jefferies & Company

INTRODUCTION

The market for derivative-based hybrid securities, also known as "structured notes," has experienced rapid growth since its infancy in 1990. The growth in this market has been largely in response to the growing needs of institutional investors during a protracted period of declining yields. These instruments, issued by corporations, banks, and governmental or quasi-governmental entities, were created to enable investors to purchase customized securities that meet specific investment parameters. Not only do these securities meet the investor's guidelines with regard to credit quality and maturity, but they also enable investors to gain access to a variety of markets in ways previously not possible. For example, through the purchase of structured notes, institutions are able to take investment positions based on currency exchange rate views, expected yield curve shifts, or the performance of virtually any market. The degree of exposure to market changes inherent in these securities can be structured in accordance with the investor's risk profile.

As the market for structured notes has recently grown at a rate greater than that for any other sector of the derivative market (particularly during the 1991–1993 period), so has the need for a more precise understanding of the performance and price sensitivity of these securities. Because the instruments described in this chapter are "synthetic" debt securities, they can be analyzed by exploring the bond and derivative components of each instrument. In this chapter, a variety of derivative-based securities are discussed with regard to their performance under a variety of market conditions.

RETURN AND PRICE SENSITIVITY OF STRUCTURED NOTES

Several factors have significant impact on the price volatility and performance sensitivity of structured notes. These factors include: (1) leverage; (2) maturity of the security; and (3) investment basis risk (the degree to which the benchmark index of the note is correlated to the market benchmarks against which the investor's overall performance is measured).

Leverage

Leverage is often defined as the amount of exposure to changes in an index per unit of a security purchased. For example, a $10 million note may have a principal redemption that is indexed to four times the amount by which the exchange rate changes between two currencies. In other words, the market value impact of exchange rates on this leveraged investment is equivalent to the market value impact experienced on a $40 million investment. As leverage increases, so does the sensitivity of the return.

Maturity of the Security

Like traditional fixed-income securities, structured notes with long maturities are more price-sensitive to movements in interest rates than are similar notes with shorter maturities. Also, longer maturities make it less likely that the investor's market expectations over the life of the security will be realized due to the inaccuracy of long-term forecasts.

Investment Basis Risk

The risk incurred by an investor increases when the determinants of return on a security are unrelated to benchmarks used to measure the investor's overall portfolio performance. This basis risk can cause a structured note to dramatically outperform or underperform the overall market.

Following are discussions of several popular derivative-based investment structures. Each security is explored with regard to its overall structure, derivative components, and the hedges required to create the security.

INVERSE FLOATING-RATE NOTE

Description

One of the most widely used investment structures since the late 1980s has been a security that offers enhanced returns to investors with bullish views on the fixed-income markets. The security, referred to as an Inverse Floating-Rate Note (IFRN), pays a coupon that increases as the level of interest rates to which the coupon is indexed decreases. Like many derivative-based securities, IFRNs typically provide an immediate current coupon benefit to investors who are willing to take a position that is contrary to market expectations with regard to the direction of interest rates. IFRNs are most popular in economic environments with low inflation and steep positively shaped yield curves, which reflect the expectation of rising rates. IFRNs may also be indexed to interest rates in an inverted yield curve environment. In such cases, the interest rate view implied by an IFRN is in agreement with the forward market.

The coupon on an IFRN is typically determined pursuant to a formula that takes the form of a fixed-rate less a variable-rate index or a multiple of a variable-rate index. The coupon on the IFRN is subject to a minimum of zero percent or, in certain instances, a minimum coupon greater than zero percent is guaranteed. The type of IFRN issued in the corporate fixed-income market is analyzed in this chapter. It should be noted that these securities behave in a similar manner to, but are distinct from, the inverse floater class of securities included in many mortgage-related securities.

Exhibit 1 shows the terms of a typical IFRN with a table showing how movements in LIBOR would affect the coupon.

Issuer's Hedge of Note

Issuers of structured notes enter into hedges to eliminate exposure to the market view inherent in the notes. A typical hedge consists of a swap in which

EXHIBIT 1   IFRN Terms

Face Amount:	$100,000,000
Maturity:	2 years
Coupon on Note:	12.77% − 2 × LIBOR actual/360 day count basis
Variable Rate Index:	6-month LIBOR
Current 6-Month LIBOR:	3.5%
Interest Rate Resets:	Semi-annually
Initial Coupon:	5.77%
Minimum Coupon:	0%

Coupon Table	
USD LIBOR	Coupon
5.50%	1.77%
5.00%	2.77%
4.50%	3.77%
4.00%	4.77%
3.50%	5.77%
3.00%	6.77%
2.50%	7.77%
2.00%	8.77%
1.50%	9.77%

the issuer receives swap payments that completely offset the coupon that the issuer pays on the note. In return, the issuer pays a simple floating or fixed rate over the life of the note.

The party with whom the issuer of a structured note executes the hedge is a swap dealer, typically a highly rated financial institution. In order to provide a hedge for the issuer, the swap dealer must hedge its own risk by entering into offsetting swaps as described below, or by purchasing and selling interest rate futures contracts. The dealer manages this hedge portfolio, consisting of swaps and securities, on an ongoing basis. For simplicity, the numerical examples below do not include bid/offer spreads that would be required by the dealer.

Exhibit 2 demonstrates the cash flow involved in an IFRN from the perspectives of the investor, the issuer, and the swap dealer.

A swap dealer supplying the hedge for this note must first offset the one leg of the swap in which it pays a fixed rate and receives LIBOR − 0.10

EXHIBIT 2   Transaction Cash Flows

percent (the issuer funding target). In order to do so, the swap dealer pays LIBOR – 0.10 percent on a swap and receives a fixed rate of 4.24 percent actual/360 day count basis. The 4.24 percent rate is based on the assumption that the two-year bid side swap rate (versus LIBOR flat) equals 4.34 percent on an actual/360 day count basis.

The swap dealer must also offset the coupon so that the issuer is fully hedged. When the investor receives a coupon 12.77 percent – 2 × LIBOR, the investor is essentially receiving 12.77 percent and paying 2 × LIBOR. In order to hedge this cash flow, the dealer pays LIBOR twice and receives two fixed rates of 4.34 percent each. The two rates plus 4.34 percent for the first swap total 12.92 percent. (The 12.92 percent rate is higher than the 12.77 percent fixed component of the coupon mentioned earlier. The 0.15 percent difference is discussed below.)

Because the coupon of the note is limited to a minimum of 0 percent, the dealer purchases an interest rate cap on LIBOR at an interest rate of 6.385 percent (referred to as the cap strike). The 6.385 percent cap strike is equal to 12.77 percent divided by 2. By purchasing a cap on twice the face amount of the note, the dealer is able to guard against a rise in LIBOR over the prescribed rate. The cost of this cap accounts for the missing 0.15 percent (see Exhibit 3).

Benefits and Risks

The IFRN described herein provides investors with a significant above-market initial coupon in a positively sloped yield curve environment. The above-market initial coupon is the result of receiving a multiple of the high fixed swap rate that a swap counterparty pays versus LIBOR, for a swap with a term equal to the maturity of the note. A multiple of LIBOR is subtracted from the fixed rate. By definition, the LIBOR level is lower than the longer-term swap rate due to the positively sloped yield curve. The two times leverage in the struc-

EXHIBIT 3   Summary of Cash Flows on Dealer Hedge

Receive Fixed versus	
LIBOR on Swap	1 × 4.24% (fixed)
Pay Floating Rate	1 × LIBOR − 0.10% floating
Receive Fixed versus	
LIBOR on Swap	2 × 4.34% (fixed)
Pay Floating Rate	2 × LIBOR
Pay Cap Premium	0.15% per annum
Payment Summary	• Fixed
	4.24% + 4.34% + 4.34% − 0.15% = 12.77%
	• Floating
	LIBOR − 0.10% + LIBOR + LIBOR
	• Dealer Pays Coupon to Issuer
	12.77% − 2 × LIBOR, subject to
	minimum of 0%
	• Dealer Receives Coupon from Issuer
	LIBOR − 0.10%

ture provides the investor with coupon sensitivity that is twice that of the movement in LIBOR. In addition to coupon sensitivity resulting from the leverage, the notes are also price sensitive due to the extended duration created by the leverage. Although the maturity of the note is two years, the duration is actually 5.71 years, as shown below.

Duration of 2-year note with 4.34% coupon:	1.90 years (times two)
Duration of 2-year note with 4.24% coupon:	1.91 years
Total duration:	5.71 years

The long duration of this instrument increases its price sensitivity.

Variations

In addition to being indexed to LIBOR, IFRNs may be indexed to virtually any rates that can be hedged in the cash or derivative market. For example, investors may take advantage of a bullish view on short-, medium-, or long-term interest rate benchmarks (e.g., Prime, Fed Funds, five-year swap rates, or 10-year Treasury rates or even a basket of different rates). The leverage may also vary to reflect the investor's risk profile with regard to desired volatility, and the fixed component of the formula may also step up or down over time in accordance with the investor's view on future interest rate movements. Investors with bullish views on foreign markets, but who are restricted from investing in foreign securities, may also purchase an inverse floating rate note that is indexed to foreign interest rates but paid in U.S. dollars.

For example, an investor with a bullish view on two-year Canadian rates may purchase an IFRN indexed to Canadian rates. The note would be reset semiannually, which would enable an investor to benefit from future declines in two-year Canadian rates.

INDEXED AMORTIZING NOTE

Description

The Indexed Amortizing Note (IAN) is an innovation of the hybrid securities market, which first experienced wide popularity in early 1992. Initially, buyers of these securities were traditional investors in Collateralized Mortgage Obligations (CMOs) and high-grade callable agency notes. The investor universe has grown to include corporate bond buyers as well.

IANs are fixed-rate debentures whose face amount may decline prior to the stated maturity, depending on the level of a specified interest rate, such as three-month LIBOR. As the specified rate declines, or even if it remains stable, the IAN will amortize prior to its stated maturity, which is usually between three and five years. Unlike CMOs with similar average life characteristics, IANs have very short stated maturities, beyond which the security cannot extend. Although an IAN may be the obligation of a corporation or bank, the vast majority of IANs that have been placed through 1993 are obligations of U.S. government agencies. Yields on these securities are significantly higher than yields on fixed-rate bonds of comparable credit quality. IANs also have characteristics, such as the short-stated maturity and well-defined amortization schedule, that make them preferable to CMOs for many investors. An IAN's amortization is determined based on reference to specific interest rate movements rather than measurements that are more difficult to define, such as mortgage prepayment speeds.

The issuer of an IAN is hedged to obtain simple LIBOR-based funding through a swap that mirrors the security's structure (see Exhibit 4). The swap

EXHIBIT 4

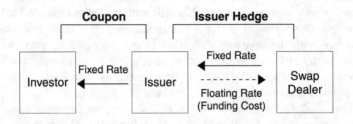

All issuer hedge terms, including any amortization, mirror the note terms.

used to hedge this structure is actually a series of options on swaps. The IAN structure is most attractive to investors (i.e., the fixed-rate coupon is highest relative to market rates) when swap option volatility is high and the yield curve is steep, as the options embedded in the IAN are the most valuable in such an environment.

Example

Face Amount of Note:	$100,000,000
Stated Maturity:	5 years
Coupon:	2-year Treasury + 0.90%
Interest Payments:	Monthly
Lock-out Period:	2 years
Reference Index:	3-month LIBOR, set 5 banking days prior to each payment date
Current 3-mo. LIBOR:	3.5%
Clean-up Call:	10%
Issuer:	U.S. Government Agency

Average Life Sensitivities

Reference Index LIBOR	Quarterly Amortization	Average Life Years
3.5%	100%	2
4.5%	100%	2
5.5%	18.30%	3
6.5%	6.40%	4
7.5%	0.00%	5

178

The IAN in the example described above has a coupon equal to the two-year Treasury yield + 0.90 percent and will mature in two years as long as LIBOR is at or below 4.5 percent at the end of two years. If LIBOR rises above 4.5 percent, the final maturity and average life will extend beyond two years. No amortization can occur prior to two years due to the lock-out provision. Amortization may occur on each of the subsequent payment dates according to the LIBOR settings, as shown above. If, for example, at the end of two years, LIBOR is set at 6.5 percent, 6.40 percent of principal will amortize on that quarterly reset date. If LIBOR were to remain at this level, the average life of the IAN would be four years, based on the amount of principal that amortized quarterly. The final maturity will not be beyond five years under any circumstances. Pursuant to the clean-up call provision, if less than 10 percent of the original principal amount is outstanding, the note will automatically mature.

Benefits and Risks

Investors have found IANs attractive for a number of reasons. Primary among them has been the high yield combined with relatively short-stated maturity. In addition, many investors prefer a bond with amortization tied directly to a specified interest rate rather than to mortgage prepayments, as in the case with CMOs. This characteristic allows the investor to know with absolute certainty how the bond will perform in any given interest rate environment. For added protection, most IANs have significant lock-out periods (often one to three years) during which no amortization can occur. Finally, as with the other hybrid securities described in this chapter, the characteristics of the IAN (average life, stated maturity, interest rate index, lock-out period, etc.) can be tailored to meet the investor's specific needs. As in the case with CMOs, IANs are subject to variations in average life, which may lower the security's return.

Exhibit 5 is an analysis of the variability of an IAN's maturity and a comparison of the total return of an IAN to that of a straight bullet security. The shaded rows compare the total return of an IAN, under several rate assumptions, to the total return of a Treasury note.

Variations

An IAN can vary in stated maturity and lock-out period from the one described above, with yield enhancement declining as the lock-out period approaches the maturity. In addition, the reference rate index may be a constant maturity Trea-

EXHIBIT 5 Total Return and Duration Analysis of Index Amortizing Note[1]

Projected 3-Month LIBOR Rate[2]	Average Life (Years)	Total Return at Maturity	Modified Duration	Constant Maturity Treasury		
				Modified Duration	Total Return	
3.2500%	2.00	4.75%	1.90			
3.5000%	2.00	4.75%	1.90			
3.7500%	2.00	4.75%	1.90			
4.0000%	2.00	4.75%	1.90			
4.2500%	2.00	4.75%	1.90			
4.5000%	2.00	4.75%	1.90	1.91	3.89%	2.00-year Treasury
4.7500%	2.06	4.75%	1.95			
5.0000%	2.17	4.89%	2.05			
5.2500%	2.39	5.02%	2.24			
5.5000%	3.02	5.08%	2.77	2.80	4.33%	3.00-year Treasury
5.7500%	3.19	5.16%	2.92			
6.0000%	3.41	5.21%	3.10			
6.2500%	3.68	5.24%	3.32			
6.5000%	4.00	5.22%	3.60	3.62	4.84%	4.00-year Treasury
6.6637%	4.14	5.22%	3.71			
6.7500%	4.21	5.22%	3.77			
7.0000%	4.44	5.19%	3.96			
7.2500%	4.71	5.13%	4.18			
7.5000%	5.00	5.03%	4.42	4.38	5.38%	5.00-year Treasury
8.0000%	5.00	5.06%	4.42			
8.5000%	5.00	5.08%	4.42			
9.0000%	5.00	5.18%	4.42			

Total Return and Duration Analysis
Assuming Implied Market Forward Rates

IAN	3.23	5.40%	2.945	Coupon: 4.82%	
2.00-yr Treasury	2.00	3.94%	1.915	Coupon: 3.92%	
5.00-yr Treasury	5.00	5.30%	4.378	Coupon: 5.20%	

1. A to AA issuer.
2. 3-month LIBOR rate at the end of second year.

sury rate or a swap rate. Most IANs to date have used LIBOR as the reference index because the swap market applies a higher option volatility to LIBOR than it does to longer rates. This high volatility in turn provides a higher yield to the investor. The bond described above has stable average life characteristics, as the note will not shorten to an average life of less than two years nor can it lengthen beyond its five-year stated maturity. The investor may choose a less stable bond (e.g., shortest average life of one year, longest average life of seven years) in exchange for receiving a higher yield. In addition, greater yield is also achievable if the investor accepts a lower quality credit such as a corporation or bank issuer rather than a governmental agency.

An innovation in this structure is to add a "knockout" feature to the IAN as added protection for the investor. If LIBOR is below the "knockout strike" (a specified interest rate) on the "knockout date" (generally 9 or 12 months after settlement), the IAN will mature on the lockout date. This feature was developed for investors who have the view that rates will stay low for 9-12 months but are much less comfortable taking a view on the level of interest rates at the end of two years.

SYNTHETIC CONVERTIBLE NOTE

Description

A synthetic convertible note (SCN) typically consists of a fixed-rate security and an option on the performance of an equity index or specific stock. As described herein, the SCN provides the investor with a low fixed-rate coupon and pays a minimum of par at maturity. In addition, the SCN offers the opportunity to earn more than par if the value of the stock or index (the "index") is above a predetermined level at maturity. The investor will receive greater than par at maturity only if the value of the index exceeds the strike. Regardless of the extent of any decline in the index value, the investor will receive a minimum of par.

Exhibit 6 shows the terms of an example SCN on a stock index.

Hedge Assumptions

The issuer is hedged by receiving swap payments equal to the note coupons in addition to a payment at maturity that is equal to the amount of principal redemption in excess of par. The issuer pays LIBOR – 0.10 percent (the issuer's funding cost) in return. The swap dealer hedges itself by paying LIBOR – 0.10 percent and receiving a fixed rate of 2 percent on a swap that offsets its payment

EXHIBIT 6 SCN Terms

Face Amount of Note:	$10,000,000
Maturity:	5 years
Coupon on Note:	2%
Option Strike:	1.1*MV Settlement
Principal Redemption Formula:	Par plus Par * $\dfrac{\text{(MV Mat.} - 1.1 \times \text{MV Settlement)}}{\text{MV Settlement}}$
	Subject to a Minimum of Par
	(investor receives 100% of the amount by which the level of the index increases in excess of 10%)
Swap Dealer Pays Issuer:	2% semi-annual coupon plus Principal Redemption Formula minus Par
Issuer Pays Swap Dealer:	LIBOR − 0.10%
Index Definition:	Broad Index of industrial stocks
MV Mat:	Market Value of Index at maturity
MV Settlement:	Market Value of Index at settlement

to the issuer. For discussion purposes, assume that the 2 percent interest rate received is approximately 4 percent per annum below the "at-the-market" swap rate that a dealer would normally receive in return for paying LIBOR − 0.10 percent. The 4 percent per annum swap rate differential is equal to a present value amount of approximately 17 percent. The swap dealer must therefore receive an up-front payment on the hedge, in an amount equal to the 17 percent present value figure, in order to be made whole when entering into this swap. This payment is therefore available to purchase call options on the desired market index (under the assumption that the investor pays par for the security even though the fixed-income component of the note is valued at 83 percent).

With the up-front payment, the dealer then buys a call option on the index for the benefit of the issuer. The option gives the dealer the right to buy the market index at a specific strike price at maturity. The option will expire worthless if, at maturity, the index value does not exceed the strike. In this instance, the investor will receive a minimum of par at maturity. If the index value exceeds the strike at maturity, the investor will receive more than par from the issuer. The amount received by the investor in excess of par is paid by the issuer from the proceeds of the exercise option (see Exhibit 7).

EXHIBIT 7

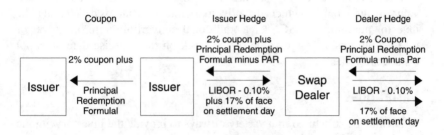

Summary of Dealer Hedge Cash Flows

Dealer receives fixed rate versus
  LIBOR − 0.10% on swap: 2%
Up-front payment to Dealer
  (based on off-market swap):   17%
Dealer pays for option: (17%)
Payment Summary: a) Dealer pays to Issuer 2% and
                                             excess Principal Redemption
                                          b) Issuer Pays to Dealer LIBOR −
                                             0.10% plus 17% of face
                                             amount

Principal Redemption Table

Basket Value	Principal Redemption	Annual IRR
−10%	100%	0%
0%	100%	0%
+10%	100%	0%
+20%	110%	3.85%
+50%	140%	8.72%
+100%	190%	15.27%

Benefits and Risks

Like a convertible fixed-income security, the SCN provides investors with a fixed coupon and additional upside if the value of a stock index rises above a specified level. Unlike a traditional convertible obligation that is convertible into the stock of the issuing company at a specific price and point in time, the SCN discussed herein pays an amount at maturity based on the increased value of the stock to which the principal amount is indexed. Whether the investor purchases an SCN or a traditional convertible note, the investor receives no upside if the value of the stock on the exercise date does not exceed the strike.

Variations

SCNs may be structured in a variety of ways to provide the investor with the flexibility to obtain principal upside based on the performance of an index, a specific stock, or a selected basket of stocks. In addition, the issuer can select the specific exercise strike desired, rather than being able to select only from available convertible notes.

INTEREST DIFFERENTIAL NOTES

Description

Interest Differential Notes (IDNs) are hybrid securities that are popular among investors who wish to establish a position referencing the differential between interest rates of two different countries. In the U.S., most differential notes are denominated in U.S. dollars and do not expose the investor to the risk of non-dollar denomination. As with other indexed notes, variations of the interest differential notes exist. The first involves variable coupons and a fixed redemption amount. A second variation pays a fixed coupon and a principal redemption that varies in accordance with the level of reference interest rates. IDNs may also be indexed to rate differentials across currencies, or within one currency and across maturities in order to create a yield-curve trade.

Example: Deutsche Mark LIBOR versus U.S. Dollar LIBOR Differential Note

Maturity: 2 years
Coupon formula: (2 × DM LIBOR) minus (2 × USD LIBOR)
                   minus 4.95%

The return of this note is linked to the spread between DM LIBOR and USD LIBOR. As the spread between the two interest rates widens, the coupon increases. Conversely, the coupon declines as the spread narrows.

This structure allows an investor to take advantage of the relationship of yield-curve slopes between different currencies. For example, the fact that the DM yield curve is inverted (downward sloping) and the U.S. yield curve is positive (upward sloping) implies that short-term DM rates are expected to fall while a rise in U.S. rates is expected. Combining the two yield curves in an Interest Differential Note allows an investor to avoid taking a position on the absolute level of rates in either country, and instead take a view on the relative levels of the interest rates in two countries. The Interest Differential Note permits the investor to earn a high yield in return for taking a view of future short-term U.S. and German interest rate movements that is contrary to the expectations implied in the yield curves of those countries.

To analyze an IDN, the investor should consider the note to be equivalent to a fixed-rate note plus a double indexation to the interest differential. The effect of the double indexation to the interest differential is to create two long positions in a two-year, U.S.-dollar, fixed-rate note and two short positions in a DM fixed-rate note. The short position in the DM note is such that the DM exchange rate risk is removed and the investor is exposed only to DM interest rate risk.

The issuer's swap hedge is composed of both U.S. dollar interest rate swaps and DM interest rate swaps. To provide for the structure outlined in Exhibit 8, the swap dealer will, in effect, take opposing (i.e., receiving fixed on one swap and paying fixed on the other swap) positions in DM and USD interest rate swaps. In addition, since the coupon may never fall below zero, the hedge incorporates an option on the spread between DM and USD LIBOR.

Exhibit 8 is an analysis of the return of a DM-USD IDN under a variety of interest rate scenarios.

The exhibit shows that the Interest Differential Note offers a 269 bp p.a. yield pickup relative to the two-year U.S. Treasury note, assuming that the differential between DEM LIBOR and USD LIBOR remains constant through the final coupon reset date. The table also highlights the significant increase in yield offered by the note as the spread between the two indexes increases. Even if the differential were to tighten, the return of the note exceeds that of the UST so long as the differential narrows at a rate less than 180 bp per annum.

Benefits and Risks

IDNs allow investors to take views on interest rates abroad without exposing themselves to currency risk in those countries. The U.S. dollar denomination

EXHIBIT 8

Coupon Formula:	(2 * DEM LIBOR – 2 * USD LIBOR) minus 4.95%
Current DEM LIBOR:	9.2500% Actual/360
Current USD LIBOR:	3.3750% Actual/360
Current LIBOR Rate Differential:	5.875% Actual/360
Initial Coupon:	6.8000% Actual/360
Current 2.0-yr Treasury:	4.20% S.A. 30/360
Yield spread over UST if LIBOR differential remains constant:	2.69% S.A. 30/360
Assumed discount rate for PV Differentials:	4.50% S.A. 30/360

Per Annum Change in LIBOR Spread (bp per ann)	LIBOR Spread at Last Reset	P.V. Benefit versus UST	Per Annum Benefit versus UST
300	10.38%	13.57%	7.17%
250	9.63%	12.16%	6.43%
200	8.88%	10.75%	5.68%
150	8.13%	9.34%	4.93%
100	7.38%	7.92%	4.19%
50	6.63%	6.51%	3.44%
Unchanged 0	**5.88%**	**5.10%**	**2.69%**
–50	5.13%	3.69%	1.95%
–100	4.38%	2.27%	1.20%
–150	3.63%	0.86%	0.46%
Break-even –180	**3.17%**	**0.00%**	**0.00%**
–250	2.13%	–1.64%	–0.87%
–300	1.38%	–2.35%	–1.24%
–350	0.63%	–2.98%	–1.57%

of IDNs is attractive, as relatively few investors are willing to expose their portfolios to currency fluctuations while implementing interest rate positions.

They may also be structured to provide exposure to any part of the yield curve. For example, the indexation may be structured based on the differential between 10-year rates in Germany and the U.S. A combination of maturities in the two currencies would also be possible. Finally, combinations of different maturities in the same currency may also be put together, allowing investors to take yield curve views in foreign or domestic bond markets. The securities often permit investors to earn potentially above-market yields on high credit quality securities in return for the market risk of the interest differential.

The basic risk of an IDN is that the interest differential could move in a direction opposite to that which would benefit the investor. For example, if in the case of the coupon indexed IDN the differential between DM LIBOR and USD LIBOR narrows, the coupon declines.

Variations

Principal Indexed Interest Differential Note

Maturity: 2 years

Coupon: 4% (Fixed)

Principal
Redemption
Formula: $100\% + 15 \times \{0.70\% - (\text{FF swap rate} - \text{DM swap rate})\}$

This note pays a fixed coupon and pays a variable redemption amount at maturity that is indexed to the spread between seven-year French franc swap rates and seven-year Deutsche mark swap rates. If the spread widens above 70 bp, the redemption value is below par; and if the spread is less than 70 bp, the redemption value exceeds par. The degree to which the redemption value exceeds or is less than par is the result of a 15 times multiple of the change in the spread.

The principal indexed notes provide a means to take advantage of the expected convergence of long-term French franc and Deutsche mark rates. With the decline in inflation in France and the concurrent rise in German inflation during 1992 and 1993, investors began to expect French rates to fall below German rates. In anticipation of such an event an investor might purchase the bond described. By purchasing this note the investor is taking a view only on the interest rate spread without taking currency exposure to either the French franc or the Deutsche mark. The seven-year swap rates are used as proxies for long-term yields in the two currencies.

This note can be reconstructed and evaluated as a fixed-rate, two-year, U.S.-dollar-denominated note with indexation to forward swap rates. The exposure to the indexation is straightforward in that a 1 bp narrowing in the spread results in a 0.15 percent increase in the redemption value of the security. The trade is hedged by entering into a swap in which the dealer receives a fixed rate on a forward-starting French franc interest rate swap and pays the fixed rate on a forward-starting Deutsche mark interest rate swap.

Constant Maturity Treasury (CMT) Yield Curve Indexed Floater

Coupon: 4.95% + (CMT 2-yr – CMT 10-yr)
Maturity: 2 years

The CMT curve floater has a fixed redemption value at par and variable coupons indexed to the spread between two-year and 10-year U.S. Treasury yields. As the yield curve flattens (i.e., the spread narrows), the coupon of the note increases. Likewise, a steepening of the yield curve would result in a lower coupon. The coupons reset quarterly, enabling the investor to earn higher returns over time to the extent that the yield curve flattens.

Rising inflation expectations and the expectation of higher short-term rates relative to longer rates create an argument for a flattening of the yield curve. One way of capitalizing on such an expectation without taking actual long and short positions in the Treasury market is through the purchase of a note indexed to the yield differential between two-year and 10-year Treasuries.

The CMT curve floater enables the investor to take a view on the differential between two rates (in this case both within the same currency) rather than taking a view on the absolute level of rates. The structure can be viewed as a combination of a two-year, U.S.-dollar note and an indexation of each coupon to the shape of the yield curve. The note is hedged by taking long and short positions in Treasuries designed to create forward rates for each coupon reset date.

SUMMARY

The preceding discussion of structured notes is intended to provide an understanding of the hedge components required to create these securities. The principles used in structuring the securities described here have been applied to hundreds of other structured notes. Exhibit 9 summarizes several of the most popular structures in 1993. These include a variety of structures based on an historically steep U.S. dollar interest rate curve and a group of structures based on high real foreign interest rates, with coupons inversely tied to European, Japanese, or other foreign interest rates, but paid in U.S. dollars. These inverse floating rate notes allowed investors to take a view on falling

EXHIBIT 9 Popular Structures

Interest Rate Environment	Generic Structure Name	Coupon	Investor View
Steep U.S. $ interest rate curve	Yield Curve Notes	CMT minus LIBOR	Interest rate curve will not flatten as quickly as forwards imply.
Steep U.S. $ interest rate curve	Prime Notes	Prime minus LIBOR	Spread between Prime and LIBOR will not narrow as quickly as forwards imply.
Steep U.S. $ interest rate curve and high volatility	Range Notes/ Accrual Notes	Above-market coupons paid every day LIBOR is within a pre-set range	Interest rates will remain steady to moderately higher.
Steep U.S. $ interest rate curve	SURF's/ Deleveraged Floaters	50% CMT plus Spread	Interest rate curve will not flatten as quickly as forwards imply.
Steep U.S. $ interest rate curve	Ratchets/ One-Way Floaters	LIBOR plus Spread-Coupon can increase a maximum of 25 bp/ quarter, and can never decrease.	Interest rates will increase slowly and steadily.
High real European interest rates	Inverse floating rate note (IFRN)	Fixed rate minus DM LIBOR, paid in U.S. dollars.	Interest rates in Europe will decline faster than forwards imply.
High real Global interest rates	Basket Note	Fixed rate minus (Sum of Foreign interest rates), paid in U.S. dollars	Some interest rates may increase, but on average foreign rates will decline.

international interest rates and at the same time eliminated the currency risk associated with buying non-dollar bonds.

Continued innovation in the derivatives market will no doubt lead to increased diversity among the investment alternatives available to institutions.

Several different methods of evaluating the performance of these securities were used throughout this chapter. The appropriate means of analyzing and evaluating return is specific to each investor and is a function of the benchmarks against which each investor measures a security's performance.

7

Corporate Exposure Management: An Alternative Approach

Azam Mistry
Vice President, Capital Markets Marketing, Midland Bank
Hongkong and Shanghai Bank Group

The management of market exposure by corporations, defined as hedging and related activities in the foreign exchange, interest rate, and commodity markets, is now a widely accepted function of treasury departments in most multinationals. However, controversy and debate continue to surround much of the activities undertaken by these groups in the interest of reducing risk to the corporation and its shareholders. Criticisms ranging from accusations of unhealthy and needless speculation to views that espouse financial market efficiency and denounce attempts to manage exposure as misdirected or even futile. Senior management disquiet and suspicion are abundant: dissatisfaction with the prospect of cash-flow losses on hedge transactions matched solely by accounting profits; reproach for hedging activities that invariably look unnecessary or badly timed in retrospect; the impression that certain risks are being managed to the deliberate exclusion of others; and a feel that, over time, financial and other market-related risks will average out, leaving the true profitability of the corporation to be determined by the performance of its mainstream activities.

These are muddy waters. Is there some form of clear thinking or appeal to first principles that may be useful? Specifically, what are the legitimate aims and parameters of a policy of exposure management? Is there a conceptual theme that one may usefully develop?

DEFINING THE MULTINATIONAL FIRM

Let's go back to basics. It seems reasonable to define today's global corporation as an entity generating both positive and negative cash flows in a variety

The views expressed by the author in this chapter are entirely his own and do not represent the views of his current or previous employers.

of currencies in addition to its own base currency, and possessing assets and liabilities dispersed geographically and by currency of original denomination. The interaction of these assets and liabilities creates cash flows whose expected magnitude and uncertainty represent the value of the firm, embodied by the price of its stock.

The corporation employs some element of choice between differing asset and liability "mixes" in terms of the cash flows that may be expected to arise directly from their usage. This is no easy choice, since the cash flows resulting from differing mixes are difficult to predict.

Further, the magnitude and uncertainty of the cash flows themselves may be impacted directly by various decisions. Such decisions involve issues like input costs and output pricing, including agreements to fix either of these magnitudes for varying periods of time.

Thus defined, the firm's value is a dynamic function of its expected cash flows and asset-liability mix. Management seeks to influence this value through decisions made at various levels and by different functional groups. Strategic choices relating to mainstream corporate activities like manufacturing, input sourcing, equipment configuration, marketing and distribution, capital expenditure, R&D, human resource optimization, etc., serve to alter the mix and efficiency of assets and liabilities, impact costs and revenues, and vary the speed and magnitude of cash flows.

However, focusing purely on financial decisions made in treasury and related departments, it is easy to see that exposure management through foreign exchange, interest rate, and commodity market activities can have a major impact on the cash flows and asset-liability configuration of the corporation. Foreign exchange hedging may be used to fix the value in base currency of future cash inflows and outflows at either positive or "negative" cost; it may also serve to protect the base-currency translated value of net investments abroad. Interest rate market activity through debt issues, cash management, swaps, and other transactional hedges is capable of locking in (or varying) the level of interest rate costs or earnings for different periods of time. Commodity market activities can fix the cost of input materials and hedge against fluctuations in output prices for varying periods of time.

Viewed in this manner, exposure management activities represent an additional set of levers for use by management in varying the expected return and variability of the firm's stock price. While these activities are subject to the same shortcomings as other control mechanisms, they may be operated somewhat independently, although within the constraints imposed by mainstream corporate operations. Significantly, through altering the configuration of risk and reward that ultimately represents the appeal of the stock to investors, exposure management may serve as an instrument that aligns the corporation's risk-reward configuration with the preferences of its stockholders.

THE CONVENTIONAL APPROACH AND ITS EVOLUTION

The conventional style of exposure management finds its origins in the micro approach to managing risk. Exposure is recognized and eliminated on a transaction by transaction basis or in a manner that treats every major corporate project or program as an individual and separable event in the organization's life. This is most clearly demonstrated by activities that aim at covering foreign exchange exposure arising from purchases of raw materials and components from overseas, or equivalently, by hedging through forward foreign exchange contracts the exposure arising from firm sales commitments denominated in a non-base currency. In addition, corporations often tend to view specific projects or ventures as individual profit activities that require for evaluation purposes that exposure directly relating to the venture be hedged in its entirety.

This form of itemized thinking has led to an attempt to view the balance sheet and income statement—indeed, the entire activity of the corporation—as something amenable to a checklisting of exposure and nonexposure items. More damagingly, such thinking has in the past engendered the feeling that it is both possible and desirable for all exposure-entailing items to be hedged in their entirety. The tendency here has been to focus primarily on the objective of risk elimination with somewhat less emphasis given to the costs involved. Note that these costs are variable over time and can be high. For example, the hedging forward of high interest rate foreign currency receivables, the locking in of input materials through commodity hedging in a positive price curve environment, the decision to pay fixed interest rates on long-term debt in a steep yield curve situation—all these can entail high costs relative to current levels. In some cases, it is conceivable that the high cost of covering exposure would make it preferable to accept a certain degree of risk. Cost considerations must enter into the determination of both the amount and the manner of hedging activity undertaken.

These issues have long since led to changes in the rationale and practice of exposure management, encompassing the three areas of foreign exchange, interest rate, and commodity market activities. In the field of foreign exchange management, the now-common practice of aggregating and netting out exposure across activities and functional divisions aims at reduc-

193

ing the number of hedging transactions and the costs involved. Secondly, a methodology of hedging foreign exchange risk using proxy currencies has evolved. This involves the use of a smaller basket of currencies in which hedges are placed, such currencies representing a proxy for the actual currencies in which exposure arises. Again, the objective is to reduce costs through finding hedge currencies that are both closely correlated with the exposure currencies and that involve lower hedging costs. A further refinement involves netting revenues against costs where these items are denominated in closely correlated foreign currencies. An example might involve a U.S. corporation that earns revenues in EMS (European Monetary System) member currencies from sales in Europe and also pays import or other costs denominated in similar EMS currencies; in this situation, the costs may be netted against the revenues, leaving only the balance to be hedged.

Further, both the time horizon and scope of foreign exchange exposure management have increased. Risk reduction activities in this area now encompass not merely transactional exposure but also translation and foreign earnings exposure in future years. It is argued that the translation of net overseas investment represents a risk to the corporation in more than a pure year-end accounting sense. This is clearly seen if one regards a foreign investment as an asset potentially disposable at any point in time; from this perspective, foreign exchange hedges that protect the value in base currency of this asset are justified.

As regards foreign earnings, the need to provide protection against future overseas profits deteriorating in base currency terms seems reasonable. Typically, these exposures are managed through the use of currency swaps, utilizing both the principal re-exchange and the coupon flows as the operational components of the hedge. Clear choices exist as to the currency, maturity, and custom configuration of the hedge; all of these have a direct bearing on hedging costs and efficiency.

The key issues here that require treasury management consideration relate to (1) the specific amounts of net overseas investment and future earnings from offshore operations that should be hedged back into the base currency and (2) the future period of time over which both translation and foreign earnings exposure should be eliminated through hedging activities. Note that any judgment on these matters must make implicit assumptions about the accuracy of forecasts about future foreign cashflows and continuing ownership of foreign assets. The inevitable uncertainty involved implies that decisions taken regarding these parameters will ultimately reflect to some degree the risk tolerance and cost-conservatism of the treasury department and that of the corporation's senior management.

In the field of interest rate management, attention is focused primarily on the cost and configuration of debt, and—to a lesser extent—on the liquidity and return profile of surplus funds. The key issues here involve the appropriate fixed-floating interest rate proportion of debt carried by the corporation and the tenor of this debt. These magnitudes may be varied through the use of interest rate and currency swaps that enable flexible switching between fixed and floating rate obligations in a variety of currencies. Additionally, interest rate swaps and related instruments like futures and FRAs (Forward Rate Agreements) are increasingly being used on both the debt and asset side to optimally manage the short-term profile and liquidity of the corporation.

Treasury management teams face difficult decisions relating to the appropriate mix of fixed and floating interest rate debt obligations carried and the maturities of such debt. Differing mixes and maturities entail different interest rate costs and risks; these change as the slope and position of the yield curve alters over time. Consider that in a given situation, a conservative corporation may choose to maintain nearly 100 percent of its debt in long maturities at fixed interest rates, and may accordingly execute swap strategies designed to enable it to reach this position; in the same circumstances, a less conservative company may decide instead on a 50-50 mix. However, in a steeply positive yield curve environment the high cost of taking the 100 percent option may perhaps cause the first institution to realign its strategy towards a partial floating-rate debt portfolio. Arguably, the second corporation may similarly change its tactics in the interest of achieving lower interest costs through an increased floating-rate debt strategy operated at the short end of the yield curve. Of course, in both cases the immediate reduction in cost is likely to be accompanied by an increment of risk through possible higher interest costs in the future, as indeed the shape of the yield curve implies.

The point really is that the specific response of any institution in these or other circumstances is virtually impossible to predict. This is because few objective guidelines exist as to what the appropriate fixed-floating rate proportion should be, even for a given environment with rigorously defined parameters. In actual practice, most corporations tend to reach their equilibrium positions largely through judgmental criteria and the weight of precedence.

The newest area of exposure management involves the use of commodity market derivatives, especially commodity swaps, futures, and options. These instruments are typically used to fix the cost of input materials purchased by corporations and to hedge against declines in the price of output products, especially where the commodity component of these products is high. For example, a corporation that purchases large quantities of aluminum on a monthly basis, invoiced regularly against a market index, may elect to enter an aluminum swap whereby it pays a fixed price over the period of the swap in return for receiving a monthly average price relating to the same index. This effectively locks in the cost of purchasing aluminum during this period. Similar transactions may be executed using options, futures or hybrid derivative structures to hedge commitments on purchased inputs or, alternatively, on sales of output. Again, the key issues here involve the period of time for which costs or output prices are fixed, and the proportion of total commitments that are fixed through hedge mechanisms such as these.

It is clear that the evolution and wider scope of exposure management has forced treasury departments to face certain thorny issues and difficult choices. Much of the confusion stems from a failure to recognize the wider role and perspective of exposure management and a reluctance to award these activities their true role. The conceptual inconsistency that results leads directly to contradictions and the incessant debate familiar to participants in the field.

CONVENTIONAL CONFUSION

The state of conflict and debate is best seen through a review of the comments often heard in treasury and related circles:

"We Hedge Everything. We Never Speculate."

This seemingly innocuous policy statement makes strong claims. In its most rigorous interpretation, it enjoins certain ground rules:

- It is inappropriate to undertake market transactions not directly related to exposure faced by the corporation.
- All firm commitments must be fully hedged in an efficient manner.
- Hedges should not be subject to removal and replacement during a period of continuing exposure.
- Attempts to optimally time the execution of hedges are both improper and futile.

The first imperative seems reasonable enough: In general, it is not appropriate for an institution to speculate in financial or other markets unless this activity is part of its stated mission. However, the second instruction makes unrealistic demands. It is often impractical or even impossible to hedge certain exposures completely. In some cases, the necessary instruments or markets may not exist or may not be fully developed, making it necessary to execute an imperfect hedge that substitutes a residual but lower risk for the original exposure. Examples include proxy-currency and proxy-instrument hedging as well as the use of mismatched dates or amounts between the exposure and the hedging vehicle (as in the case of futures hedging). Additionally, cost considerations may influence the hedging decision. If the cost of a perfect hedge is inordinately high, the wisdom of executing such a strategy may be legitimately questioned; instead, a less perfect hedge structure that provides what is judged to be adequate protection may be selected.[1]

Clearly, corporations do not "hedge everything." For instance, most institutions borrow funds in the money markets on a floating rate basis, implicitly "speculating" on the future trend in interest rates. They choose to leave unhedged portions of their anticipated earnings flows denominated in foreign currencies, thereby tacitly taking views on future foreign exchange movements. They also choose not to fix in advance the prices of their input raw materials and supplies over the foreseeable future, thereby assuming that future price movements will not unduly damage profitability. This inaction is usually a response to both the uncertainty regarding future corporate cash-flows and needs as well as the cost of executing longer hedges. Is there not a degree of speculation in the decision to do nothing or in the decision to hedge only on a partial basis?

Imperfect and partial hedges such as those described above do not seem to fulfill the requirements of a stated policy of "full and efficient" hedging, nor do they comply with the strictures of a policy intended to be entirely free of speculative elements. For instance, the reduction of pure market risk through imperfect hedges leaves behind residual risk of a somewhat different nature. The strategy relies for its success on the assumption that certain market relationships will continue to hold or else change only in a favorable manner and direction. Tactics like these essentially involve an element of speculation about market magnitudes.

Again, a decision to hedge partially, or not at all, will usually reflect unavoidable constraints and necessarily involve speculative issues and judg-

---

1. There is clear evidence that conservative corporations have followed this line of thinking: in the mid-1980s, several structures were developed to enable corporations to cover forward foreign exchange risk in developing country currencies, including the Mexican peso. These hedges involved exorbitant forward exchange rate costs due to high foreign interest rates, and it is significant that few institutions chose to enter such transactions.

ments. Such actions are both necessary and prudent. If they appear improper in any sense, it is only because the field of exposure management is more complex than it seems. A fuller appreciation of the underlying issues reveals the hollowness of statements that blindly espouse the need to hedge completely and avoid speculative considerations in their entirety.

As regards the last two statements, it should be acknowledged that a great deal of controversy exists regarding the "active" management of hedging activities, i.e., the attempts to initiate, raise, and replace hedges at appropriate times so as to maximize gains or minimize losses. Those who oppose these practices usually refer to considerations of market efficiency and the often misstated conviction that it is impossible to "beat the market" consistently. This is in fact the incorrect formulation of a sophisticated argument (for one thing it seems to suggest the strange conclusion that it is impossible to underperform the market as well!). The truth (or at least the theory) is that in the long run it is impossible to beat the market while accepting the same degree of risk that market movements entail. If one wishes to beat the market, it is necessary to undertake higher levels of risk. In the context of hedging activity, this implies that a policy of active management of hedges will experience a greater proportion of failures (and successes), i.e., there will be more hits and misses than a passive hedging policy would entail.

In the long run, active hedge management will reflect a higher degree of risk than passive hedging activities and will provide higher returns (or reduced hedging costs) commensurate with this risk. This means that the choice of hedging strategy adopted (which in general aims first and last at the reduction of risk to the corporation) itself has a bearing on the degree of risk reduction achieved. In commonsense terms, this has intuitive appeal: An exposure management policy that allows for hedge removal and replacement in accordance with judgments as to future market movements may result in lower hedging costs, but will do so only through the acceptance of a risk greater than that entailed by a policy of passive hedging. This is a provocative area and one that goes to the heart of arguments that follow, but it is not appropriate to enter into it at present. For the moment, it is sufficient to note that, once again, these considerations show that the subject of exposure management is not really amenable to the kind of black-and-white thinking that one may easily be seduced into adopting.

"Why Did You Hedge?"

This is invariably a retrospective statement. It usually represents a response to circumstances where a specific hedge appears to have been unnecessary due to market movements resulting in a favorable outcome for the underlying exposure and a loss-making consequence for the hedge strategy. In a nutshell, and with the benefit of hindsight, the hedge was not needed. Or was it?

This common statement reflects either a futile lamentation or a serious misconception about the role and function of hedging activities. It is important to accept the nature of any individual or collective set of hedges as a form of insurance policy against risks that may or may not arise. To the extent that such risks do not in fact materialize, it is appropriate to view the cost of hedging, i.e., the loss made on the hedge and other related outgoings, as an insurance premium paid to reduce risk. From this perspective, the claim that a given hedge appears to have been in retrospect unnecessary is tantamount to the assertion that any individual carrying a life insurance policy has in fact wasted money, to the extent that he or she is still alive and should not have undertaken the insurance.

Hedging activities, like insurance, are to be regarded as necessary costs paid to mitigate risk to the entity concerned. The value of these is clearly seen if one considers that these actions enable a risk-reducing entity such as a corporation to achieve a greater degree of certainty as to future successful economic performance, albeit at a cost. Ultimately, such activities are of value to parties with an interest linked to the success and continued healthy existence of the entity whose protection is achieved.

However, two significant issues need to be recognized. Firstly, the cost should not be such that these parties would consider it inappropriate or excessive in any sense. Obviously, there are difficulties here in that different parties may have differing perceptions about what constitutes an appropriate cost. Secondly, and closely linked to the first issue, the degree of risk-reduction should be in some sense congruent with that desired by the interested parties. These are difficult issues that raise complex questions; however, what is clear is that a correct stance taken on both issues—however arrived at—is capable of providing a cost-risk trade-off that correctly aligns the entity insured or hedged with the disposition and objectives of interested parties.

"In the Long Run, It Will Even Out. These Levels Will Come Back."

This statement seems to embody a naive faith in the cyclical nature of market movements, based on observations that certain market magnitudes tend to revert to equilibrium levels over time. There is perhaps some truth to the premise that financial markets experience mean-reversion in the long run, particularly with regard to real rather than nominal magnitudes. However, the suggestion is that hedging activity is to some degree unnecessary since these allegedly symmetrical market fluctuations will ensure that, for a relatively unhedged firm, the good years will cancel out the bad ones, leaving a satisfactory picture in the long run. Quite apart from the fact that this statement places blind faith in the regularity and timing of market fluctuations, it ignores the very real problem of risk arising to the corporation in the short term.

If the position of an unhedged or underhedged corporation is "correct" in some long-term sense, it is only correct in the same sense that a stopped clock is correct twice a day, or indeed, 730 times a year. In the real world, a corporation is judged at least partly by its short-term viability and performance, as evidenced by fluctuations in its stock price. The need to provide continuous or ongoing protection of some sort cannot be ignored.

The statement does, however, have a deeper implication: It seems to suggest that a degree of risk acceptable to the corporation exists. This is a point worth following further.

"Our Investors *Want* This Risk."

This is a sophisticated argument, which, as we will see, goes to the heart of the issues involved. The point made is that investors who acquire the shares of a corporation do so in order to earn returns commensurate with the acceptance of a certain degree of risk, and, more specifically, make their investment decision in anticipation of precise types of risks.

For example, consider a shareholder who purchases the stock of a U.S. corporation that relies for most of its revenues on profitable exports to other countries or through successful operation of its overseas subsidiaries. Such an investor may have made the investment decision based on clear expectations about various magnitudes, including, perhaps, a perception that the U.S. dollar will weaken against the currencies of the corporation's trading partners. If the corporation then chooses to hedge forward all its foreign currency revenues into dollars or to hedge a substantial part of its future foreign earnings, these actions would directly contradict the objectives of the investor. To put it more broadly, when an investor chooses to purchase the stock of a U.S. corporation that prospers when the dollar depreciates against other currencies, he or she may be making the decision on the basis that the stock is equivalent in part to a short-dollar foreign exchange position, and that such a position is an appropriate addition to a diversified investment portfolio. Hedging actions by the corporation aimed at neutralizing or reducing the impact of a depreciating dollar on its operations may work directly against the investor's overall objectives.[2]

Another example might include a shareholder purchasing stock in a highly-leveraged corporation in the belief that interest rates will fall, raising the price of the stock through decreased interest costs and improved cash flow. If this corporation were to take a decision to fix the interest rates on all or a large portion of its debt through the use of say, interest rate swaps, this would again frustrate the investor's objectives, especially if the implicit investment assumption made was that the corporation would maintain the existing portion of its debt portfolio on a floating rate basis in order to take advantage of declining interest rates.

If one accepts the spirit of this argument (and it is a compelling argument), several important issues present themselves. Since any given policy of exposure management entails differing risks and costs, the choice of the appropriate strategy raises several difficult questions. The corporation is faced with the near-impossible problem of determining the specific objectives and risk-reward preferences of the majority of its shareholders. The question that needs answering relates to the image of the corporation in the eyes of its investors, and raises issues concerning information flow to the investment community and the resulting correctness of perceptions about the corporation's activities. Does the investor view the corporation as an entity that benefits from a strengthening or weakening dollar? Is the stock perceived as one that responds favorably to bullish or bearish interest rate scenarios? Does the corporation's shareholder community see its investment as a play on commodity price levels? Assuming that such information is available, should the corporation direct its activities toward satisfaction of the objectives of its existing shareholder base or should it focus its exposure management activities (and perhaps other efforts) in such a way as to attract other types of

---

2. Arguments of this genre have long been common in academic circles. The area of most debate has involved diversification of corporate activities through acquisitions and mergers. The theoretical view has been that corporations acting purely in the interest of their shareholders should not diversify or switch activities on a large scale, since investors have clearly made a decision to invest specifically in the existing operations of the corporation. In other words, a chemical company should not move into the natural gas exploration business through acquisition or otherwise, since its shareholders have demonstrated that their investment is directed towards the chemical business only. If these shareholders wished to diversify their investment portfolios, they would do so through direct acquisition of shares in natural gas exploration companies.

investors? If information flows are near-perfect, implying that investors are fully aware of the risks being accepted commensurate with the current hedging policy (or lack of it), should any changes be made at all, even if adherence to this policy may entail severe performance problems for the corporation?

The comments reviewed above will sound all too familiar to those involved in corporate treasury activities. The issues raised serve to emphasize that the real challenge in exposure management relates not to the choice of hedging structure adopted from the wide menu of simple and hybrid mechanisms now available from commercial and investment banking institutions, or to the issues of timing and active management of hedges, but to inevitable decisions regarding the amount of exposure hedged and the period of time for which hedge protection is appropriate. If the corporation is viewed as a vehicle that exists primarily to serve the interests of its shareholders, these decisions must be made against the backdrop of assumptions about the objectives of these shareholders, the efficacy of information flows to these individuals and institutions, and, finally, the legitimacy of actions taken by the corporation in order to shift its investor base towards alternative entities.

To arrive at criteria upon which to base these decisions, it is useful to acquaint ourselves with the basics of formal portfolio management theory, especially insofar as it describes the actions of investors seeking to develop optimal investment strategies in their portfolios.

A PRIMER ON PORTFOLIO THEORY

Classic portfolio theory states that an investor equipped with the requisite information will make rational choices among alternative investment opportunities based solely on the expected return and the risk attached to each. If two (or more) investment alternatives exist, each with the same degree of risk but differing expected returns, the investor will choose the investment with the higher return. Similarly, if two investment opportunities offer the same expected returns but differing risks, the investor will select the investment that entails less risk. Obviously, if one investment offers a higher return with lower risk than the other, it will invariably be chosen over the latter. However, if one investment has a higher expected return and a higher risk, the choice is not clear; ultimately, the decision will depend on the investor's preferences, i.e., his attitude to risk and return. Since this is a matter involving the personal characteristics of the investor, the outcome cannot be objectively forecast: It is a function of the individual evaluation of risk versus return on the part of the investor concerned.

Exhibit 1 summarizes these conclusions. The vertical axis denotes the expected returns of stocks A, B, C, and D. The horizontal axis plots the risk associated with each stock, embodied by the standard deviation, a statistical measure of the volatility of stock price returns (the standard deviation represents the square root of variance, which is the average of the squared deviations from the mean stock price return).

In Exhibit 1, stocks B and C are clearly preferred to stock A: stock B has the same return as stock A with lower risk, while stock C has the same risk as stock A but a higher expected return. As between stocks A and D, stock D has a higher return and lower risk and is therefore the preferred investment. However, a clear choice cannot be made between stocks B, C, and D: stock B has a lower degree of risk but also a lower return than stocks C and D. Stock C has a higher return than both B and D, but also entails a higher risk. Note that a simple graphical rule may be adopted here: If a stock on the graph lies in the quadrant to the northwest of another stock, it will be unambiguously chosen over that stock. This is clearly displayed by the choice of stocks B, C, and D over stock A. As stated earlier, the choice made by an investor between stocks B, C, and D cannot be objectively forecast. The outcome will depend on the investor's personal risk-return preferences.

EXHIBIT 1

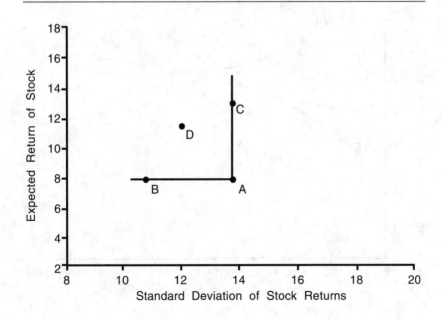

The theory is extended to apply to combinations of "portfolios" of stocks and other investment instruments, with the same rules regarding return and risk being observed. Exhibit 2 shows portfolios of investments graphed according to their expected (portfolio) returns and volatility.

Using the northwest rule described earlier, it is possible to identify those portfolios that would be chosen by a rational investor over other portfolios; these would be the portfolios with the most northwesterly positions on the graph. Portfolio theory denotes these as "efficient" or "undominated" portfolios, since they are superior to other investment portfolios. The line connecting these portfolio positions on the graph is called the "efficient frontier," denoted in Exhibit 2 as the line EF. The portfolios lying along this line are sometimes described as being "mean-variance efficient." A rational investor would choose only between portfolios of stocks falling along this frontier; any other portfolio chosen would represent a suboptimal investment decision. The exact portfolio selected along the frontier would depend on the investor's risk-return preference, i.e., the rate at which the investor would accept increased risk for increased return. This is illustrated graphically by the investor's indifference curve, a tool of traditional microeconomic theory,

EXHIBIT 2

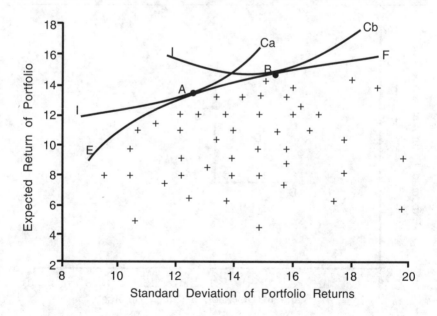

shown in Exhibit 2 as IC_a. The point of tangency between the indifference curve and the efficient frontier represents the portfolio chosen by a given investor. Thus investor A, with preferences denoted by his indifference curve IC_a, would select portfolio A, while investor B, who has a greater tolerance for risk as denoted by his indifference curve IC_b, would choose portfolio B.

APPLICATION TO EXPOSURE MANAGEMENT

Investors with access to information about the expected returns and risks of investment opportunities are assumed to behave in accordance with the tenets of this theory. In particular, it is assumed that an investor would select an investment portfolio chosen only from those located along the efficient frontier, and further, that the specific choice made would reflect the investor's risk-return preferences and objectives. In making this decision, the investor would rely on the expected return and risk associated with each stock in the portfolio and the historical relationship between these stocks, revealed through (a) historical stock volatilities and correlations in the past, and/or (b) explicit information, statements, and analyses relating to each corporation whose stock is considered for inclusion in the portfolio.

In actual practice, institutional investors make formal application of the theory in order to establish efficient investment portfolios and to define for their own investors/beneficiaries the degree of risk associated with these investments. Mathematical techniques such as portfolio optimization are usually employed, utilizing historical data regarding stock returns and volatilities over varying periods of the past in order to identify appropriate efficient portfolios. An investment fund will often explicitly state its policy regarding risk in either qualitative or quantitative terms and sometimes estimate in advance the return expected in exchange for accepting this degree of risk. In fact, even if investors do not explicitly or quantitatively identify expected returns and risks it is obvious that investment decisions tacitly recognize them. To these investors, it is important that corporations whose stocks are included in the portfolio follow policies designed to maintain the risks and expected returns associated with their stocks. Specifically, actions taken by the corporation to reduce risk at the cost of decreased returns (or to increase risk in the interest of achieving higher returns) may be inappropriate as far as investor objectives and preferences are concerned. One absurd extreme, for example, would involve a corporation that reduces risk and return to a degree that approaches the return on risk-free investments such as U.S. government Treasury Bills.

What are the implications for exposure management policy? Since exposure management activities aim specifically at reducing risk to the corporation with a concomitant incurrence of cost, it is clear that these activities are capable of making inappropriate adjustments in risk and return as far as investor interests are concerned. A corporation with major overseas activities may, for example, "overhedge" its currency exposures, resulting in an investment profile incongruent with the perception of its investors that it is a stock well geared to overseas growth and foreign currency appreciation. A debt-laden corporation that employs hedging strategies to fix the interest rates on its borrowings prior to the onset of a period of falling yields will frustrate the intention of investors who see it as an entity whose stock price is likely to appreciate due to lower interest charges. A corporation utilizing large amounts of raw materials that establishes substantial commodity hedges to lock in the price levels of its future requirements will fail to adequately exploit a period of falling commodity prices, frustrating investors who believe that such declines would substantially increase its profitability. Conversely, but equivalently, a corporation that fails to hedge itself adequately in an environment of potentially adverse market conditions would mislead investors who believed in its ability to appropriately safeguard its profits.

Exposure management policies (indeed, all corporate policies) should optimally aim at achieving no more and no less than that expected by investors. In an ideal world with perfect information flows and absolute efficiency of control by management, it may be argued that a corporation would be managed exactly in line with shareholder objectives. Manufacturing, marketing, pricing, acquisition and disposal of business—all corporate activities would be coordinated in such a manner as to result in the expected return-risk configuration that all or a majority of shareholders have clearly expressed themselves as desiring. Exposure management policy would be directed so as to facilitate achievement of this overall risk-reward profile; the interaction of alternative hedging policies with other corporate actions would be known, and the optimal exposure management policy would be clearly identified.

Unfortunately, such an ideal world does not exist. Mainstream corporate activities like manufacturing, marketing, capital investment, etc., are incapable of fine tuning; furthermore, the potential effects upon stock price volatility and returns from varying decisions relating to these is unknown, perhaps even unknowable, due to the limited experience of the past and the near impossibility of carrying out controlled experiments. Consequently, these policies must be treated to some extent as given parameters. Exposure management, however, may be utilized as an "overlay" to such mainstream corporate policies and may be directed towards a role of neutrality as far as the overall risk-return profile of the corporation is concerned. If this rationale is adopted, it means that the selection of an appropriate mix of hedging strategies must ignore mainstream corporate policies and focus on providing that hedge policy that results *in itself* in a degree of risk equivalent to that desired by the corporation's shareholders.

What is the practical application of this statement? Consider the question of interest rate policy relating to the appropriate mix of floating rate and fixed rate debt obligations. If the history of stock price action, or (for the moment) some other appropriate analysis of investor preference, has shown that the shareholders of a corporation desire, or are willing to accept, a risk or volatility reflected by a standard deviation of stock price returns of say, 14 percent, then the correct proportion of fixed to floating rate debt would be that which has historically shown a volatility of 14 percent. Effectively, it is assumed that the cost implied by the adoption of such an interest rate policy would be acceptable to shareholders.

Consider the area of translation exposure or future foreign earnings exposure. The leading question relates to the proportion of total foreign exposure that should be hedged. If a hedge ratio of, say, 70 percent of total exposure would have in the past resulted in a volatility or risk measured by a standard deviation of 14 percent, equivalent to that deemed acceptable to shareholders, then that 70 percent ratio is in fact the appropriate policy parameter. The hedging costs implied by the adoption of such a 70-30 ratio would implicitly be those acceptable to shareholders. In a similar fashion, the appropriate hedging policy for commodity exposure management could be identified; the same analysis could be applied to find the appropriate ratio of hedged and unhedged commodity exposures that should be adopted by the corporation.

A more sophisticated application, using certain assumptions, could assist in finding the proper mix of proxy currencies used to hedge foreign earnings and translation exposure, and to identify the appropriate duration of hedge instruments and the time horizon over which protection should be maintained. In selecting these parameters, the tenets of portfolio theory would be closely followed and an efficient frontier of hedge strategies would be identified, as shown in Exhibit 3. (Note that this diagram is the same as that in Exhibit 2, except that the y axis shows negative expected return, i.e., expected hedging costs, plotted against standard deviation along the x axis.) If a given hedge strategy involved the same risk as other strategies but at lower expected cost, then it would be selected over these. This is shown in

EXHIBIT 3

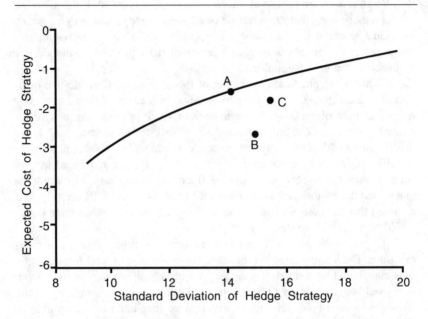

Exhibit 3, where hedging structure A located on the efficient frontier EF is clearly preferable to strategies B and C. In general, only efficient hedge strategies, i.e., mean-variance efficient structures would be employed.

Restricting the selection of hedge strategies to those located on the efficient frontier provides an initial decision rule to assist in setting exposure management policy. For example, if a corporation that has historically employed a 70-30 fixed-floating rate debt strategy were to find that a 60-40 ratio resulted in either lower risk at the same cost, the same risk at lower cost, or lower risk at lower cost, then the corporation could legitimately change its policy in the interest of its shareholders. If this rationale were applied to different areas of exposure management, the corporation would employ only those hedging policies that were found to be mean-variance efficient, i.e., found to lie along the efficient frontier.

SERVING DIFFERENT MASTERS

Difficult and provocative questions arise, however, when one attempts to choose between strategies located *along* the frontier. In theory, the appropri-

EXHIBIT 4

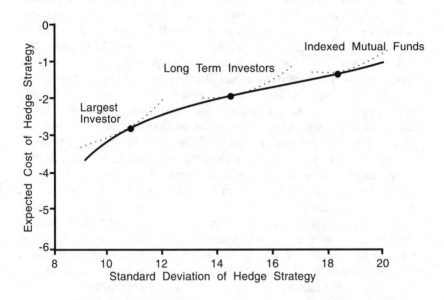

ate policy would be found at the point of tangency between the collective indifference curves of the corporation's shareholders and the efficient frontier, as described earlier. However, it is not easy to define a collective indifference curve for all shareholders, since different investors possess varying risk-reward preferences. Exhibit 4 shows theoretical equilibrium points for different groups of investors. Which of these alternative policies should the corporation choose? Or, to put it another way, which group of investors is the one whose interests the management of the corporation may legitimately serve?

The question of identifying correctly those shareholders who represent the most important beneficiaries of the corporation is a difficult one to answer. The management of a company may judge that the interests of its largest shareholder(s) legitimately represent the higher priorities for the setting of policy. Communication with these shareholders to ascertain their objectives and preferences may then provide a useful guide to corporate policy, including exposure management policy; this is particularly true if these shareholders are of an institutional nature and are able to clearly articulate their aims. Alternatively, corporations may find it appropriate to respond to the objectives of their longer-term investors, choosing policies that sacrifice short-term gains and accept a higher degree of more immediate risk in exchange for successful long-term performance. Or again, a corporation may choose to prioritize the interests of a broad band of investors, whose preferences and objectives are reflected directly by the behavior of a wide equity market index; in this case, the company may adopt policies that embody the same degree of risk or volatility as that displayed by the index over time.

There are other means by which a corporation may seek to identify appropriate exposure management policies. These center around the issue of information—the accuracy of information disseminated by the corporation about its activities and policies and the information relating to preferences implicitly or explicitly disclosed by shareholders. For example, consider that a corporation with heavy involvement in energy and related activities would constitute a stock judged by investors to be an energy sector investment. To the extent that these shareholders expect risk (and returns) consistent with energy stock price movements, the corporation may adopt hedging policies with the same degree of volatility as that displayed by an energy sector index. If the corporation concerned is a conglomerate with diversified operations, it might be possible for its management to adopt a risk profile comparable to that displayed by a competitor with a similar portfolio of businesses.

Alternatively, the company may choose to maintain the degree of volatility that its own stock return has experienced in the recent past, or perhaps during periods of outstanding performance or wide share ownership. In such instances, the corporation is effectively seeking to align itself with the preferences revealed by existing and potential investors through price action in the markets.

A more direct approach may involve publicizing the corporation's exposure management policies: Management may reveal in investor briefings and press releases that the corporation intends to conduct hedging policies so as to maintain, for example, an earnings profile that responds favorably to dollar declines in foreign exchange markets, interest rate declines in the domestic economy, upward trends in certain commodity price levels, etc. If this idea seems peculiar, it is worth noting that these are essentially the same informational parameters that professional investment managers are obliged to provide to their (large) investors; whether communicated in quantitative or qualitative terms and whatever the degree of freedom allowed to the manager in deviating from such stated policies, these investment guidelines are invariably sketched for investors in some detail. In practice, however, few corporations provide such specific information, relying instead on investor efforts and experience allied with stock analysts' findings to adequately inform their shareholders.

The crux of these arguments then is that the choice of hedging strategy need not be overly concerned with issues like "beating the market," seeking to identify and eliminate as much exposure as possible, adopting complex hybrid strategies that provide an implicit play on future market direction, attempting to optimally time the execution and raising of hedges, or analyzing in retrospect the wisdom of loss-making hedge strategies. Emphasis should be placed instead on the objectives of defining shareholders' risk tolerance and return expectations, communicating the true profile of the corporation's operations (including hedging strategies), and formulating exposure management policies so as to align the institution's performance profile with shareholder expectations.

IMPLEMENTING AN "INVESTOR-FRIENDLY" POLICY

The specifics of the process described above may now be made clearer.

1. The corporation should identify the prevalent perceptions of its investor community about the risk level of its stock price. This may be done through recognizing the relevant group(s) of shareholders whom the corporation feels legitimately represent its priority ownership, and by acknowledging the expectations, objectives, and preferences of these groups. Alternatively, the corporation may choose to examine the impressions relating to its image among investors in general, namely, the perceptions concerning the primary industrial sector(s) in which it operates, the extent to which it is viewed as an institution with interests geared to world markets, the prevailing opinions held by existing and potential investors as to the sensitivity of its costs and revenues to changing conditions in interest rate, foreign exchange, and commodity markets, etc. Various sources for such information exist, including stock analyst opinions, shareholder discussions, published stock betas, inclusion in certain market indices, and so on.

2. Following step 1, the corporation will be in a position to identify the degree of risk or volatility that the external investor world associates with its stock price. A specific risk level or a risk band may then be

assigned as a target exposure volatility which senior management should seek to maintain.

3. This target volatility or risk may then be used to derive investor-appropriate exposure management policies. The corporation would examine its interest rate, foreign exchange, and commodity hedging strategies to determine what mix of the exposure management policies employed in each area would achieve as a whole the required target risk level. To achieve this, mathematical optimization techniques utilizing historical data relating to interest rate, foreign exchange, and commodity price volatilities and correlations over an appropriate period in the past would be employed. Ideally, each functional exposure area would not be analyzed in isolation. Instead, due attention would be given to the interaction, or correlation, between rates and prices in the three markets.

For example, the optimization would take note of the manner in which a particular foreign currency interest rate has fluctuated with the exchange rate of that currency against the base currency, or the tendency of a certain commodity price to move in line with a particular currency exchange rate. The result would be an efficient frontier of hedge policies, each embodying a different combination of interest rate, foreign exchange, and commodity management policies. This would illustrate the different levels of risk and return that would have been achieved in the past through different combinations of hedging strategies.

An example of this output is provided in Table 1 and graphed in Exhibit 5 on pages 214 and 215. Note that strategies D and F do not lie on the efficient frontier in Exhibit 5, implying that they are not viable candidates. The strategies A, B, C, E, G, H, and I are mean-variance efficient and represent legitimate choices, depending on which level of risk is considered suitable. Note further that the example assumes a hedge horizon of five years for all strategies; this is adopted for simplicity. In practice, the period of the hedge strategy could itself be optimized in a similar manner, although this may involve some data constraints.

In this example, if the corporation wished to maintain a risk level equivalent to a standard deviation of 14 percent, it would adopt strategy E as shown in the table, implying a hedging cost of 2.75 percent per annum. This would involve an optimal exposure management policy that hedged 43 percent of translation exposure and 63 percent of foreign earnings exposure over the five-year hedging horizon; the corresponding interest rate policy adopted would require that 60 percent of the corporation's debt be carried on a fixed interest rate basis, and 43 percent of commodity exposures would be covered.

THEORETICAL AND PRACTICAL PROBLEMS

The rationale proposed does present certain problems, both from a theoretical and an implementational point of view.

1. Firstly, the methodology described ignores the volatility arising directly from the mainstream activities of the corporation, i.e., the volatility of costs and revenues, both domestic and overseas, relating to the everyday business of the institution. Consequently, all correlations between these excluded cash flows and the market rates and prices included in the analysis are omitted. While this exclusion is less than satisfactory, it is justifiable owing to the near impossibility of accurately estimating these volatilities and correlations.[3]

2. No consideration is given to the possible "feedback" effect of an optimal exposure management policy on the behavior of the stock price itself. It is conceivable that such an effect may cause an undesirable shift in the risk-return profile of the stock. While the magnitude of any possible shift is impossible to estimate in advance, the corporation may be able to avert sharp variations in stock price behavior by avoiding sudden changes in its current exposure management policy. A good indicator for monitoring alterations in stock price action is the beta value, a measure of the correlation between the stock price movements and changes in an equity market index, such as the S&P 500.

3. No mention has been made of the period over which market volatilities should be measured for inclusion in the optimization. This period should be lengthy enough to cover different trends in market

---

3. The same problem arises in the area of portfolio management. Fund managers who hold investment portfolios of foreign equities, bonds, and other overseas assets often tend to make their initial investment decisions based solely on foreign currency-denominated returns and risks; subsequently, they implement foreign exchange hedges as an overlay strategy, usually employing optimization criteria. In doing this, they implicitly ignore the correlations between foreign currency-denominated asset returns and exchange rate movements. This is identical to the approach described above.

TABLE 1   **Hedging Strategies for Exhibit 5**

| Hedging Strategies | Foreign Exchange | | Interest Rate | Commodity Exposure | Expected Hedging Costs per Annum | Standard Deviation of Hedging Policy |
	Translation Exposure	Foreign Earnings Exposure	Percentage of Total Debt	Percentage of Total Hedged		
Strategy A	35% hedged	93% hedged	92% Fixed	56%	-4.50%	9.15
Strategy B	39% hedged	85% hedged	84% Fixed	67%	-3.70%	11.20
Strategy C	38% hedged	70% hedged	71% Fixed	55%	-3.30%	12.50
Strategy D	50% hedged	54% hedged	76% Fixed	58%	-4.28%	13.20
Strategy E	43% hedged	63% hedged	60% Fixed	43%	-2.75%	14.01
Strategy F	49% hedged	61% hedged	51% Fixed	41%	-3.60%	14.86
Strategy G	59% hedged	48% hedged	42% Fixed	32%	-2.33%	15.75
Strategy H	63% hedged	39% hedged	49% Fixed	25%	-2.18%	17.03
Strategy I	72% hedged	28% hedged	59% Fixed	29%	-2.10%	18.05

EXHIBIT 5

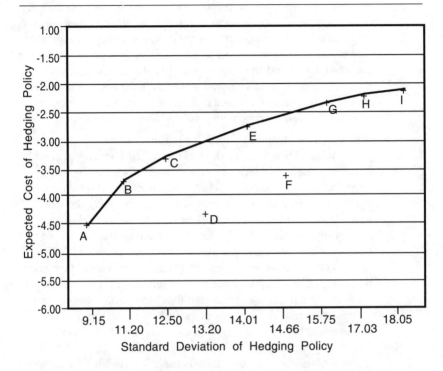

magnitudes, but not so long as to reflect institutional structures and circumstances no longer prevailing. In general, a period in the recent past covering three to five years would be considered appropriate for this analysis.[4]

4. Another important question relates to the frequency of adjustments made to hedging policy in response to subsequent optimizations car-

---

4. A related problem involves the degree of confidence that should be placed on the stability of volatilities and correlations over time. The implicit assumption made is that future volatilities in market rates and prices will continue to resemble those observed in the period from which optimization data are drawn. Or, to put it another way, it is assumed that the period over which market volatilities are measured is sufficiently representative of the future period in which optimization results are to be applied.

ried out. The initial optimization will be based on the original profile of exposure carried by the corporation; as these exposures change, new optimizations will have to be run in order to adjust hedging policy. A monthly re-examination of the exposure policy through regular optimization would appear to be sufficient. It is important for the corporation to avoid frequent changes in policy since these may prove to be expensive: Transactional costs in the form of bid-offer spreads may be excessive, and undesirable cash outflows may result from the frequent raising of loss-making hedge strategies.

5. A potential problem may arise if the optimal exposure management policy selected results in a risk level for the stock incongruent with its current return. If the risk level is "correctly" chosen by management, but appears too high in relation to the expected return (implying that the corporation is in some sense underhedged), the return will rise through a fall in the stock price, other things being equal. Conversely, if the risk level is too low, resulting in an excessive stock return in relation to the risk involved, the return will fall through an appreciation in the stock price. In both cases, the market will ensure that the appropriate level of return is achieved, although some changes in the composition of the corporation's shareholder group may result. The price assumption here is that the corporation's management has made a correct identification of the level of risk that may be legitimately associated with the stock. Given the correctness of this assumption, modest changes in shareholder composition should be regarded as acceptable.

6. The most basic issue involved in this approach, however, relates to the separate entityhood of the corporation and the separation of management and ownership that the corporate structure provides. Senior management thinking and action may sometimes be unrelated to the direct interests of shareholders. This may be evidenced not merely in the relatively straightforward situation where management and shareholder interests are directly opposed, but also in the case where management views itself as a better judge of what is beneficial to the corporation (and therefore its shareholders) than the shareholders themselves.

For example, consider the situation where the pursuance of an investor-appropriate exposure management policy as dictated by an analysis such as that described above is likely to lead to performance problems for the corporation over a period of time. Management may judge that the shareholders are somehow incorrect in requiring (through their implicit or explicit preferences) that such a policy be followed, and may consequently ignore the preferences of these shareholders by adopting an alternative policy. This may ultimately lead some of the corporation's shareholders to either mandate a change in senior management or to sell their stock holdings in the company and invest the proceeds elsewhere; the latter alternative seems to imply that management may be able to direct its shareholder composition towards the kind of investors it deems appropriate.

It is difficult to judge if the corporation's management is acting legitimately in taking such actions. Clearly, however, this issue arises in other areas of corporate policy, including, for example, the decision to diversify operations, divest business segments, reduce or augment dividends, undertake large capital expenditures, etc. Perhaps the best thing to say is that if one accepts some role for senior management in guiding and interpreting shareholder intentions in the light of the former's better-informed position, it is permissible to allow some degree of latitude to management in applying and fine-tuning exposure management and other policies, subject to the broad consensus of shareholders.

APPLICATION OF THESE TECHNIQUES BY CORPORATIONS TODAY

This chapter has argued for an application of portfolio theory and practice to the area of exposure management. Such an application provides a solution to current controversies regarding exposure management policy, or at least a clearer perspective of the role and scope of hedging activities, as described earlier. The question arises as to what extent such theory is actually being utilized by corporations today.

In many institutions, the functions of treasury exposure management and pension fund management are getting closer. This collaboration has been encouraged by the increased use of derivatives and other hedging instruments by pension fund managers and the realization that both functions utilize the same markets and counterparties. The similarity between treasury departments engaged in the hedging of translation and foreign earnings exposure arising from overseas operations and pension fund managers covering similar exposure from foreign bond and equity portfolios has not gone unnoticed.

Exchange of ideas and personnel resources has also facilitated greater cooperation. This interaction has resulted both in attempts to apply the tenets of portfolio theory to exposure management as well as efforts to transplant techniques used in exposure management to pension fund activities.

Several commercial and investment banks now offer optimization techniques and advisory services supporting the application of portfolio theory to their corporate treasury customers. Some of these are comprised purely of optimization methods applied to different exposures faced by the corporation, aimed at identifying the efficient frontier of hedging strategies as a menu for treasury decisions to focus upon. Others include quantitative and qualitative (even judgmental) techniques that embody directional forecasts for market magnitudes. Treasury departments are free to incorporate these techniques into their exposure management methodology, or even to mandate the advising financial institution to execute and manage the chosen hedge strategy (this is identical to the portfolio manager's decision to employ a specialized overlay manager, as described in footnote 3).

Corporate treasuries are notoriously secretive about their hedging strategies. However, it would appear that several large corporations are now experimenting with optimization methods drawn directly from classic portfolio theory. At a minimum, these institutions may be utilizing the methodology to determine the position of their current strategies in mean-standard deviation space, and perhaps to adjust these policies so as to achieve efficient frontier positions. Beyond this, it may be surmised that some corporations are employing these techniques to justify altering their positions along the frontier, with the objective of changing the cost-risk trade-off between alternative strategies. As for the rationale utilized by corporations to determine which of the optimal exposure management policies to adopt, it is only possible to speculate, but it is more than likely that considerations such as those described above are receiving serious attention.

8

Interest Rate Risk Management: The Risk Point Method

Ravi E. Dattatreya
Senior Vice President, Sumitomo Bank Capital Markets, Inc.

Raj S. Pundarika
Debt and Derivatives Marketer, Paribas Capital Markets

SUMMARY

Interest rate risk management is a major component of any comprehensive risk management program.[1] *Duration* is a popular tool employed by sophisticated users for interest rate risk measurement. By effectively using it, an institution can all but eliminate basic market risk, which is no longer a major concern. Among the other types of interest rate risk, we focus on *yield curve risk,* which has attained importance recently. To model yield curve risk, we use a form of price sensitivity relative to a specific hedge instrument. This number, called the *risk point,* helps us use a variety of hedge instruments to better handle yield curve risk.

It is appropriate to look at the risk point concept as a more complete description of risk than just as a way to handle yield curve risk. This view is supported by the fact that the risk point method is useful in several situations. It can accurately highlight yield curve risk in an asset/liability context. In portfolio management, it can help us evaluate bond swap opportunities more precisely. In structured investment, it can help replicate portfolios in indexing applications and in developing efficient benchmarks. It can provide a superior

1. We thank E. Sundar Panduranga of UBS Securities for help in building certain models and examples. We also thank Joe Brennan and John Fox of Sumitomo Bank Capital Markets for their helpful comments.

selection of bonds in dedicated portfolios. It can help create more robust immunization strategies. It leads to more accurate hedge design in trading. Finally, it also provides more insight into the current crop of exotic investments.

We recommend that the risk point method be used as an integral part of a comprehensive risk management program.

INTRODUCTION

Institutions, i.e., investors as lenders and corporations as borrowers, assume various types of financial risk. These include liquidity risk, credit risk, currency and interest rate risk, and option or convexity risk. In this chapter we will focus on interest rate risk. In addition, we will show how the concepts developed apply to many other types of risks as well.

It is important to view interest rate risk as an integral part of a comprehensive risk management program.[2] Risk management can be defined as a systematic approach that attempts to provide a degree of protection to the institution from risk and makes such risk acceptable. Any complete interest rate risk management program, therefore, should provide the necessary framework for the implementation of the 4 Ms of risk management: measurement, monitoring, modification, and management.

> *Measurement* defines exactly what types of risks will be managed under the program. For each risk, the appropriate risk measures and acceptable procedures for measurement are defined.

> *Monitoring* sets forth the mechanics of locating which parts of the institution are sources of different forms and quantities of risk and the frequency with which these risks will be measured and reviewed. It puts in place the necessary systems and procedures to ensure that the information can be and is obtained when desired.

> *Modification* provides the risk manager with the tools necessary to modify any particular risk to desired levels. For example, here is where we determine whether futures or swaps are appropriate instruments for the institution and the limits on quantities and purposes for which these will be used. In actual use, optimization by the risk manager, i.e., selection of tools and quantity, is also done here.

---

2. Risk management is known as Asset Liability Management (ALM) in many contexts.

Management is the collection of policies and procedures for the exercise of the other three Ms. Here we define the upper and lower[3] bounds for each risk category as well as the conditions under which an action will be required to initiate the modification step. In addition to routine policy, this part of risk management includes some emergency powers for the risk manager and guidelines as to how and when these powers can be used. As an example, the emergency powers could include relaxation of the limits on the tools or amounts that can be employed.

In a way, we can compare risk management to a form of insurance. It can shield the institution from risk where its assumption is necessary. For example, in the absence of automobile insurance, we would probably find the risks of driving a car unacceptable. It is insurance that makes it possible for us to drive. The main function of risk management is similar: It is to enable the institution to be in business, that is, to assume the necessary risks. For example, it facilitates a bank to make long-term loans that are in demand regardless of whether long-term funding for the loan is available, by providing acceptable techniques to hedge the resultant interest rate risk. It enables a multinational corporation to engage in business overseas, shielding the firm from changes in exchange rates. In general, the more leveraged an institution, the more critical risk management is to that institution. This is because its net worth then is a small fraction of the size of its assets, and even modest market moves can result in wide swings in the net worth. Risk management is therefore simply the process of preservation of net worth.

The function of risk management is not just protection from risk. The safety achieved through it also opens up opportunities for enhancing the net worth. An effective risk management program can make it possible for an

---

3. The goal of risk management is not risk elimination. Lower bounds for risk are required as risk and reward are interrelated. In most cases, risk cannot be eliminated, only transformed, anyway. This fact was realized best by corporations that issued (or converted via interest rate swaps to) fixed rate debt just before the long rally in the bond market in the early 1990s. Even though these corporations had fixed rate debt, which is considered a no-risk situation in most cases, they soon realized the risk in fixing as the market rates plummeted and they found themselves paying higher-than-market coupons on their debt or on interest rate swaps. One way to look at this situation is to consider both fixed rate and floating rate as risky: the former when rates fall, and the latter when rates rise. For more discussion of this topic, see Ravi E. Dattatreya, Raj E. Venkatesh, and Vijaya E. Venkatesh, *Interest Rate and Currency Swaps,* Probus Publishing, Chicago, 1994.

institution to take on positions that would have been considered too large or too risky in the absence of the protection offered by risk management. Such a program can also enable an institution to enter into new business areas as the demands of the marketplace change and grow. In many cases these businesses would have been beyond the reach of the institution without the comfort of the insurance provided by risk management.

Every manager has two fundamental priorities. The first priority is to protect and preserve the existing business or investment and provide damage control.[4] The second priority is to enhance the returns, strengthen the business, and enrich the institution. Risk management, as discussed above, can be a vital ally to the manager in fulfilling these two needs.

There are several types of financial risk. These include interest rate risk, currency risk, credit risk, liquidity risk, and option or convexity risk. Among these, some risks, e.g., interest rate risk and option risk, fall neatly within the risk management framework, mainly because it is possible to quantify the risks easily and appropriate hedging vehicles are available. Any acceptable risk management policy will also help measure and monitor liquidity risk and provide suitable strategies for its management. Other risks are more complex to manage. Consider credit risk. It is difficult to manage it in the traditional sense. It is best controlled by limiting it before it is assumed.

The focus of our attention in this chapter will be the quantifiable risks, interest rate risk in particular. As a consequence, we will be dealing mainly with risks associated with fixed income assets and liabilities.

MEASURES OF INTEREST RATE RISK

As a first step in developing a framework for risk management, we have to define interest rate risk and determine an acceptable way to measure it. Let us briefly review the basic definitions.

Interest Rate Risk[5]

We measure interest rate risk by considering *price sensitivity*, that is, the change in the value of an asset or liability cash flow in response to a change in interest rates. More precisely, price sensitivity is expressed as the dollar

---

4. Damage control is where emergency powers are used most often by the risk manager.
5. For a thorough discussion of interest rate risk measures and convexity, see Ravi E. Dattatreya and Frank J. Fabozzi, *Fixed Income Total Return Management*, 2nd Ed., Probus Publishing, Chicago, 1994.

change (or, some times, a percentage change) in value for a unit change in interest rates. This unit is most often one basis point or 100 basis points.

Different fixed income instruments have different levels of interest rate risk. Various risk measures are available, each with its own advantages and problems.

Maturity

The term to maturity is an indicator of interest rate risk. Longer maturity bonds usually move more in price than shorter maturity bonds. However, this ordering does not always hold. Maturity takes into account only the timing of the final principal flow in a fixed rate bond, and ignores other important information such as the size and timing of other cash flows. The actual interest rate sensitivity depends upon these factors and therefore, maturity, though sometimes useful, is only an approximate indicator of risk. Maturity is also not a cardinal measure, that is, it does not *quantify* risk.

Duration

It is possible to blend information contained in the size and timing of all cash flows into one number, called *duration*, that can be a more useful measure of risk. Duration is the weighted average time of all of the cash flows, the weights being the present values of the cash flows. For bonds with only one cash flow, e.g., zero coupon bonds and money market instruments, duration is equal to maturity. For others, duration will be shorter than maturity.

It turns out that by slightly adjusting duration by dividing by a factor $(1 + Y)$ where Y is the annual yield to maturity of the bond in decimal form, we get *modified duration* which is exactly equal to the price sensitivity of the bond as we have defined above. Since the adjustment factor is very close to one, duration and modified duration can be used interchangeably in most situations. This is also justified because duration is an approximate measure anyway. By this reasoning, we diligently avoid the common temptation to dwell on the (inconsequential) difference between the two durations.

We can also think of duration of a security as the maturity of a zero coupon bond of equal price sensitivity.[6] This definition is a more general one

---

6. We choose zero coupon bonds for this comparison since these bonds, unlike coupon-bearing bonds, can have durations of arbitrary magnitude. In other words, there is a limit on how large the duration of a coupon bond can be; zero coupon bonds have no such limit.

in that it can be used with more complex securities such as options and with leveraged positions. For example, if the duration of an option is 150, it simply means that the price sensitivity of the option is equal to that of a zero coupon bond of maturity equal to 150 years. Some instruments (e.g., options) can have negative duration, which can be represented by short positions in zero coupon bonds.

Dollar Duration

Duration represents the *percentage* change in value in response to a change in rates. By weighting duration by the value of a holding, that is, by multiplying the market value of a holding by its duration (expressed as a decimal percentage), we get dollar-weighted duration. Known as *dollar duration*, this number represents the actual dollar change in the market value of a holding in a bond in response to a 100 basis point change in rates. When expressed as a dollar change per one basis point move in rates, dollar duration is sometimes called the *price value of a basis point*, or *PVBP*. Other than the factor of 100, there is little difference between dollar duration and PVBP.

The major advantage of using dollar duration is that it is additive. The concept, therefore, extends easily from individual securities to portfolios. The dollar duration of a portfolio is simply the (algebraic) sum of the dollar durations of the individual holdings.

Convexity

Duration (or dollar duration) is not a constant. It changes as a result of changes in market rates and because of the passage of time. For simple fixed coupon bonds, the dollar duration increases when the rates fall. That is, as the market rallies (i.e., as rates fall), for each successive basis point move down, the bond price increases at an increasing rate. Similarly, if rates increase and the market declines, the rate of decline slows down as the rates rise. This property is called *convexity*. It is a desirable property in an asset since the price sensitivity changes in a way beneficial to the holder of the asset.

There are certain securities with option-like features such as callable corporate bonds and mortgage backed securities[7] that show a contrary behavior: Their duration can fall in rallying markets and increase in falling markets.

---

7. Most of the exotic securities in the current crop have negative convexity. To compensate the investor for this, they offer attractive, relatively higher current yields.

This property, called *negative convexity*, is not a desirable property in an asset, unless suitably compensated, as the price sensitivity moves in a way not beneficial to the holder.

In most situations, convexity is a second order effect, that is, its influence on the price behavior of a bond is small compared to that of duration. However, for large moves in market rates, for highly leveraged positions, and where option-like features are involved, convexity can be important.

YIELD CURVE RISK

Several years of use of the duration concept has imparted the ability to most financial institutions to all but eliminate market risk via prudent hedging activities. As a result of this, other residual risks have gained prominence. Some of these risks can be dominant in many situations; among them, the most important is *yield curve risk*, which deserves a detailed treatment. In particular, yield curve risk can be significant in portfolios containing options, some mortgage derivative, and most exotic securities.

As usually stated, duration of a fixed income asset (or liability) is the price sensitivity relative to its own yield. Therefore, when we use duration for hedging purposes, we are implicitly assuming that the yield levels of the various assets and liabilities move in parallel, that is, in equal amounts. In fact, however, different credit, coupon, or maturity sectors of the market move differently in terms of their yield. This difference is known as the *basis risk* among the sectors. Basis risk with respect to different maturity sectors is also known as *yield curve risk* and represents changes in the yield curve that are not parallel shifts. These include the so-called reshaping shifts, e.g., twists, pivoting moves, steepening, and flattening.

In general, basis risk is difficult to measure and hedge.[8] Most hedging vehicles address market risk,[9] e.g., changes in the Treasury rates, not basis risk. It is possible to take the view that only market risk is hedgeable and treat

---

8. Actually, in practice, basis risk refers to any risk that is not hedgeable or is not hedged. If a risk can be quantified and acceptably managed, e.g., yield curve risk in our case, then that risk is no longer a part of the generic basis risk.
9. This makes sense because a hedging instrument, in order to ensure its wide usage, should represent the broad market rather than a specific security or too narrow a sector. Otherwise, it would suffer a severe lack of liquidity, and the cost of hedging would be unacceptably high.

basis risk as a prudent business risk that an institution has to take. This is the only approach in dealing with certain types of basis risk, e.g., credit risk.[10]

A risk measure can be considered more complete compared to a simple measure such as duration if we can incorporate some of the important basis risks. Fortunately, it is possible to address yield curve risk in many acceptable ways. By necessity, such a broader risk measure will be more than just one number.

One method is to divide assets and liabilities into smaller maturity baskets and analyze each basket separately. If each basket covers a sufficiently small maturity range, then we can assume that the yield curve risk is acceptably small within that range. In a hedging application, we would use hedging instruments suitable for that maturity range to match dollar durations. In an asset/liability context, if each basket or sector is matched, using appropriate hedges as required, then the assets and liabilities are matched as a whole because of the additive property of dollar duration. To the extent that the yields of all assets and liabilities as well as the hedging instruments used within a sector move in step, this approach is satisfactory.

There is a problem, however. It turns out that an asset of a given maturity might react to changes in rates in another maturity. Consider, for example, a 10-year bond with a coupon of 10 percent. The cash flow from this bond occurs every six months throughout its life. Since the value of a bond is simply the sum of the present values of the individual cash flows, it stands to reason that the value of the 10-year bond could be influenced by rate changes not just in the 10-year maturity but also in all shorter maturities representing the cash flows.

In this context, it is appropriate to clarify what we mean by a "rate." In fixed income analysis, we use two types of reference interest rates: full coupon rates and spot or zero-coupon rates. Full coupon rates are analogous to the yield to maturity on bonds trading at or close to par, e.g., the yield on an on-the-run (current coupon) Treasury. The spot rate for a given maturity, on the other hand, is the yield on a zero coupon bond with that maturity. When dealing with individual cash flows, e.g., for discounting, it is appropriate to use spot rates; when dealing with bonds trading near par, full coupon rate can be used.

Since a bond is just a collection of cash flows, its yield is a complex blend of the individual spot rates corresponding to the coupon and principal

---

10. Recently, however, derivative instruments for managing certain types of credit risk are being developed.

flows. Given the spot rate curve, we can easily determine the coupon yield curve. Conversely, a given spot rate is a complex blend of all shorter-maturity coupon rates. Given the coupon rate curve, we can determine the spot rate curve. In summary, a given spot rate depends upon all intermediate coupon rates; a given coupon rate depends upon all intermediate spot rates.

The value of a 10-year par bond, then, responds to all intermediate spot rates, but depends only on the 10-year coupon rate. Thus, to hedge a 10-year par bond, all that we need is another 10-year bond, e.g., the current 10-year Treasury. If we wish to use zero coupon bonds for hedging, then a 10-year zero coupon bond and smaller amounts of all intermediate maturity zero coupon bonds will be required for hedging. Similarly, a single cash flow occurring in the tenth year can be efficiently hedged by a 10-year zero coupon bond. On the other hand, if we wish to use current coupon Treasuries for hedging, then, in addition to the 10-year Treasury, we will also need shorter maturity Treasuries.

If the bond we are hedging is not priced at par, then it behaves like the combination of a 10-year full coupon and a 10-year zero coupon bond. For example, a $100 million holding of a 9 percent bond selling at 90 can be viewed as the sum of $90 million of a 10 percent par bond and $10 million of a zero coupon bond.[11] Thus the sensitivity of the 10-year discount bond is the sum of that of each of its components. The hedge for a bond not near par, therefore, is a blend of the hedges for a zero and that for a full coupon bond.[12]

In summary, then, an asset (or a liability) of a given maturity might respond to spot or coupon rate changes in other shorter maturities. Therefore, we need to do more than simply group the assets and liabilities in maturity sectors.

One way to handle this problem is to first break down each asset and liability into its cash flow components. Then the individual cash flows can be grouped into maturity buckets. Now, the price sensitivity of each sector is more clearly defined, at least with respect to spot rates corresponding to each sector.

The cash-flow approach provides very valuable insight into the relative natures of the assets and the liabilities. However, it represents risk in terms of

---

11. In both cases, there is an annual cash flow of $9 million and a payment at maturity of $100 million.

12. Similarly, a 10-year premium bond can be decomposed into a slightly larger amount of a par bond and a short position on the zero coupon bond.

spot rate, that is, in terms of zero coupon bonds, which are rarely used for hedging. A more sophisticated approach is the *risk point method*, discussed below.[13]

TOWARD A MORE COMPLETE RISK MEASURE: THE RISK POINT CONCEPT

Since risk is a measure of change in value, it stands to reason that risk management and security valuation ought to be closely related. Therefore, it is advantageous to use a model that integrates these two aspects. The risk point method attempts such integration. It also has the practical advantage that it measures risk relative to available hedging instruments.

We define the *risk point* of a security or portfolio with reference to a specific hedge instrument. For this reason, it can also be called *relative dollar duration*.[14] It represents the change in the value of the security or portfolio due to a one basis point change in the yield of the hedge. If we divide the risk point by the dollar duration or PVBP of the hedge, we get the dollar amount of the hedge instrument to be used as a hedge. This hedge amount will protect

---

13. Other approaches are available in literature. See for example: Chambers, D., and W. Carleton, "A Generalized Approach to Duration," in *Research in Finance,* Volume 7, JAI Press, Greenwich, CT, 1988; Thomas S. Y. Ho, "Key Rate Durations: Measures of Interest Rate Risks," *J. of Fixed Income,* September 1992; Khang, C., "Bond Immunization When Short-term Rates Fluctuate More Than Long-term Rates," *J. Financial and Quantitative Analysis,* 14 (1979), pp. 1085-1090; Litterman, R., and J. Scheinkman, "Common Factors Affecting Bond Returns," *J. Fixed Income,* June 1991, pp. 54-61; Reitano, Robert, "Non-Parallel Yield Curve Shifts and Durational Leverage," *J. Portfolio Management,* Summer 1990, pp. 62–67.

The discussion of the risk point concept here builds on the work reported in [1] Ravi E. Dattatreya, "A Practical Approach to Asset Liability Management," Sumitomo Bank Capital Markets Report, 1989; [2] Ravi E. Dattatreya, "A Practical Approach to Asset Liability Management," in F. Fabozzi and Atsuo Konishi, *Asset Liability Management,* Probus Publishing, Chicago, 1991; and [3] Ravi E. Dattatreya, Raj E. Venkatesh and Vijaya E. Venkatesh, *Interest Rate and Currency Swaps,* Probus Publishing, Chicago, 1994. See also: Ravi E. Dattatreya and Frank Fabozzi, *Fixed Income Active Total Return Management,* Rev. Ed., Probus Publishing, Chicago, 1994; and Ravi E. Dattatreya and Scott Peng, *Structured Notes,* Probus Publishing, Chicago, 1994.
14. We prefer, however, the former terminology. In the context of modern financial markets, the temporal meaning of duration is no longer relevant.

---

the portfolio against risk from small changes in the market sector represented by the hedge instrument.[15]

Unlike PVBP or dollar duration, which measures the *total* interest rate risk, the risk point measures only one component of the total risk. This component represents the risk due to a change in rates in a given maturity sector. Thus, to determine a complete risk or hedge, we need a full set of risk points, relative to a set of hedge instruments. From this set of risk points we can determine the portfolio of hedge instruments that will hedge a given portfolio.

The risk point method consists of three main steps:

- We first list the hedge vehicles that we are willing to use.

- We then apply a model that values the assets and liabilities relative to the prices of the hedge vehicles.

- We change the yield or price of one of the hedge instruments by a small amount, keeping all other yields and prices the same. With the new yield, we revalue the portfolio. The change in its value (expressed as dollars per one basis point[16] change) is the risk point of the portfolio. We get the amount of the hedge instrument needed for hedging by simply equating the PVBP of the hedge to the risk point of the portfolio.[17]

This procedure is explained more fully in the next section.

AN IMPLEMENTATION
OF THE RISK POINT METHOD

The essential part of the risk point method is a model that values the assets and liabilities relative to the hedge instruments chosen. In order to be able to

---

15. In defining the framework for risk measurement, we focus more on hedge instruments than on specific market segments or yield curve sectors. The reason for this is that it is of little use to look at risk for which there is no tool for hedging or management. In addition, there is no loss of generality in our approach because almost all major sectors that are sources of risk are well represented by hedge instruments.
16. One basis point could refer to another appropriate small unit, e.g., 1 tick for Eurodollar futures, 1 percent for volatility in the case of options, etc.
17. It is also possible to express the risk point as a hedge-equivalent, i.e., the actual amount of the hedge required. The vector of risk points, then, would simply be the hedging portfolio. Representation of the risk point as a relative dollar duration has the advantage that alternative hedge instruments can be easily substituted.

deal with a variety of assets and liabilities, the set of hedges chosen must also be broad. An example of a practical implementation of the method follows.

Hedge Instruments

For our example, we include all the current coupon Treasury bonds and notes in the set of hedge instruments that we consider. T-Bills are included to handle cash flows occurring in the short term.

Valuation Model

We will use a simple, but effective, valuation model. The procedure will be to value each financial instrument as the sum of the discounted present values of the cash flows generated by the instrument. We must first determine the *discount function*, i.e., all the discount factors that will be used for this procedure. This is a two-step process.

In the first step, to obtain appropriate spreads to evaluate cash flows from corporate bonds, we include spreads from the interest rate swap market.[18] The composite rate, i.e., the sum of the Treasury yield and the spread, is called the *par bond yield* (see Table 1).[19,20] It represents the yield on par bonds of the credit quality represented by the spreads used. We then use linear interpolation[21] to generate the *par curve*, i.e., par bond yields at all maturities (see Column 3, Table 2).

The second step is to determine the zero curve, or, equivalently, the discount factors, from the par curve. Discount factors can be derived sequentially from the par curve one after another. This process is called *bootstrapping*. This procedure builds the zero curve in a step-by-step or inductive manner.

---

18. By setting the spreads to zero, we can use the results to the Treasury market. Spreads from other markets (e.g., Single-A corporate bonds) can be used if necessary.
19. The Treasury yields and swap spread used are obtained from market data as of 3.00 p.m. New York time on May 9, 1994. Each data point is represented on a semi-annual pay, 30/360 basis. Note that the familiar seven-year Treasury is absent because they are no longer planned to be issued.
20. Alternatively, in the short end, it is possible to use LIBOR to determine the composite rate directly. In this case, care should be taken to ensure that the day count conventions are handled correctly.
21. We could use more sophisticated interpolation. However, linear interpolation gives acceptable results and is used widely in the interest rate swap market.

TABLE 1   The Hedging Instruments with Yields

Maturity (Years)	Treasury Yield	Spread (b.p.)	Total
0.5	4.932	28	5.212
1	5.520	29	5.810
2	6.234	31	6.544
3	6.563	35	6.913
5	7.074	32	7.394
10	7.466	41	7.876

For each maturity, it uses the fact that the price of a bond is the sum of the present values of all the cash flows (coupon and principal) from the bond. It is best illustrated using algebraic notation.

Suppose we have already determined the first n semi-annual discount factors, $f_1, f_2, ..., f_n$. Then the discount factor for the next period, $f_{(n+1)}$, is determined using the following relationship:

$$1 = c \times f_1 + c \times f_2 + ... + c \times f_n + (1 + c) \times f_{(n+1)}$$

where the left-hand side, 1, represents the price of par, c is the semi-annual coupon payment (one-half of the par rate), and $(1 + c)$ represents the final payment with principal and interest for a par bond maturing at the end of the $(n+1)$th period. Each of the factors of the form $(c \times f_1)$ represents the present value of a cash flow. The relationship simply says that the sum of the present values of all cash flows is equal to the price of the bond. The required discount factor, $f_{(n+1)}$, is therefore given by:

$$f_{(n+1)} = \frac{\left[1 - \left(c \times f_1 + c \times f_2 + \cdots + c \times f_n\right)\right]}{(1+c)}$$

Or,

$$f_{(n+1)} = \frac{\left[1 - c \times \left(f_1 + f_2 + \cdots + f_n\right)\right]}{(1+c)}$$

Thus, given the par curve, if we know the first discount factor, we can compute all other discount factors sequentially. The first discount factor is easy to determine since the six-month par rate is also a six-month zero rate since a six-month (semi-annual) bond has just one cash flow.

From the discount factors, it is easy to compute the zero rates. The nth zero rate, z_n, is related to the nth discount factor, f_n, via the relationship:

$$f_n \times \left(1 + \frac{z_n}{2}\right)^n = 1$$

assuming semi-annual compounding. The interpolated par curve (Column 3), the discount function (Column 4), and the zero rates (Column 6) are all shown in Table 2.[22]

Once the discount function or the spot rate curve is known, the value of any security is simply the sum of the present values of its cash flows, discounted at the appropriate spot rate. This is shown in Table 3 for a 10-year bond with a coupon of 10 percent. Each present value (Column 5) is simply the product of the cash flow (Column 4) and the corresponding discount factor (Column 2). The total PV, 114.740102, is the value of the bond.

Determination of Risk Points

To determine the risk point corresponding to a given hedge, the following steps are taken: First, the yield on the hedge instrument is changed by one basis point. Then the spot rates are recomputed using this new price for the particular hedge instrument, keeping the prices (and yields) for all other hedges the same as before. The value of the asset (or liability or portfolio) is now recomputed. The change in the value of the asset due to the change in the yield of the hedge gives us the risk point of the asset relative to that hedge instrument. This procedure is repeated for all hedge instruments in the set of hedges chosen. The risk point relative to a hedge can be used to determine the amount of the hedge to be bought (or sold) to hedge it against changes in the price of that hedge.

To illustrate this procedure, let us increase the yield on the 10-year Treasury from 7.466 percent (from Table 1) by one basis point to 7.476 percent. The composite rate changes from 7.876 percent to 7.886 percent. The new discount functions and zero rates are recomputed as in Table 4 (compare

---

22. The reader can obtain useful insight into the concepts and procedures by actually working out a number of examples. To facilitate this, we have also shown the intermediate values of the cumulative discount factors for ease of computation. In addition, we have provided all the values to several decimal places so that the reader can verify her work.

23. Note that the change in the 10-year rate impacts the discount function and the zero rates only beyond year 5.

TABLE 2   Bootstrapping: Getting the Zero Curve from the Par Curve

Maturity	Par Yields	Interpolated Par Yields	Discount Factor	Cumulative Factor	Zero Rates
0.5	5.212	5.212000	0.974602	0.974602	5.212000
1	5.810	5.810000	0.944257	1.918859	5.818712
1.5		6.177000	0.912552	2.831411	6.194689
2	6.544	6.544000	0.878608	3.710019	6.576629
2.5		6.728500	0.846701	4.556720	6.768333
3	6.913	6.913000	0.814349	5.371069	6.964043
3.5		7.033250	0.783565	6.154633	7.091448
4		7.153500	0.752934	6.907567	7.221785
4.5		7.273750	0.722504	7.630071	7.354956
5	7.394	7.394000	0.692321	8.322392	7.490986
5.5		7.442200	0.665550	8.987942	7.541282
6		7.490400	0.639435	9.627377	7.593429
6.5		7.538600	0.613973	10.241350	7.647266
7		7.586800	0.589156	10.830505	7.702698
7.5		7.635000	0.564977	11.395483	7.759674
8		7.683200	0.541431	11.936914	7.818175
8.5		7.731400	0.518511	12.455425	7.878204
9		7.779600	0.496207	12.951632	7.939786
9.5		7.827800	0.474514	13.426147	8.002961
10	7.876	7.876000	0.453423	13.879569	8.067783

with Table 2[23]). The computation of the new value of the 10 percent bond under study is shown in Table 5 (compare with Table 3). The value of the bond has fallen from 114.740102 to 114.667571, that is, by 0.072531. This number is the change in dollars for every $100 par holding of the bond. This is the risk point for the 10 percent bond relative to the 10-year Treasury.

The risk point is usually computed for a given par holding of a security. In analytical situations where the par holding is hypothetical, it is convenient to express it as dollars per $10,000 par holding.[24] This makes the risk point number roughly comparable to duration or dollar duration. The risk points for

---

24. Change in value for a 1 b.p. move on a $10,000 par holding is equal to 100 times the change in value for a 1 b.p. move on a $100 holding. The latter represents the PVBP or dollar duration.

TABLE 3   Value of a 10%, 10-Year Bond

Maturity	Discount Factor	Zero Rates	Cash Flow	Present Value
0.5	0.974602	5.212000	5.00	4.873009
1.0	0.944257	5.818712	5.00	4.721286
1.5	0.912552	6.194689	5.00	4.562759
2.0	0.878608	6.576629	5.00	4.393041
2.5	0.846701	6.768333	5.00	4.233503
3.0	0.814349	6.964043	5.00	4.071745
3.5	0.783565	7.091448	5.00	3.917823
4.0	0.752934	7.221785	5.00	3.764668
4.5	0.722504	7.354956	5.00	3.612519
5.0	0.692321	7.490986	5.00	3.461606
5.5	0.665550	7.541282	5.00	3.327749
6.0	0.639435	7.593429	5.00	3.197177
6.5	0.613973	7.647266	5.00	3.069864
7.0	0.589156	7.702698	5.00	2.945778
7.5	0.564977	7.759674	5.00	2.824887
8.0	0.541431	7.818175	5.00	2.707157
8.5	0.518511	7.878204	5.00	2.592553
9.0	0.496207	7.939786	5.00	2.481037
9.5	0.474514	8.002961	5.00	2.372570
10.0	0.453423	8.067783	105.00	47.609370
			Total PV:	114.740102

this bond relative to all the other hedges are shown in Table 6 (Column 5) on this basis, i.e., for a $10,000 par holding. Also shown here are a few other results that should be of interest to risk managers. Column 6 shows the fraction (as a percentage) of the total risk represented by any given sector. For example, approximately 95.4 percent of the risk in this bond is in the 10-year sector. Column 6 expresses the risk point as a percentage of the total value of the bond. The numbers in this column are similar to duration. These two columns, along with the risk points themselves, form a more complete picture of the risk in the 10 percent bond under consideration. Exhibit 1 shows a graphical depiction of the risk points. We call the collection of risk points the *risk profile* or the *risk point profile*.

TABLE 4   New Zero Curve After Incrementing 10-Year Yield

Maturity	Par Yields	Interpolated Par Yields	Discount Factor	Cumulative Factor	Zero Rates
0.5	5.212	5.212000	0.974602	0.974602	5.212000
1.0	5.810	5.810000	0.944257	1.918859	5.818712
1.5		6.177000	0.912552	2.831411	6.194689
2.0	6.544	6.544000	0.878608	3.710019	6.576629
2.5		6.728500	0.846701	4.556720	6.768333
3.0	6.913	6.913000	0.814349	5.371069	6.964043
3.5		7.033250	0.783565	6.154633	7.091448
4.0		7.153500	0.752934	6.907567	7.221785
4.5		7.273750	0.722504	7.630071	7.354956
5.0	7.394	7.394000	0.692321	8.322392	7.490986
5.5		7.443200	0.665506	8.987898	7.542511
6.0		7.492400	0.639344	9.627243	7.595897
6.5		7.541600	0.613830	10.241072	7.650990
7.0		7.590800	0.588957	10.830029	7.707698
7.5		7.640000	0.564721	11.394750	7.765973
8.0		7.689200	0.541114	11.935864	7.825799
8.5		7.738400	0.518130	12.453994	7.887182
9.0		7.787600	0.495762	12.949756	7.950151
9.5		7.836800	0.474003	13.423759	8.014749
10.0	7.886	7.886000	0.452845	13.876605	8.081033

PROPERTIES OF RISK POINTS

Table 6 also shows the sum of all the risk points, called the *total risk*.[25] This number, 7.600610, is similar[26] to the PVBP for the bond, as it represents the change in the value of the bond due to a parallel move up of the yield curve by one basis point. If this is expressed as a percentage of total value of the

---

25. Note however, since some risk points can be negative and some positive, the magnitude of total risk does not always indicate the risk level of an instrument. See, for example, the discussion of the CMS note below.

26. Similar, but not exactly equal, since the PVBP computation starts with a flat yield curve.

TABLE 5   Change in the Value of the 10%, 10-Year Bond

Maturity	Discount Factor	Zero Rates	Cash Flow	Present Value
0.5	0.974602	5.212000	5.00	4.873009
1.0	0.944257	5.818712	5.00	4.721286
1.5	0.912552	6.194689	5.00	4.562759
2.0	0.878608	6.576629	5.00	4.393041
2.5	0.846701	6.768333	5.00	4.233503
3.0	0.814349	6.964043	5.00	4.071745
3.5	0.783565	7.091448	5.00	3.917823
4.0	0.752934	7.221785	5.00	3.764668
4.5	0.722504	7.354956	5.00	3.612519
5.0	0.692321	7.490986	5.00	3.461606
5.5	0.665506	7.542511	5.00	3.327532
6.0	0.639344	7.595897	5.00	3.196721
6.5	0.613830	7.650990	5.00	3.069148
7.0	0.588957	7.707698	5.00	2.944785
7.5	0.564721	7.765973	5.00	2.823603
8.0	0.541114	7.825799	5.00	2.705569
8.5	0.518130	7.887182	5.00	2.590650
9.0	0.495762	7.950151	5.00	2.478812
9.5	0.474003	8.014749	5.00	2.370017
10.0	0.452845	8.081033	105.00	47.548774
			New PV	114.667571
			Old PV	114.740102
			Change:	–0.072531

bond (Table 6, Column 7, last row), then we get a number similar to the duration of the bond.

At first blush, it seems as though total risk will increase or decrease based upon the selection of hedge instruments. However, the risk point method is quite robust, and under most conditions handles arbitrary selection of hedge instruments well. For example, let us delete the five-year Treasury from the hedge instrument list and recompute the par curve, zero curve, and the risk points. Table 7 shows the new risk points and total risk. Note how the risk in the seven-year sector has been redistributed between the three-year and the 10-year sectors.

TABLE 6   Risk Points for the 10% Bond

Maturity (Years)	Treasury Yield	Spread (b.p.)	Total	Risk Point	Percent of Total Risk	Percent of Total PV
0.5	4.932	28	5.212	–0.002566	0.033757	–0.002236
1	5.520	29	5.810	–0.009118	0.119968	–0.007947
2	6.234	31	6.544	–0.021308	0.280349	–0.018571
3	6.563	35	6.913	–0.055563	0.731037	–0.048425
5	7.074	32	7.394	–0.258960	3.407101	–0.225693
10	7.466	41	7.876	–7.253094	95.427787	–6.321324
			Totals:	–7.600610	100.000000	–6.624196

The risk points have another interesting property. Consider again the 10 percent coupon, 10-year bond above. The collection of risk points actually represents a portfolio of hedging Treasuries, called the *hedge portfolio*. This portfolio has the property that its risk is the same as that of the bond. When a portfolio is designed so as to match the risk of another, then the former is called an *immunizing* or *duration-matching* portfolio. In addition, the cash flow from this portfolio is close to that of the cash flow from the bond. When a portfolio is designed so that its cash flows match that of another, the former is called a *dedicated* portfolio. The hedge portfolio is always immunizing or duration matching. The larger the number of hedge instruments, the closer the hedge portfolio comes to a fully dedicated portfolio.

There is one difference between the dedicated portfolio in this context and the one used in structured investments. In the latter, only positive holdings are considered, whereas in our hedging portfolio, negative holdings, i.e., short positions, are quite common.

TABLE 7   Risk Points with a Smaller Set of Hedges

Maturity (Years)	Treasury Yield	Spread (b.p.)	Total	Risk Point	Percent of Total Risk	Percent of Total PV
0.5	4.932	28	5.212	–0.002584	0.033865	–0.002251
1	5.520	29	5.810	–0.009182	0.120353	–0.007999
2	6.234	31	6.544	–0.021457	0.281247	–0.018692
3	6.563	35	6.913	–0.242119	3.173593	–0.210917
5						
10	7.466	41	7.876	–7.353835	96.390943	–6.406137
			Totals:	–7.629176	100.000000	–6.645995

237

TABLE 8   Risk Points Profile of Some Common Investments

Maturity (Years)	10-Year Par Bond	10-Year 3% Bond	10-Year 15% Bond	10-Year 0% Bond	14.50% Annuity	5-Year Par Bond	3-Year Par Bond	3, 10 Dumbbell
0.5	0.000000	0.005890	−0.008606	0.009514	−0.017515	0.000000	0.000000	0.000000
1	0.000000	0.020933	−0.030583	0.033812	−0.062249	0.000000	0.000000	0.000000
2	0.000000	0.048917	−0.071469	0.079013	−0.145466	0.000000	0.000000	0.000000
3	0.000000	0.127555	−0.186362	0.206034	−0.379316	0.000000	−2.685351	−1.753771
5	0.000000	0.594487	−0.868566	0.960251	−1.767856	−4.160751	0.000000	0.000000
10	−6.938302	−6.215646	−7.994128	−5.771025	−2.148999	0.000000	0.000000	−2.406980
Totals:	−6.938302	−5.417864	−9.159714	−4.482402	−4.521401	−4.160751	−2.685351	−4.160751

TABLE 9   Risk Points for Mortgage Backed Securities

Maturity	Sequential PO	Sequential IO	Companion PAC Bond	Z-PAC Bond	Z Bond
1	2.712990	−1.067860	−0.087954	−0.227987	0.084370
2	0.105150	−0.751634	−0.312604	−0.462619	0.176150
3	−0.881439	0.727920	−1.991636	−0.900864	0.408440
5	−0.791930	−0.190383	−8.828908	−0.149317	1.440020
10	−8.551698	6.211113	−10.083130	0.164040	−17.569742
Totals:	−8.137903	5.143436	−26.806461	−1.725013	−14.650842

Finally, risk points are additive, in two ways. The risk point in any sector for a portfolio can be computed easily by simply adding the risk points in that sector of all bonds in the portfolio. In addition, we can quickly compute the risk point for a broader sector by adding the risk points for all the smaller sectors within.

Table 8 and Table 9 show[27] the risk points for various common fixed income investments.

It is interesting to look at the risk profile for an exotic structure.[28] In Table 10, we show the profile for a three-year note that pays coupons equal to the five-year swap rate less a fixed spread. Such a note is called a CMS note or Constant Maturity Swap rate note. The coupon on the note is reset semi-annually. Simple duration analysis will treat the note essentially as a floating rate instrument, implying a small duration or risk. The risk point profile (Table 10, Column 5, and Exhibit 1), however, reveals that the CMS note has negative and positive risks. In fact, the note is bullish on rates up to three years and bearish on rates beyond that. In particular, the note has risk in the five- and 10-year maturities even though it only has a three-year maturity.

APPLICATIONS OF THE RISK POINT METHOD

The risk point method, being a more complete and comprehensive measure of interest rate risk, can be used wherever other simple measures such as duration are currently being used. We provide here a brief review.

---

27. The data in Table 9 for mortgage-backed securities were computed by Thomas Ho of Global Advanced Technology Corporation, New York.
28. The risk point analysis of exotic securities is covered in detail in Ravi E. Dattatreya and Scott Peng, *Structured Notes,* Probus Publishing, Chicago, 1994.

TABLE 10   Risk Point for a CMS Note

Maturity (Years)	Treasury Yield	Spread (b.p.)	Total	Risk Point
0.5	4.932	28	5.212	−0.058520
1	5.520	29	5.810	−0.208950
2	6.234	31	6.544	−0.484468
3	6.563	35	6.913	−2.831432
5	7.074	32	7.394	2.280450
10	7.466	41	7.876	1.512276
			Total:	0.209356

Hedging

This is the most common use of duration, and therefore, of risk points. Common duration analysis not only gives us just a crude approximation for the hedge, but it also fails to provide critical information as to which hedge instruments are optimal to use. On the other hand, the risk point method correctly identifies the major risks in a portfolio and directly generates the portfolio of hedge instruments best suited for the hedging task. Since the starting point for the risk point method is the selection of hedge instruments, we have full control over which hedge instruments will be considered for hedging from the outset.

The par amount of any hedge instrument required to hedge a portfolio can be determined by dividing the risk point of the portfolio by the PVBP[29] of the hedge instrument. For example, consider the 10 percent coupon bond again. For every $100 of the bond, we need $104.5370 (7.253094/6.938302) of the 10-year Treasury as a component of the hedge.

Indexing

As a structured portfolio methodology, indexing is quite common. Indexing requires one to manage a portfolio in such a way that the returns from the portfolio track that from a given bond index, e.g., various Lehman Brothers indexes or the Merrill Lynch Government Bond Index. A common technique is to purchase, as far as possible, the same bonds as in the index in the same

---

29. Note that the PVBP of a hedge is equal to its risk point relative to itself. For example, from Table 8, the PVBP of the 10-year Treasury is $6.938302. Note that this PVBP is slightly different from the traditional definition. One reason is that the latter starts out with a flat yield curve rather than the actual yield curve.

EXHIBIT 1   Risk Point Profile of a CMS Note

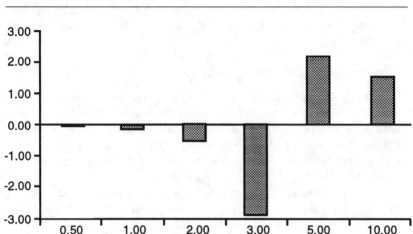

proportions. The effectiveness of this technique is limited, because indexes almost always have too many bonds in them and most of these are not available at fair prices in the quantities required. An alternative is to manage the portfolio duration to match the published duration of the index as closely as possible. This technique allows the manager to pick bonds that are relatively cheap for the portfolio.

Situation

A portfolio manager is running an indexed fund tied to an index with a duration of five years. Given the bearish mood of the market, the manager decides to keep the duration of the fund short, at 4.5 years. Rates do climb. However, the manager finds that the fund has barely kept up with the index, and has not outperformed the index as expected. Further analysis reveals that the yield curve has steepened as the rates rose. The fund holds a relatively large amount of 10-year bonds, which have suffered a loss. Thus, duration matching in normal situations and using a shorter duration in a bearish market provide no guarantee that expected results will be obtained. The reason is that duration is an oversimplification.[30]

---

30. In this context, we can compare duration to the mean of a distribution. A normal distribution with small variance can be represented satisfactorily by its mean. This is an ideal situation. If the variance is large, or if the distribution is skewed, then we need more parameters to describe or represent the situation. The farther the distribution from the ideal, the less meaningful the mean. Similar is the case with duration.

A superior way to index is to first determine[31] the full risk point profile of the index and then manage the fund against this profile as a guide. Then the manager will know what types of yield curve bets are implied in the fund's portfolio.

Immunization and Dedication

Another popular application of duration is in immunization. If we are managing a portfolio in order to meet a specific liability in the future, immunization calls for balancing the portfolio so that the duration of the portfolio equals the duration of the liability. This procedure is based on a parallel shift assumption for yield curve moves. Therefore, it is subject to the same types of surprises suffered by the index fund manager above.

A more robust approach is to determine the risk point profile of the liability and match this to the risk profile of the portfolio. In this sense, immunization is not much different from index fund management.

In dedicated portfolios, a common strategy is to cash-match in the early years and use immunization in later years. Again, this strategy can be made more robust by using risk point matching rather than just duration matching in the back years.

Benchmarking

In many industrial corporations, the performance of the liability portfolio is measured against a benchmark portfolio. In many ways, this procedure resembles indexing. Again we recommend use of the risk point profile for managing the liabilities. Perhaps the creation of the benchmark portfolio itself can benefit from this method.

Scenario Analysis

One use of duration is in scenario analysis. Under parallel shift assumptions, we can quickly determine the change in the value of a portfolio from its duration. This use of duration is limited to parallel shifts and fails to reveal risks due to reshaping shifts of the yield curve. Using the risk point profile of the portfolio, it is easy to carry out scenario analysis, including yield curve twists and other reshaping shifts.

---

31. In the absence of published information on the risk points for an index, the profile can be estimated by looking at a simplified portfolio representative of the index.

For example, in the case of the 10 percent coupon bond above (Table 6), if the 10-year rate moves up by 10 b.p. and the five-year rates move up by 5 b.p. and the other rates are unchanged, then the change in the value of a $10,000 holding can be estimated to be $73.825740 (10 × $7.253094 + 5 × $0.258960).

Bond Swap Transactions

A common bond swap transaction is to swap a bond (a bullet) for a pair of bonds (the dumbbell) in such a way that the duration of the dumbbell is equal to that of the bullet. Even though it is difficult to match the risk point profiles of the bullet and the dumbbell, the profiles provide accurate clues as to where the risks and bets in the transaction might be.

EXTENSIONS

The application of the risk point method is not limited to securities with simple, known, and fixed cash flows. It is in fact a general approach and can be used to hedge virtually all instruments. As long as a security can be valued relative to a set of hedge instruments, the method is applicable. For example, suppose that we are considering an option on a 10-year zero coupon bond. Then, we can easily determine the risk point for the option by first determining the change in the price of the zero relative to the current 10-year Treasury. Secondly, we determine the corresponding change in the price of the option due the change in the zero price. This directly gives us the risk point of the option relative to the current 10-year Treasury.[32]

The concept can also be extended to include risks other than interest rate risk. For example, suppose that we would like to hedge the option on the 10-year zero coupon bond against changes in volatility. We would choose a hedge instrument that responds to volatility, such as an option on the current 10-year Treasury. To determine the risk point, called the *volatility risk point*, which can be defined in various ways, we compute the change in the value of the hedge as well as the option on the zero per unit change in the volatility.

---

32. The risk point for the option relative to the 10-year Treasury is the product of (1) the risk point of the option relative to the zero and (2) the risk point of the zero relative to the 10-year. Mathematically, we can restate this relationship as follows: $d(\text{option})/d(10\text{-year UST}) = [d(\text{option})/d(\text{zero})] \times [d(\text{zero})/d(10\text{-year UST})]$.

The ratio of the two represents the risk point of the option relative to the hedge with respect to volatility. This number is the number of units of the hedge-instrument required to hedge the option on the zero to protect against changes in volatility.

In addition to volatility risk, we can similarly define risk points for stock market risk, exchange rate risk, commodity price risk, credit risk, etc. The two key factors in such extensions are the availability of appropriate hedge instruments and a valuation model.

Convexity

We can also extend the idea of duration-like risk point to convexity. Convexity basically measures the non-linear relationship between the cause (change in the reference rate) and the effect (value or price of a security). One way to measure the non-linearity is to look at the difference between a linear estimate and the actual value. In Table 11, we show the difference between the change in the value of the 10 percent bond for a 10 basis point change in the yield of a hedge (Column 6) and 10 times the change in value for a 1 basis point change in yield (i.e., the risk point, Column 5). The result, Column 7, can be called the *convexity points*.

There is another way to determine convexity, as in Table 12. We can move the entire yield curve[33] by a small amount (10 basis points) and re-compute the risk points. The difference between the risk points computed before (Column 5) and after (Column 6) is the parallel shift. The result will represent a type of convexity points.[34]

It is difficult to pinpoint exactly how the convexity points ought to be used, as convexity itself is a second-order effect. Nonetheless, we recommend their use, even for just monitoring purposes, by the risk manager. This is especially so when exotic securities are involved.

CONCLUSION AND SUMMARY

In this chapter, we have presented the risk point concept as a more complete measure of interest rate risk than other commonly used measures such as

---

33. There are a number of degrees of freedom in selecting the type and magnitude of the yield curve shift. The actual shift chosen is influenced by specifics of any particular situation.
34. This set of convexity points is considered more useful in certain circumstances.

TABLE 11   Convexity Points—I

Maturity (Years)	Treasury Yield	Spread (b.p.)	Total	Risk Point	Convexity Points
0.5	4.932	28	5.212	–0.002566	0.000011
1	5.520	29	5.810	–0.009118	0.000043
2	6.234	31	6.544	–0.021308	0.000118
3	6.563	35	6.913	–0.055563	0.000405
5	7.074	32	7.394	–0.258960	0.003621
10	7.466	41	7.876	–7.253094	0.137062
			Totals:	–7.600610	0.141261

TABLE 12   Convexity Points—II

Maturity (Years)	Treasury Yield	Spread (b.p.)	Total	Risk Point Before	Risk Point After	Change or Convexity
0.5	5.032	28	5.312	–0.002566	–0.002420	0.000145
1	5.620	29	5.910	–0.009118	–0.008604	0.000514
2	6.334	31	6.644	–0.021308	–0.020116	0.001192
3	6.663	35	7.013	–0.055563	–0.052492	0.003072
5	7.174	32	7.494	–0.258960	–0.245042	0.013919
10	7.566	41	7.976	–7.253094	–7.205489	0.047605
			Totals:	–7.600610	–7.534163	0.066447

duration. The concept adds value in almost all situations where duration is used, including: hedging, immunization, dedication, indexation, bond swapping, and scenario analysis. The risk point concept is especially valuable in the management of portfolios, including options and most of the complex modern financial instruments. We recommend that the risk point method be used as an integral part of a comprehensive risk management program.

In risk management, as in most important situations, our policy is to reject the black box approach. By providing more insight into the nature of risk, the risk point method takes us one step away from the black box, and one step closer to our ideal.

9

Primitive Securities: Portfolio Building Blocks

Thomas S. Y. Ho
President, Global Advanced Technology Corporation

Perhaps the most important principle in the bond market is the law of one price: two bonds that have identical cash flows should have the same price. This principle enables us to determine bond value from the bond's cash flows. Also, it forms the theoretical foundation to many practical applications. Arbitrage strategies, portfolio immunization, and securities pricing are just a few examples.

According to the law of one price, bullet payments (or zero-coupon bonds) are the basic building blocks to any fixed cash flow pattern. We can replicate such a security by holding a portfolio of bullet payments. When we can price the bullet payments, we can analyze and value these securities. This approach is useful as long as the bond is option-free, so the bond cash flow is deterministic.

Yet many bonds include embedded options. Corporate bonds have call and put options. Mortgage-backed securities and collateralized mortgage obligations are affected by the homeowner's prepayment option. Many interest rate swaps have cash flows that depend on the path of interest rates. Insurance products have lapse (or withdrawal) features. Moreover, dynamic portfolio strategies are, in essence, bonds with embedded options. For example, portfolio insurance is a portfolio with a put option.

Copyright © 1993 *The Journal of Derivatives,* Winter, 1993. Published by Institutional Investor. Reprinted with permission.

The author thanks Tom McAvity for suggesting the research on primitives and other insights, Andy Davidson for conversations on CMO valuation, and his colleagues at GAT, particularly Vern Budinger, Bill McCoy, Yury Geyman, Marcy Joseph, and Basil Rabinowitz.

This article considers how to develop basic building blocks for these and other bonds. The building blocks are called "primitive" securities.

Much of bond research deals with pricing. A pricing model provides a consistent framework in which to determine fair value. The theory of primitive securities expands that framework by decomposing fair value into its components, which themselves can be thought of as securities.

Ho [1992b] describes how a bond value can be disaggregated into the Treasury equivalent value and the option value. This approach focuses on decomposition of a bond into its option and option-free components, but it does not provide details on the type of option. Is the option path-dependent? When does the option have the highest impact on the bond price? These are some of the questions that our approach can answer.

This article contributes to the literature in two basic ways. First, it provides the framework to manage a portfolio as a set of cash flows. In recent years, many portfolio strategies have been based on the total return approach, using a relatively short investment horizon, and relative valuation, which depends on the risk and return trade-offs as specified by the return distribution. When bonds are complex and illiquid (CMOs, for example), this total return approach is often ineffective. Managing a portfolio on a cash-flow basis provides more control over portfolio risks and allows implementation of strategies that can exploit liquidity cycles.

Another important contribution of this article is a unifying framework for bond analysis and portfolio strategies. There are many synthetic securities, bond strategies, and bond types (a dizzying number in the CMO market alone). A consistent framework for comparison is required to analyze these securities, or bond strategies. Effective duration or convexity has proven to be inadequate, because bonds or strategies differ from each other in ways beyond their sensitivity to instantaneous shifts of the yield curve.

In discussion of the theoretical framework of the analysis and the methodology for decomposing a bond into a portfolio of primitive securities, we prove that if two option-free bonds have the same "pathwise values," they must also have the same cash flows. We develop an operational version of the theory and apply it to analyze different bond types to show how to identify the option risks of a bond using the analytical tool of the "primitive profile." We then discuss four applications in risk management.

I. BASIC FRAMEWORK

The underlying economic structure of the model in this article is in the spirit of Ho and Lee [1986]. The bond or strategy cash flows are contingent on the movement of the term structure. We first list the basic assumptions of the term structure movement model.

Basic Assumptions

1. The market is frictionless. There are no taxes or transaction costs, and all securities are perfectly divisible.

2. The market clears at discrete points in time, which are set at regular intervals, indexed by n. For simplicity, we treat each period as a unit of time. We define a discount bond of maturity T to be a bond that pays \$1 at the end of the Tth period, with no other payments to its holder.

3. The bond market is complete in the sense that there exists a discount bond for each maturity n.

4. At each time step n, there are a finite number of states of the world. For state i, we denote the equilibrium price of the discount bond of maturity T by $P(T; i, n)$. This function, the discount function, completely describes the term structure of interest rates in the ith state at time n.

5. $P(T; 0,0)$ is the initial discount function, which is consistent with the observed spot yield curve of the Treasury securities market. The discount functions $P(T; i, n)$ follow a binomial movement model such that there is no portfolio strategy using the discount bonds that can generate arbitrage profits.

A model with these assumptions is a single-factor arbitrage-free rate movement model. Ho and Lee [1986]; Black, Derman, and Toy [1990]; Heath, Jarrow, and Morton [1992]; and Pederson, Shiu, and Thorlacius [1990] present specific interest rate models that satisfy the five assumptions. Our results do not depend on the particular interest rate movement model, as long as the movements are arbitrage-free, satisfying these five assumptions.

Definition of a Bond

From the binomial lattice of term structure movements, we can construct a binomial lattice of interest rate movements. The one-period interest rate, $r(i, n)$, is defined,

$$r(i, n) = -\ln P(1; i, n) \tag{1}$$

Exhibit 1 is a numerical example, Example A, of a binomial lattice of interest rates. This example uses one year as a unit of time and considers interest rate movements out to five years. The lattice is called "a four-period lattice," emphasizing the four movements in five years. Note that while the one-period interest rates are shown here, at each state and time we actually have a full discount function specified according to an arbitrage-free interest rate model, from which the one-year rates have been drawn.

A rate path, or "scenario," can be represented by a string of 1s and 0s, where 1 means the one-year rate goes up in that period, and 0 denotes a falling rate. The length of the interest rate path is the length of the string. For example, the two-period path 01 represents the path that falls to 9 percent and then rises back to 10 percent. In Example A, there are $2^4 = 16$ distinct interest rate paths of length 4. The complete set of interest rate paths of a binomial lattice is called the "path space."

For our purposes, we do not make a distinction between a *bond* and a *bond strategy*. Both are simply represented by assigning a stream of cash flows to each of the possible rate paths in an unambiguous way. Because the payout of a bond can be path-dependent, we need to take the whole rate path into consideration, not just the time and state of the binomial lattice.

A bond (or bond portfolio) can be fully described by the linear combination of its payouts for each path. If two bonds have identical payouts along every rate path, they are the same. This means that, for a particular lattice, a countable number of bonds can form the basis for all possible bonds, and any given bond can be replicated by a portfolio containing only these basis bonds.

The dimension of the bond space for an n-period binomial lattice of interest rates, denoted by B_n, is equal to the total number of basis bonds with maturity n or less, which is in turn equal to the number of distinct paths of all lengths up to n.

As there are 2^k rate paths for each length k,

$$B_n = 2 + 2^2 + 2^3 + \cdots + 2^k + \cdots + 2^n, \text{ or}$$
$$B_n = (2^{(n+1)} - 2) \tag{2}$$

Any bond or portfolio of bonds can be represented as a portfolio of the basis bonds. But no basis bond can be reproduced by a portfolio of the other bonds in the basis. To show this result, we assign a unique ordering to the payouts of a bond for each state and time period.

EXHIBIT 1   A Four-Period Binomial Lattice of Interest Rates

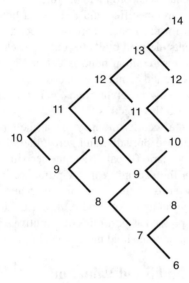

Linear Ordering of Scenarios

Since there are B_n scenarios that represent all possible interest rate paths for which the payouts of a bond must be specified, we need to have a systematic way of ordering them. We suggest a system in which all rate paths with length up to the length of the binomial lattice are ordered according to three priority rules.

Path A ranks higher than Path B if

- Rule 1: A has a shorter length.

- Rule 2: A has more down movements, i.e., more 0s.

- Rule 3: A has an earlier down movement than B, i.e., counting from the left, the first 0 along A occurs before the first 0 along B.

Rule 1 ensures that the bond that has an earlier maturity ranks higher. Rules 2 and 3 ensure that all paths that end at the same point (i.e., the same date and interest rate) should be close to each other, and that we count the falling rate scenarios first.

Consider Example A again. For $n = 4$ and $B_n = 30$, Exhibit 2 shows the ordering of the 30 scenarios according to the rules.

Once the paths are specified and ordered, a bond is unambiguously defined by its payout for each one. Therefore, a bond can be expressed as a vector with B_n elements, defined by its payouts in each of the scenarios. For example, a two-year zero-coupon bond is defined by the vector that pays $100 in scenarios 3, 4, 5, and 6, and zero otherwise.

Exhibit 3 shows how different bonds and strategies for $n = 3$ can be represented by their cash flow vectors.

A "primitive" is a security that pays $1 at the terminal point of a scenario, when that scenario prevails, and zero otherwise. For example, the primitive security of scenario 01 pays $1 in the second year if rates fall in the first year and rise in the second year. (A primitive is in fact an "Arrow-Debreu security," in terms of the economics literature, which pays $1 in a specific state of the world and 0 otherwise.) From Exhibit 3, we can see that all "bonds" can be expressed as portfolios of primitives. The entries of a bond cash flow vector are simply the holdings in each of the primitives.

Pathwise Values and Bond Valuation

Since a bond has a set of cash flows along each interest rate path, we can calculate the present value for each cash flow by discounting by the successive one-period rates along the path. For a binomial lattice of period n, there are $P_n = 2^n$ "pathwise values" for each bond.

EXHIBIT 2 Interest Rate Scenarios for the Path Space of a Four-Period Binomial Lattice

Path Number	Path	Path Number	Path	Path Number	Path	Path Number	Path
1	0	7	000	15	0000	23	1001
2	1	8	001	16	0001	24	1010
		9	010	17	0010	25	1100
3	00	10	100	18	0100	26	0111
4	01	11	011	19	1000	27	1011
5	10	12	101	20	0011	28	1101
6	11	13	110	21	0101	29	1110
		14	111	22	0110	30	1111

EXHIBIT 3   Bond Cash Flow Vectors

Path Number	1	2	3	4	5	6	7	8	9	10	11	12	13	14
Scenario	0	1	00	01	10	11	000	001	010	011	100	101	110	111

Securities (defined below):

	1	2	3	4	5	6	7	8	9	10	11	12	13	14
Primitive for path 01	0	0	0	1	0	0	0	0	0	0	0	0	0	0
0-Primitive	-1	0	1.09	1.09	0	0	0	0	0	0	0	0	0	0
Zero-Coupon	0	0	0	0	0	0	100	100	100	100	100	100	100	100
Option	0	0	0	0	0	0	0	0	0	0	1	1	1	3
One-Year Roll	0	0	0	0	0	0	129.5	129.5	131.9	131.9	134.3	134.3	136.8	136.8
Path-Dependent	0	0	0	0	0	0	0	1	-1	0	0	0	0	0

Notes:

"Path number" is the number of the scenario under the linear ordering described above.

"Scenario" defines the movements of rates through the lattice, 0 indicates a down movement, and 1 indicates an up movement

"Primitive for 01" is the primitive that pays $1 in scenario 01.

"0-primitive" is a zero-value strategy that borrows $1 when the rate falls in the first period and invests the money in a one-year bond.

"Zero-coupon" is a three-year zero-coupon bond. At the end of year 3, the bond pays $100 irrespective of the rate path.

"Option" is a three-year European call option on the interest rate, with a strike level of 10%.

"One-year roll" is a strategy that rolls over a one-year bond. Starting with $100 invested at 10%, at the end of one year we receive $110 and then roll over into another one-year bond yielding the prevailing rate. After a second rollover, we receive the total cumulated cash amount at the end of the third year.

"Path-dependent" is a path-dependent security, which has a different payoff if the rate falls then rises versus rises and then falls.

Ho [1992b] shows that the bond value is the mean of all the pathwise values, as long as the binomial lattice is arbitrage-free. Hence, the pathwise value is a decomposition of the bond fair value. Clearly, two bonds are distinct from each other if they have different pathwise values. If two bonds have the same pathwise values, we say that the bonds are "equivalent." They need not have identical cash flows, as we will discuss below, although they should be similar.

Consider two bonds, an asset and a liability. If the asset and the liability are equivalent, they must have the same market value, because they have the same pathwise values. Further, when interest rates move over time according to the binomial lattice, the asset value always equals the liability value, even though the cash flows are not matched. This is because if two bonds have the same pathwise value at the outset, they must also have the same pathwise value in any of the future nodes on the binomial lattice.

When we consider all possible bonds, there will be many that involve offsetting cash flows. The bond labeled "0-primitive" in Exhibit 3 is an example of such a bond, because it involves receiving $1 if the rate goes down to 9% in the first period, and then paying back $1.09 for certain one period later. This "bond" should have no current market value. Further, such bonds have no value along any interest rate path, nor can any combination of them have a pathwise value.

The set of all bonds that have no pathwise value forms a vector subspace. We call these bonds 0-primitives. Now we can derive the decomposition proposition.

Bond Space Decomposition

PROPOSITION 1: DECOMPOSITION. Let the subspace of all 0-primitives be denoted by K_n, where n is the number of periods in the binomial lattice. Then the dimension of the subspace K_n is

$$dim\ K_n = B_n - P_n \qquad (3)$$

Proof. Given a binomial lattice of period n, calculating the pathwise value is a linear mapping from the B_n dimensional bond space to the space of $2^n = P_n$ values. This mapping is surjective, with the kernel being the vector subspace K_n. The results then follow from basic linear algebra theory. (See Hartley and Hawkes [1970].)

QED.

254

There are P_n bonds that have positive (valuable) pathwise values, and they are independent of each other. These bonds are called v-primitives, and their basis is given in Proposition 2. Any bond can be replicated by a portfolio of v-primitives and 0-primitives.

The main insight of Proposition 1 is that there may be many bonds in the bond space, but the important ones are the v-primitives, which determine the bond's value. Exhibit 4 shows how the bond space is decomposed into v-primitives and 0-primitives.

If there is a systematic way of determining a set of bonds that forms a basis for the space of v-primitive securities, then, given any bond, we can determine the portfolio of these basis v-primitives whose values must sum to the bond value. As the following proposition shows, the solution to this important question is surprisingly simple.

PROPOSITION 2: THE v-PRIMITIVE BASIS. A basis for the space of v-primitives can be formed from bonds that have no payout except at the end of a single rate path, where the last entry of the path is zero. The set of all the basis v-primitives is the set of all these bonds plus the bond that pays $1 in scenario 1.

Sketch of Proof. Using Exhibit 2 and referring to Exhibit 3, we can generate the primitives as in Exhibit 5. These vectors are clearly linearly independent, as each has a payout for only one path. By the way they have been defined, the total number is half of the dimension of the bond space, plus one. That is, $b_n/2 + 1$. The dimension of the v-primitive space is 2^n, so the set of 2^n v-primitives defined according to Proposition 2 forms a basis of the space.

QED.

EXHIBIT 4 Decomposition of the Bond Space into v-Primitives and 0-Primitives

Lattice Periods	Number of Paths	Dimension of Bond Space	Number of v-Primitives	Number of 0-Primitives
2	4	6	4	2
3	8	14	8	6
4	16	30	16	14
5	32	62	32	30

EXHIBIT 5 Cash Flow Vectors for v-Primitives and 0-Primitives for Three-Period Lattice

Interest Rate Scenario

	1	2	3	4	5	6	7	8	9	10	11	12	13	14
Path Number	1	2	3	4	5	6	7	8	9	10	11	12	13	14
Scenario	0	1	0	1	0	1	0	1	0	1	0	1	0	1
v-Primitive Basis Bonds														
0	1	0	0	0	0	0	0	0	0	0	0	0	0	0
1	0	1	0	0	0	0	0	0	0	0	0	0	0	0
00	0	0	1	0	0	0	0	0	0	0	0	0	0	0
10	0	0	0	0	1	0	0	0	0	0	0	0	0	0
000	0	0	0	0	0	0	1	0	0	0	0	0	0	0
010	0	0	0	0	0	0	0	0	1	0	0	0	0	0
100	0	0	0	0	0	0	0	0	0	0	1	0	0	0
110	0	0	0	0	0	0	0	0	0	0	0	0	1	0
0-Primitive Basis Bonds														
0*	1	0	-1.09	-1.09	0	0	0	0	0	0	0	0	0	0
1*	0	1	0	0	-1.11	-1.11	0	0	0	0	0	0	0	0
00*	0	0	1	0	0	0	-1.08	-1.08	0	0	0	0	0	0
10*	0	0	0	0	1	0	0	0	0	0	-1.10	-1.10	0	0
0**	1	0	0	0	0	0	-1.17	-1.17	-1.199	-1.199	0	0	0	0
1**	0	1	0	0	0	0	0	0	0	0	-1.221	-1.221	-1.24	-1.24

These v-primitives, together with the 0-primitives, form a basis for all bond cash flow vectors. This basis, of course, is not unique but can be chosen in a way that is convenient to analyze bonds.

To complete the discussion of the decomposition of a bond, we now specify a basis for the 0-primitive subspace. As Proposition 3 shows, these bonds are also surprisingly simple to represent.

PROPOSITION 3: THE 0-PRIMITIVE BASIS. Consider a v-primitive. Now construct a bond that receives $1 just like that primitive, but then reinvests it immediately and pays all proceeds back in a future period. As each of these bonds represents a strategy of receiving a dollar, reinvesting at the prevailing interest rate, and repaying all proceeds at a later date, the pathwise value must always be zero. The set of all such bonds that can be constructed by considering all the v-primitives and all the future reinvestment dates forms a basis of the space of 0-primitives.

Exhibit 6 illustrates how Propositions 2 and 3 lead to a complete basis for the bond space, for a two-period lattice.

EXHIBIT 6   v-Primitive and 0-Primitive Basis Bonds for a Two-Period Lattice

Path						
Number	1	2	3	4	5	6
Scenario	0	1	0	0	1	1
		0	1	0	1	

Cash Flows of Basis Bonds

v-Primitives

0	1	0	0	0	0	0
1	0	1	0	0	0	0
00	0	0	1	0	0	0
10	0	0	0	0	1	0

0-Primitives

	1	0	$-(1 + r_{1d})$	$-(1 + r_{1d})$	0	0
	0	1	0	0	$-(1 + r_{1u})$	$-(1 + r_{1u})$

r_{1d} denotes the interest rate after a down move in period 1.
r_{1u} denotes the interest rate after an up move in period 1.

PROPOSITION 4: COMPLETE DECOMPOSITION OF A BOND. A bond is defined by its cash flow for each interest rate path. Therefore, a bond can be represented by a cash flow vector b, of length B_n. Construct a square matrix D of size $B_n \times B_n$, as in Exhibit 6, where the columns represent the interest rate scenarios and the rows give the cash flows of the basis v-primitive and 0-primitive bonds. Call this matrix the decomposition matrix.

Let the vector x denote the holdings of each of the basis bonds such that the cash flows from the portfolio are identical to those of the bond whose value is being decomposed along all interest rate paths. The vector x represents a decomposition of the bond into equivalent positions in the v-primitive and 0-primitive basis bonds. Then, we have:

$$x \cdot D = b$$

or

$$(x_0, x_1, x_2, \ldots, x_m) \begin{vmatrix} D_{00} & \ldots & D_{0m} \\ \cdot & \ldots & \cdot \\ \cdot & \ldots & \cdot \\ D_{m0} & \ldots & D_{mm} \end{vmatrix} = (b_0 \ldots b_m) \qquad (4)$$

where $m = B_n$.

D is an invertible matrix by construction, and therefore we can solve for x. Further, if we are just given the pathwise values of the bond, without knowing the bond's cash flows, we can calculate the portfolio holdings of the primitives. The result will be consistent with Equation (4).

The decomposition of a bond according to Proposition 4 provides important insight into its structure. The most important insight is that we can calculate the pathwise values for any given bond. Now, let us consider the converse of the question. If we know the pathwise values, how much do we know about a bond?

Proposition 4 says that once we know the pathwise values for a given bond, we know the holdings of the v-primitives that will produce an equivalent bond. Therefore, we know the basis bonds that can build its value. Now, if we have additional information about the bond, for example, the bond type (zero-coupon, callable under specified conditions, etc.), so that we can unambiguously determine the composition of the 0-primitives, then we have a complete solution.

The most important example of this argument applies to option-free bonds. Within the class of option-free bonds, we have shown that we can unambiguously decompose a bond into its v-primitives and 0-primitives. Therefore, it follows that if two option-free bonds have the same pathwise values, the two bonds must have the same cash flows.

This result has important implications for portfolio immunization strategies. Kao and Geyman [1993] verify this result empirically and apply the methodology to design immunization strategies.

II. ANALYZING BOND VALUES

Here we implement the primitive securities framework to analyze actual bonds. In practice, the binomial lattice of a pricing model is often based on a one-month step size, and the bond maturity may be up to 30 years. Therefore, the number of primitive securities would be astronomically large ($2^{361} - 2$), and decomposition of the bond value by constructing all of the primitives is impractical.

To implement the basic idea of primitives in valuing actual bonds, we use the linear path space (LPS) approach (see Ho [1992b]). LPS is a structured sampling technique to condense a binomial lattice with many periods into a lattice of manageable size.

We begin with the full binomial lattice with one-month time steps, and partition the path space into term segments, at one, three, five, seven, 10, 20, and 30 years. Then, at each term, we partition the full set of interest rate levels (12M + 1 of them for any M-year term) into a much smaller set of "gates." As a simple example, in Exhibit 1, the five interest rates possible after four periods might be partitioned into three gates: [6, 8], [10], and [12, 14].

We can now classify a path by the sequence of gates it goes through. This defines an equivalence class. The number of paths in a given equivalence class as a proportion of the total number of primitive paths is the path weight for that class.

For each class, we choose a representative path (the one going through the midpoint of each of its gates). The (approximate) "pathwise value" for a bond is then the present value of its cash flow along the representative path for its equivalence class. (Davidson and Herskovitz [1991] also discuss the choice of scenarios to analyze bond values. They refer to the "gates" as "buckets.")

Finally, we multiply the pathwise values by their corresponding weights and sum to obtain the (approximate) bond value. With an increasing number of paths, in the limit the sum converges exactly to the bond price.

The gates are structured so that each representative path must rise, fall, or stay on the same level in the binomial lattice of arbitrage-free interest

259

rates. Therefore, the structured sample forms a trinomial process, and a representative path can be uniquely represented by a string of +s, 0s, and –s, where these symbols indicate, respectively, that the rate rises, stays constant, or falls for that segment of the path.

The trinomial lattice constructed from market interest rates on February 20, 1993, is given in Exhibit 7. The rates shown are the 10-year Treasury spot rates derived from the Ho-Lee arbitrage-free term structure model. We extend the rate tree out to seven years.

Primitive Profiles

Now we can decompose a bond price into the primitive values. First, we order the states analogously as in Section I. Then we calculate the present value of the bond cash flow along each segment of the representative path, and the corresponding "primitive weight." The primitive weight is the present value of the payout along the path multiplied by the probability of that path and divided by the total value of the bond.

In other words, the primitive weight tells us what proportion of the bond's value can be attributed to the cash flows it receives along the specified interest rate path. The primitive profile is the distribution of the primitive weights for each term segment. It will become the major tool for analysis in this framework.

EXHIBIT 7   The 10-Year Treasury Rate (%) in the Trinomial Linear Path Space Lattice, as of February 20, 1993

Term	0	1	3	5	7
Date	2/93	2/94	2/96	2/98	2/00
Rates					15.62
				13.08	13.05
			10.29	10.45	10.52
		7.97	8.51	8.72	8.84
	6.63	7.06	7.62	7.86	8.01
		6.15	6.73	7.01	7.18
			4.98	5.31	5.54
				2.78	3.09
					0.67

260

Primitive weights have some important properties. First, the primitive weights for a bond portfolio are simply the weighted averages of the primitive weights for each bond in the portfolio, with the weighting proportional to each bond's market value. Second, a large spike among the primitive weights indicates that the bond is risky, because it "invests" heavily in a single scenario.

The Primitive Profile for an Actual Callable Bond

Exhibit 8 shows the primitive profile of an actual callable corporate bond issued by Southern Bell Telephone. Each panel shows the primitive weights for the different scenarios in each term segment as indicated by the heights of the bars. The sum of the primitive weights for the term segment is shown in the upper right-hand corner of each panel.

For example, analysis of the Southern Bell bond indicates that 23.48 percent of the bond's market value is attributable to the cash flows expected in the first year, and the profile shows that this is largely because the bond is called in one year when rates fall.

A callable corporate bond is often analyzed by trying to value the embedded option on the underlying principal and coupons. The primitive profile takes a different approach. We determine a "benchmark bond," which is a portfolio of option-free zero-coupon bonds that behave most like the bond in question. This is accomplished by calculating the sum of the primitive weights for each term. This aggregate value determines the proportion of the investment attributable to cash flows that could occur at that term. We then suppose the same proportions are invested in a portfolio of zero-coupon bonds of those maturities.

For example, in the first panel of Exhibit 8 the broken line shows the primitive weights that would be computed for a one-year zero-coupon bond on the three possible scenarios (−, 0, +). These weights are scaled so that their total is 23.48. As the panels show, the benchmark portfolio for this bond holds 23.48 percent of each dollar invested in a one-year zero, 13.01 percent in a three-year zero, and so on.

The primitive weights for the zero-coupon bond are depicted by the broken lines in each panel of the primitive profile. The differences between the primitive weights for the zero-coupon bonds under the different scenarios and those of the bond under investigation depict the uncertain nature of the bond's cash flow. The effect of the bond's option feature can then be seen by comparing the pattern of primitive weights at each term with the weights that would be calculated for the option-free zero-coupon bond of that maturity.

EXHIBIT 8   Southern Bell Telephone

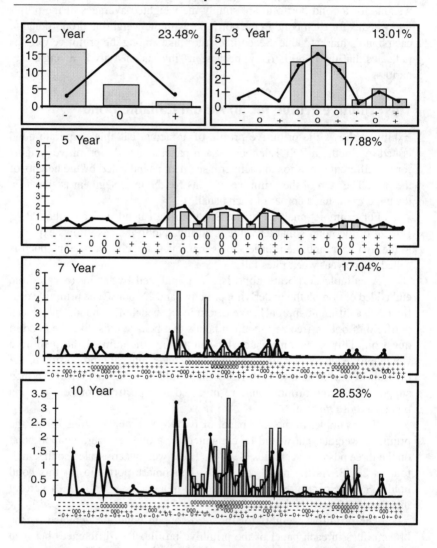

Here, the primitive profile for the Southern Bell bond clearly demonstrates the impact of the call provision on the bond's behavior. Compare the primitive weight on the falling rate path 0 − − at the five-year term with the weight on the 0 − − primitive in the benchmark portfolio.

Using the benchmark bond, we have a much better method to value the bond. Further, if we wish to control the risk using dynamic hedging strategies, for example (see McCoy [1993]), this methodology allows us to minimize the hedging risks. In using a binomial arbitrage-free model, we use the "risk-neutral" probabilities to determine the "expected" value that is consistent with relative valuation. In this context, the benchmark bond is in fact the "expected" cash flows of the bond, under the risk-neutral probabilities.

Unlike effective duration and convexity numbers, or key rate duration profiles, the primitive profile is relatively stable as the interest rate level changes. This is because the primitive profile depicts the payoffs in all scenarios, and these payoffs specify the bond type. When market interest rates change, the prices of the bonds adjust accordingly, but the general pattern of the profile would not change.

Analysis of Path Dependence: Pass-Throughs and PACs

There has been much discussion about the embedded option in mortgage-backed securities. Let us consider a new-issue 7.0 percent GNMA pass-through. Note in Exhibit 9 that the primitive profile of the pass-through differs from that of the benchmark bond, summarized as:

Year	1	3	5	7	10+
Benchmark Bond	8.02	22.02	21.22	17.35	31.61

The results show that the 7.0 percent GNMA has significant payments at the 10-year term and beyond. At the five-year term, however, we see that scenario 0 – – has significant prepayments.

A Planned Amortization Class (PAC) bond is a collateralized mortgage obligation (CMO) that is protected from prepayment risks by the existence of "support tranches," i.e., other CMO classes to which the prepayment risk is effectively transferred. Therefore PACs are considered to have relatively stable cash flows. The primitive profile can identify the scenarios where the protection fails, and the effect of the prepayments that will occur in those cases.

Consider two PAC bonds. Bond A is a well-supported PAC, while Bond B is poorly supported. The bonds and the benchmark bonds are summarized in Exhibit 10.

According to the primitive profiles of these PACs in Exhibits 11A and 11B, Bond A has more payments in the longer terms than Bond B. The

EXHIBIT 9   GNMA Pass-Through 359/30 7.00

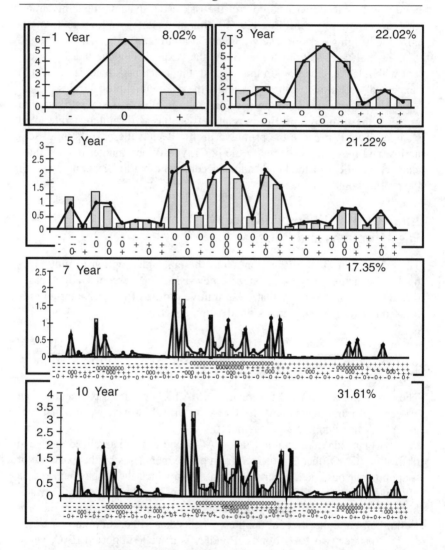

analysis shows that Bond A is well protected. Interest rates would have to fall for five years to produce high prepayments. By way of contrast, the results show that Bond B has significant prepayment risk and much less stable cash flows.

EXHIBIT 10   PAC Bonds A and B

Bond	Benchmark Bond Primitive Weights				
	1	*3*	*5*	*7*	*10+*
A FN92-210 KA	6.45	13.05	12.33	17.35	50.76
B FN92-65 E	6.62	23.13	34.78	16.68	18.74

Analyzing the FNMA 92-65 E PAC

FNMA 92-65 E in many ways is typical of PAC bonds. The deal was settled on May 29, 1992, backed by 30-year 8.50s (GWAC 8.95 percent), and was priced assuming a prepayment speed of PSA 200 (i.e., at 200 percent of, or twice as fast as, the Public Securities Association standard). The PAC E bond has a coupon of 7.5 percent, with stated weighted average life (WAL) of 10 years. The stated PAC collar (the range of prepayment speeds for which the WAL should hold) was 90–250 PSA. The deal has experienced high prepayments in the past year, and as a result the effective collar has drifted to 101 to 241 PSA.

At speeds of 100 to 200 PSA, the bond pays according to the planned amortization window, i.e., principal repayment expected in years 2001 to 2003. At the high speed of 500 PSA, however, the WAL shortens to 3.5 years; at the slow speed of 50 PSA, the WAL lengthens to over 10 years.

Analysis of the PAC bond shows:

Duration	5.23 years
Convexity	–0.13
Option Cost	34 basis points

The call risk lowers the duration below the WAL of the amortization window. The negative convexity and the option cost also confirm the presence of call risks. But, under what scenarios would we experience the impact of the call?

The primitive profiles provide us with more detailed information. In Exhibit 11B for FN 92-65 E, we see first that there is no call risk in the first year, but that the risk is high if the rate falls to 6.15 percent. If rates remain at that level, significant prepayments would occur for the next five years. The cash flow is particularly sensitive to a whipsaw of rates between three and five years.

Consider the two scenarios 0+– and 0–+. In the first scenario, the interest rate stays at 7.06 percent, then rises to 8.51 percent and falls to 7.86 percent in the fifth year, while the 0–+ path drops instead to 6.73 percent and

EXHIBIT 11A   FNMA 92-210 KA PAC

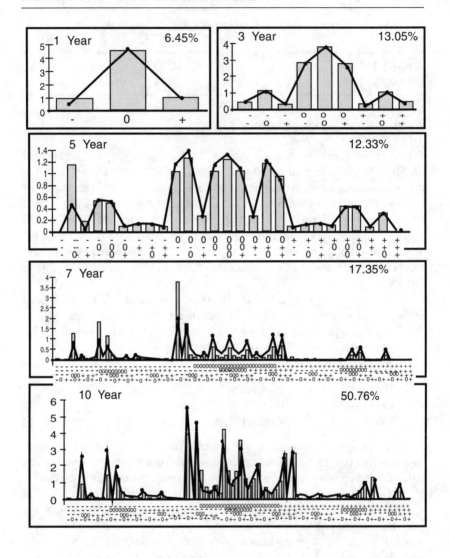

EXHIBIT 11B   FNMA 92-65 E PAC

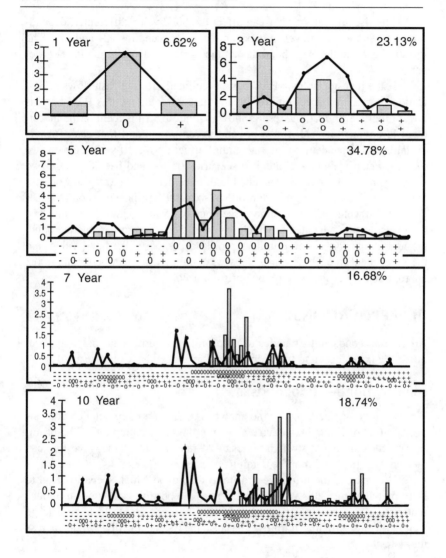

subsequently rises to 7.86 percent. The second scenario has much more impact on the bond.

The rise and fall of rates can affect the bond value differently, depending on when the rate movements occur. Consider scenarios 00– and –00. The results show that the PAC bond has a much greater payout in the former scenario.

If the investor holds a PAC bond specifically for the cash flows scheduled to be received according to the amortization window, this PAC bond is not appropriate. In fact, the results show that only 18.74 percent of the investment is paying for cash flows beyond seven years, and that cash flow is unstable and dependent on the rate path. Further, in the 10-year segment, we see that much weight is allotted to scenarios 0+0+0 and 0++00. These two scenarios have experienced sustained high rates, leading to extension of payments. In this case, the primitive profile also quantifies the extension risks.

When we invest in an option-free bond, we want to know how much of the investment is allocated to which payment. For an option-embedded bond, the idea is the same. The primitive profile decomposes the bond value into the investment in each scenario. This way, the investor can better judge the appropriateness of the bond to the portfolio need.

III. APPLICATIONS

Analysis of bonds and strategies using primitive securities has many applications. We have chosen to focus on four risk management examples.

Identifying the Hidden Risks

The primitive profile provides the analytics to direct a more detailed analysis of a CMO. For example, we have shown in the PAC example that the primitive profile can identify which whipsaw of rates affects value. Investors can then analyze the bond in more detail using vector analysis.

We can use the primitive profile to determine which scenarios lead to large prepayments. This way we can better plan portfolio strategies to reduce that risk. For example, it would generally be undesirable to have a large weight on any particular primitive, because the risk is not "diversified" across the states.

Profiting from Liquidity Cycles

In portfolio management, if we can assure that an asset and a liability are matched in primitive weights, then the cash flows are relatively matched. For this reason, we do not need to buy or sell bonds solely on the basis of risk management needs. We can trade bonds to enhance portfolio value. If we can succeed in controlling the risks, we can exploit the liquidity cycles of the bonds by buying when they are cheap, with the comfort that we will not be forced to sell when the market is illiquid.

Controlling Interest Rate Risks Beyond Duration and Convexity

Both effective duration and convexity have been used extensively in bond analytics. These static measures assume small instantaneous yield curve shifts. While they provide valuable information to investors, the information is often inadequate. The primitive securities approach enables us to analyze bonds on a cash-flow basis, allowing a better understanding of their characteristics.

For example, where immunization is concerned, instead of matching the target levels of portfolio duration and convexity, this research suggests that we can implement pathwise immunization. When we anticipate interest rate movements, instead of just lengthening or shortening duration, we can position the portfolio to bet on specific scenarios.

Managing Embedded Options

Our methodology allows determination of the base case cash flow in order to specify precisely the effect of embedded options. McCoy [1993] has shown how to strip the options from a bond and replicate them, using key rate durations for dynamic hedging. We have shown that the base case cash flow need not be the underlying coupons and principal of the bond.

The advantage of this approach is clear. The portfolio approach clearly separates the overlay strategies that deal with the uncertainty of the portfolio cash flows from the basic portfolio management. Using the benchmark bond, we have kept the overlay portfolio value to a minimum.

IV. CONCLUSIONS

For bonds that are free of explicit options, investors pay special attention to the sinking fund structure in corporate bonds and private placements, the amortization features in commercial mortgages, and the payment windows in PACs. By knowing the payments and the yield curve, investors can decompose an investment into bullet-payment components in order to analyze values and strategies. For option-embedded bonds, no analogous framework has been proposed.

Our main contribution is to extend the analytical framework of bond valuation to determine the building blocks of a bond's value when there are embedded options. The primitive securities approach views a bond as a portfolio of primitives. This way, we can identify the scenarios that the bond is "betting" on.

Further, we can easily extend the primitive securities analytics to portfolio strategies. In this general framework, we need not make a distinction between a bond and a strategy. They are both defined by their cash flows under different interest rate scenarios. As a result, we can define the appropriate timing for buying and selling bonds.

This approach has a number of advantages. First, it provides a more detailed specification of a bond's risk exposure. It provides a screening process to identify the basic areas of bond risk exposure. Second, the primitive securities approach enables us to define the embedded option risks. As a result, the analytics can identify the appropriate portfolio strategies to manage the option risk effectively. Third, this approach can properly identify the path-dependent nature of bonds. In today's markets, there are many bonds that are path-dependent, giving value to an approach that identifies the behavior of these bonds.

This article suggests several new avenues of research in providing only a framework to analyze a bond portfolio strategy as a portfolio of primitive securities. It may give some impetus to a study of bond portfolio strategies under a general consistent framework.

REFERENCES

Black, F., E. Derman, and W. Toy. "A One-Factor Model of Interest Rates and Its Application to Treasury Bond Options." *Financial Analysts Journal,* January-February 1990, pp. 33–39.

Davidson, A., and M. Herskovitz. "Twist and Shift: Valuing Path Dependence of MBS." Merrill Lynch & Co., November 1991.

Hartley, B., and T.O. Hawkes. *Rings, Modules and Linear Algebra.* London: Chapman and Hall, 1970.

Heath, D., R. Jarrow, and A. Morton. "Bond Pricing and Term Structure of Interest Rates: A New Methodology for Contingent Claim Valuation." *Econometrica,* 60 (1992), pp. 77–105.

Ho, T.S.Y. "Key Rate Durations: Measures of Interest Rate Risks." *Journal of Fixed Income,* September 1992a.

Ho, T.S.Y. "Managing Illiquid Bonds and the Linear Path Space." *Journal of Fixed Income,* June 1992b.

Ho, T.S.Y., and S.B. Lee. "Term Structure Movements and Pricing of Interest Rate Contingent Claims." *Journal of Finance,* 41 (1986), pp. 1011–1029.

Kao, D., and Y. Geyman. "Immunization Strategies and Pathwise Valuation." Working paper, Global Advanced Technology Corporation, 1993.

McCoy, W. "Bond Dynamic Hedging and Value Attribution: Empirical Evidence." Working paper, Global Advanced Technology Corporation, 1993.

Pederson, H., E. Shiu, and A. Thorlacius. "Arbitrage-Free Pricing of Interest Rate Contingent Claims." *Transactions of the Society of Actuaries,* 41 (1990).

10

Managing Illiquid Bonds and the Linear Path Space

Thomas S. Y. Ho
President, Global Advanced Technology Corporation

Beyond the large and liquid Treasury market and the generic mortgage-backed pass-through market, most bond markets are illiquid. Managing illiquid bonds, particularly bonds with embedded options, deserves special attention.

To value an illiquid collateralized mortgage obligation tranche, for example, we need to identify the performance of the bond along some interest rate paths. But which paths should we select? To analyze the ability of illiquid assets (for example, commercial mortgages) to support an insurance liability portfolio, what scenarios should we use in the scenario tests? How can we construct cash flow matching strategies using mortgage-backed securities? What interest rate scenarios should we use for testing surplus adequacy and portfolio management?

Much recent research has been devoted to pricing and analyzing interest rate-contingent claims such as interest rate options, callable bonds, mortgage-backed securities, and collateralized mortgage obligations. (See, for example, Brennan and Schwartz [1979], Courtadon [1982], Cox, Ingersoll, and Ross [1985], Jamshidian [1990], and Vasicek [1977].) Pricing models are used to identify the embedded option value and the option-adjusted spread.

Copyright © 1992 *The Journal of Fixed Income,* June, 1992. Published by Institutional Investor. Reprinted with permission.

The author thanks Tom McAvity and Kin Tam for invaluable suggestions and insights, as well as Mark Wainger, Chang Liu, and Yury Geyman for their assistance in testing the models throughout the project.

Analytics have been developed to identify the market value sensitivity (for example, effective duration) to the yield curve shifts.

Yet, when a bond cannot be traded, what does the market price mean? How should investors use the effective duration measure? How should the recent approach of "market valuation" be related to the more standard scenario testing? Despite the importance of these issues in managing illiquid bonds, no in-depth research has dealt with them.

The methodologies to analyze illiquid bonds to date are inadequate. For example, to test the surplus adequacy of an insurer, New York State Regulation 126 suggests seven interest rate scenarios to simulate the performance of the surplus. As the bonds in both the asset and liability portfolios of an insurer include increasingly complex embedded options, are seven scenarios enough?

As both banking and insurance industries move toward market value accounting, how should the accounting results be evaluated and used when there is no market for many of the assets and liabilities? Are the results consistent with those of scenario tests? In implementing a dynamic strategy in replicating a particular portfolio, managers often only use effective duration and other "market valuation" analyses. This approach would not be adequate when the portfolio has significant illiquid bond holdings, and when the portion of liquid assets is not sufficient to support the required trading level.

This article provides a framework of analysis for illiquid bonds. Its main result is that, within the context of an arbitrage-free interest rate movement model, the model price is the average value of the present value of the cash flows along all the interest rate paths. That is, if enough rate paths are taken in scenario testing, the market value is the present value of all scenarios.

But the choices are too extensive for an exhaustive selection of paths. Our model of the path space called Linear Path Space (LPS) is a sample of paths that can be generated under a specified recursive procedure (not randomly generated paths), with paths ordered according to importance. The LPS model has useful properties for scenario simulations.

Applications beyond relating scenario simulations to valuations extend to development of portfolio strategies. The model can be used to formulate immunization and dedication strategies using illiquid bonds with embedded options.

PATHWISE VALUATION

Arbitrage-free valuation has become a standard methodology in modern financial theory. For pricing an option-free cash flow, the methodology is relatively simple. A portfolio of zero-coupon bonds can be constructed so that the portfolio of bonds has payoffs identical to the option-free cash flow. Then the value of the cash flow should be the same as the portfolio value. Such is the case even if the cash flow is illiquid. (Often a spread is added to the cash flow to account for the illiquidity.) This approach is in essence discounting along the spot curve.

The pricing of bonds with embedded options in an arbitrage-free framework is more complicated. An interest rate movement model is called an arbitrage-free rate movement model if the pricing of options satisfies put-call parity or any other arbitrage conditions. In particular, if a bond, with option embedded or not, can be created synthetically by continually revising a portfolio of bonds, then the price of the bond equals the portfolio value.

The methodology of using continuous hedging to price the option-embedded bonds, in the same spirit as the pricing of stock options in the Black-Scholes model, is called the "relative valuation" approach. According to the relative valuation approach, securities are priced so that arbitrage is not possible with other securities.

Recently, another valuation approach has been used to price mortgage-backed securities. This approach generates an interest rate path from an interest rate movement model. The cash flow payoffs of a bond along the interest rate path can then be determined and discounted. The average of the present values along all the interest rate paths is the bond price. This methodology can be extended to any type of bond, with embedded options or not.

Therefore, given an arbitrage-free rate movement model (for examples, see Ho and Lee [1986], Black, Derman, and Toy [1990], Heath, Jarrow, and Morton [1990], and Pederson, Shiu, and Thorlacius [1989]), an option-free bond can be priced three ways: discounted along the spot curve, relative valuation, or pathwise valuation, and the results will all be consistent. In fact, for any bond (option-embedded or otherwise), the bond can be priced by relative valuation and pathwise valuation, as long as all the cash flows along a rate path are generated by rules consistent with the backward substitution procedure rules.

Proposition 1

Pathwise valuation of zero-coupon bonds is consistent with the backward substitution approach.

We can illustrate this result with a simple numerical example. The example is a binomial lattice of a one-year rate over a three-year horizon. A rate path in the binomial lattice is represented by a string of +s and –s, with + meaning that the rate goes up in that period, and – denoting a falling rate. Example 1 is given in Exhibit 1 and Table 1.

EXHIBIT 1 Binomial Lattice

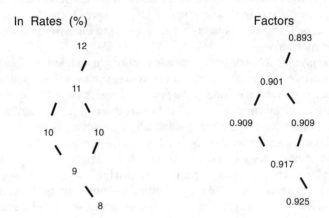

In Rates (%)   Factors

TABLE 1   Example of Proposition 1

Term of Zero-Coupon	Rate Path	Pathwise Value	Average
1	na	0.909	0.909
2	+	$0.819 = 0.909 \times 0.901$	
	−	$0.833 = 0.909 \times 0.917$	0.826
3	− −	$0.771 = 0.909 \times 0.917 \times 0.925$	
	− +	$0.758 = 0.909 \times 0.917 \times 0.909$	
	+ −	$0.744 = 0.909 \times 0.901 \times 0.909$	
	+ +	$0.731 = 0.909 \times 0.901 \times 0.893$	
			0.751

To verify that pathwise valuation is the same as backward substitution, we see that

$$0.909 \times 0.5 \times (0.901 + 0.917) = 0.826.$$

Similar calculations show that 0.751 is the price of the three-year zero-coupon bond according to the backward substitution approach. The proof of the proposition is presented in Appendix A.

TABLE 2   Example of Proposition 2

Rate Paths	Pathwise Value	Average
– –	0.833×0	
– +	0.833×0.009	
+ –	0.819×0.009	
+ +	0.819×0.025	
		$0.0088 = 0.0353/4$

Proposition 2

Pathwise valuation of a European option is consistent with relative valuation.

An extension of Example 1 will illustrate this result. Assume a European call option expiring in two years, with a strike price of 0.90, on a three-year zero-coupon bond. Using the binomial lattice for factors, we see that the payoffs of the option for the three states are: 0.0, 0.009, and 0.025. Hence, the pathwise values of the option are as in Table 2.

It can be verified that the option price calculated by backward substitution is also 0.0088. The proof of Proposition 2 is presented in Appendix B.

Proposition 3

Pathwise valuation is consistent with early exercise of American options. The proof is in Appendix C.

Proposition 3 is the more general result of both Propositions 1 and 2, but we present all three results here for clarity of exposition. These results are important for several reasons. First, they link the valuation of securities with scenario analysis, which is often used to study how a portfolio behaves along a particular interest rate path. These results show the relevance of scenario analyses for pricing. Second, valuation models are often used to study small shifts of the yield curve. By relating the price to scenario analysis, we can study the value of illiquid bonds by studying the cash flow of these bonds along interest rate paths. Third, these results enable us to construct portfolio strategies.

PATH SPACE STRUCTURE

Central to modern bond pricing models and scenario testing is the selection of interest rate paths in an arbitrage-free framework. An interest rate path typically is a vector of one-month spot rates for 30 years. Hence a rate path is a vector of $360 = 12 \times 30$ entries. The entries are rates selected from the binomial lattice of the interest rate model. For our purposes, when we select a rate path, we also attach to each spot rate the binomial lattice of arbitrage-free rates starting from that spot rate. A rate path in our discussion means the spot curves and subsequent movements assigned to each spot rate along the path.

There are 2^{360} possible paths. The set of all these paths is called the path space. The purpose of specifying the path space structure is to determine a set of paths that portfolio managers can use for pricing, scenario testing, and portfolio strategy testing. This set of rate paths (scenarios) should have the following properties:

1. Consistency with standard scenario testing, including interest rate levels remaining the same, rising, falling, or whipsawing, as in Regulation 126, which assumes seven basic scenarios: level, up then level, down then level, up instantaneous, down instantaneous, up whipsaw, and down whipsaw. The scenarios should have these seven as a subset.

2. Convergence to market value. The scenarios should be nested so that on the basic level the model is consistent with Regulation 126, but more and more paths can be used until the valuation converges to the bond value.

3. The convergence process should be systematic. Generation of paths leading to convergence must rest on a mathematical procedure, not on ad hoc specification of the scenarios.

4. Efficiency. The convergence process has to be efficient so that the path selection is consistent with variance reduction procedures. Therefore, a minimal number of paths is needed to converge onto the price.

5. Completeness. The path space should be partitioned so that all the paths in the path space can be accounted for.

6. Generalizable. The procedure must be easily extended to fit other requirements so that researchers can extend the path selection procedure to other structures without destroying the basic concepts.

A model of the path space must have the properties above so that it can be used for pricing, simulation, and structuring portfolio strategies.

LINEAR PATH SPACE MODEL

Linear path space modeling is a procedure for selecting a sample of paths and linear ordering of their importance in valuation. The first step is partitioning all the possible paths into equivalent classes. All the paths within each class should be "similar" to each other. Then, within each class we select a representative path. In relatively insignificant classes we can ignore representative paths. Then we rank representative paths by the "order" of the equivalent class (the relative size of the equivalent class). We basically classify paths by whether they rise, fall, or remain unchanged within a specified period in the future. Specification of the linear path space begins by stating these periods in the future.

We first divide the term (0 to 30 years) into segments consistent with the "key rates" often used by practitioners. So the term segment is a vector $T(i)$ i = 1, 2, 3...7 (12, 36, 60, 84, 120, 240, 360). There are seven segments. The first segment is (0, 11), the second (12, 35)..., and the seventh is (240, 359). For reasons to be explained later, we try to keep $T(i)$ divisible by two. The length of the ith segment is defined as $L(i) = T(i) - T(i-1)$, $T(0) = 1$.

Of course, more generally, a linear path space can be specified by any term segments. For clarity in presentation, we specify a particular linear path space using actual numbers, although the basic model can be easily modified or extended. Exhibit 2 shows the partitioning of the path space.

The state space at the end of each segment is called the key state space. The first key state space has 12 states ($i = 0...11$), the second has 36 ($i = 0...35$), and so on to ($i = 0,...,n-1$). We next partition the key state spaces in such a way that the partitioning can be generated recursively (Property 3), and is consistent in practice with level scenarios and symmetric up and down scenarios (Property 1).

We first divide the first key state space into three equal partitions (up, level, down): (0, 3), (4, 7), and (8, 11). In partitioning the second state space, we need to keep the first partition the same as the second to ensure that there are level rate movements. Then the remaining states on both ends of the second state space become the remaining partitions. Hence the 36 states of the second key state space are partitioned into five parts, each part represented by the highest and the lowest states of each partition: (0, 11), (12, 15), (16, 19), (20, 23), (24, 35).

Similarly, partitioning of the third state space is given by (0, 11), (12, 23), (24, 27), (28, 31), (32, 35), (36, 47), (48, 59). For the Kth key state space, there are $2K + 1$ partitions. Therefore there are always an odd number of partitions, yielding a middle partition with the other partitions symmetric

EXHIBIT 2   Linear Path Space

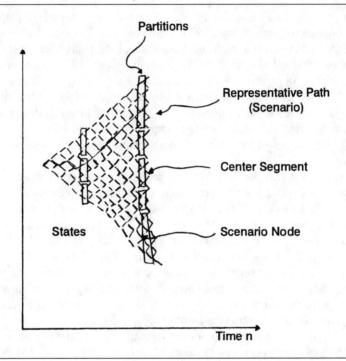

Linear Path Space partitions the binomial path space so that the representative paths (scenarios) form a trinomial lattice.

on both sides. The middle partition is called the center segment of the Kth key state space; there are K partitions above and K partitions below. Therefore, $(K, J) - K < J < K$ uniquely defines each partition.

Next we define the recursive generation of linear partitioning. Given the ith key space partition, the $(K + 1)$th key space partition is; beyond the first partition $(0, T(K + 1) - T(K) - 1)$, create the second and following partitions up to the $(2K + 2)$th partitions simply by adding $T(K + 1) - T(K)$ to all the entries to the Kth partition. The $2(K + 1) + 1$ partition is $([T(K + 1) + T(K)]/2, T(K + 1) - 1)$. Each partition can be represented by (I, J) or by (i, l, u), where l and u are the lower and the upper limit of a partition.

Each interest rate path (a vector of 360 entries) must pass through one and only one partition of each key state space. Hence the total interest rate path space is partitioned by $[J(1), J(2), ..., J(7)]$, where $-K < J(K) < K$. $J(K)$ specifies the order of the segment of the partition of the key state space.

For example, $(1, -2, 4,....,)$ is the class of paths that goes through the first segment above the center segment of the first key partition; then the paths continue to pass through the second segment below the center segment of the second key state partition; and finally pass through the fourth segment above the center segment. Note that many of these partitions are null spaces, with no interest rate path belonging to the partition. There are $3 \times 5 \times 7 \times \cdots \times 15$ equivalent classes, but many of them have no rate path belonging to the equivalent class.

The linear path space considers only the equivalent classes where $J(K)$ can be -1, 0, or 1. That is, the linear path space considers only rate paths that go down, stay level, or go up to another scenario node, and therefore they stay relatively stable within each term segment. As a result, there are 3^7 equivalent classes in the linear path space.

EQUIVALENT CLASSES OF THE LINEAR PATH SPACE AND THEIR ORDERING

Here we define the representatives of the scenario classes (called scenarios) and calculate the number of paths in each class to all the paths in the path space (called the order of the scenario).

We define $| i, l, u |$ to be a midpoint operation where:

$| i, l, u | = (u - l)/2$ if an integer and keep the value positive,
$\quad\quad\quad = $ next higher integer of $x = (u - l)/2$ if $x > T(i)/2$,
$\quad\quad\quad = $ next lower integer otherwise.

The scenario nodes are defined as the node $n(i, J) = (T(i) - 1, | i,l,u | = | i,J |)$ on the binomial path space.

A branch $b(i, J, K)$ is the shortest interest rate path that links the node $(i - 1, J)$ to the node (i, K). The branch is defined as for each j, $T(i) - 1 < j < T(i + 1) - 1$, $y = | i,J | + (| i + 1,J | \times j)/[T(i) - T(i - 1)]$. Then the state corresponding to the jth month is the integer of y. The branches that connect the segments represent the representative path of the equivalent class.

Given a representative path, we can calculate the number of paths in the equivalent class to which this representative belongs. Each scenario can be represented by a vector of seven entries with each entry being −1, 0 or 1. (0,0,0,0,0,0,0) represents the "level" scenario, where the interest rate level experiences minimal change in the next 30 years within the arbitrage-free rate movement model.

At this point, we still have numerous scenarios ($3^7 = 2{,}187$) in the linear path space. We need to have a procedure that systematically reduces the number of scenarios for scenario testing. Selection of scenarios can be accomplished by linear ordering them in descending order. The number of scenarios to be used for testing will depend on how well these scenarios explain the valuation of the securities.

A partial list of the ordering of the linear path space is presented in Table 3 on pages 284 and 285. For simplicity in presenting the basic idea of the linear path space, we consider all the paths only up to the 10th year. Complete analysis of the path space for 30 years is a straightforward extension of the analysis.

The first column in Table 3 is the numbering of the scenarios. The second column identifies the scenarios by code. The third column presents the percentage of the number of paths in the equivalent class of all the paths in the path space. The fourth column presents the cumulative order of the scenarios. The fifth column shows the percentage that the number of paths of each equivalent class represents of all the paths of the linear path space, called the weight of the scenarios. The sixth column is the cumulative weights. By definition, the cumulative weights should approach one at a decreasing rate.

The results are somewhat surprising. First, the linear path space represents 89.9 percent of all the paths, as the cumulative order of the scenarios shows. Second, the first 29 and 73 scenarios represent over 50 percent and 75 percent of all the interest rate paths. These are manageable sample sizes for scenario analysis. Also, nearly all the paths pass through the two segments above and below the center segments. Indeed, paths that extend beyond these segments represent zero weights.

Consider the June 28, 1991 spot curve and the implied volatilities of 14 percent for the one-year rate and 10 percent for the 10-year rate. The one-month spot rates on the scenario nodes are given in Exhibit 3. Because the yield curve is upward-sloping, the rates in the level scenario rise slowly. The lattice of rates also shows the effect of mean reversion of rates. When interest rates are high, in a scenario of high rates, we see that the level of interest rates falls slightly.

In Exhibit 3, we can see generally how the linear path space represents the seven scenarios of Regulation 126. The seven scenarios and their propor-

**EXHIBIT 3   The Prevailing One-Month Spot Rates
at the Scenario Nodes**

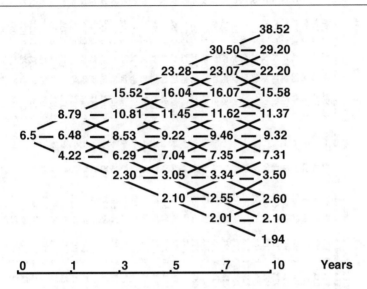

tions to all the paths (weights) of Regulation 126 are given in Table 4 on page 286.

If the scenarios can be represented by the seven scenarios in the linear path space, we can actually calculate the proportion of paths represented by these scenarios. The proportion is 10.38 percent. The "level" scenario is clearly the dominant scenario, representing close to 50 percent of the paths represented by the seven scenarios. Therefore, the seven scenarios seem to represent a relatively small portion of all the possible paths used to value a security.

LINEAR PATH SPACE AND PATHWISE VALUATION

For a particular bond, option embedded or otherwise, one can determine the cash-flow payout of the bond along an interest rate path. The present value of the cash flow can be discounted along that particular interest rate path, with the resulting value called the pathwise value. But the scenario represents a proportion of paths in the path space. Therefore, the weighted sum of the pathwise values (using the scenario weights) would determine the security

TABLE 3   Linear Path Space

#	Code	% Ttl. Path	% Cumul.	% Path Cnsdrd	% Cumul.
1	00000	5.82%	5.82%	6.47%	6.47%
2	0000-	2.94%	8.76%	3.27%	9.75%
3	0000+	2.94%	11.71%	3.27%	13.02%
4	000-0	2.32%	14.02%	2.58%	15.60%
5	000+0	2.32%	16.34%	2.58%	18.17%
6	00-00	2.31%	18.65%	2.57%	20.74%
7	00+00	2.31%	20.96%	2.57%	23.31%
8	0-000	2.28%	23.24%	2.54%	25.85%
9	0+000	2.28%	25.52%	2.54%	28.38%
10	0-00-	1.45%	26.97%	1.61%	30.00%
11	0+00-	1.45%	28.42%	1.61%	31.61%
12	000-+	1.44%	29.85%	1.60%	33.21%
13	000-+	1.44%	31.29%	1.60%	34.80%
14	0-0-0	1.32%	32.61%	1.47%	36.27%
15	0-0-0	1.32%	33.93%	1.47%	37.74%
16	0-00-	1.29%	35.22%	1.43%	39.17%
17	0+00+	1.29%	36.51%	1.43%	40.60%
18	0-00+	1.26%	37.76%	1.40%	42.00%
19	00-0+	1.26%	39.02%	1.40%	43.40%
20	00-0+	1.21%	40.23%	1.35%	44.75%
21	0+00+	1.21%	41.45%	1.35%	46.10%
22	00+00	1.21%	42.65%	1.35%	47.44%
23	00+-0	1.21%	43.86%	1.34%	48.78%
24	0-+00	1.19%	45.05%	1.33%	50.11%
25	0+-00	1.19%	46.24%	1.33%	51.43%
26	0-0+0	1.16%	47.40%	1.29%	52.72%
27	0+00-	1.16%	48.56%	1.29%	54.01%
28	000--	1.02%	49.58%	1.13%	55.15%
29	000-+	1.02%	50.60%	1.13%	56.28%
30	00++0	0.99%	51.59%	1.10%	57.38%
31	00--0	0.99%	52.58%	1.10%	58.48%
32	0+0+0	0.96%	53.54%	1.06%	59.55%
33	0-0+0	0.96%	54.49%	1.06%	60.61%
34	-0000	0.82%	55.31%	0.91%	61.52%
35	+0000	0.82%	56.13%	0.91%	62.43%
36	00-+-	0.73%	56.86%	0.81%	63.25%
77	-00+0	0.33%	76.56%	0.37%	85.15%
78	0+--+	0.27%	76.83%	0.30%	85.46%
79	0-+--	0.27%	77.10%	0.30%	85.76%
80	-+00-	0.27%	77.38%	0.30%	86.06%
81	+-00+	0.27%	77.65%	0.30%	86.37%
82	+-00-	0.27%	77.92%	0.30%	86.67%
83	-+00-	0.27%	78.19%	0.30%	86.97%
84	+-+00	0.27%	78.45%	0.30%	87.26%
85	-+-00	0.27%	78.72%	0.30%	87.56%
86	0---+	0.24%	78.96%	0.27%	87.83%
87	0+++-	0.24%	79.21%	0.27%	88.10%
88	0-+++	0.23%	79.43%	0.25%	88.35%
89	0+---	0.23%	79.66%	0.25%	88.60%
90	-0+0+	0.22%	79.88%	0.25%	88.85%
91	+0-0-	0.22%	80.10%	0.25%	89.10%
92	+00-+	0.21%	80.31%	0.23%	89.32%
93	-00+-	0.21%	80.51%	0.23%	89.55%
94	+-0+0	0.20%	80.72%	0.23%	89.78%
95	+-0-0	0.20%	80.92%	0.23%	90.01%
96	-00-+	0.20%	81.12%	0.22%	90.23%
97	+00+-	0.20%	81.32%	0.22%	90.45%
98	+0-0+	0.19%	81.51%	0.21%	90.66%
99	-0+0-	0.19%	81.70%	0.21%	90.87%
100	-0+0+	0.19%	81.88%	0.21%	91.08%
101	+0-0+	0.19%	82.07%	0.21%	91.28%
102	-0+0-	0.17%	82.24%	0.19%	91.48%
103	+0+0-	0.17%	82.42%	0.19%	91.67%
104	+0-0-	0.17%	82.58%	0.18%	91.85%
105	-0-0+	0.17%	82.75%	0.18%	92.04%
106	+--00	0.16%	82.91%	0.18%	92.22%
107	-++00	0.16%	83.07%	0.18%	92.40%
108	++0-0	0.16%	83.23%	0.17%	92.57%
109	-0-0+	0.16%	83.38%	0.17%	92.75%
110	0+---	0.15%	83.53%	0.17%	92.91%
111	0-+++	0.15%	83.69%	0.17%	93.08%
112	0-++-	0.15%	83.83%	0.16%	93.24%
153	++-+0	0.08%	88.25%	0.08%	98.16%
154	++0-0	0.08%	88.32%	0.08%	98.23%
155	--0+0	0.08%	88.39%	0.08%	98.31%
156	+-++0	0.07%	88.45%	0.07%	98.39%
157	+---0	0.07%	88.52%	0.07%	98.46%
158	-0++-	0.07%	88.59%	0.07%	98.53%
159	+0--+	0.07%	88.65%	0.07%	98.61%
160	+0+--	0.06%	88.72%	0.07%	98.68%
161	-0-++	0.06%	88.78%	0.07%	98.75%
162	-+++-	0.06%	88.84%	0.06%	98.81%
163	--++-	0.06%	88.89%	0.06%	98.87%
164	++-0+	0.05%	88.95%	0.06%	98.93%
165	--+0-	0.05%	89.00%	0.06%	98.99%
166	+++-+	0.05%	89.05%	0.06%	99.05%
167	+--++	0.05%	89.10%	0.06%	99.11%
168	+++--	0.05%	89.16%	0.06%	99.17%
169	+++-+	0.05%	89.21%	0.06%	99.22%
170	++0+0	0.05%	89.25%	0.05%	99.28%
171	-0-++	0.05%	89.30%	0.05%	99.33%
172	++0+-	0.05%	89.35%	0.05%	99.38%
173	---++	0.04%	89.39%	0.05%	99.43%
174	-0++-	0.04%	89.44%	0.05%	99.48%
175	+0---	0.04%	89.48%	0.05%	99.53%
176	+++-+	0.04%	89.52%	0.04%	99.57%
177	+---+	0.04%	89.55%	0.04%	99.61%
178	+--+-	0.03%	89.58%	0.04%	99.64%
179	-+++-	0.03%	89.61%	0.03%	99.67%
180	++--+	0.03%	89.64%	0.03%	99.70%
181	+++--	0.03%	89.67%	0.03%	99.73%
182	--0++	0.03%	89.69%	0.03%	99.77%
183	++0--	0.03%	89.72%	0.03%	99.80%
184	+++-0	0.03%	89.75%	0.03%	99.83%
185	++--0	0.03%	89.78%	0.03%	99.86%
186	--+++	0.02%	89.79%	0.03%	99.88%
187	+++--	0.02%	89.81%	0.02%	99.90%
188	0+++-	0.01%	89.82%	0.01%	99.91%

TABLE 3 (continued)

#						#						#					
37	00+-+	0.73%	57.59%	0.81%	64.06%	113	0+---	0.15%	83.98%	0.16%	93.41%	189	0-0-	0.01%	89.84%	0.01%	99.92%
38	+0+00	0.67%	58.26%	0.75%	64.81%	114	++0+0	0.15%	84.12%	0.16%	93.57%	190	--00-	0.01%	89.85%	0.01%	99.94%
39	-0-00	0.67%	58.93%	0.75%	65.55%	115	+-0-0	0.15%	84.27%	0.16%	93.73%	191	-+00+	0.01%	89.86%	0.01%	99.95%
40	0-+0-	0.62%	59.56%	0.69%	66.25%	116	+++0-	0.14%	84.41%	0.15%	93.88%	192	-+---	0.01%	89.87%	0.01%	99.96%
41	0+-0+	0.62%	60.18%	0.69%	66.94%	117	+-0+	0.14%	84.54%	0.15%	94.04%	193	++---	0.01%	89.88%	0.01%	99.97%
42	0+-+0	0.61%	60.79%	0.67%	67.61%	118	+0+	0.14%	84.68%	0.15%	94.19%	194	-0-0-	0.01%	89.89%	0.01%	99.98%
43	0+-0-	0.61%	61.39%	0.67%	68.29%	119	+0+	0.14%	84.82%	0.15%	94.34%	195	+0+0+	0.01%	89.89%	0.01%	99.99%
44	0-0+-	0.59%	61.98%	0.66%	68.94%	120	+++0	0.14%	84.95%	0.15%	94.49%	196	0+0+0	0.00%	89.90%	0.00%	99.99%
45	0+0-+	0.59%	62.57%	0.66%	69.60%	121	+-+0	0.14%	85.09%	0.15%	94.64%	197	0-0--	0.00%	89.90%	0.00%	99.99%
46	0+0+0	0.58%	63.15%	0.65%	70.24%	122	-00++	0.13%	85.22%	0.15%	94.79%	198	-0-00	0.00%	89.90%	0.00%	99.99%
47	0+0+0	0.58%	63.74%	0.65%	70.89%	123	+00+	0.13%	85.36%	0.15%	94.94%	199	-0-0+	0.00%	89.90%	0.00%	99.99%
48	0-0-+	0.54%	64.28%	0.60%	71.49%	124	+-0+	0.13%	85.48%	0.14%	95.08%	200	00+++	0.00%	89.90%	0.00%	100.00%
49	0+0+-	0.54%	64.82%	0.60%	72.09%	125	-+0+	0.13%	85.61%	0.14%	95.22%	201	00---	0.00%	89.90%	0.00%	100.00%
50	+-000	0.53%	65.35%	0.60%	72.69%	126	-++-0	0.12%	85.73%	0.14%	95.35%	202	+0+-+	0.00%	89.90%	0.00%	100.00%
51	-+000	0.53%	65.89%	0.60%	73.28%	127	+++0	0.12%	85.85%	0.13%	95.48%	203	-0+--	0.00%	89.90%	0.00%	100.00%
52	--000	0.52%	66.41%	0.58%	73.87%	128	+0+	0.11%	85.96%	0.13%	95.61%	204	+00++	0.00%	89.90%	0.00%	100.00%
53	++000	0.52%	66.93%	0.58%	74.45%	129	-0++	0.11%	86.07%	0.13%	95.73%	205	-00--	0.00%	89.90%	0.00%	100.00%
54	00+--	0.50%	67.43%	0.55%	75.00%	130	+0++	0.11%	86.18%	0.13%	95.85%	206	0+++0	0.00%	89.90%	0.00%	100.00%
55	00+-+	0.50%	67.93%	0.55%	75.55%	131	-0+	0.11%	86.29%	0.12%	95.97%	207	0---0	0.00%	89.90%	0.00%	100.00%
56	-00-0	0.49%	68.42%	0.55%	76.10%	132	-0-0	0.10%	86.39%	0.12%	96.09%	208	-+++-	0.00%	89.90%	0.00%	100.00%
57	+000+	0.49%	68.91%	0.55%	76.65%	133	-0+0	0.10%	86.49%	0.12%	96.21%	209	-++++	0.00%	89.91%	0.00%	100.00%
58	+000-	0.46%	69.38%	0.52%	77.17%	134	--00-	0.10%	86.59%	0.11%	96.32%	210	0+++-	0.00%	89.91%	0.00%	100.00%
59	-000+	0.46%	69.84%	0.52%	77.68%	135	++00-	0.10%	86.69%	0.11%	96.43%	211	+-0-0	0.00%	89.91%	0.00%	100.00%
60	00++-	0.43%	70.27%	0.47%	78.16%	136	+0++	0.10%	86.79%	0.11%	96.54%	212	+-0+0	0.00%	89.91%	0.00%	100.00%
61	00+-+	0.43%	70.69%	0.47%	78.63%	137	+0+	0.10%	86.89%	0.11%	96.64%	213	-0-0-0	0.00%	89.91%	0.00%	100.00%
62	+000-	0.42%	71.11%	0.46%	79.09%	138	--+00	0.09%	86.98%	0.10%	96.75%	214	-++++	0.00%	89.91%	0.00%	100.00%
63	-000+	0.42%	71.52%	0.46%	79.55%	139	++00	0.09%	87.07%	0.10%	96.85%	215	-0-++	0.00%	89.91%	0.00%	100.00%
64	0+-++	0.38%	71.91%	0.43%	79.98%	140	+0++	0.09%	87.16%	0.10%	96.94%	216	-0+-+	0.00%	89.91%	0.00%	100.00%
65	0+0--	0.38%	72.29%	0.43%	80.41%	141	+0+-	0.09%	87.25%	0.10%	97.04%	217	+0+-+	0.00%	89.91%	0.00%	100.00%
66	0-+++	0.37%	72.66%	0.41%	80.82%	142	-++0+	0.09%	87.34%	0.10%	97.14%	218	-+++-	0.00%	89.91%	0.00%	100.00%
67	0-++-	0.37%	73.03%	0.41%	81.23%	143	+--0+	0.09%	87.42%	0.10%	97.24%	219	--+++	0.00%	89.91%	0.00%	100.00%
68	0-+0-	0.37%	73.39%	0.41%	81.64%	144	+++-0	0.09%	87.51%	0.10%	97.34%	220	--00	0.00%	89.91%	0.00%	100.00%
69	0++0-	0.37%	73.76%	0.41%	82.04%	145	+--+0	0.09%	87.60%	0.10%	97.44%	221	+++00	0.00%	89.91%	0.00%	100.00%
70	-0-+0	0.36%	74.12%	0.40%	82.44%	146	-++0	0.09%	87.69%	0.09%	97.53%	222	+++-0	0.00%	89.91%	0.00%	100.00%
71	+0+-0	0.36%	74.48%	0.40%	82.84%	147	+--0+	0.08%	87.77%	0.09%	97.63%	223	+++-0	0.00%	89.91%	0.00%	100.00%
72	-0-0-	0.36%	74.83%	0.39%	83.24%	148	-0+-	0.09%	87.86%	0.09%	97.72%	224	+++-0	0.00%	89.91%	0.00%	100.00%
73	0-++0	0.36%	75.19%	0.39%	83.63%	149	+0++	0.08%	87.94%	0.09%	97.81%	225	---0+	0.00%	89.91%	0.00%	100.00%
74	0-+-0	0.35%	75.54%	0.39%	84.02%	150	+-++	0.08%	88.02%	0.09%	97.91%	226	---+	0.00%	89.91%	0.00%	100.00%
75	0++-0	0.35%	75.90%	0.39%	84.42%	151	+++	0.08%	88.10%	0.09%	98.00%	227	+++++	0.00%	89.91%	0.00%	100.00%
76	+00-0	0.33%	76.23%	0.37%	84.79%	152	-++-0	0.07%	88.18%	0.08%	98.08%	228	++0++	0.00%	89.91%	0.00%	100.00%

285

TABLE 4   Regulation 126 Scenarios

Type	Description	Representation	Weights (%)
Level	Rate Remains Unchanged	00000	5.82
500 Rise	Rise Until Year 10	0+0+0	1.32
Pop Up	300 Instantaneous Rise	10000	0.82
+ Whipsaw	500 Rise in Year 5, then Fall	0++−−	0.14
500 Fall	Fall Until Year 10	0–0–0	1.32
Pop Down	300 Instantaneous Fall	−0000	0.82
− Whipsaw	500 Fall in Year 5, then Rise	0−−++	0.14

value. However, ordering of the paths of the linear path space means that we do not need to calculate all the pathwise values. Because the cumulative weighted pathwise value should converge to the underlying value, we can examine the speed of the convergence.

To analyze the convergence of pricing, we consider the spot curve estimated as of June 28, 1991, as above. Tables 5A and 5B on pages 288–290 present the convergence of valuation on benchmark securities; a 10-year zero-coupon bond and a five-year zero-coupon bond. The results show that the linear path space does lead to convergence of value. Moreover, the convergence is fast. The results show that the first 176 paths and 24 paths can price the 10-year and the five-year zero-coupon bonds within 0.5 percent.

Table 6 on page 291 compares the prices of European call options on a 20-year zero-coupon bond expiring in 10 years and call options on a 10-year zero-coupon bond expiring in five years at different strike prices. Results show that the pathwise valuation approach does converge to the theoretical value computed by backward substitution. As one might expect, the convergence is better for in-the-money options than for out-of-the-money options.

We should emphasize that the linear path space approach is not a better methodology than the backward substitution approach in pricing optimally exercised interest rate options. The comparison made here is simply used as a benchmark test.

PATHWISE VALUATION PROFILE

The performance profile (or price/yield relationship) is a standard tool in analyzing bond value with respect to the shift of the yield curve. The performance profile is a plot of the bond price against the instantaneous parallel shift of the yield curve. Such a pathwise valuation profile can depict the level of duration and convexity of the bond, and therefore is useful for formulating dynamic strategies.

A similar plot can be used for managing illiquid bonds. We can plot the pathwise value of the bond against the average shift of the rate path. This shift is defined as the average of the differences of each spot rate along the rate path from the "level" scenario. As there may be two scenarios having the same shift but different pathwise values, the plot would be a scattered plot. Even a scattered plot would reveal much about the behavior of the bond or portfolio strategy.

According to the main result, the fair price is the average of all the pathwise values. A horizontal line drawn through the fair price becomes the break-even line for the scenarios. Scenarios above the line are profitable scenarios, while those below the line are unprofitable. Identifying the scenarios that result in profitability, and quantifying the profits, allows investors to make better buy or sell decisions.

Exhibit 4A on page 292 depicts the pathwise valuation profile of a 10-year zero-coupon bond. The first 33 paths (which represent over 50 percent of the path space) from the linear path space are used in the plot. The curve AB is the performance profile of the bond. As expected, the pathwise profile is a scattered plot around the performance profile. The bond price is also similar to that of the present value along the level scenario.

Exhibit 4B depicts the profile of the European call option on a 20-year zero-coupon bond with 10 years to expiration, at a strike price of 50. In this case, the price of the option exceeds the pathwise value of the "level" scenario, which is zero. Indeed, the option would result in a loss much more often than not, although the potential profit is significant.

In comparison with the performance profile AB in Exhibit 4A, the plot of the pathwise valuation is much more scattered than that of the zero-coupon bond. For example, two paths with average shifts of 180 basis points from the level scenario have very different present values: one at 11 and the other at zero.

Upon closer examination, the result shows that in one case the rate falls immediately at the beginning but not to a level sufficient for the option to

TABLE 5A Linear Path Convergence

#	Code	Weights (A)	Prsnt Val 10 Yr Zero	Cumul. Sum(A*B)
1	00000	6.47%	0.4345	0.0281
2	0000-	3.27%	0.4473	0.0427
3	0000+	3.27%	0.4220	0.0565
4	000+0	2.58%	0.4020	0.0669
5	000-0	2.58%	0.4696	0.0790
6	00+00	2.57%	0.3861	0.0889
7	00-00	2.57%	0.4889	0.1015
8	0+000	2.54%	0.3704	0.1109
9	0-000	2.54%	0.5097	0.1239
10	0++00	1.61%	0.2925	0.1286
11	0--00	1.61%	0.6454	0.1390
12	000-+	1.60%	0.4561	0.1463
13	000+-	1.60%	0.4139	0.1529
14	0-0-0	1.47%	0.5953	0.1616
15	0+0+0	1.47%	0.3171	0.1663
16	0-00+	1.43%	0.3494	0.1713
17	0-00-	1.43%	0.5402	0.1790
18	00-0-	1.40%	0.5182	0.1863
19	00+0+	1.40%	0.3643	0.1914
20	00-0+	1.35%	0.4749	0.1978
21	00+0-	1.35%	0.3975	0.2032
22	00-+0	1.34%	0.4524	0.2092
23	00+-0	1.34%	0.4173	0.2148
24	0-+00	1.33%	0.4530	0.2208
25	0+-00	1.33%	0.4168	0.2264
26	0-+0-	1.29%	0.4951	0.2328
27	0+0-0	1.29%	0.3813	0.2377
28	000++	1.13%	0.3793	0.2420
29	000--	1.13%	0.4977	0.2476
30	00--0	1.10%	0.5711	0.2539
31	00++0	1.10%	0.3306	0.2575
32	0-0+0	1.06%	0.4003	0.2618
33	0+0-0	1.06%	0.4716	0.2667
34	-0000	0.91%	0.3590	0.2700
35	-0000	0.91%	0.5258	0.2748
36	00-++	0.81%	0.4053	0.2781
77	-00+0	0.37%	0.4865	0.3760
78	-+00+	0.30%	0.4354	0.3773
79	+-00-	0.30%	0.4615	0.3787
80	0-+--	0.30%	0.5189	0.3803
81	+-00+	0.30%	0.4091	0.3815
82	++00-	0.30%	0.3743	0.3826
83	++-00	0.30%	0.5044	0.3841
84	0-+++	0.30%	0.3638	0.3852
85	+-00-	0.30%	0.4336	0.3865
86	0-++-	0.27%	0.5856	0.3881
87	0++++	0.27%	0.3223	0.3890
88	0-+++	0.25%	0.4315	0.3900
89	-+0-0	0.25%	0.4844	0.3912
90	0+--+	0.25%	0.4375	0.3923
91	++0+0	0.25%	0.3897	0.3933
92	-00++	0.23%	0.5009	0.3945
93	+00-+	0.23%	0.3769	0.3953
94	-+0+0	0.23%	0.4147	0.3963
95	+-0-0	0.23%	0.4552	0.3973
96	++00+	0.22%	0.3258	0.3981
97	-00-+	0.22%	0.5794	0.3993
98	-0+-0	0.21%	0.5050	0.4004
99	+0-0+	0.21%	0.3924	0.4012
100	-0+0-	0.21%	0.3738	0.4020
101	+0-+0	0.21%	0.4811	0.4030
102	-0+0+	0.19%	0.4539	0.4039
103	+0-0-	0.19%	0.4159	0.4047
104	+--00	0.18%	0.3983	0.4054
105	+-+00	0.18%	0.4739	0.4062
106	0+0+-	0.18%	0.3005	0.4068
107	-0-0+	0.18%	0.6281	0.4079
108	-0-0+	0.17%	0.5700	0.4089
109	+0+0-	0.17%	0.3312	0.4094
110	0+---	0.17%	0.4774	0.4102
111	-0+++	0.17%	0.3954	0.4109
112	-+0-0	0.16%	0.5346	0.4118
153	-0+-0	0.08%	0.6195	0.4337
154	+++-0	0.08%	0.2828	0.4359
155	++0-0	0.08%	0.3047	0.4342
156	-0+-0	0.07%	0.4451	0.4345
157	-+++0	0.07%	0.3410	0.4347
158	+0--+	0.07%	0.4241	0.4350
159	+0+--	0.07%	0.3410	0.4353
160	-0-++	0.07%	0.5536	0.4356
161	+---0	0.07%	0.5535	0.4360
162	+--0-	0.06%	0.6057	0.4364
163	-+++-	0.06%	0.4181	0.4367
164	+-+++	0.06%	0.5558	0.4370
165	++-0+	0.06%	0.3117	0.4372
166	++-+-	0.06%	0.4515	0.4374
167	+-+-+	0.06%	0.4165	0.4377
168	-+-++	0.06%	0.4533	0.4380
169	+-+--	0.06%	0.3396	0.4382
170	++0--	0.05%	0.3401	0.4383
171	-+0+-	0.05%	0.5551	0.4386
172	++0-+	0.05%	0.2875	0.4388
173	-0++-	0.05%	0.6566	0.4391
174	+0+-+	0.05%	0.4628	0.4393
175	-0+++	0.05%	0.4079	0.4395
176	-++-+	0.04%	0.4432	0.4397
177	-++-+	0.04%	0.4259	0.4399
178	-0++-	0.03%	0.6017	0.4401
179	+++-+	0.03%	0.5222	0.4402
180	-++++	0.03%	0.3615	0.4403
181	-+++-	0.03%	0.6297	0.4405
182	-+++0	0.03%	0.5288	0.4407
183	++--0	0.03%	0.3570	0.4408
184	++0+-	0.03%	0.3137	0.4409
185	+0+-+	0.03%	0.2998	0.4410
186	-++--	0.02%	0.5444	0.4411
187	++++-	0.02%	0.3468	0.4411
188	-0-0-	0.01%	0.7157	0.4412

TABLE 5A (continued)

#	path	%	val 1	val 2	#	path	%	val 1	val 2	#	path	%	val 1	val 2
37	00-+-	0.81%	0.4657	0.2819	113	++-0+	0.16%	0.3531	0.4123	189	++00+	0.01%	0.2391	0.4412
38	+0-+00	0.75%	0.2835	0.2840	114	0++--	0.16%	0.3518	0.4129	190	++--	0.01%	0.3676	0.4413
39	-0-00	0.75%	0.6658	0.2890	115	0-++	0.16%	0.5367	0.4138	191	+0+0+	0.01%	0.2598	0.4413
40	0-+0-	0.69%	0.4663	0.2922	116	+-+-0	0.15%	0.4705	0.4145	192	0++0+	0.01%	0.2681	0.4413
41	0++-0	0.69%	0.4048	0.2950	117	++-+0	0.15%	0.4667	0.4152	193	--00-	0.01%	0.7778	0.4414
42	0-++-0	0.67%	0.4895	0.2983	118	+++-0	0.15%	0.4045	0.4158	194	0-+-	0.01%	0.6938	0.4415
43	0-++0	0.67%	0.3856	0.3009	119	+00++	0.15%	0.3995	0.4164	195	0--++	0.00%	0.5136	0.4415
44	0-0+-	0.66%	0.4855	0.3041	120	+++-0+	0.15%	0.3853	0.4169	196	---++	0.00%	0.8845	0.4415
45	0+0-+	0.66%	0.3888	0.3066	121	-+-0+	0.15%	0.4899	0.4177	197	+++0-	0.00%	0.1998	0.4415
46	0+0+-	0.65%	0.4400	0.3095	122	-00++	0.15%	0.4726	0.4184	198	--0-	0.00%	0.8845	0.4415
47	0+0+-	0.65%	0.4291	0.3123	123	+0-++	0.15%	0.4012	0.4190	199	--0-	0.00%	0.1678	0.4415
48	+-000	0.60%	0.4212	0.3148	124	+-0-+	0.14%	0.4421	0.4196	200	++++0	0.00%	0.1451	0.4415
49	0+0--	0.60%	0.3361	0.3168	125	+0+-	0.14%	0.4270	0.4202	201	-0-++	0.00%	0.7473	0.4415
50	-+000	0.60%	0.4482	0.3195	126	0+0++	0.13%	0.5891	0.4210	202	0+0++	0.00%	0.2906	0.4415
51	0-0-+	0.58%	0.5617	0.3229	127	+0-++	0.13%	0.3848	0.4215	203	0---+	0.00%	0.7244	0.4415
52	--000	0.58%	0.7236	0.3271	128	-0-++	0.13%	0.4905	0.4221	204	0+++0	0.00%	0.2317	0.4415
53	++000	0.55%	0.2609	0.3286	129	+++0	0.13%	0.3204	0.4225	205	0+++-	0.00%	0.2529	0.4415
54	00-++	0.55%	0.3074	0.3303	130	+0++0	0.12%	0.3125	0.4229	206	0----	0.00%	0.1894	0.4415
55	-00-0	0.55%	0.4394	0.3327	131	-0-+	0.12%	0.6041	0.4236	207	--+	0.00%	0.8464	0.4415
56	00+--	0.55%	0.6141	0.3361	132	+0-0	0.12%	0.4366	0.4242	208	+0+0+0	0.00%	0.2246	0.4415
57	-000-	0.52%	0.4296	0.3384	133	-0-+0	0.12%	0.4324	0.4247	209	+++++	0.00%	0.2450	0.4415
58	+000+	0.52%	0.5573	0.3413	134	+-0++	0.12%	0.3677	0.4251	210	--+-0	0.00%	0.7873	0.4415
59	00--+	0.47%	0.3387	0.3431	135	++00-	0.11%	0.2765	0.4254	211	-+--+	0.00%	0.6333	0.4415
60	00++-	0.47%	0.5388	0.3456	136	--00+	0.11%	0.6827	0.4261	212	++0+0	0.00%	0.2067	0.4415
61	+000-	0.46%	0.3504	0.3473	137	+0-0-	0.11%	0.5134	0.4267	213	0----	0.00%	0.7469	0.4415
62	00+0+	0.46%	0.3696	0.3490	138	++-0+	0.10%	0.3758	0.4271	214	+++-0	0.00%	0.2312	0.4415
63	-000+	0.43%	0.5107	0.3513	139	+++-0	0.10%	0.4385	0.4275	215	00---	0.00%	0.6139	0.4415
64	0-0++	0.43%	0.4581	0.3533	140	+0--	0.10%	0.4305	0.4279	216	+++-+	0.00%	0.7428	0.4415
65	0+0--	0.41%	0.4121	0.3551	141	+0--	0.10%	0.4825	0.4284	217	+++++	0.00%	0.2118	0.4415
66	0-+0+	0.41%	0.6089	0.3576	142	+++-00	0.10%	0.3303	0.4288	218	--0	0.00%	0.8845	0.4415
67	0+0-	0.41%	0.3100	0.3588	143	++-0+	0.10%	0.4603	0.4292	219	-00--	0.00%	0.6602	0.4415
68	+0-00	0.40%	0.4755	0.3608	144	--+00	0.10%	0.5715	0.4298	220	++++-	0.00%	0.7469	0.4415
69	0++--	0.40%	0.3970	0.3624	145	+-0-	0.10%	0.5023	0.4303	221	--0-+	0.00%	0.8122	0.4415
70	+0-00	0.39%	0.4040	0.3640	146	+0++	0.10%	0.3913	0.4307	222	-0--0	0.00%	0.7705	0.4415
71	0++++	0.39%	0.4673	0.3659	147	+0+-	0.10%	0.4101	0.4311	223	+++++	0.00%	0.1583	0.4415
72	0+++-	0.39%	0.4191	0.3675	148	++-+	0.09%	0.4805	0.4315	224	+0+--	0.00%	0.2592	0.4415
73	0++-0	0.39%	0.4504	0.3693	149	+++-0	0.09%	0.3929	0.4319	225	00+++	0.00%	0.2451	0.4415
74	+0-+00	0.39%	0.5525	0.3714	150	+0-++	0.09%	0.3527	0.4322	226	00+++	0.00%	0.3029	0.4415
75	-0-+0	0.39%	0.3417	0.3728	151	-0+-	0.09%	0.5353	0.4327	227	-0+--	0.00%	0.7175	0.4415
76	+00-0	0.37%	0.3880	0.3742	152	--+-0	0.08%	0.6675	0.4332	228	--0-0	0.00%	0.8374	0.4415

TABLE 5B   Valuation of Five-Year Zero-Coupon

Path	Code	Weight (A)	Present Value 5-Year Zero-Coupon (B)	Cumulative Value Sum (A×B)
1	000	0.2394	0.677502	0.162194
2	00–	0.0958	0.662706	0.225681
3	00+	0.0958	0.696186	0.292376
4	0–0	0.0938	0.635644	0.352001
5	0+0	0.0938	0.725919	0.420092
6	0–+	0.0494	0.653195	0.452360
7	0+–	0.0494	0.710066	0.487437
8	–00	0.0337	0.615620	0.508184
9	+00	0.0337	0.745612	0.533311
10	0++	0.0280	0.762591	0.554663
11	0––	0.0280	0.608204	0.571693
12	+–0	0.0220	0.699568	0.587084
13	–+0	0.0220	0.659615	0.601595
14	–0+	0.0149	0.632598	0.611021
15	+0–	0.0149	0.729328	0.621888
16	–0–	0.0127	0.589026	0.629369
17	+0+	0.0127	0.783279	0.639316
18	–+–	0.0110	0.645210	0.646413
19	+–+	0.0110	0.718861	0.654321
20	++0	0.0084	0.851475	0.661473
21	––0	0.0084	0.541937	0.666026
22	+––	0.0068	0.684290	0.670679
23	–++	0.0068	0.677806	0.675288
24	++–	0.0037	0.814692	0.678302
25	––+	0.0037	0.569315	0.680409
26	+++	0.0000	0.889937	0.680409
27	–––	0.0000	0.509804	0.680409

TABLE 6   Option Price Comparison

Strike Price	Price by Roll Back	Price by Path Selection
Call on a 20-Year Zero-Coupon Bond Expiring in 10 Years		
$50.00	$ 0.69	$ 1.04
$40.00	$ 2.34	$ 2.61
$30.00	$ 5.66	$ 6.04
$20.00	$ 9.91	$10.24
$10.00	$14.26	$14.63
Call on a 10-Year Zero-Coupon Bond Expiring in Five Years		
$70.00	$ 0.49	$ 0.70
$60.00	$ 3.72	$ 3.88
$50.00	$10.07	$10.08
$40.00	$16.86	$16.82
$30.00	$23.65	$23.63
$20.00	$30.44	$30.43
$10.00	$37.24	$37.24

provide any payoff. In the other case, the rates do not change until the last time segment, although the rate then falls significantly, resulting in high option payoffs even though on average the rates do not shift that much.

The pathwise valuation profile can identify scenarios where an investment is profitable and by how much. Profitability depends to a great extent on the scenarios and not only on the interest rate shift, particularly for interest rate options. Further, when the profile is applied to assets and liabilities combined, we can see how to control for the risk of embedded options.

APPLICATIONS TO PORTFOLIO STRATEGIES

Three applications of LPS to portfolio strategies include scenario analysis, pathwise immunization, and pathwise dedication. The last two applications are extensions of the more standard immunization and dedication strategies to allow an effective use of illiquid option-embedded bonds.

**EXHIBIT 4A   Pathwise Valuation Profile,
10-Year Zero-Coupon Bond**
AB is the performance profile.

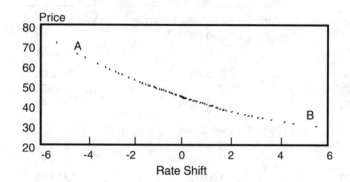

**EXHIBIT 4B   Pathwise Valuation Profile,
Call on 20-Year Bond Expiring in 10 Years**
AB is the performance profile.

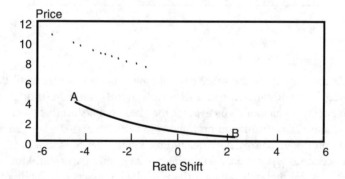

Scenario Analysis

In analyzing the performance of an illiquid portfolio or a bond, we often project the cash flow under different interest rate scenarios. We have shown that the seven scenarios of Regulation 126 seem inadequate, particularly in light of the widespread use of embedded options in assets and liabilities.

Another approach is randomly generating a large number of interest rate paths (not necessarily from an arbitrage-free model) and studying the performance of the sample. This random path approach is not satisfactory for two reasons. First, a large sample (say, 1,000 paths) is needed to make a probability inference. This makes detailed scenario analysis and formulation of portfolio strategies difficult, if not impossible.

Second, this approach focuses on analyzing the cash flow of each scenario. If the cash flow of each scenario is discounted and all present values summed, however, the average value may not be the same as the market value.

Now, on the one hand, we claim that the market value is correct in representing the future projected probable cash flows. On the other hand, scenario analysis is considered a relatively exhaustive simulation of all the probable cash flows. Yet how can the present value of the cash flows not be the same as the reported market value? There is clearly an internal inconsistency in the argument or analysis.

Linear path space, which is a set of linearly ordered scenarios, provides a natural solution. We can begin with the seven scenarios in Table 4, and then increase the number of the scenarios, calculating the cumulative present value of the pathwise values. When enough scenarios have been analyzed, the cumulative value should converge to the market value, assuming consistent valuation and scenario analysis.

Pathwise Immunization

There are many immunization strategies implemented for asset liability management and structured management. Typically, an immunization strategy is a dynamic portfolio strategy that continually adjusts the portfolio sensitivity to interest rate risk so that the portfolio can mirror the liabilities or the bogey.

For example, Kopprasch et al. [1987], Ho [1990a], and Reitano [1990] define different interest rate risk measures. Bierwag [1987] and Granito [1984] discuss the procedures for matching the risk measures in immunizing interest rate risks. It is important to immunization strategies to be able to trade when needed. Liquidity of the bonds is important.

Consider an example. Suppose the liability is a single bullet payment with a term of three years. On the asset side, we hold a callable bond with a matching effective duration initially. Now, if the interest rate level rises, the likelihood of the bond being called falls. As a result, the callable bond duration, and hence the asset duration, lengthens.

If interest rates rise farther, the market value of the callable bond (or the asset value) will fall significantly below the liability value. That is, when the liability matures, the asset cannot be sold at a price sufficient to pay off the liability.

Immunization requires continual matching of duration to avoid the asset value falling below the liability value. But asset-liability matching may require selling substantial amounts of the assets. When the assets are illiquid and are providing substantial value, the dynamic strategy may not be desirable. Pathwise immunization provides an alternative to the dynamic strategy approach.

Consider a certainty case when there is no interest rate risk. If we initially match the asset and the liability in market value, the present values of the asset and liability will always match in the future along the interest rate path, even if the cash flows are mismatched.

Where there is uncertainty in interest rate levels, we can apply an analogous argument. Assume we can enumerate all the possible interest rate paths in the future. Now, suppose we can match the pathwise value of the asset and liability for each possible path. Then, in essence, we have assured that the asset and liability present values will always match, regardless of which interest rate path prevails.

Pathwise immunization is a way to ensure that the values of the asset and liability are matched in a broad range of scenario tests. However, we must note the importance of selecting the scenarios from the linear path space. When scenarios are selected from the linear path space, the condition of matching the pathwise values of the assets and liabilities makes matching the market values of assets and liabilities a necessary condition. If random scenarios are used, the initial market values of the assets and liabilities need not match.

The solution of pathwise immunization may not be the same as that of standard immunization. Let us consider Example 1 again. We use a combination of cash and a three-year zero-coupon bond to pathwise immunize a two-year zero-coupon bond. We consider the two paths: the rate rises or falls after one year, represented by + and –, respectively.

Table 7 shows the pathwise value for each security and path. Suppose we hold x three-year bonds and c cash. In matching the pathwise values, we can solve for x and c. They are $x = 0.6666$ and $c = 0.323$. For the standard immunization strategies using duration calculation, the results are $x = 0.73$ and $c = 0.275$. It is not surprising that the results differ, as each method seeks to immunize different scenarios.

The advantages of pathwise immunization over standard immunization are clear. In immunization, investors always seek to buy inexpensive bonds.

TABLE 7   Pathwise Valuation for Two Securities

Paths	Two-Year Bond	Three-Year Bond	Cash
+	0.819	$0.744x$	c
−	0.833	$0.765x$	c

Many of these bonds are illiquid. Because the standard immunization proce-dure requires investors to buy or sell the bonds to match the risk measures continually, investors need a systematic way to determine the trade-off between liquidity and value.

For example, consider the pathwise valuation of the zero-coupon bond and the interest rate option in Figures 4A and 4B. A portfolio manager can use options to match the duration of an option-free bond portfolio, although we note that the asset and liability can be grossly mismatched over time as their pathwise valuation profiles are so different. Pathwise immunization ensures that the interest rate risk exposure is matched over time.

Pathwise immunization can be viewed as an extension of the standard immunization procedure. It requires the optimal portfolio to have a certain pathwise value of a selection of paths. These linear constraints imposed on the portfolio holdings can be additional constraints beyond the usual con-straints of matching durations. Combining the duration constraints with the pathwise value constraints in essence assures immunization for both small and instantaneous interest rate risk exposure and longer-term and larger inter-est rate shifts. This result is true for bonds whether they have embedded options or not, as we show in the numerical example above where there is no embedded option.

Pathwise Dedication

Cash-flow matching has gained broad acceptance in managing assets and lia-bilities. Assets are structured so that the cash inflows from the assets can sup-port the cash outflows of the liabilities without selling any assets. In recent years, however, most bonds have been issued with embedded options and therefore have uncertain cash flows. As a result, cash flow matching using option-embedded bonds does not eliminate the necessity of selling bonds. Standard dedication formulations can be found in Elton and Gruber [1987] and Ho [1990b].

In pathwise immunization, we can solve for the optimal solution, minimizing the cost of the portfolio so that the asset portfolio can cash-flow match the liabilities along selected interest rate paths. That is, the optimal asset portfolio must satisfy the dedication condition along each of the interest rate paths.

Note that the cash flows of an option-free bond are the same in different scenarios, but such is not the case for option-embedded bonds. If such an optimal solution exists, the assets would satisfy the dedication conditions over a range of interest rate path scenarios even though the assets have embedded options.

Pathwise dedication is similar to pathwise immunization in that both techniques ensure that the asset and liability management constraints are maintained along each selected interest rate path. The difference is that pathwise immunization may call for bonds in the asset position to be sold or cash borrowed to fund the liability at a given time. Hiller and Eckstein [1990] have discussed the importance of using alternative procedures to standard dedication methodology when the bonds have embedded options.

To illustrate the use of pathwise dedication, consider an example. For simplicity, suppose the liability schedule is relatively straightforward, a constant annual payment of 100 for 10 years. We also assume a zero reinvestment rate for simplicity. This assumption, while unrealistic, does not affect our general conclusions. Using a mix of corporate bonds and mortgage-backed securities for the optimization in Table 8, we derive the solution for the standard dedication as below.

The total portfolio market value is 695.98. The corporate bonds in this dedicated portfolio have minimal embedded options, and their cash flow is interest rate-insensitive. Such is not the case with the 15-year GNMA. This mortgage-backed is selected because of the sufficiently wide option-adjusted spreads. Its disadvantage, however, is that its cash flow is dependent on the

TABLE 8   Standard Dedication

Size (Par)	Description	Coupon	Maturity	Rating
3.75	Boise Cascade	8.375	8/94	BBB
49.43	AT&T	5.500	1/97	AA
227.27	Chemical NY Corp	9.750	6/99	A–
389.83	GNMA 15	10.000		

interest rate level. If interest rates rise, the assumed projected cash flow would no longer hold, and the asset portfolio cash flow might not be able to pay for the liability cash outflow.

For pathwise, dedication, we consider dedicating under scenarios in which rates rise and rates fall in addition to level scenarios. Therefore, the optimal solution is the portfolio with the least cost that can still assure sufficient cash inflow to support the liability schedule when rates rise or fall. The solution is provided in Table 9.

The total portfolio market value is 710.52. Note that the pathwise dedication portfolio is more expensive, because the portfolio assures enough cash to pay for the liabilities under different scenarios. More importantly, the result shows that the GNMA 15 is less desirable in pathwise dedication because the liability is interest rate-insensitive, while the GNMA has embedded options. Significantly more of the Boise Cascade bond is bought in pathwise dedication because of its shorter maturity.

The advantages of pathwise dedication are clear. While the solution seems more expensive, in fact pathwise dedication may provide a cheaper solution in general because many portfolio managers now avoid using certain option-embedded bonds in dedication, which restricts their choices. Pathwise dedication enables managers to consider more bonds.

Indeed, if portfolio managers use only bonds with negligible embedded options, pathwise dedication should provide a cheaper solution. This is because, if both assets and liabilities have no embedded options and their cash flows are interest rate-insensitive, a pathwise dedication solution is the same as the standard dedication solution. Allowing a larger universe of bonds as candidates can only reduce the cost of the solution. Such is the case in the example above. If the liability schedule is dedicated with non-callable Treasury issues, the cost would be 720.

TABLE 9   Optimal Pathwise Solution

Size (Par)	Description	Coupon	Maturity	Rating
24.87	Boise Cascade	8.375	8/94	BBB
44.41	AT&T	4.375	10/96	AA
29.16	Western Airline	10.750	6/98	A–
243.58	Chemical NY Corp	9.750	6/99	A–
383.48	GNMA 15	10.000		

Furthermore, the optimization procedure lets us determine the trade-off between the cheapness of the bond and the interest rate sensitivity of the cash flow. Unlike some optimization procedures whose solution would constrain certain portions of the portfolio to include bonds with embedded options, pathwise dedication solves for the optimal portfolio, which depends on the cheapness of the security and the instability of the cash flow relative to the liability.

SUMMARY AND CONCLUSIONS

We show first that pathwise valuation is consistent with relative valuation, so that scenario simulations with rate paths taken from an arbitrage-free rate model are consistent with market valuation. A model of the path space called the linear path space provides a systematic procedure for selecting a set of interest rate scenarios. The path space is partitioned further into equivalent classes where each of the scenarios is a representative path. The number of paths in each equivalent class provides a way of linearly ordering these scenarios.

By appropriate weighting of the scenario paths, the linear path space offers convergence with efficiency. Typically, 180 paths are needed to value long-dated bond options. Path generation can be made systematic, and all the paths can be accounted for by the partition. Definition of the path space is general. Term segments can always be shortened for further refinement of the partition. The level of refinement desired will depend on the applications and the assets and liabilities.

Three applications of the linear path space are: scenario testing, pathwise immunization, and pathwise dedication. These applications are a necessary extension from the standard approach when the assets are both illiquid and option-embedded.

There are other applications of the linear path space model. One major application could be a systematic analysis of the interest rate risk exposure embedded in collateralized mortgage obligations (CMOs). CMO tranches are diverse in their characteristics, and they can be quite interest rate-sensitive. The pathwise valuation procedure can provide valuable insight into their behavior.

Another application is in formulating portfolio strategies. Insurance issuers often use scenario analysis in managing interest rate risks. A systematic procedure for selecting interest rate scenarios would allow development of asset-liability portfolio management strategies.

APPENDIX A

Proposition 1

Pathwise valuation equals the backward substitution approach for zero-coupon bonds.

Proof

Let $r(i,n)$ be the one-period spot rate at time n and state i. Then $f(i,n) = 1/[1 + r(i,n)]$ is the discount factor.

First, we want to establish that the proposition is true for a one-year bond. For the pathwise value, there are two rate paths but the same value $f(0,0)$. Hence the pathwise values in both cases are $100 \times f(0,0)$. Therefore, the average is also $100 \times f(0,0)$. For the backward substitution approach, there are two possible outcomes, but they are both 100. Therefore the average of the two outcomes is 100, and the value is $100 \times f(0,0)$.

Next, we consider a two-year bond. According to the binomial lattice, there are three possibilities: rate rises and rises, rises and falls, and falls and falls. The paths are $f(0,0)f(1,1)$, $f(0,0)f(1,1)$, $f(0,0)f(0,1)$, and $f(0,0)f(0,1)$. Hence, the pathwise value is $[f(0,0)f(1,1) + f(0,0)f(0,1)]100/2$.

By the backward substitution approach, we have

$$\text{value} = 100 \ ([f(1,1) + f(0,1)]/2)f(0,0)$$

Hence, the two methodologies produce the same results for two-year bonds.

Now we can complete the proof by induction. Suppose that the proposition is true for all zero-coupon bonds with maturity T. Consider the case where the maturity is $T + 1$. Consider we are at the node point $(1,1)$. Pricing the zero-coupon bond from the node point $(1,1)$ by backward substitution or by pathwise valuation must be equivalent by the induction assumption. Let the price be $p(1,1)$. Similarly consider the node point $(0,1)$, and let the price be $p(0,1)$.

By the induction assumption, $p(1,1)$ = average of all the paths $f(*,1)f(*,2)...f(*,T+1)$, and the same with $p(0,1)$.

But the backward substitution procedure shows that the initial value is

$$p(0,0) = f(0,0)100[p(1,1) + p(0,1)]/2 \tag{1}$$

Because $p(1,1)$ and $p(0,1)$ are the average pathwise values of all the paths starting at nodes $(1,1)$ and $(0,1)$, respectively, Equation (1) therefore is also the pathwise valuation from the initial node $(0,0)$.   QED

APPENDIX B

Proposition 2

Backward substitution and pathwise valuation are equivalent for European options.

Proof

Proposition 2 differs from Proposition 1 only in that the terminal condition of the backward substitution does not have a constant payoff of 100 in general for European options. Otherwise, there is no difference.

The proof for Proposition 1 does not rely on constant payoff at the terminal condition. Therefore, the proof applies to European options by extension.

QED

APPENDIX C

Proposition 3

Backward substitution and pathwise valuation are equivalent for American options.

Proof

American options differ from European options by the early exercise rules. Consider a one-period case. Early exercise in this case is the same as the terminal condition. Hence the two approaches are the same. Consider the two-year case. Suppose that there are early exercises at some of the states at the end of the time one period. But, by the induction assumption, the values at each of the nodes are the same irrespective of which methodology is used.

If all the values are the same at all the states, we can then consider these values to be boundary conditions. Then Proposition 2 shows that the two methodologies are equivalent for the subsequent periods. This argument can then extend to any time T, and the induction argument completes the proof.

QED

REFERENCES

Bierwag, G.O. *Duration Analysis: Managing Interest Rate Risk.* Cambridge, MA: Ballinger, 1987.

Black, F., E. Derman, and W. Toy. "A One-Factor Model of Interest Rates and its Application to Treasury Bond Options." *Financial Analysts Journal,* January–February 1990, pp. 33–39.

Brennan, M., and E. Schwartz. "A Continuous-Time Approach to the Pricing of Bonds." *Journal of Banking and Finance,* 3 (1979), pp. 133–155.

Courtadon, G. "The Pricing of Options and Default-Free Bonds." *Journal of Financial and Quantitative Analysis,* 17 (1982), pp. 75–100.

Cox, J., J. Ingersoll, and S. Ross. "Theory of the Term Structure of Interest Rates." *Econometrica,* 53 (1985), pp. 385–407.

Elton, E.J., and M.J. Gruber, *Modern Portfolio Theory and Investment Analysis,* 3rd ed. New York: Wiley, 1987.

Granito, M.R. *Bond Portfolio Immunization.* Lexington, MA: D.C. Heath, 1984.

Heath, D., R. Jarrow, and A. Morton. "Bond Pricing and the Term Structure of Interest Rates: A Discrete Time Approximation." *Journal of Financial and Quantitative Analysis,* 25 (1990). pp. 419–440.

Hiller, R., and J. Eckstein. "Stochastic Dedication: Designing Fixed Income Portfolios Using Massively Parallel Benders Decomposition." Harvard Business School Working Paper, November 1990.

Ho, T.S.Y. "Key Rate Durations: A Measure of Interest Rate Risk Exposure." Working Paper, Salomon Brothers Center, May 1990a.

Ho. T.S.Y. *Strategic Fixed Income Investment,* Homewood, IL: Dow Jones-Irwin, 1990b.

Ho, T.S.Y., and S.B. Lee. "Term Structure Movements and Pricing Interest Rate Contingent Claims." *Journal of Finance,* 41 (1986), pp. 1011–1029.

Jamshidian, F. "Bond and Option Evaluation in the Gaussian Interest Model." *Research in Finance,* Vol. 9 (1990).

Kopprasch, R., W. Boyce, M. Koenigsberg, A. Tatevossian, and M. Yampol. "Effective Duration of Callable Bonds," New York: Salomon Brothers, 1987.

Pederson, H., E. Shiu, and A. Thorlacius. "Arbitrage-Free Pricing of Interest Rate-Contingent Claims." *Transactions of the Society of Actuaries,* 41 (1989), pp. 231–265.

Reitano, R. "Non-Parallel Yield Curve Shifts and Durational Leverage." *Journal of Portfolio Management,* 62 (Summer 1990).

Shiu, E.S.W. "Immunization—The Matching of Assets and Liabilities." In *Advances in the Statistical Sciences VI: Actuarial Sciences,* I.B. Mac-Neill and G.J. Umphrey, eds. Dordrecht, Holland: D. Reidel Publishing Co., 1987. pp. 145–166.

Vasicek, O. "An Equilibrium Characterization of the Term Structure." *Journal of Financial Economics,* 5 (1977), pp. 177–188.

PART II

Corporate and Investor Viewpoint

Street Myths about Customers and Customer Myths about the Street

Laurie S. Goodman
Senior Vice President, Paine Webber

A quiz for readers employed by Wall Street firms (True or False):

1. A price inquiry arises because a customer has a real interest in a derivative product.

2. Accounting treatment, balance sheet treatment, and capital treatment drive transactions.

A quiz for readers employed by the buy side (True or False):

3. Wall Street firms have a model that prices all securities consistently across all sectors.

4. If prices differ substantially from theoretical values, and prices differ substantially between firms, it is because Wall Street firms try to rip customers off on trades.

Readers employed by Wall Street firms probably answered yes to questions one and two. Readers employed by the buy side probably answered yes

The author would like to thank Jane Brauer and Joe Hanosek for helpful comments on an earlier draft.

to questions three and four. The correct answer to all questions was no. Readers employed by the buy side who took the sell side quiz, would correctly answer no to questions one and two, while sell side participants would correctly answer no to questions three and four. These incorrect statements are myths that the sell side and the buy side hold about each other. In this paper, we dispel each of these myths. We begin with street myths about customers.

MYTH #1: A Price Inquiry Arises Because a Customer Has a Real Interest in a Derivative Product

The reality is very different. The buy side is using swaps to assess relative value across securities or markets. One technique to evaluate difficult securities is to recreate them using combinations of other securities. Let us use as an example an inverse floater created as part of a CMO. An inverse floater is a security whose coupon is of the form:

$$\text{Coupon} = A + (B \times \text{Index})$$

where A and B are constants.

The multiplier, B, is often referred to as the leverage. LIBOR is the most common index, although inverse floaters off alternative indices such as the Eleventh Federal Home Loan Bank district cost of funds (COFI) and one-, five-, seven-, and 10-year Constant Maturity Treasury Indices have also been created.

Inverse floaters are very difficult to evaluate, because they represent a synthetically leveraged bond position. To see this, one must realize that inverse floaters are created by dividing a fixed rate mortgage into two pieces: a floater and an inverse floater. Thus, if one took $100 million of FNMA 8 percent bonds (FNMA 8s), and split the bonds to create $50 million of a floater at LIBOR + 120 basis points and $50 million of an inverse floater, the coupon of the inverse floater would be 14.8 − LIBOR. One could also split the FNMA 8s by creating $80 million in floaters paying LIBOR + 120 and $20 million in inverses, paying 35.2 − (4 × LIBOR). This medium leverage inverse floater can be thought of as going long FNMA 8s and funding 80 percent of the position at the floating rate on these securities (LIBOR + 120 basis points). Even though the investor owns only $20 million inverse floaters, they have the price risk on $100 million FNMA 8s.

One way often used to make relative value decisions in mortgages is to use option adjusted spread analysis. This analysis essentially measures, after taking account of the options, how much one must raise or lower risk-free interest rates in order to duplicate the price on a bond. Thus, a FNMA 8 may have an option adjusted spread (OAS) of 81. This may reflect a spread to the zero coupon Treasury yield curve of 98, less 17 basis points for the embedded options. Inverse floaters usually show up on this type of analysis as being very attractive, because functional OAS analysis does not take into account the leverage used. Leveraged transactions cannot be directly compared to unleveraged transactions. In order to see this, consider a world in which bond payoffs are uncorrelated with interest rates and dependent only on a flip of the coin, as shown in Exhibit 1. The risk-free bond pays 6 percent interest regardless of whether heads or tails is flipped. The bond has an OAS of zero. Bond A pays 7 percent interest if heads is flipped, 5.5 percent interest if tails is flipped. This bond has an OAS of 25. (Intuitively, its average yield is 6.25 percent, and there are no options.) Bond B pays 8.5 percent if heads is flipped and 4.5 percent if tails is flipped. The bond has an OAS of 50 (an average return of 6.5 percent and no options). On a relative value basis, it would look as if Bond B is the cheapest alternative. In fact, one can use a combination of

EXHIBIT 1   Evaluating Inverses

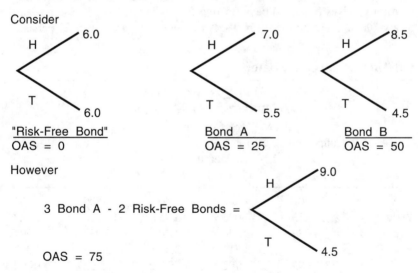

Be Careful Using OAS on Inverse Floaters

Consider

H 6.0 / T 6.0	H 7.0 / T 5.5	H 8.5 / T 4.5
"Risk-Free Bond"	Bond A	Bond B
OAS = 0	OAS = 25	OAS = 50

However

3 Bond A - 2 Risk-Free Bonds =   H 9.0 / T 4.5

OAS = 75

So OAS is not "arbitrage free" in leverage space.

Bond A and the risk-free bond in order to produce an alternative that strictly dominates Bond B. By combining three of Bond A minus two of the risk-free bonds, the payoff function would be 9 percent if one flips heads, and 4.5 percent if one flips tails. The OAS on this combination is 75 (average yield 6.75, no options). Thus, the OAS on an inverse floater is not a good way to make relative value decisions. The fact that higher leverage should require a higher OAS is not captured by the OAS methodology.

If we can't use OAS to make relative value decisions, we can try to recreate the cash-flow profile using combinations of other securities. Consider the inverse floater shown in Exhibit 2. This inverse floater was selected because its average life profile is fairly stable across a wide range of PSAs or prepayment projections. The collateral backing this deal is FHLMC Gold Five-year balloons. The coupon formula takes the form:

$$\text{Coupon} = 27.9 - (3 \times \text{LIBOR}) \text{ Floor} = 0$$

The price of the security was 103-22 at the time the 10-year Treasury was 7.47. The security appears to have a very attractive base case yield of 14.09 percent at 300 PSA.

In order to replicate this inverse floater, one could think of purchasing a four-year Treasury note with a 7.5 percent coupon, trading at a price of 103, and simultaneously entering into three interest rate swaps, in which the investor receives fixed and pays floating for four years. The investor would receive three times the four-year fixed swap rate (7.0 percent), or 21 percent,

EXHIBIT 2   Inverse Floater

Deal FHLMC 1151 G SI
Collateral FHLMC Gold Five-Year Balloon
8% Coupon
Coupon on Inverse = $27.9 - (3 \times \text{LIBOR})$ floor = 0
10-Year Treasury = 7.47
Price = 103-22

PSA	200	300	400	500	600
Yield	14.215	14.091	13.951	13.796	13.622
Avg. Life	4.283	3.824	3.408	3.032	2.694
Mod. Dur.	2.985	2.711	2.459	2.229	2.017
Begin Pay	3/15/92	3/15/92	3/15/92	3/15/92	3/15/92
Final Pay	10/15/95	10/15/96	10/15/96	10/15/96	10/15/96

308

and pay three times LIBOR. The net cost of the swap would be zero. The cost of the package is the net cost of the Treasury security (103) plus the net cost of the swaps (0). The cost of the package, at 103, is 22/32 less than the inverse floater. If we amortize 22/32 over four years, it would be worth 20 basis points per annum. The coupon on this replicated portfolio is:

	Coupon on four-year note	7.5
plus	Coupon on four-year fixed swaps	21.0
plus	Coupon value of 22/32	.20
minus	Coupon on floating side of swap	$3 \times$ LIBOR
	Total	$28.70 - (3 \times$ LIBOR$)$

This equals $28.70 - (3 \times$ LIBOR$)$. The coupon on the inverse floater is $27.9 - (3 \times$ LIBOR$)$, 80 basis points lower than the replicated portfolio. The 80 basis point differential was roughly equal to the cost of three LIBOR caps (necessary to fix the floor at zero). So the net coupons on the replicated portfolio and the inverse floater are the same, but the replicated portfolio has much less negative convexity and is therefore a better value.

Thus, using the swap market to help make a relative value judgment on this difficult-to-evaluate security was very useful. It allowed us to decide that the inverse floater, while initially appearing to have an attractive yield, could easily be recreated with more desirable characteristics using a combination of bond and swap positions. This analysis can be easily applied to other inverse floaters. For those floaters with extreme negative convexity, it may be necessary to write options in the replicating portfolio. If one used this type of analysis extensively, one would find some inverse floaters are attractive, while others are unattractive.

Dealers should be aware that the buy side is increasingly using derivative markets to evaluate securities with unusual return profiles. Other examples of this include taking the return profile of a "hard to evaluate" security and adding derivatives to give the security the same return profile as a security we recognize. For example, a support tranche of a CMO could be evaluated by buying options (both puts and calls) in order to create a symmetric bond-like profile.

MYTH #2: Accounting Treatment, Balance Sheet Treatment, and Capital Treatment Drive Transactions

In reality, trades are decided upon based on one factor: Does it economically make sense? Accounts will pick up a trade they want to do and find the favorable way to do it. Accounting and capital treatment are often the excuse for turning down a trade the portfolio manager does not believe economically makes sense.

Two examples will make this point clear. In the past two years there have been quite a few securities issued in the U.S. markets with dollar payoffs, in which the payoffs are dependent upon the performance of foreign bond markets. The securities are often issued by agencies of the U.S. government or high-quality corporations. There is a good deal of investor interest in these issues. The reason is many U.S. portfolio managers who are benchmarked against or judged against a U.S. index are prohibited from holding foreign bonds. They are prohibited from entering into a swap involving foreign bonds. However, many money managers would like to invest in what they hope will be high rate of return securities that are not included in their benchmark. In May, 1991 SLMA, an agency of the U.S. government, issued a two-year Swiss Franc LIBOR floating rate note. It was initially priced at par, and paid a quarterly coupon of three-month Swiss Franc LIBOR minus 105 basis points. Note that the investor has no currency exposure in this bond; the only bet being taken is that Swiss Franc LIBOR minus 105 basis points will be higher than Dollar LIBOR.

Why would SLMA issue a bond denominated in Swiss Franc LIBOR? The answer is that SLMA does not have the economic risk on this position. They have done a swap in order to achieve sub-LIBOR financing. Thus, on each coupon payment date, SLMA will receive from the swap counterparty Swiss Franc LIBOR – 105 basis points and make a payment to the swap counterparty based on dollar LIBOR (For example, LIBOR – 25 basis points). SLMA will in turn pay the investors Swiss Franc LIBOR – 105 basis points. This is equivalent to SLMA having issued debt at LIBOR – 25 basis points.

In July 1992, a similar security was offered allowing investors to take an explicit bet that Swiss Franc LIBOR would widen relative to U.S. LIBOR in the next 12 months. At this point it appeared that European nations could not possibly lower interest rates because of exchange rate pressures. The security was a AAA-rated two-year medium term note, priced at par, paying a generous initial coupon of 6.07 percent. The coupon is reset quarterly at twice the Swiss Franc LIBOR-U.S. Dollar LIBOR differential minus 4.45. Thus, if Swiss Franc LIBOR was 94 percent while dollar LIBOR was 3.5 percent, the coupon would be:

$$(2 \times (9 - 3.5)) - 4.45 = 4.55$$

The fourth reset was at the end of the first year; at that point the reset is for a full year and is based on annual rate differentials. All coupons are subject to a 0 percent floor.

For this security, a group of investors who wanted this payoff was identified. The originators did not find an issuer who was willing to agree to this payoff structure. They found an issuer who was willing to raise funds at slightly less than his normal borrowing costs, in exchange for having both a security and a swap on his books. The issuer of this security is actually paying approximately LIBOR for the funds. Through a swap, the economic risk of this security rests with a swap counterparty. The swap counterparty has hedged the risk as part of a derivative book.

These types of securities have advantages for issuers and investors. Issuers are able to fund more cheaply than would otherwise be the case. Investors are able to take positions in markets they otherwise do not deal in, offering them additional opportunities to enhance performance. It also creates additional risks. When investors seek securities outside their field of expertise, they must understand the risks they are taking. Investors who purchased the first security fared very well; the differential between Swiss Franc LIBOR and U.S. LIBOR widened dramatically during the first 15 months of the security's life. By contrast investors who purchased the second security could not have timed it worse; they purchased the security at the peak differential and will receive a zero coupon at the next reset.

At other times, a security structure is not the most desirable way to hold a position; investors would much prefer to hold a similar position off-balance sheet. A good example of this is the market for index amortizing rate swaps (IAR Swaps). An index amortizing swap is a swap whose maturity extends when interest rates rise. The amortization on the swap is driven by the index rate (usually LIBOR). The profile of this type of swap is shown in Exhibit 3. In this example, if the index rate rises 100 basis points or less after the lockout, the swap completely amortizes. As interest rates rise more than 100 basis points, the amortization rate slows. Customer inquiry on this is one-sided; customers want to receive the fixed rate and pay LIBOR. As of this writing, the fixed rate was the two-year Treasury + 190 for a security with a five-year final. The large spread on this security is compensation for its negative convexity; that is when interest rates rise, its duration extends, exactly when it is least desirable for the fixed rate receiver.

This type of position often competes with CMO tranches of mortgages for a place in a portfolio. On sequential tranches of CMOs (often called payers), the average life will extend as prepayments fall (interest rates rise) and contract as prepayments rise (interest rates fall). The negative convexity is comparable to that on an IAR.

When accounts are deciding between a CMO tranche and an IAR swap, there are a number of considerations. The first is that the economics of the

EXHIBIT 3   Five-Year Final Index Amortizing Rate (IAR) Swap Average Life Graph

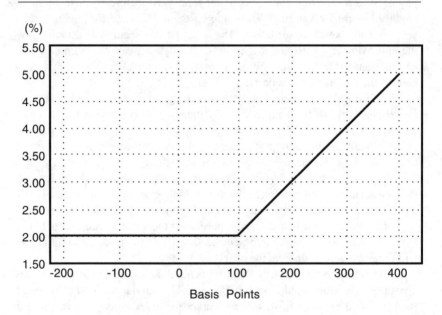

Basis Points

two are similar but not identical; a CMO depends on prepayments that are driven far more heavily by the 10-year Treasury than short-term rates. By contrast, the IAR is usually driven by LIBOR. Secondly, the IAR is dependent solely on interest rates, while a CMO is based on prepayment rates, which are primarily dependent on interest rates but are also dependent on other factors. Aside from the differences in structure, CMOs are securities and IARs are off-balance sheet items. Some banks are worried about FASB 115, requiring them to disclose the mark-to-market value of all securities positions. The change in the market value of off-balance sheet items does not have to disclosed.

An account would not enter into an IAR swap in order to have an off-balance sheet item. The account would consider first whether spreads were attractive enough to purchase a negatively convex instrument. If they were, the alternatives to doing so would be considered. The off-balance sheet aspect would be an advantage or a disadvantage depending on the account.

We have now looked at two street myths about customers and shown they are bogus; we now turn to customer myths about dealers.

MYTH #3: The Street Has a Pricing Model That Prices All Securities Consistently Across All Sectors

The reality is that derivatives dealers have different models for different purposes. Attempts are made to try to price the particular instrument in question by focusing on its salient features.

There are three major types of models that are used for the pricing of instruments that contain options:

- "Closed form" expressions
  Modified Black-Scholes
- Interest rate "trees"
  —Recombining and non-recombining
  —Single and multi-factor
- Monte-Carlo simulation

"Closed form" expressions come in two types: yield-based modifications of Black-Scholes and price-based modifications of Black-Scholes. The Black-Scholes option pricing formula was initially developed for options on common stock: The option price was dependent on the current stock price, the strike price on the option, a (constant) interest rate, the time to expiration, and the volatility of the stock. The stock was assumed to be lognormally distributed with constant volatility.

In the early days of the cap market, "yield-based" modifications to Black-Scholes were used extensively to price caps and floors. It was assumed that three-month LIBOR was lognormally distributed with constant volatility, while the rate of interest used to discount future cash flows was constant. This is a fundamental inconsistency, as a constant discount rate implies interest rates are non-random, in which case LIBOR is deterministic. If one used the "yield-based" modification, it is possible to calibrate the model to obtain reasonable prices. This is done by using smaller implied volatilities for longer-maturity, high-strike caps than for shorter-maturity, lower-strike caps. Essentially, on longer-maturity, high-strike caps, the price is being severely overestimated by using a constant interest rate. Using a lower volatility allows one to "correct" for this effect.

Price-based modifications to Black-Scholes allow the model to be used to price options on bonds or futures. One assumes the bond price is lognormally distributed with constant volatility and the rate of interest used to discount all futures cash flows is constant. This methodology has three inconsistencies. As in the yield-based modifications, there is a fundamental inconsistency because the constant discount rate implies the bond price is nonrandom. Second, the bond price being fixed (par) at maturity violates the lognormality assumption. Third, as the bond matures, its price volatility must decline, violating constant volatility. Nonetheless, the price-based modifications to Black-Scholes work well when the option is European and the option maturity is small in relation to the underlying assets' life. Thus, a price-based modification to Black-Scholes would be acceptable for a three-month option on the long bond, but would be very bad for a six-month option on a two-year note. The price-based modifications are in wide use for short-term options pricing.

The whole yield curve or arbitrage-free approach to option pricing was developed in 1986 by Ho and Lee, and enhanced by Black, Derman, and Toy; Hull and White; and Heath, Jarrow, and Morton. This approach essentially relies on the construction of a binomial, single-factor interest rate tree. At each node of the tree, interest rates can either move up or down. The arbitrage-free interest rate tree is constructed so as to match the prices on Treasury securities. In a recombining tree, a down-up movement is the same as up-down movement. This applies only to path-independent securities, where the payoff is only dependent on where rates are now, not on how you got there. For path-dependent securities, a down-up movement would produce different results from an up-down movement. Recombining trees are in wide use for cap and floor pricing, callable bond pricing, and the pricing of short-term options. In a one-factor model, the yields on securities of different maturities are perfectly correlated. It is important to realize this does not mean all yield curve changes are parallel; rather long-term rates move less than short-term rates, but all rates move in tandem.

Neither two-factor trees nor non-recombining trees are in wide use because they are computationally inefficient. Non-recombining trees, in which a down-up movement is not the same as an up-down movement, are computationally difficult, as the number of paths grows rapidly. In a recombining tree that starts at time $t = 0$, there will be $n + 1$ nodes at time n. Thus, at time three, there will be four nodes. In a nonrecombining tree, there will be $2**n$ nodes, or eight nodes at time three. These trees would, however, be very valuable for the pricing of path-dependent options. Two-factor models, which allow interest rates across different maturities to be less than perfectly correlated, are computationally inefficient, as the number of paths grows rapidly. Nonetheless, a number of dealers have two-factor models under development, and we would expect increased reliance on these instruments to price yield curve options and "better of" options going forward.

Most commonly, options that cannot be valued using a single-factor recombining tree, such as the options embedded in mortgage-backed securities, yield curve options, "better of" options, periodic caps, and IARs, are priced using Monte-Carlo simulation techniques. These prices are often checked against those produced using a two-factor model, to make sure the Monte-Carlo simulation is being calibrated correctly. This type of simulation, which consists of running hundreds of paths, is very quick and computationally efficient, but not necessarily arbitrage-free.

Over the next several years, as our technology improves, we would expect to see increased reliance on multi-factor models and less reliance on Monte-Carlo simulation.

MYTH #4: The Street Tries to Rip Customers Off on Trades, Since Pricing Can Differ Substantially Between Dealers and Substantially from Theoretical Values

In fact, there are four major reasons why pricing may differ between dealers:

- Transactions costs associated with hedging are not zero;
- Positions often cannot be replicated easily in cash markets and involve less than perfect hedging.
- Many derivative products receive only one-way inquiry, so a swap desk cannot lay off the other side of the trade;
- Risk profiles and/or balance sheet limitations constrain the ability of individual dealers to take positions in products with one-way inquiry; when the risk profile begins to fill, offers deteriorate rapidly.

We use two products to illustrate these points. The first product is a forward yield curve swap in which the customer receives a long-term rate reset every six months (for example, 10-year CMT or the 10-year swap rate) and pays LIBOR. The swap begins five years in the future. Essentially, the current yield curve is so steeply upward sloping that the forward yield curve is essentially flat between years five and 10. Exhibit 4 shows the difference in the implied forward rates between six-month LIBOR and the 10-year swap rate. Until year five, the differences are large; they average 161 basis points. Between year five and year 10 they average only 20 basis points.

Now let us consider the hedging on the forward swap. The swap dealer wants to create the following hedge in order to offset the position in which he is paying (short) the 10-year swap rate and receiving (long) six-month LIBOR beginning in five years:

Long	Short
10-year swap rate in 5 years for 6 months	6-month LIBOR in 5 years
10-year swap rate in 5.5 years for 6 months	6-month LIBOR in 5.5 years
10-year swap rate in 6 years for 6 months	6-month LIBOR in 6.0 years
* * * *	* * * *
10-year swap rate in 9.5 years for 6 months	6-month LIBOR in 9.5 years

How does a dealer hedge a position such as this? In a forward swap in which the fixed rate does not reset, the dealer can simply be long (short) a longer maturity swap and short (long) a shorter maturity swap in order to duplicate the forward position. In this case, however, both sides of the swap reset every six months. Essentially the dealer is long 15–20 year swaps and short 5–10 year LIBOR. However, the 15–20 year government sector is quite illiquid, and the swap market does not go out past 10 years. In this deal, any hedge the dealer desk undertakes is leaky—that is, it entails considerable basis risk. The best hedge turns out to be a long position in Treasury securities in the 15–20 year sector and a short position in 5–10 year swaps, but the dealer is still exposed to a considerable amount of risk.

This example illustrates all the points discussed above: The position cannot be easily replicated in cash markets and the hedge must be rebalanced, there are transactions costs associated with the rebalancing, and the inquiry is all one way; all customers want to pay six-month LIBOR and receive the 10-year swap rate.

Another example of a product in which the risks cannot be perfectly hedged is the index amortizing swaps (IARs) discussed earlier. The IAR can be thought of as a standard fixed-floating swap plus a path dependent combination of forward caps written by the investor. Thus, in this product, the swap desk has essentially purchased caps. This risk can be partially offset by writing non-path dependent options through the cap book. Again, the position

**EXHIBIT 4 Difference Implied Forward Rates
Six-Month LIBOR vs. 10-Year Swap Rate**

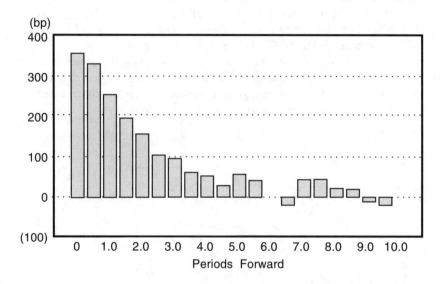

cannot be perfectly replicated, the hedge must be rebalanced, and the inquiry is all one way: all customers want to receive fixed and pay floating.

A swap desk will have some appetite for products such as those above. As the book grows, depending on how comfortable a desk is with the hedging, the offerings may deteriorate. Other dealers may not have filled in their risk profiles for that particular product, creating seemingly wide disparities across different dealers. Thus pricing may diverge considerably from theoretical values and may be very different between dealers.

CONCLUSION

In this paper we have looked at dealer myths about customers and customer myths about swap dealers. Dealers must realize that customers are looking at a wide array of derivative products across different markets and are using values in one market to help assess value in another. Moreover, they are deciding what trades they want to do based on economic considerations, and are choosing the "best" form to execute from an accounting and regulatory framework. Accounting and regulatory considerations do not drive trades; more often than not they are excuses for trades customers do not feel make economic sense.

Customers often don't realize that all transactions are hedged; pricing will depend on how comfortable the dealer is with the pricing and how easily the product can be hedged. Many products sold now cannot be perfectly hedged, and have only one-way inquiry, often creating disparities between dealers in their pricing. It is important for customers to realize that a given trade may not fit the book of a given dealer at a specific point in time; this does not mean that dealer is always less aggressive in its pricing.

Soda, Snacks, and Swaps: Use of Derivatives at PepsiCo, Inc.

Edward P. Krawitt
Director, Treasury Centre, Lawson Mardon Packaging,
a division of Alusuisse Lonza Holding AG

INTRODUCTION

Although market participants know the phenomena by a number of names, structured transactions in the fixed income capital markets have generally come to mean a combination of a debt issue and an interest rate swap resulting in a new synthetic liability. The first such financing occurred during the early years of the swap market, when two entities, one with fixed rate payments, the other with floating, would exchange their interest payment obligations. The issuer of fixed rate debt had floating rate payments, and the issuer of floating rate debt had fixed rate obligations. Subsequently, swap trading desks grew to not only match counterparties but also to assume payment risks and obligations. At the same time, the use of interest rate swaps by liability managers has grown from the hedging of discrete transactions to adjusting the overall interest rate risk of an entire liability portfolio.

Structured transactions have an important role in reducing the interest costs of PepsiCo's debt portfolio. The primary motivation for PepsiCo to use a structured transaction is to obtain synthetic debt at cheaper cost than a direct issue. Examples are swapping debt into a floating rate obligation at a

Edward P. Krawitt was Manager, Capital Markets, PepsiCo, Inc. The opinions expressed are those of the writer and not necessarily those of PepsiCo, Inc. Mr. Krawitt is currently with Lawson Mardon Packaging, a division of Alusuisse-Lonza Holding AG.

better rate than PepsiCo's commercial paper program or swapping into fixed rate debt at less than a direct term issue. Along with cheaper financing come risks, such as credit exposure to a swap counterparty, and benefits, such as accessing a new investor base.

Although this chapter is limited to a discussion about structured financings, PepsiCo also uses interest rate swaps as one of its tools for overall liability management. The swap market provides PepsiCo with a quick and efficient way of adjusting the risk profile of our debt portfolio. Floating rate debt is easily converted to fixed—and back again—which adjusts the duration of the entire portfolio. While the swap market does not relieve PepsiCo from refunding risk, we are able to better control interest rate risk as well as take advantage of structured financing arbitrages.

A SIMPLE EXAMPLE

A straightforward example of a structured transaction is a PepsiCo $100,000,000 one-year fixed rate medium-term note swapped to a commercial paper based floating rate obligation. The proceeds retired commercial paper yet kept the same interest rate risk profile. See Exhibits 1 and 2.

This "plain vanilla" note had no special appeal for a specific buyer and generally sold to money market investors. The motivation was primarily from an arbitrage in the swap and note markets. At the time of the deal, swap spreads were relatively wide and could more than cover PepsiCo's fixed payment obligations on the one-year note. The result is synthetic 30-day commercial paper at a spread below the Federal Reserve composite rate and competitive with PepsiCo's cost of commercial paper.

In this case, synthetic commercial paper enables PepsiCo to reduce its refunding exposure by pushing out the need to raise new funds to a year from daily or monthly. Although still exposed to the vicissitudes of index fluctuations, PepsiCo smoothed out its exposure to swings in its own commercial paper postings.

EXHIBIT 1   The Simple Transaction: One-Year Fixed to Floating

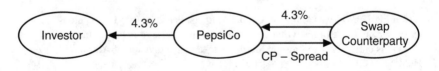

EXHIBIT 2   CP – Spread

Note Terms

Par Amount	$100,000,000
Settlement	1 week from trade date
Maturity	1 year
Coupon	4.3%
Coupon Payment Frequency	Semi-annually
Principal Repayment	At maturity
Fee to Agent	0.125%

Swap Terms—to Commercial Paper Based Floating Rate

Notional Amount	$100,000,000
Effective Date	1 week from trade date
Termination Date	1 year
Issuer Receives	4.3% fixed
Payment Frequency	Semi-annually
Issuer Pays	Commercial Paper less Spread
Payment Frequency	Semi-annually
Calculation	Daily average, monthly compound of 30-day Federal Reserve Composite for commercial paper on a money market yield basis
Up-front Fee to Issuer	0.125%

This transaction has no fancy features and is a pure play on swap spreads. PepsiCo can easily convert the obligation back to fixed by unwinding the swap or layering on another swap in which PepsiCo receives floating and pays fixed.

As part of the structuring of the transaction, the up-front fee received by PepsiCo for the swap exactly offsets the agent's fee for placing the note. This enables PepsiCo to receive net proceeds of par.

ROLES IN A STRUCTURED TRANSACTION

The four roles in the market consist of (1) a debtor or issuer such as PepsiCo, who issues the debt and has the obligation of making all interest and principal obligations; (2) the investor or buyer, who often wants to purchase an asset

EXHIBIT 3

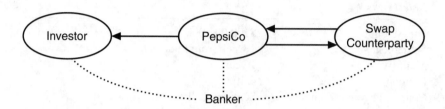

with particular attributes; (3) a swap intermediary or counterparty, who makes the deal happen by converting the investor's asset into a liability that fits the debtor's financing strategy; and (4) a banker, who brings the parties together and structures the deal. See Exhibit 3.

Generally, the process works as follows: An investor wants exotic debt, a banker finds a company to sell it, the issuer swaps the debt with a counterparty to obtain desired financing levels. Implementing the process includes evaluating credit risk, pricing nuances, and understanding the mechanics in the derivative markets.

The Issuer

Issuers of structured transactions range from government agencies and large finance companies that are constantly in the market for debt to industrial companies that tap the capital markets on a less frequent basis. Usually such issuers will have large debt portfolios with the capacity to absorb new structures as the market presents opportunities. The capacity may be from a continuous need for debt from maturing issues, as is often the case with finance companies, or may be from a reallocation of debt through synthetic, or structured means. An example is retiring commercial paper with synthetic floating rate debt.

The motivation for a company to issue exotic debt and swap it into a traditional obligation is usually to obtain a lower all-in financing cost. All else being equal, an investor will pay extra for a structured transaction, and, after allowing for various administrative costs and the cost of an interest rate swap, an issuer should obtain cheaper debt. A qualitative reason for synthetic debt is tapping a new investor base.

To evaluate the attractiveness of any transaction, the issuer must compare the proposal with the alternatives. Common benchmarks for floating rate debt are the commercial paper index and LIBOR. By comparing the total cost of a transaction, including commissions, fees, legal expenses, filing costs, and other intangible burdens with the issuer's cost of commercial paper versus the CP index for commercial paper issuers or with LIBOR for LIBOR-based borrowers, a company can quickly ascertain the relative cost or savings of a structured transaction.

In addition to the favorable economics of a deal because of investor demand, short-lived market opportunities, or "axes," arise from swap counterparties as well. These often occur when a swap house is long or short a position—fixed versus floating, a particular currency, or volatility—and will offer attractive rates on the opposite side to remove the risk.

Other reasons for an issuer to engage in a structured transaction is a preference for using synthetic financing over the direct markets. A good example is that of a large issuer of commercial paper (CP) who is in the market daily. The CP issuer posts daily rates that fluctuate according to overall market conditions and the credit quality and investor demand for that particular issuer. The commercial paper index, the Fed Composite, fluctuates according to overall market conditions. By issuing debt and swapping it into a floating rate obligation below the CP composite, the issuer will remove rate fluctuations due to company-specific events from its financing cost.

In the above example, PepsiCo reduced its dependence on demand for its commercial paper. The one-year maturity for the structured deal versus 30-day maturity for commercial paper reduced its refinancing risk.

Any purchase of debt by an investor includes credit risk, for which the investor is compensated by a spread above riskless debt. When a debt issuer becomes a party to an interest rate swap, the issuer immediately incurs the risk of the swap counterparty. A default by the swap counterparty will destroy the original economics of the deal. Consequently, the issuer must actively evaluate the credit of its counterparties when structuring a transaction.

Investors

The motivation for investors varies. Common reasons are to match a liability, make a bet on a particular market or rate, or access a market into which an investor is statutorily prohibited. These are all specific needs of an investor that are generally not natural liabilities for an issuer.

Investors with a liability stream, such as an insurance company, may want assets to match estimated payouts. Choices include buying a portfolio of securities structured to match the liability schedule or a single note with the return of principal tailored to match liabilities. Interest on the note may be fixed or floating, and the debtor can swap the obligation to a fixed or floating interest rate. Advantages for such an investor include better pricing, lower transaction costs, and quick access to the investment.

Investors who want to bet on a particular rate, spread, or any type of relationship in the capital markets can do so by buying a structured transaction. An issuer will fill the need provided the issuer can swap the debt to a desired liability and the deal has favorable economics. An investor who thinks swap spreads will widen can link the interest payment rate to a swap spread. Investors who think rates will stay constant can buy collared notes— notes that are floating but have a floor and a ceiling on the rate.

Any investor with any view can have a tailor-made security with all of the return accruing to the investor's scenario and selling off the rest. For example a "lower of" note returns the maximum coupon when interest rates stay at a given level. See Exhibit 4.

This is an example of structure for an investor who has a strong view that rates will not vary much from 6.7 percent. The coupon of this transaction is a function of three-month LIBOR and structured so that it attains a maximum when LIBOR is at 6.7 percent. As the graph in Exhibit 5 shows, the investor had a view that three-month LIBOR would stay at approximately 6.7 percent. To obtain the healthy rate above LIBOR relative to the issuer's base level, the investor effectively sold the rights to any better returns back to the issuer.

A standard fixed or floating note would not have given the investor the desired yield. Although the investor could have obtained the same return profile by buying a standard fixed or floating note and layered on swaps, the investor may be prohibited from using interest rate swaps or may have just wanted one security. In addition to the embedded option value in the structure, additional arbitrage came from the investor's need to "pay up" to obtain a custom-made security.

Not wanting to make the opposite bet, PepsiCo issued the note and in turn "sold" those rights to a swap counterparty in order to receive a financing cost of the CP index less a spread.

Swap House

Swap dealers started as brokers for counterparties and would line up two companies interested in swapping their interest obligations. This evolved into the swap house being the counterparty and taking on the credit risk of the other side. Conversely, an issuer of debt who swaps the debt takes the credit risk of the swap house.

EXHIBIT 4   A "Lower of" Note: The Investor Predicts Flat Rates

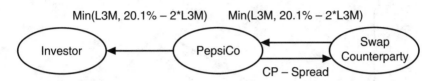

Min(L3M, 20.1% − 2*L3M)   Min(L3M, 20.1% − 2*L3M)

Investor   PepsiCo   Swap Counterparty

CP − Spread

Note Terms

Par Amount	$25,000,000
Settlement	1 week from trade date
Maturity	2 years
Coupon	Lower of 3-month LIBOR and 20.1% − 2 × 3-month LIBOR with a minimum rate of 0%
Coupon Payment Frequency	Quarterly
Principal Repayment	At maturity
Fee to Agent	0.250%

Swap Terms—to Commercial Paper Based Floating Rate

Notional Amount	$25,000,000
Effective Date	1 week from trade date
Termination Date	2 years
Issuer Receives	Lower of 3-month LIBOR and 20.1% − 2 × 3-month LIBOR with a minimum rate of 0%
Payment Frequency	Quarterly
Issuer Pays	Commercial Paper less Spread
Payment Frequency	Quarterly
Calculation	Daily average, monthly compound of 30-day Federal Reserve Composite for commercial paper on a money market yield basis
Up-front Fee to Issuer	0.250%

EXHIBIT 5 Coupon of "Lower Of" Note

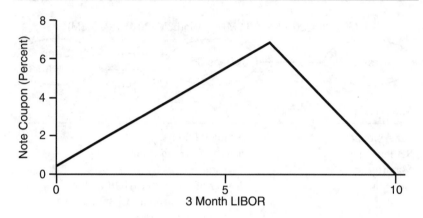

A swap dealer's role is to provide fixed income derivative instruments as tools for interest rate management. The dealer's role within the context of structured transactions is to provide market knowledge, help initiate and structure transactions, and take the counterparty role for an interest rate swap to complete the deal for an issuer.

Swap dealers will often make markets in a number of rates and currencies and to hedge their positions they may be aggressive bidders for a particular portion of the market. When this happens a swap house will initiate a transaction, for example to "buy" volatility to return their portfolio to a neutral position.

The aggressiveness of bidding for swap business versus market levels is a function of a dealer's books and its knowledge of the product. If a dealer paid fixed rate legs of swaps and finds itself long, it may become an aggressive payer of floating rate legs to bring its position to a neutral level. Just like an investor of securities and an issuer of debt, swap dealers monitor and adjust their duration and other risk measures. Consequently, when they put on or take off trades to change the profile of their portfolio, they may pay above market rates of which the other side, such as an issuer with a structured transaction, can take advantage.

When PepsiCo issued its capped floating rate notes, volatility was high, and PepsiCo effectively "sold" the caps to a swap counterparty for less than PepsiCo "bought" the caps from the investor. This arbitrage existed because a swap dealer was short volatility. See Exhibit 6.

EXHIBIT 6 Capped Floaters—Selling the Embedded Volatility

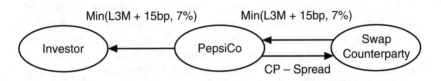

Note Terms

Par Amount	$100,000,000
Settlement	1 week
Maturity	2 years
Coupon	3-month LIBOR plus 15 basis points, maximum of 7%
Coupon Payment Frequency	Quarterly
Principal Repayment	At maturity
Fee	0.25%

Swap Terms—to Commercial Paper Based Floating Rate

Notional Amount	$100,000,000
Effective Date	1 week
Termination Date	2 years
Issuer Receives	3-month LIBOR plus 15 basis points, maximum of 7%
Payment Frequency	Quarterly
Issuer Pays	Commercial Paper less Spread
Up-front Fee to Issuer	0.25%

This capped floater is similar to a standard LIBOR-based floating rate note except that the note has a maximum coupon of 7 percent. Economically, it is the same as the investor buying a two-year floating rate note with a coupon of 7 percent and selling two-year caps based on three-month LIBOR with a strike of 6.85 percent. Conversely, issuing this note is comparable to issuing a standard two-year LIBOR note and buying two-year caps. Selling the caps without the swap would have left PepsiCo with LIBOR-based financing.

The investor's compensation for selling the caps is the additional spread above LIBOR for each of the periodic coupon payments. Without the cap feature, this note would have had a coupon of about three-month LIBOR flat or through LIBOR. Thus, the investor receives an extra 15 basis points for the potential future rate give-up. This investment makes sense for an investor who is bullish on rates. If the investor's outlook of flat to lower rates proves to be true, then the additional yield will boost the investor's return. It's not for free, however; with the yield capped at 7 percent, a rise in rates over the two-year period will put the option, which the investor is short, out-of-the-money. See Exhibit 7.

Like the previous example, this is an instrument for a portfolio manager to manifest an explicit view of the market.

PepsiCo swapped this structure to a CP based floating rate obligation that met its financing targets and extended the refunding requirements out to two years from a monthly rollover of funds. Although PepsiCo embedded the sale of the caps with the basis swap of LIBOR to CP in a single swap, the transaction could have been broken into two pieces with two counterparties: the sale of the interest rate cap to one and the swap to another. Depending on a counterparty's appetite to buy volatility and receive LIBOR floating, separating the swap into two pieces could enable an issuer to net a better rate.

As structured financings grow more and more exotic with different currencies, rates, and embedded options, the necessary tools with which to evaluate these structures must keep up with the sophistication of the products. A

EXHIBIT 7   Coupon Rate on Capped Floater

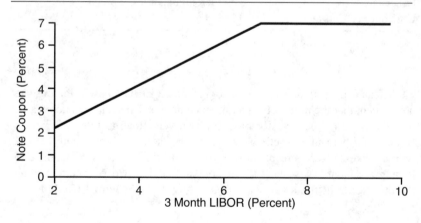

swap dealer will only be as aggressive with pricing a transaction as its ability to evaluate the transaction. The dealers with sophisticated analytics and an understanding of the risk in the more complicated structures will generally have the most aggressive bids and the willingness to participate in such transactions.

In order to be at the cutting edge of security design, the role of good swap dealers is to have both market knowledge and the ability to analyze complicated structures within the context of a changing market.

Bankers

Bankers, who are often swap counterparties, play an important role as agents in the structured transaction process. The dealer may be an investment or commercial bank, an underwriter or an agent, affiliated with a swap house, or working primarily in an advisory capacity. One of a dealer's roles is to keep a pulse on state-of-the-art financial technology in order to serve both investing clients and issuing clients.

Dealers identify buyers and sellers of exotic securities. By maintaining relationships with buyers who have special needs for custom-tailored securities and with issuers who have the capacity to issue structured financings, dealers bring both sides together. Dealers also provide much of the innovation in the capital markets and do so to satisfy both needs. The combination of knowing customer needs, capital markets acumen, analytical resources, and the ability to distribute debt makes investment bankers an important part of expanding capital market liquidity.

An investment bank initiated the following PepsiCo note launch due to its relationships with both the buyer of the note and PepsiCo, the issuer. By knowing current swap markets, the investor's level of acceptable credit risk and view of Canadian dollar interest rates, and PepsiCo's financing targets, the bank structured the transaction to satisfy each party's goals.

With the note detailed in Exhibit 8, the buyer is manifesting a view of Canadian interest rates and country risk while avoiding currency risk, since the coupon payments and principal repayment are in U.S. dollars. The buyer expected an easing in Canadian rates; the inverted coupon structure pays a higher coupon as rates fall. By linking the coupon to Canadian rates, the buyer was able to diversify its exposure to U.S. rates. Not wanting currency exposure, the buyer opted for coupon payments in U.S. dollars. Pricing and maintaining this swap involves a dynamic hedging process that is a function of U.S. and Canadian interest rates as well as foreign exchange rates.

EXHIBIT 8   Inverse C$BA Notes—A Buyer's View
of Canadian Rates

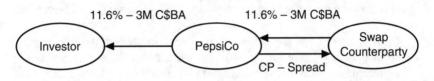

Note Terms

Par Amount	$15,000,000
Settlement	1 week
Maturity	2 years
Coupon	11.6% – 3-month Canadian dollar Bankers Acceptance rate
Coupon Payment Frequency	Quarterly in U.S. dollars
Principal Repayment	At maturity
Fee	0.25%

Swap Terms—to Commercial Paper Based Floating Rate

Effective Date	1 week
Termination Date	2 years
Issuer Receives	11.6% – 3-month Canadian dollar Bankers Acceptance rate
Payment Frequency	Quarterly
Issuer Pays	Commercial Paper less Spread
Up-front Fee to Issuer	0.25%

As part of a transaction, bankers may take on additional roles such as underwriting a transaction. A bank or bank affiliate may also be the counterparty for the swap. After the transaction, the dealer often serves as the calculation agent, helps with repricing or coupon resetting, and may make a market in the security.

STRUCTURING

Structuring a deal consists of addressing the economic and legal issues. The economics of a deal are a function of the cash flows, namely payment of interest and principal on the debt and the receipt and payment of interest on the two legs of the swap.

In structuring these deals, PepsiCo looks to save on interest costs while making sure the liability fits within its financing strategy. For a floating rate transaction, this usually means the widest spread below the index. To readily compare floating rate structured transactions to its direct commercial paper alternative, PepsiCo often links its financing to a spread below the Federal Reserve CP composite rate, the standard CP index.

Structured transactions that result in net fixed rate debt must be competitive with PepsiCo's cost of fixed rate funds. Structured transactions bring other advantages over the direct markets, too, including a diversification of funding sources and helping maintain the scarcity value of public debt issues.

By exactly matching the interest receipt of a swap to the interest obligations on the debt, the issuer need not make any assumptions about amortizations of cash flows or the cost of carry for interim interest payments. For example, a note with semi-annual fixed rate payments but with quarterly fixed rate receipts will expose the issuer to the cost of carry for the fixed payments. Matching interest payments and swap receipts will enable the issuer to focus on the desired economics of the swap payment, which will fall within the issuer's financing plan.

All of the above examples match the swap receipt to the note payment. Also matching are the swap fee and the note commission, so that the issuer receives par. The up-front fee to the issuer from the swap counterparty compensates the issuer for the commission paid to the agent for selling the debt. Matching these two cash flows eliminates the need for amortization assumptions for the note fee.

Although the debt and the swap are economically linked, they are legally separated. The guts of the debt documentation are contained in the description of the interest calculation, which would appear in the filing with the SEC for a registered transaction. This is usually a prospectus supplement for a discrete shelf takedown or a pricing supplement for a medium-term note. The guts of the swap documents are the swap confirmation letters. For the interest payment and swap receipt to match, the language describing each must match. This means using the same day count, payment conventions, and sources for looking up indices. For a floating rate note, nuances such as what

**EXHIBIT 9   The Leveraged Inverse Floater: Big Kick
as Rates Drop**

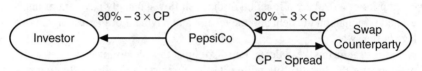

Note Terms

Par Amount	$100,000,000
Settlement	1 week from trade date
Maturity	1 year
Coupon	30% – 3 times CP, where CP is the 30-day Commercial Paper index, reset daily, compounded monthly, minimum coupon of 0%
Coupon Payment Frequency	At maturity
Principal Repayment	At maturity
Fee to Agent	0.25%

Swap Terms—to Commercial Paper Based Floating Rate

Notional Amount	$100,000,000
Effective Date	1 week from trade date
Termination Date	1 year
Issuer Receives	30% – 3 times CP, where CP is the 30-day Commercial Paper index, reset daily, compounded monthly, minimum coupon of 0%
Payment Frequency	At termination
Issuer Pays	Commercial Paper less Spread
Payment Frequency	At termination
Calculations	Daily average, monthly compound of 30-day Federal Reserve Composite for commercial paper on a money market yield basis
Up-front Fee to Issuer	0.25%

screen the floating rate comes from, Telerate or Reuters, for example, can make the difference between cash flows matching or missing. A mismatch will alter the economics and original expectations of the deal.

Although not usually a problem with standard fixed rate payments or common floating rate payments such as LIBOR-based swaps, daily reset notes are more problematic, with particulars of the compounding method and rate cut-off day becoming important.

PepsiCo issued a CP-based levered inverse floater. This investment appealed to one bullish on interest rates but constrained by regulatory constraints from buying a long-duration instrument. As rates fell, the note payout increased. See Exhibits 9 and 10.

For this note, the interest accrues until maturity. The corresponding swap receipt accrues until the termination date. Consequently, all the rate-setting conventions including source of rates, rate cutoff, method of averaging, and method of compounding must match. Any differences could compound to affect the economics of the transaction.

Economically, this is an interesting note issue, because one can look at the coupon as a combination of:

Paying 30% on $100MM or 10% on $300MM,
Receiving 3 times CP on $100MM or CP on $300MM, and
Selling 3 $100MM 10% CP caps or one $300MM 10% cap.

EXHIBIT 10 Levered Inverse Floater

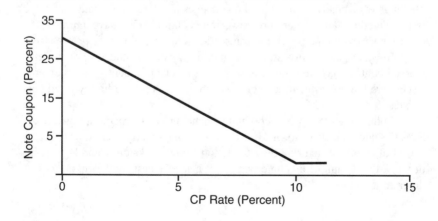

Conversely, to offset this one can decompose the swap into

> Receiving 10% on $300MM notional,
> Paying CP flat on $300MM, and
> Buying a $300MM 10% cap.

And to pay floating, paying CP less a spread on $100MM notional.

Legally, the debt portion of a structured transaction can be any type of liability, including discrete shelf takedowns, medium-term notes, Eurobonds, private placements, or foreign issues. Many medium-term note programs, including PepsiCo's, have standard language designed to accommodate a variety of different types of fixed or floating rates and should have the flexibility to issue any type of debt. Consequently, once an issuer has a medium-term note program registered with the SEC, the legal requirements for the debt consist of filing a pricing supplement that describes the particulars of a single debt issue for the SEC and the investor.

The documentation for a swap usually consists of a master agreement and swap confirmation letter between the two counterparties. The confirmation letter contains the details of the swap including all of the—sometimes intricate—definitions and particulars for calculating the swap receipt and payments. These definitions must match the debt to maintain the integrity of the structured transaction.

Credit Concerns

While the terms of any particular security will compensate an investor for a lower rating, the general idea behind structured transactions is for investors to obtain assets whose return is based on changes in interest rates rather than the issuer's credit quality. Therefore, lower-rated entities often have a more difficult time accessing the structured transaction market.

In other words, investors are making a rate bet and do not want to worry about the creditworthiness of the issuer. Consequently, popular note issuers are the government agencies, sovereign issuers, and highly rated corporates.

In the same vein, when obtaining financing via a structured transaction, PepsiCo does not want to make a bet on a counterparty's credit. Despite a surfeit of care in structuring the transaction from an economic and legal point of view, the default of a counterparty will instantly destroy the economics of the transaction.

The market value of interest rate and currency swaps will vary depending on current interest and foreign exchange rates and the structure of the swap. A basis swap—from one floating index to another—will not have much sensitivity to rate movements relative to a fixed-to-floating swap. Currency swaps can have dramatic shifts in their market value, since both interest rates and FX rates have an effect. PepsiCo swapped its Swiss Franc issue to a fixed rate dollar obligation for interest and principal payments. See Exhibit 11.

EXHIBIT 11 The Swiss Franc Deal: A Currency Swap

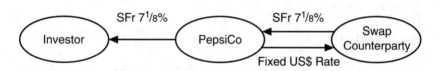

Note Terms

Par Amount	SFr100,000,000
Settlement	4 weeks from trade date
Maturity	3 years
Coupon	$7^1/_8\%$
Coupon Payment Frequency	Annually
Principal Repayment	At maturity

Swap Terms—to US Dollar Fixed Rate

Notional Amount	SFr100,000,000
Effective Date	4 weeks from trade date
Termination Date	3 years
Issuer Receives	$7^1/_8\%$
Payment Frequency	Annually
Issuer Pays	Fixed U.S. dollar rate
Payment Frequency	Annually
Final Payment	Fixed U.S. dollar amount for Swiss Franc principal payment

The value of the swapped principal repayment provides the bulk of the market value of the swap and is dependent on exchange rates and U.S. and Swiss yield curves. As Exhibit 12 shows, shifts from the Swiss Franc/Dollar rate can cause large movements in market value. Movements that are in-the-money for PepsiCo create a credit exposure to the swap counterparty.

Issuers must constantly evaluate the credit quality of their swap counterparties with respect to their absolute rating, their rating relative to any particular deal, and their rating relative to the issuer's overall exposure to the institution.

Certain derivative structures do not entail any credit risk to an entity, such as a sale of caps. Others will likely have little credit risk over the life of a deal, such as a basis swap between 30-day commercial paper and one-month LIBOR. Others, particularly long-dated fixed/floating currency swaps, can have tremendous fluctuations in market value and thus credit exposure to the counterparty.

Post Deal

After a deal, the parts of a structured transaction are legally independent. From an economic point of view they are linked, and often from an accounting view they are linked through hedge accounting treatment. This independence brings flexibility to an issuer. Two examples are liquidating an in-the-money swap to book a gain or assigning a swap to reduce credit risk.

Comparing a structured transaction versus its alternatives in the direct issue market brings up a number of differences:

> Credit exposure—the issuer is exposed to the swap counterparty as discussed above.

> Mark-to-market—under rule FASB 107, the issuer must disclose the current value of all financial instruments, the swap as well as the debt.

EXHIBIT 12 Value of Swap to PepsiCo with Two Years to Maturity

SFr/$ FX Rate	Market Value
1.15	$16.3MM
1.26	$8.4MM
1.53	($5.1MM)
1.76	($13.7MM)

Disclosure—the debt will likely be disclosed by the issuer, in financial statements and through public filings with the SEC. Accompanying swaps, although sometimes mentioned generally, do not have their details, and thus the net financing cost, disclosed.

CONCLUSION

The growing depth and liquidity in the swap markets have enabled issuers of debt to keep up with the demands of investors of debt. PepsiCo, as an issuer, minimizes interest expense by satisfying buyers' needs for esoteric instruments and swapping its obligation back to a liability that fits its financing strategy. Structured transactions improve the liquidity of the overall capital markets by tuning the tools and financial instruments closer to the needs of their users.

Continued innovations in the debt and swap markets will further increase the use of structured transactions. As swaps become more complex, their use will pose new challenges and risks of which users must be aware. Credit risk and its proper measuring and monitoring will continue to be important as the worthiness of counterparties changes. PepsiCo will continue to use structured transactions as another tool to reduce interest cost and bring value to its shareholders.

Using Derivative Products to Manage the Risk and Return of Life Insurance Companies

Thomas A. McAvity, Jr.
Vice President and Director of Quantitative Research
Lincoln National Investment Management Company

This chapter describes how derivative products can help life insurance companies manage risk and return within an asset-liability management (ALM) framework. We begin by examining this ALM framework and then provide a brief overview of derivative products and markets. The heart of the chapter consists of case studies that illustrate how derivative product strategies have met the needs of insurers.

ASSET-LIABILITY MANAGEMENT FRAMEWORK

Besides offering traditional risk-transfer products like life and health insurance, insurers provide investment products that allow customers to accumulate capital for retirement and other needs. Hybrid products like universal life offer a combination of life insurance and capital accumulation.

Since these investment and hybrid products have been growing more rapidly than other products, insurers have experienced dramatic growth in their invested assets, in the ratio of invested assets to surplus, and in the portion of net operating income generated by investment spreads. Many insurers now find that managing the level and downside risk of investment spreads has become their most important challenge.

Managing an Investment Spread Business

Insurers operate as investment intermediaries when they sell fixed investment products backed by the general account. Most of the money being invested is funded by customer deposits and premiums. The insurer uses the investments to manufacture the cash flows required by the liabilities. The insurer's net investment revenue or margin is the spread between investment income and the income credited to the customers. Over the lives of the liabilities and the related assets, the insurer's financial goal is to earn sufficient margin to recoup acquisition costs and periodic expenses and earn sufficient profit to achieve the desired return on capital and other resources employed.

With a fixed product, the insurer guarantees an interest rate (or specified index for computing return) at time of sale. The rate may be explicitly stated or implicitly used in calculating the size of the deposit required to fund the stream of future benefits that the insurer is obligated to pay (e.g., a pension buyout annuity, structured settlement, or typical immediate annuity). The rate may be committed for the entire term of the product (e.g., a guaranteed investment contract or GIC) or for a portion of the term, subject to adjustment by the insurer from time to time thereafter (e.g., a single-premium deferred annuity or SPDA). Such adjustments may be based on the insurer's experience with the underlying investment portfolio or simply on market requirements.

Operating as an investment intermediary can be viewed as a special case of operating as a risk intermediary. Consider an insurer that sells GICs and buys a diversified portfolio of fixed income investments with cash flows that match the liability cash flows, including the extra spread required to cover expenses and profit. The incremental yield obtained on the fixed-income investments in relation to U.S. Treasuries can be viewed as premiums covering the risks of default, rating downgrade, and spread widening. These premiums are analogous to premiums collected on term life insurance. In each case, the premium should cover not only the expected claims or losses but also compensate the insurer for bearing downside risk.

By diversifying the specific risks of issuers and industries, the insurer narrows the probability distribution of future default experience, just as a term insurance writer diversifies mortality risk. In each case, no matter how well diversified the population, the insurer is left with the systematic risks, respectively, of rising general levels of default or mortality as the result of system-wide changes or events, e.g., the arrival of an epidemic or of a deep recession. These systematic risks can be measured by simulating future cash flows for a set of scenarios that spans the range of uncertainty for each systematic risk.

Managing Return and Risk to Net Worth

Asset-liability management should focus on managing net worth under uncertainty while satisfying constraints. For a life insurance company engaged in more than one investment spread business, management of net worth requires a two-tier financial engineering approach: (1) for each product line, create integrated investment and product strategies with a desirable performance profile across all possible scenarios and (2) for each scenario, roll up all product lines into the corporate "portfolio" and reconsider the respective levels of activity and component strategies in light of the aggregate performance profile. Derivative products can be valuable tools for enhancing risk-reward profiles at both levels.

The performance profile of the strategy for a single product line must be evaluated in the context of the whole portfolio of product lines, because total risk is reduced to the extent that risk exposures are weakly or negatively correlated across the portfolio. At the levels of the legal entity and holding company, the portfolio of product-line activities should be balanced to achieve the most attractive profile of economic results while meeting constraints over the natural time horizon of the business. A company's capacity for risk is proportional to its capital. For a given level of capital, its appetite for risk is a function of management philosophy and constraints imposed by constituents. The optimal weighting of product-line activities and the optimal mixture of strategies will vary with capital, risk aversion, management's views of likely future events, and its level of confidence in those views.

The traditional concept of an efficient frontier of optimal asset allocations based on the prospective mean and variance of asset returns is inappropriate for two reasons. First, return on assets must be combined with return on liabilities to determine whether the company has increased net worth. Instead of maximizing asset returns in relation to asset risk, insurers should maximize return on net worth in relation to risk to net worth. The risks assumed at the asset or liability level are levered at the surplus level by the ratio of assets or liabilities to net worth. For example, a one-year duration mismatch between assets and liabilities translates into a 15-year surplus duration if invested assets are 15 times net worth.

Second, the use of variance as a proxy for downside risk is appropriate only for symmetric return distributions. Variance is the average of the squared deviations from the mean, whether up or down. For many insurance product lines, the profile of results combining assets and liabilities has more downside risk than upside potential because of options embedded in both assets and liabilities. To isolate downside risk, the insurer must use more discriminating measures like downside semivariance, which averages the squared downside deviations from the mean. The concept of semivariance can be generalized to measure deviations from a specified target or threshold, rather than the mean.[1]

Variable Products

Like an open-ended mutual fund, a variable product usually passes through to the end-user the experience of a managed pool of money. The risk of underperformance is passed through to the customer, along with the potential for outperformance. A variable annuity or variable universal life policy offers the functionality of a mutual fund or family of mutual funds within the "wrapper" of an annuity or a variable universal life policy.

Although fixed and variable products pose very different risks to the insurer and the customer, they address a common challenge to the insurer: to meet customer needs and expectations while avoiding unnecessary and uncompensated risks. To create the cash flows necessary to meet a given set of customer needs, the insurer must identify the most suitable investment strategy or style, select or create a benchmark index representing that style, and manage the investment strategy in relation to that benchmark.

Regulatory, Accounting, and Tax Frameworks

Insurers operate within regulatory, accounting, and tax frameworks that differ from those governing commercial and investment banks and nonregulated corporations. These differences represent material advantages and disadvantages in the competition for the sale of investment products and investment management services.

State insurance laws and regulations are intended to protect the customer by requiring fair products, realistic benefit illustrations, and reasonable sales compensation and by mitigating the risk of insolvency. The latter objec-

---

1. Apart from computational complexity, Markowitz (1959) prefers semivariance to variance because variance is an adequate proxy for downside risk only if the return distribution is normal or if the investor's utility function is quadratic. Quadratic utility functions are difficult to defend. Harlow and Rao (1989) propose the generalized Mean-Lower Partial Moment (MLPM) model specifying downside risk as deviations below the investor's target or minimum acceptable rate of return. Later, Harlow (1991) finds substantial differences between the mean-variance efficient frontier and the mean-semivariance efficient frontier for asset classes with skewed distributions.

tive is addressed through reserve requirements, cash-flow testing, risk-based capital (RBC), and constraints on the use of asset classes perceived as risky. Guarantee Fund Associations provide the ultimate safety net for customers by redistributing insolvency losses to competitors.

Regulators and rating agencies evaluate the financial stability, profitability, and claims-paying ability of life insurers through the lens of statutory accounting, which differs markedly from the accounting models applied to commercial banks, investment banks, and nonregulated financial corporations. Liabilities are valued using a combination of legally required methods and discount rates and the Actuarial Standards of Practice.

Actuaries are required to perform cash-flow testing to assure that statutory reserves are adequate to cover potential future obligations in a variety of interest rate and economic scenarios.

The amount of risk-based capital required is a function of the liability profile and the mixture and diversification of invested assets. Regulators will monitor the ratio of available capital to required capital and take measured action to the degree that this RBC ratio falls too low.

The National Association of Insurance Commissioners (NAIC) is in the process of creating a new Model Investment Law that updates and broadens the existing restrictions on investments, including derivative products. Part of the impetus behind the law is to close some barn doors that allowed a few companies to self-destruct. Close examination of these defaults shows a common cause—an abusive disregard of the need to diversify risks. This restrictive tone, however, is being attenuated by the valuable process of discussion and mutual education taking place between the industry and the regulators as work on the Law progresses.

In the area of derivative products and other innovations, the education process is critical not only to regulators but also to senior management and Board members. Before the education process progressed, some regulators tended to view derivatives and other innovations as risky and requiring much tighter restrictions than other more familiar practices that are actually much riskier. For example, earlier drafts of the model investment law were unduly liberal in the permitted concentration of exposure to the credit risk of a single domestic issuer (3 percent of invested assets for a BBB-rated issuer) and unduly restrictive in the exposure to the credit risk of a swap counterparty or foreign issuer (1 percent for a AAA-rated counterparty).

Insurers are subject to unique tax rules. Life insurance products provide customers with a tax advantage called "inside buildup"; for example, earnings credited to an annuity contract are typically not taxed until they are distributed to the customer. The death benefit paid on life insurance is not taxable income to the estate of the person dying. Life insurers are also taxed differently than competitors under the Internal Revenue Code.

The Challenge: Building Economic Net Worth While Meeting Expectations of Constituents

Insurers must manage risk and return in the context of not only economic reality but also the perceptions of constituents, including regulators, rating agencies, distributors, agents, customers, and shareholders. While real risk may be measured in terms of downside exposure to the economic value of the firm's net worth, perceived risk is measured primarily in terms of the adequacy of surplus and the pattern of historical GAAP and statutory income.

Regulators and rating agencies use measures of risk and formulas for estimating required capital that are based on simplified ratios and rules of thumb using information required on the statutory accounting "blank." These measures necessarily fall short of the economic realism attainable with a well-conceived in-house risk management and capital allocation system grounded in more detailed data and more discriminating segmentation of products.

We can view "cosmetic capital" as the amount of capital necessary to comply with the expectations of these external constituents, and "internal" or "economic" capital as the amount necessary to absorb downside risk in the company's own decision models. They will typically not be equal. Cosmetic capital requirements represent constraints that must be met along any scenario.

Reinsurance

For a growing company, available surplus can be an important constraint. Insurers may use reinsurance to avoid undue concentration of risk and to allow a limited amount of surplus to support a larger and more diversified book of business. For example, an insurer may have life insurance in force in amounts ranging from $10,000 to $50,000,000. For policies on any one life with exposure exceeding the company's retention policy, say $1,000,000, the company may obtain reinsurance for the excess, avoiding undue concentrations of risk and stabilizing the volatility of potential claims in any year. The reduction in risk achieved through this "excess-loss" reinsurance allows the company to insure more lives, achieving greater diversification of risk and economies of scale. Reinsurance also supports a credit to the reserves for the liabilities and reduces the requirement for surplus. Unless the cost of the reinsurance is too high relative to the price at which the underlying policies have been sold, the potential profile of the company's future operating results has probably been improved.

Reinsurance is not always structured as "excess-loss" over a deductible amount. With "quota-share" reinsurance, the reinsurer basically participates pro rata or symmetrically in the profits and losses of a block of business, albeit with possible variations in profitability as the result of how the allowances and profit-sharing are negotiated. Ceding companies constrained by limited capital use quota-share reinsurance to expand their in-force business to realize economies of scale and build market share and franchise value.

We will see in the next section that derivative products can be used to reduce risk in ways very similar to reinsurance. Derivatives include instruments with symmetric payoffs, like quota share reinsurance, and asymmetric payoffs, like excess-loss reinsurance.

OVERVIEW OF DERIVATIVE PRODUCTS

The idea of using derivative products to transfer risk started many years ago with forward contracts on commodities. Forward contracts are bilateral agreements that allow a buyer and a seller to reduce their risk by fixing the price of a transaction prior to the delivery date. Terms of a forward contract may be customized to suit both parties. They are "over-the-counter" as opposed to "exchange-traded" derivative products.

Over-the-Counter Derivatives

In the past decade, the over-the-counter (OTC) derivatives market has grown from less than $1 trillion to over $10 trillion. Some of the most common products are forwards, swaps, options, caps, and floors. Most OTC derivative transactions or "deals" are done between a customer and a dealer. Brokers provide a means for dealers to trade with one another without giving up as much information about market prices, flows, and buy and sell interest.

In the OTC market, each party to the transaction relies on the creditworthiness of the counterparty to honor future obligations. Most swaps provide only for exchange of periodic payments based on differentials between two interest rates or returns, not of principal. The amount of counterparty risk at a given time in the future is simply the replacement cost—i.e., market value—of the deal, if the counterparty should default at that time. The market value of a swap is generally a modest percentage of notional amount. Dollar for dollar, counterparty risk is greater for longer-dated transactions, for options purchased from the counterparty, and for currency swaps, which do include final payments representing currency-driven changes in the value of the notional amount.

Generally, OTC trades are documented on a standard confirmation form that is linked to a master agreement between the parties. In the United States and an increasing number of foreign jurisdictions, laws honor the provision typically set forth in the master agreement providing for netting of obligations across all deals between the two parties, thereby reducing the probable size of the counterparty risk over time.

Forward Contracts

Consider agricultural commodities. In the spring, it is uncertain what the price of a crop will be in the fall. The prevailing or "spot" price in the spring is irrelevant, because the crop can't be delivered until fall. This uncertainty creates risk for both farmers and users of the crop. Each growing season, a farmer's ability to cover costs and earn an adequate income is at risk if prices are too low at time of delivery. A processor's costs are at risk if prices are too high.

For each party, entry into a forward contract locks in a mutually agreeable price. The forward contract is an example of a symmetric derivative product. From the farmer's perspective, it eliminates the risk that the spot price may be lower at harvest time but sacrifices the opportunity for incremental profit if the spot price turns out to be higher. The processor also eliminates risk but forsakes potential savings. Since each party is averse to risk, there is room for both parties to feel that they are getting a good deal.

To illustrate this point, let's assume that the farmer and the processor have the same subjective probability distribution for the price per bushel at harvest-time:

Probability	Price
10%	4.00
25%	5.00
30%	6.00
25%	7.00
10%	8.00
Expected Price	6.00

Using this distribution, they would agree on its $6.00 expected value (the probability weighted average).

Now, let's define the "certainty equivalent"[2] as the price at which each party is indifferent between the alternatives of locking in a sure thing or retaining the risk. Risk aversion is subjective; it depends on individual circumstances and attitudes. The more averse to risk the farmer is, the lower the price he will accept as a certainty equivalent; in this case, the farmer may be willing to accept a price as low as $5.25 to remove his risk. Likewise, the more risk averse the producer is, the higher the forward price he is willing to agree to pay, perhaps $6.35 in this case. For each party, the difference between the expected value and the certainty equivalent is the premium he or she is willing to pay to transfer the risk. For two risk-averse parties with the same view of the probability distribution of prices at delivery, there is a range of prices satisfactory to both parties.

Exchange-Traded Futures

Like forward contracts, exchange-traded futures contracts have a symmetric payoff. When futures began trading on exchanges, the buy and sell interest provided by hedgers was supplemented by marketmakers ("locals") and speculators, improving liquidity. Liquidity is critical to allow continuous trading and stable prices even when hedgers don't enter the market simultaneously.

Exchange-traded contracts require a certain trading volume to be viable, as illustrated by the failure of three contracts on NASDAQ-traded OTC stocks in the mid-1980s. When a new contract fails to attract trading volume, potential users avoid taking positions out of fear of poor liquidity, including wide bid-offer spreads and the risk of adverse market impact should they elect to offset their positions.

Conversely, high volume tends to be self-sustaining. The most successful exchange-traded contracts are designed to track closely the price performance of heavily traded underlying markets. Variety is sacrificed because of

---

2. In *Theory of Games and Economic Behavior,* von Neumann and Morgenstern (1947) propose certainty equivalents and utility functions as key elements of a theory of risk analysis and decision-making under uncertainty. It is rational for a risk-averse investor to seek to maximize expected utility across all feasible scenarios, assigning subjective probabilities to the scenarios. The use of summary measures like mean and downside semivariance to define an efficient frontier of optimal strategies is equivalent to maximizing expected utility under restrictions on the return distribution and the form of the utility function.

the need to focus trading volume in one or at most a few standardized contracts for each broad market.

The available times to expiration are limited to the extent of active buy and sell interest and are generally shorter than those available in the over-the-counter market. Eurodollar contracts are traded at quarterly intervals out to 10 years, with volume and liquidity declining as the term to expiration increases beyond five years. The U.S. Treasury Bond contract is traded in quarterly expiration dates out to two years but has significant volume and open interest only in the first year. The U.S. Ten-Year Note contract is traded out only one year, and interest in the last two quarterly contracts is minimal. Futures contracts exist or are in the process of being created on most of the active debt and equity markets globally.

The futures exchanges protect participants from counterparty risk through the use of initial and variation margin. Initial margin is like a good-faith deposit. Variation margin is the daily settlement in cash of any profit or loss based on marking buyers' and sellers' positions to market. Suppose that an insurer buys a future at a price of $100. If the price rises to $104, the company will receive variation margin of $4. If the price then drops to $101, the insurer will have to pay variation margin of $3.

There is a symbiotic relationship between the OTC and exchange-traded markets. OTC dealers use exchange-traded futures and options to hedge or replicate many of the OTC products they provide to customers. The growth in the OTC derivatives market has contributed to, rather than subtracted from, the growth of the listed futures and options markets. In each of these markets, volume is large compared to trading volume in many of the underlying cash markets.

For example, trading volume for exchange-traded futures and options on U.S. interest rates was over 221 million contracts in 1993, up 16 percent from 1992. In the U.S. Treasury Bond contract alone, volume grew to 79.4 million contracts in 1993, up 13 percent from 1992. With a face amount of $100,000 per contract, that 1993 volume represented the equivalent of almost $8 trillion of Treasury bonds! The 64.4 million volume in Eurodollar contracts translates into an even larger $64 trillion dollar value, because each contract represents a face amount of $1,000,000. Eurodollar contracts are the primary hedging vehicle for interest rate swaps out to five years.

Volume on foreign exchanges is growing even faster than in the United States and is already almost as great. Futures and options trading abroad totaled 517.6 million contracts in 1993, up 33.5 percent from 1992. In the United States, 1993 volume totaled 521.3 million, up 13.3 percent. Of the total of 1.039 billion contracts traded worldwide in 1993, 774 million or 74.5

percent were financial futures. Of the financial futures, interest rate futures accounted for the largest share (510 million or 65.9 percent) and the fastest growth rate (29.1 percent vs. 1992).

Options

Options may be traded on an exchange or OTC. Options provide asymmetric payoffs. Suppose that instead of selling his crop forward at $5 per bushel, a farmer buys the option to sell the crop at $5 per bushel. If the final price is less than $5 per bushel, the farmer exercises the option and sells his crop to the writer of the option for $5 per bushel. However, if the price exceeds $5 per bushel, the farmer lets the option expire worthless and sells the crop in the spot market for the higher price. The asymmetric payoffs of options are like excess-loss reinsurance, in which the reinsurer assumes responsibility for paying the excess of any claim over the amount of risk retained by the ceding company.

The asymmetric payoff patterns provided by options are not typically available in the underlying cash markets. There exist exchange-traded options on many individual stocks as well as on many stock and bond indexes. The over-the-counter derivatives market can provide virtually any conceivable customized option, and it provides times-to-expiration that extend much longer than listed markets.

Insurers buy assets with embedded options like mortgage-backed securities and callable bonds. They also embed options in many of their products. For example, in a typical single-premium deferred annuity (SPDA), the customer has the option to withdraw 10 percent of the account value annually with no penalty and the balance at a declining penalty that disappears after five to eight years.

Like the prepayment option embedded in each mortgage in an MBS, these withdrawal options are not efficiently exercised by customers. One of the biggest challenges for the insurer is to estimate how customers will behave under various interest rate scenarios with respect to these options. Given that big moves in interest rates can actually change market practices, as we saw in the residential mortgage industry over the last two years, we know that simple statistical extrapolation of historical data ("data mining") is inadequate to predict future behavior.

Fixed annuity and universal life products provide that the credited rate will not fall below a guaranteed minimum, typically 3 percent to 6 percent. With falling interest rates, these guarantees become valuable to customers and costly to insurers.

Listed and OTC options allow an insurer to hedge many of the risks assumed in existing investment strategies and product designs. Even if they don't use these tools, insurers can examine the cost of hedging embedded options as a rational basis for evaluating the richness or cheapness of investment opportunities and for pricing their products.

The market price of options on bonds and interest rates is a function of forward rates and the volatility or uncertainty surrounding the rate on which the option's value will be determined. Volatility is usually expressed in percentage terms. For example, if the one-year Treasury yield is 4 percent and the implied volatility of an option on that note is 25 percent, then that volatility is equivalent to 25 percent of 4 percent or 100 basis points. Usually, the volatility of the yield of a Treasury note is higher for shorter maturities and lower for longer maturities.

HEDGING A FIXED DEFERRED ANNUITIES BUSINESS AGAINST THE RISK OF RISING INTEREST RATES

Single, flexible, and periodic premium deferred annuities (SPDAs, FPDAs, PPDAs) have provided much of the growth of general account investment portfolios in the U.S. life insurance industry in the last decade. They now account for a major portion of investable assets for many life insurers, and the surplus allocated to them typically accounts for a major part of total company surplus. The substantial downside risk of these products represents an important strategic problem for many insurers. This case study illustrates how derivatives can be used to improve the risk-reward profile of an important line of business.

A typical SPDA guarantees an interest rate to the customer for the first year. Because this "new money rate" is the primary basis of competition for new deposits, it is often more generous than would be supported by prevailing investment yields, given the spread that the insurer must earn over time to recoup acquisition costs and make the desired profit. The extra amount might take the form of an explicit bonus or "teaser."

After the first year, the insurer has the valuable option of deciding what "renewal rate" to credit, providing considerable leeway in recouping any teaser and in managing the interest rate margin under normal conditions. This option is constrained, however, by the customer's option to withdraw his or her money and the adverse effect that abusive renewal rate practices would have on new sales.

Withdrawal Option

Most SPDAs grant customers the option to withdraw their money. Although outright withdrawals are subject to tax, a competitor can arrange a convenient tax-free exchange to another deferred annuity. SPDAs typically permit partial free withdrawal annually and withdrawal at any time of the full account value less a surrender charge. Surrender charges are typically structured to recapture the unamortized portion of acquisition costs over the first five to eight years after issuance. A typical surrender charge schedule begins at 7 percent for the first year and declines 1 percent per year to 1 percent in the seventh year.

Some surrenders will occur because customers die, become disabled or unemployed, or simply want or need the cash. This base level of non-interest sensitive withdrawals will be increased by interest-sensitive withdrawals when the insurer's renewal rate is uncompetitive with the new money rate offered by competitors.

For SPDA providers who invest in relatively long maturities, uncom-petitive renewal rates are most likely to occur in the event of a sustained uptrend in interest rates. Suppose that over the past five years, an insurer has invested the proceeds of each annuity sold into seven- and 10-year notes. The insurer now has a laddered portfolio with maturities ranging from two to 10 years. If interest rates rise over a sustained period, the effective rate at which income is generated by such a portfolio of fixed-rate investments (the "port-folio earned rate") will increase only to the extent that cash generated by new deposits and by maturities, prepayments, and interest from in-force assets can be reinvested at higher prevailing market rates. Since maturities will only amount to 12 to 15 percent per year, the yield on the portfolio will lag behind prevailing market yields, and the market value of the portfolio will fall below its book value, creating a dilemma for the insurer.

If the insurer maintains a constant margin between the portfolio yield and the renewal rate, that rate will become increasingly uncompetitive, and withdrawals will increase. Although surrender charges will offset most of the writeoff of the unamortized balance of Deferred Acquisition Costs for GAAP purposes, the insurer still has to cope with funding cash outflows with the sale of bonds whose market value is less than book value. This policy is also likely to reduce the sales of new annuities.

If the insurer sets the renewal rate higher than would be permitted by a policy of maintaining a constant net interest margin, current statutory and GAAP income will suffer. If rates rise fast and long enough, the required sub-sidy may exceed the amount of gross margin for which the product was origi-nally priced, causing a negative gross margin.

The resolution of the dilemma is to strike a balance that achieves the least unattractive tradeoffs between high current operating losses and excessive surrenders. The shortfall in operating income will be proportional to the gap that opens up between (1) the rate actually credited and (2) the renewal rate that the insurer can afford to pay, which depends on the portfolio earned rate. Within this framework, we can isolate the need for cash flows from a hedging strategy as those necessary to keep the shortfall within desired tolerances.

Hedging with CMT and CMS Caps

The role of a hedge is to generate the cash flows needed to offset potentially adverse experience. It is helpful to visualize the operation of the hedge along those scenarios in which projected shortfalls exceed tolerances. In this case, out-of-money caps on the five-, seven-, and 10-year constant maturity Treasury (CMT) and swap (CMS) rates allow an insurer to limit the size of its downside risk to an acceptable level at a cost of about 15 basis points per year. The hedge serves a function similar to excess-loss reinsurance, in which the ceding company retains the first loss but uses reinsurance to limit that loss to a tolerable level.

Although the most common interest rate caps are driven by LIBOR, caps based on CMT and CMS rates are more suitable for this hedge and are usually cheaper. CMT and CMS rates are suitable because they track the new-money rates offered on competing annuities. To back newly sold SPDAs, insurers usually buy bonds and mortgages with maturities of five to 10 years, typically gravitating towards the highest yield attainable. To address the possibility that the yield curve may invert in the future, some caps may be bought on the two-year CMT or CMS and/or LIBOR.

Setting the size and strike prices of the cap hedge is a financial engineering problem best done in a comprehensive simulation model of the assets and liabilities managed according to specified decision rules over time. Such a model provides the framework for considering not only cap hedges but also all of the other "knobs" that may be adjusted in the investment strategy, product design, and credited rate strategy. Another "knob" is the possible use of traditional and financial reinsurance.

Hedging with Yield Curve Swaps

Some insurers address the risk of rising rates by shortening duration, and then seek to make up for the lost yield through other strategies or a less competitive credited rate policy. One straightforward method of shortening the duration of a fixed-income portfolio is to enter into an interest rate swap in which the insurer pays a fixed rate and receives a floating rate. The most common floating rate is three- or six-month LIBOR, which is now about 300 basis points lower than the 10-year swap rate. If an insurer paid fixed and received LIBOR for 10 years, this differential would reduce yield sharply in the early years.

As an alternative, some insurers have entered into yield curve swaps in which they receive a floating rate equal to a fixed spread below the prevailing constant-maturity Treasury (CMT) rate or swap rate (CMS) for maturities of five, seven or 10 years. The insurer can select a swap with the desired term (or "tenor"). By selecting a swap with a delayed start, an insurer can achieve a more attractive spread than with an immediate start.

Let's illustrate the idea with an example in which the rate received by the insurer floats with the prevailing yield on the five-year "on-the-run" Treasury Note. As time passes, new five-year notes are issued and replace the old notes for purposes of the calculation. The yield received by the insurer tracks fairly well the yield at which competitors are offering new SPDAs. The spread over or under the Treasury varies with the slope of the yield curve. At this writing (April 1994), the market for this trade is to pay three-month LIBOR and receive the five-year CMT minus 130 basis points.

The insurer can pay either a fixed rate or LIBOR-floating. Paying fixed allows the insurer to acquire and retain attractive fixed-rate investments to underlie the swap. If the insurer pays LIBOR in the swap, he may find a floating or short-duration investment that offers a positive spread over LIBOR. If that spread were 80 bp, then the all-in result of the short-term investment program and the yield curve swap would be 5 CMT minus 50 bp.

Like "ground" in an electrical circuit, LIBOR represents "home base" for the U.S. dollar swap market; most swaps represent an exchange of LIBOR for some other rate or return. If the insurer pays a fixed rate instead of LIBOR, that fixed rate will be the market swap rate for a fixed-for-floating swap of that tenor.

HEDGING ASSET AND LIABILITY COMMITMENTS

In the market for guaranteed interest contracts (GICs) and other guaranteed pension products, rate competition requires providers to work for a narrow gross margin. By managing interest rate risk carefully, an insurer can minimize the allocation of surplus, thereby increasing the ratio of invested assets to surplus and allowing a modest interest margin to create an attractive return on equity.

Unlike retail products, which are sold in an almost continuous flow of smaller transactions, GICs and other guaranteed institutional products require larger discrete commitments. GICs are sold when the opportunity is available to achieve a favorable rate. Likewise, assets with the desired maturity, yield and structure become available sporadically, not typically at the same time as the opportunity to sell a GIC.

The sale of a GIC can be hedged by the purchase of U.S. Treasury Notes or STRIPs, selecting maturities that have interest rate exposures most similar to those of the GICs being hedged. As commitments are made to acquire long-term investments, an appropriate amount of these Treasuries can be sold.

Hedging with Interest Rate Futures

As a substitute for buying Treasuries, an insurer can hedge a GIC by buying exchange-traded interest rate futures on two-, five-, and 10-year U.S. Treasury Notes. Futures provide liquidity, low transaction costs, and the ability to avoid putting up cash that may not yet have been received from the GIC deposit. Using futures instead of Treasuries also provides the benefit of hedge accounting under FAS 87; under this Statement, any gain (loss) on unwinding the hedge is credited (debited) to the carrying value of the asset(s) purchased.

Alternatively, the insurer can warehouse an "inventory" of assets in anticipation of selling GICs. The short sale of Treasuries to hedge such an inventory is not permitted under insurance law. The most attractive hedge is to sell futures whenever an asset is purchased and then to offset the appropriate amount of this short position when a GIC is sold. At any given time, the outstanding futures position is a mirror image of the asset inventory. FAS 87 calls for incorporating the gain or loss on the hedge into the assets being hedged.

Each of these strategies hedges against changes in interest rates but not against changes in the spreads available in the bond and GIC markets, which are closely correlated. An insurer carrying a large inventory of hedged assets would be helped (hurt) if spreads on assets and GICs narrowed (widened) in the interval of time before GICs were sold against them. As a result, an insurer may vary the size of the inventory and tilt to positive or negative inventory positions depending on their view of the future trend in spreads on fixed income assets and GICs.

HEDGING THE RISK OF WIDENING SPREADS

Spreads on noncallable corporate bonds have fluctuated widely over the past 10 years. Such fluctuations introduce risk and opportunity into the management of a fixed income portfolio within an asset-liability framework.

Consider a block of single-premium deferred annuities sold over the past six years, on which surrender charges are declining 1 percent per year as the block ages. These SPDAs might be supported by a fixed-income portfolio consisting of 60 percent corporate bonds and private placements, 25 percent mortgage backed securities (MBSs), and 15 percent commercial mortgages. Recall that as renewal rates on these SPDAs fall short of SPDA new money rates, customers have an increasing incentive to surrender. If the yield spreads in the market should widen, a competitor attempting to lure away these deposits will have the advantage of using higher-yielding assets, over and above the effects of any increase in interest rates.

In the 1992–93 period, corporate bond spreads tightened by about 60 basis points to the narrowest levels of the decade. Similar tightening has been experienced in swap spreads, which pertain to the fixed side of a "plain-vanilla" fixed-for-floating interest rate swap. Dealers believe that this tightening is related to the slope of the yield curve; the current steepness creates an imbalance of supply and demand. Investors prefer to receive fixed to earn a higher rate. Corporations prefer to receive fixed and pay floating to reduce the cost of fixed-rate debt. It is risky to rely on historical extrapolation, however, because the swap market has been experiencing very rapid growth and broadening of its user base, causing significant changes in the underlying pattern of demand and supply.

The mid-market swap spread can be viewed as the equilibrium level at which two AA-rated counterparties are indifferent between receiving or paying fixed. The difference between the swap spread and the single-A or BBB corporate bond spread can be isolated as the incremental premium for term default risk. At this point in the economic recovery and interest rate cycle, an insurer might have a view about either the steepness of the curve or the likely trend in pure default premia.

Hedging with Spread Locks

If an insurer's primary concern is that flattening of the yield curve would cause corporate and swap spreads to widen, spread locks may be used as a hedge and as a means of actively expressing the view that spreads are likely to widen. A spread lock is an over-the-counter derivative transaction that specifies the tenor of the swap whose spread is being measured and the term over which the customer expects that spread to widen (or narrow). The dealer will offer to set the lock at the end of the term at a certain spread, which may be wider than the spot spread.

At the end of the term, if the spread is wider than the lock, the dealer owes money to the insurer. If the spread is narrower than the lock, the insurer owes money to the dealer. The amount owed is typically equal to the product of three terms: (1) the notional amount of the transaction, (2) the spread difference (actual level vs. the lock), and (3) the duration of a swap of that tenor.

For example, suppose that an insurer is concerned that 10-year single-A spreads, which are only 70 basis points, may widen. With spot 10-year swap spreads at 35 basis points, the insurer puts a spread lock of $100 million notional amount on the 10-year swap spread for one year at a spread of 38 basis points. After a year, corporate spreads and swap spreads widen by 15 basis points to 90 and 55 respectively. The cash settlement on the spread lock would be based on a favorable spread of 17 basis points and be calculated as follows: $100,000,000 \times .0017 \times 6.85 = \$1,164,500$. That payoff would offset most of the effect on market value of the 20 basis point widening of $100 million of the insurer's corporate bonds.

Spread locks may be "European style," i.e., exercisable only at the termination date, or they may allow the customer a window during which the lock can be exercised. Even before the window or termination date, a customer can typically unwind the lock at a mutually agreeable level, which will be a function of the forward swap spread then prevailing in the market.

Hedging with CMT/CMS Swaps

Another way to hedge against spread widening is to enter into a floating-to-floating swap in which the insurer pays the CMT rate plus a specified spread and receives the CMS rate. The specified spread will be based on the forward swap spreads implied by the current prices in the swap and Treasury markets. The trade is attractive if the insurer believes that swap spreads will be wider than those implied spreads. The CMT/CMS swap accomplishes the same result as a series or "strip" of European style spread locks.

HEDGING THE RISK OF FALLING RATES

For portfolios backing fixed cash flows like GICs and long-tailed fixed annuities, the use of callable corporate and mortgage-backed securities creates reinvestment risk. As conditioned as we might be to focus on inflation and high interest rates as our main fear, we must consider the possibility of an era of disinflation and even lower interest rates. Even for liabilities like SPDAs, on which the insurer enjoys the option of resetting the renewal rate, there is the danger of penetrating the level of the minimum guaranteed rate.

Sometimes, securities with call or prepayment risk are priced attractively in relation to noncallable securities of similar duration and quality. In the case of SPDAs, it may be attractive to use some current coupon or discount MBS pass-throughs and CMO tranches with some shortening risk but little or no lengthening risk, trading off some call risk to obtain more yield.

Such strategies leave some need to hedge against an extreme rally in interest rates. Insurers have used various tools to meet this need, including interest rate floors, prepayment caps, and bond warrants.

Interest Rate Floors

Interest rate floors are the mirror image of caps. They usually consist of a quarterly or semi-annual series of options ("floorlets") on a yield index like LIBOR, CMT, or CMS. On each reset date, the yield is observed; if the yield is less than the strike yield, the "floorlet" entitles the owner to receive an amount of revenue equal to the notional amount times the excess of the strike yield over the observed yield, adjusted to a quarter- or half-year.

Floorlets are priced in relation to the forward rate for the respective index. With the steep yield curves that have prevailed for the past three years, forward rates rise even more steeply than the yield curve itself in the first few years, making floors an economical way to protect portfolios from reinvestment risk.

Simulations show that the prepayment risk requires more than a simple floor structure. Payoffs must be "souped up," either by having the notional amount increase as the index drops or by purchasing a ladder of strikes to accomplish the same objective in a piecewise linear fashion.

Floors may also be used as part of a defensive strategy. An insurer with long-dated liabilities could replace some long assets with shorter assets plus floors driven by a long-maturity CMT or CMS. If rates drop significantly, the floors rise in value at an accelerating rate, protecting the portfolio from reinvestment risk and helping the combined strategy to outperform the original assets if the move is substantial. Conversely, if rates rise significantly, the floor loses value at a decelerating rate, allowing the combination to lose less value than the original assets. Only if rates are fairly stable will this strategy underperform the original long asset.

Prepayment Caps

Using floors to hedge MBS prepayments requires the investor to make assumptions about the prepayment behavior of the underlying residential mortgages. Prepayments have proven to be difficult to estimate in recent years. An alternative hedge is to use prepayment caps, which pay the owner an amount designed to meet the hedging need at each realized level of prepayments. In effect, the insurer is synthetically selling the mortgage-backeds by using this hedging method, and the dealer is stepping into his shoes in bearing the prepayment risk.

The investor has a choice between floors and other more complex products driven solely by interest rates and products that are driven by experience in the MBS market. One criterion for making this choice is the investor's view as to whether the market is overvaluing or undervaluing the prepayment option in relation to pure interest-rate options.

Bond Warrants

Bond warrants are long-dated call options on specific bonds to be issued upon exercise, typically by a corporate issuer with an investment-grade rating. Bond warrants are often cheaper than OTC swaptions of similar structure. Unfortunately, limited availability tends to restrict an end-user's ability to diversify the credit risk of such options. At least the credit risk is mitigated by the insurer owning the option: if the credit spread widens, that fact can be considered in the decision whether or not to exercise the option. This situation is the opposite of that encountered with callable bonds, where the call option works against the investor with respect to changes in both interest rates and the creditworthiness of the issuer.

CREATING SYNTHETIC ASSETS

Many insurance company investment departments have developed confidence in their expertise and access to opportunities in certain traditional sectors of the domestic fixed income markets, particularly fixed-rate public and private corporate obligations, commercial mortgages, and mortgage backed securities. Unfortunately, continued adherence to this menu limits opportunities for diversification, leaving insurers with undue concentrations of exposure to the systematic risks of interest rate movements and defaults in the U.S. The swap market allows insurers and other investors to diversify the systematic risk exposures of their portfolios while continuing to earn excess returns in the cash markets where they have expertise.

The swap market also allows insurers to seek relative value in new market sectors that may be less efficiently priced than its traditional sectors.

Foreign markets have become very attractive to some insurers as well as leading independent money managers. Asset swaps allow the investor to achieve these benefits without retaining currency risk.

Asset Swaps

An asset swap combines an existing bond or note with a swap to create a new synthetic asset suitable for an investor. If the asset is denominated in a foreign currency, the swap wraps around the asset and converts it into a dollar-based investment with either a fixed or floating interest rate. We illustrate the idea with an investment made in February 1993, and sold in February 1994.

The underlying security was a LYON (a zero-coupon convertible bond) issued by SKF, a Swedish manufacturer. The bond is denominated in European Currency Units (ECUs). When combined with the swap, it had the characteristics of a coupon-bearing, dollar-denominated corporate bond offered at a spread of 300 basis points over a par Treasury maturing on the put date. In February 1994 the insurer sold the bond and unwound the swap, taking advantage of appreciation of the hedged position to 150 basis points over Treasuries. Part of the appreciation was attributable to a substantial increase in the price of the stock during the one-year holding period.

Total Return Swaps

Some dealers offer swaps in which the insurer pays LIBOR or a fixed rate and receives the total return on a defined index or group of securities. For example, insurers have done total return swaps in which they receive the return on a bond index, a class of mortgage-backed securities (e.g., all FNMA 7 pass-through securities issued during the first quarter of 1994), or a specified portfolio of bank loans.

By using a swap structure, the insurer can invest its cash in floating or fixed-rate assets to create the cash flows for the pay side of the swap. Depending on the riskiness of the swap, the insurer might use high-quality assets or attempt to achieve an excess return by taking advantage of the strengths of its style and capabilities, e.g., with origination of private placements or consumer finance loans.

Equity-Linked Structures

In domestic and foreign equity markets, OTC derivatives can curtail downside risk by providing asymmetric exposures not available in the cash markets. An insurer can combine a zero-coupon bond with a long-dated call on an index of domestic or foreign equities to create a downside-protected exposure to the market. This same exposure can also be bought in the form of a "protected equity note," in which the option and the zero-coupon obligation are embedded in a note issued by the dealer or an unrelated third-party issuer.

An equity swap paying the return on a foreign equity index provides a result that is difficult and costly for an insurer to reproduce in the cash markets. The swap may be on a highly diversified index of equities in a country or in a "basket" of country indexes. Transaction costs, in the form of the spread charged by the dealer, may be less than would be paid by the insurer in the cash markets if the dealer or its customers enjoy preferred access, regulatory status, or tax treatment in the countries involved.

An insurer can use such exposures to enhance the returns and diversification of its invested assets and achieve a more efficient allocation of surplus. It can also use these tools to create similar benefits for customers.

Structured Notes

Structured notes are a very broad and fast-growing class of investment products that combine the flexibility of over-the-counter derivative transactions with the regulatory and accounting treatment afforded to traditional notes. Under current regulations and reporting requirements, a structured note with no risk to principal is treated like any other note issued by that issuer. No extra risk-based capital is assigned to the underlying coupon risk.

Structured notes are a delivery vehicle for OTC derivatives. They offer the advantages of convenient packaging and user-friendly regulatory treatment. Unfortunately, they usually cost more than the equivalent structure unbundled because the issuer must be induced to provide the note structure and sometimes to guarantee the performance of the counterparty on the embedded swap.

The NAIC is currently considering whether insurers should be allowed to use such unbundled derivative strategies to replicate the risk-reward exposures now allowed only in the form of cash market investments and structured notes.

CONCLUSION

The case studies illustrate how insurers can use derivative products to reduce the risks inherent in their existing asset-liability spread businesses or to enhance the profile of return versus risk across scenarios that realistically capture the major sources of risk. The suitability of risk-reducing or hedging applications is generally accepted by major insurers and regulators at this stage. However, there is still a gap in awareness that may retard the use of derivatives for equally suitable enhancement of an insurer's risk-reward profile.

Insurers are already in the business of taking risks in the products they sell and in the relationship of their investment strategies to the liability cash flows that will be required in various scenarios. Why is the risk assumed in a derivative product different? Isn't the core issue not where the risk is taken but what overall portfolio of risks is assumed?

One issue being considered by the regulators is whether insurers should be allowed to use derivatives to replicate exposures that might otherwise be assumed in the cash markets. Replication transactions would have to be reported based on substance rather than form, i.e., based on the exposures assumed rather than to swaps or options per se. It is ironic that regulators would be more concerned with permitting suitable, portfolio-enhancing replication transactions like total-return swaps while ignoring much larger risks to net worth assumed in large duration mismatches between assets and liabilities and excessive dependence on single classes of risky assets.

Of all the current regulatory requirements, the most all-encompassing, holistic measure of aggregate risk is cash-flow testing. In a perfect world, these cash-flow tests would be a byproduct of an insurer's own proprietary simulation capabilities that would be used for financially engineering investment and product strategies at the product line and corporate levels, considering not only the statutory results but also the economic and GAAP results, taking taxes into account. In this world, insurers would be aware of the lessons of modern finance and portfolio theory as they sought to achieve the optimal mix of activities.

If regulators encouraged insurers to develop such advanced risk management capabilities, they could rely on the application of these capabilities as the primary safety net protecting customers from insolvency. With more stringent and economically rational standards for cash-flow testing in place, the calculations of required risk-based capital could be based on actual risks assumed rather than coarse rules of thumb. The integrity of the cash-flow testing procedures and supporting data could be strengthened by requiring representations by the valuation actuaries and members of senior management and independent audits.

14

Structured MTNs: Adding Value Using Embedded Derivatives

Jacob Navon
Senior Vice President, The Boston Company

INTRODUCTION

Most of this book is devoted to the use of derivatives as direct obligations between counterparties such as interest rates and currency swaps, or as specific "products" such as exchange traded futures and options. Structured Medium Term Notes (SMTNs) represent another type of derivative use that has mushroomed in the past three years. This chapter will outline the approach we use to evaluate these securities at The Boston Company Asset Management, Inc. (TBC). We will discuss our rationale for using these structures, the benefits we derive, and some of the potential pitfalls. We will illustrate our points using specific examples. We will conclude that when properly crafted and valued, SMTNs can significantly enhance portfolio construction.

SMTNs: DESCRIPTION AND EVOLUTION

At the time of writing this article, hardly a day goes by without some headline appearing in the financial press discussing the whole topic of derivatives. In general this segment of financial markets is treated with suspicion, caution, and much trepidation. Derivatives are somehow feared to be enhancing systemic risk. Dire predictions of financial meltdown abound. That is, if one practitioner will experience any problems living up to obligations, the whole financial system will somehow collapse. The doomsayers handily ignore recent experience whereby the defaults of Drexel Burnham Lambert and Olympia & York and the collapse of the Bank of New England did not precipitate such domino effects upon the "tranquil" financial landscape. Yet fact does not interfere with perception. In short, derivatives are preferred to be perceived as rank financial alchemy, instruments that are somehow mysterious, dangerous, and very new. The major participants are afforded the same prejudice bestowed upon performers of medieval witchcraft in days long gone.

In contrast, consider that derivatives have existed probably as long as markets themselves. They are no more novel or strange than any other investment vehicle. Broadly defined, they are merely some kind of contract or arrangement, between consenting counterparties, about a particular asset, that does not involve directly transferring ownership of that asset between the parties at the time of execution of the contract. Such an agreement typically represents either a future obligation concerning the underlying asset or a contingent claim upon its ownership or worth. As such, the ongoing value of the contract is "derived" from the worth of the asset. Hence the name "derivatives."

In this respect, derivatives are actually similar to other financial instruments. Equities, for example, merely represent a financial contract evidencing an ownership interest in some underlying business entity. Notes and bonds represent certificates of indebtedness whereby the issuer promises to pay interest and principal back to the lender at some prescribed schedule. The value of a stock derives from the worth of the underlying business. The value of a note or bond derives from the worth of the issuer's future cash-flow promises, discounted to the present day at a rate that reflects both generally prevailing interest rates and the issuer's creditworthiness.

Stocks and bonds in their "modern" form, have been used in documented transactions for hundreds of years. The Amsterdam stock exchange has been around since the seventeenth century. But so have derivatives. Indeed, options were traded on Dutch tulip bulbs during that infamous speculative bubble. Such transactions occurred on the same Amsterdam exchange that traded equities. Looking back further in time, one can easily conjure a scenario where the prehistoric farmer pledged a portion of his "future" crop to his toolmaker counterpart in return for the present delivery of an appropriate farming implement. To our knowledge, no such transaction has ever been documented. Agricultural futures contracts, however, have been traded on exchanges in the United States for more than one hundred years.

Derivatives in general, therefore, constitute an established section of the financial mosaic. SMTNs, however, appear to be a relatively new phenomenon. They appeared first in the early 1980s. But are they really that new? No. SMTNs represent notes, typically issued from a medium term note "shelf registration," whose coupon and/or principal payments are linked to some explicit derivative position. Yet this definition would encompass callable bonds. These securities represent regular bonds where the issuer has the right (but not the obligation) to pay the holder his principal back at some point prior to the contractual maturity date. A callable bond, therefore, is nothing more than a straight bond with an embedded call sold back to the issuer. Its value should be identical to the value of the straight bond less the value of the option.

Callable bonds, however, have existed for decades. In fact until the mid-1980s, most corporate debt was issued with some associated call feature. The embedded derivative arrangements would get quite complex. Pro-rata sinking fund bonds, for example, could be analyzed as straight bonds with associated forward sales at par back to the issuer. These forwards were often further enhanced with option characteristics such as a "double-up" feature. SMTNs, thus, are merely a subcategory of a corporate bond market that has exhibited their distinctive features since its very creation.

Their "newness" derives not from the fact that they encompass embedded derivative positions. Rather SMTNs are new because their legal issuing structure, the medium term note format, is a relatively recent formulation. Medium term notes themselves have only been issued since the early 1980s. The above discussion, then, serves to place derivatives in general, and SMTNs in particular, in their proper place as mere extensions of financial markets that have existed for a very long time. This does not deny, however, that the range of usage of derivatives and SMTNs has exploded geometrically in the past few years. SMTNs have become a market that conservatively encompasses $50 billion in annual issuance domestically. Most of this growth has occurred in the past three years. The range of structures has grown as well. SMTNs extend beyond embedding simple forwards and options. Virtually every kind of market exposure has been built into one of these securities.

One can invest in notes that have exposures to currencies, domestic equities, international stocks, falling rates (here and abroad), rising rates, and commodities. These exposures can be achieved through the coupon of the instrument, its principal payment, or both. Coupon linked (CL) structures typically pay par at maturity and have the coupon vary on a regular schedule. It rises and falls with the desired exposure. Principal linked (PL) notes typically pay a fixed rate coupon, but the principal at maturity will vary with the underlying market position. In either case the exposure can be magnified by levering the derivative position. The degree of leverage can be explicitly determined at the note's creation.

TBC'S APPROACH TO SMTNs

We have utilized SMTNs primarily in our enhanced limited maturity portfolios. The ensuing discussion will describe our approach predominantly in that light. Our description of the process, consequently, should be interpreted within the context of a short-term portfolio. Such a portfolio requires careful attention to capital preservation and liquidity. We do not necessarily advocate generalizing every nuance of our approach to other investment objectives. We offer the following as a framework of how one might begin to think about utilizing SMTNs, not as a "cookie cutter" paradigm for all investment seasons.

In determining appropriate investment strategy, one must *always* first consider the investment objective! We seek to add value to limited maturity portfolios by enhancing the combined yield of our holdings. Alternatively we seek investments that can help lower the aggregate risk of the portfolio. This particular style conforms to generalized investment theory. Any novel investment must either help return in some way or reduce portfolio risk. We seek to add yield because it literally equates to return for limited maturity portfolios. Fixed income returns comprise three components: coupon income, reinvestment of cash flows, and price change. This latter component is small, by definition, for short securities. Consequently our portfolios' returns correlate very highly with coupon and reinvestment, i.e., realized yield.

Clearly, one can add yield by structuring PL notes that pay a high fixed coupon. As long as these notes mature at par or better, the holding period returns would be quite attractive. Alternatively, one could seek to add yield by structuring notes with variable coupons and that mature at par. These CL notes would outperform if the underlying exposure benefited the coupons at every reset date. We tend to use CL structures. We believe this type to be less risky for a couple of reasons.

First, we seek to avoid all principal risk in our limited maturity portfolios. We prefer instead a modest yield advantage. That added value can be easily lost when a few securities return less than full par. For this reason we limit also the degree of leverage in our SMTNs. At worst the coupon on any given holding can drop to zero. But we would always receive our principal back at maturity. Thus, while the value of the note would drop when the coupon is zero, we will recoup that loss if we continue to hold the note. As long as we properly control the diversification of our derivative exposures the aggregate yield of the portfolio should remain high at all times.

Second, we find that coupon linked SMTNs are much more difficult to create than principal linked structures. The benefit from this observation can be quite subtle. Ultimately we seek to expose our portfolios to nontraditional risk dimensions using SMTNs. We would only invest in such securities if we believed that our probability of success far outweighs the probability of underperformance. This implies we look for inefficiencies! We seek to exploit anomalies in many markets. A note that is more difficult to create requires the anomaly to be particularly large in order to appear attractive at creation. The greater the anomaly, the higher the likelihood we will benefit. In such fashion, the additional difficulty of making CL structures acts as an extra check. All other things being equal (which they never are) CL notes can improve the probability of success. By definition, this raised success expectation implies lower aggregate risk.

SMTNs can further assist portfolio risk reduction by explicitly hedging other exposures that already exist in the portfolio. For example, we purchase short corporate notes. We are consequently exposed to credit spread risk. As we will demonstrate in a later section, we have been able to create SMTNs that will explicitly benefit during periods when corporate spreads are widening. As the corporate notes lag, these SMTNs will outperform. SMTNs also greatly assist our ability to diversify short portfolios. The risk reduction benefits of diversification are well understood and need no elaboration here. Suffice it to say, however, that through SMTNs we have been able to generate exposure to markets well beyond short-term domestic U.S. interest rates or credit spreads. These are the only two risk dimensions available to traditional short-term investors. We will enumerate the various types of SMTNs we have used in a later section. But first we explain the techniques by which we evaluate these and other investments.

TBC'S APPROACH TO EVALUATING SMTNs

We consider ourselves to be a value-style investment management firm. We apply this orientation to investments in all asset classes: equities (international and domestic), bonds, and limited maturity portfolios. A value approach to investing requires that the manager first determine an appropriate "fair market" price for the security under consideration. Value managers seek to purchase assets at or below this price. Our approach to evaluating SMTNs is no different.

Exhibit 1 summarizes our methodology. We first seek to price explicitly any and all of the derivatives embedded in the note. This requires detailed knowledge of how the notes are constructed. Issuers of SMTNs rarely, if ever, want to issue the note in its final form purchased by the investor. In

EXHIBIT 1   TBC's Approach to Evaluating SMTNs

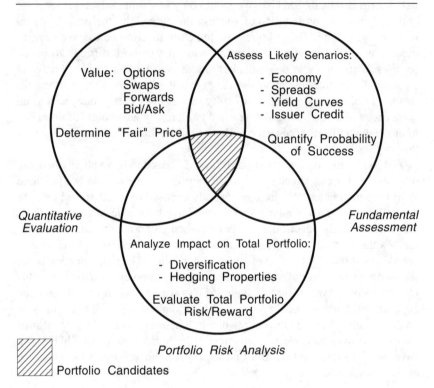

Value: Options
        Swaps
        Forwards
        Bid/Ask

Determine "Fair" Price

Assess Likely Senarios:

- Economy
- Spreads
- Yield Curves
- Issuer Credit

Quantify Probability
         of Success

Quantitative
Evaluation

Fundamental
Assessment

Analyze Impact on Total Portfolio:

- Diversification
- Hedging Properties

Evaluate Total Portfolio
          Risk/Reward

Portfolio Risk Analysis

Portfolio Candidates

almost every case, the issuer ultimately desires regular funding but at a slightly lower cost than a traditional debt instrument. Issuers consequently need to hedge all the market exposures underlying the SMTN using a variety of common derivative strategies: swaps, caps, floors, options, etc. By comparing the price of all these transactions summed together, with the terms of the SMTN, one can quickly determine whether the note at hand is fairly valued.

This value is independent of any future outcome. Our quantification merely arrives at a fair price today, given where all the relevant markets are trading now. We do not purchase any and all notes that are fairly priced, however. We next seek to assess the distribution of possible future scenarios. Here we combine a variety of quantitative and qualitative tools (such as scenario analysis) to assess the likelihood that the next investment will outperform our targets over its life. We need to determine how various likely economic influences will impinge on the market exposures underlying the SMTN. We need to understand the likely path of a variety of interest rates, term structures, volatilities, correlations, and market spreads. We do not seek to predict the one future outcome. We merely attempt to understand how the note will behave across a range of possible future scenarios. Ultimately we want to ensure that it will outperform a majority of the time.

The above two types of analysis quickly pinpoint the types of anomaly we are ultimately trying to exploit. If certain markets are misaligned, we find that either the SMTNs appear extremely cheap to fair value, or they are fairly priced but highly likely to outperform. Or both! We are not done yet, however. Having found a note that satisfies both conditions, we next analyze our existing portfolio. We need to determine the impact of the marginal investment on the aggregate risk profile of the current holdings. Too much of a good thing is still too much. This last quest can turn quite subtle. Often one may find a cheap SMTN that is likely to perform well but that has an underlying risk profile identical to other non-SMTN investments in the account. We will exemplify such situations in a later section. First we turn to two specific examples that will hopefully elaborate on the valuation methodology.

NON-DOLLAR INVERSE FLOATING RATE NOTES

We have made a substantial allocation to this type of structure. These notes exemplify our approach particularly well. We will show how a diversified portfolio of these investments satisfies our three major conditions: They can be purchased at extremely attractive levels, they can be expected to outperform, and they truly diversify relative to traditional risk dimensions. Non-dollar Inverse Floating Rate Notes (IFRNs) are simply securities, whereby the coupon *rises* as some foreign interest rate *falls*. Exhibit 2 demonstrates one such note we have purchased that is linked to the Stockholm Inter Bank Offered Rate (STIBOR), a short-term Swedish interest.

The SMTN we bought matured in two years and paid a coupon that reset every three months. The reset formula was 13 percent minus three-month STIBOR subject to a minimum coupon of zero. Clearly as Swedish rates fell, our coupon would increase. We paid par. But did we buy value? To perform that quantitative analysis, we will examine the note from the issuer's perspective. Let us assume that the issuer really wanted to raise floating rate funds at a U.S. rate attractive to them. In effect the issuer contracted with us to pay 13 percent every quarter and receive from us three-month STIBOR at

EXHIBIT 2 Non-Dollar Inverse Floating Rate Note

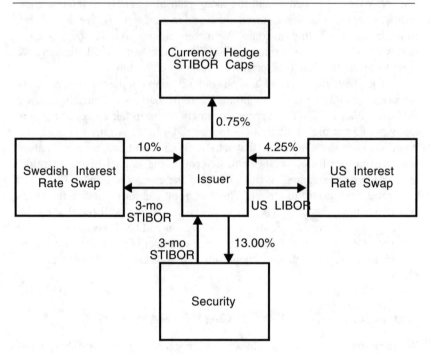

the then prevailing rates. Since the minimum coupon is zero, the issuer effectively also sold us 13 percent STIBOR caps. How could such an issuer hedge themselves?

To the extent that the issuer was receiving three-month STIBOR they needed to hedge that component. They could utilize an interest rate swap (IRS) in Sweden. The issuer could contract to pay three-month STIBOR and receive 10 percent at the time of issue. Such swaps, moreover, are denominated in Swedish Krone. The issuer, then, needed to hedge themselves in the forward currency market to convert the cash flows into dollars. In addition, the issuer had to buy back the caps. We determined that these hedges together were worth 0.75 percent per annum. These transactions served to fix the issuer's coupon obligation in U.S. dollars. They would have to transact an additional IRS in the United States in order to convert the fixed payments into floating ones. At the time, the issuer could receive 4.25 percent vs. paying three-month U.S. LIBOR. Let us summarize.

The issuer has hedged the STIBOR exposure, and receives and pays the same amount. Instead they received 10 percent plus 4.25 percent from the two IRSs and paid 0.75 percent for the caps and currency forwards. The issuer thus received a net of 13.5 percent (10 + 4.25 − 0.75). They also contracted to pay U.S. LIBOR. How did we determine that this represented good value? We must account for the 0.5 percent apparently "left on the table" (13.5 percent net received from the hedges less the 13 percent paid into the note). First remember that the issuer would only conduct this transaction if they could meaningfully save on their traditional funding cost. The issuer of our note was rated AAA, so at the time they could issue at LIBOR flat to less 0.125 percent using a traditional floating rate note. We determined that this issuer would seek to save between 0.125 and 0.25 percent by talking to a variety of syndicate desks and to some of our own large corporate clients. Thus one half of the "missing" 0.5 percent accounts for the "issuer cost." The issuer would want to keep 0.25 percent to net out a LIBOR less 0.25 percent funding cost for them.

That still leaves 0.25 percent unaccounted for. But we have not considered transaction costs yet. To issue this particular SMTN, there are five transactions: an underwriting of a two-year note, two interest rate swaps, a strip of caps, and a currency forward hedge. In effect we have transacted all of these trades at an average bid/ask spread of five basis points (0.05 percent). This is well within the normal quote of about 10 basis points for these types of derivatives. *By accounting for all the pieces at fair market prices separately, we could satisfy ourselves that we were getting attractive execution.* It does not matter if the issuer was actually getting a higher savings and the dealer even tighter spreads, or vice versa. As long as we could independently verify the pieces, and conclude that the "remainder" was cheap, it does not matter where the real savings occurred in practice. The same note with a reset formula of 12.5 percent minus three-month STIBOR would be too expensive. Conversely, one priced at 13.5 percent less three-month STIBOR would have been cheaper still.

Our note was cheap regardless of what happened subsequently to Swedish interest rates. But cheap investments do not in and of themselves guarantee success. Any security bought at a low price can still underperform if the price declines or the expected income does not materialize. To determine whether we could expect superior performance, let us highlight the fundamental analysis. This note was purchased in early 1993, well after the collapse of the Exchange Rate Mechanism (ERM) in the fall of 1992. Readers might recall that the Swedish government tried to tie the exchange rate of the Krone to the ERM in anticipation of joining the European Economic Com-

munity. When the ERM collapsed, there was a run on the Krone as speculators attacked the currency in anticipation of its decline. Central bankers first
tried to defend the exchange rate by buying Krone in the open market. They
quickly ran out of reserves. The Swedish government then tried to defend its
currency by raising interest rates (short-term rates reached 500 percent). This
almost destroyed their banking system. The government subsequently abandoned these futile efforts and quickly lowered rates to mitigate the effects of
recession created by these policies.

At the time of our purchase, Swedish rates had fallen somewhat and
their yield curve was relatively flat (short-term rates were approximately at
the same level as ones further out in the maturity spectrum). The recession
had worsened, and even a cursory economic analysis suggested that rates had
more room to fall. The likelihood that they would rise rapidly again was quite
small. The only visible prior cause for high rates, tight monetary policy, had
been abandoned. Thus we could reasonably expect to earn increasingly higher coupons over time. While this analysis was quite "easy," we are not holding ourselves out as experts on the Swedish economy. Timing the note to a
period when the yield curve was flat and expected to steepen into a positive
slope was quite important to our probability evaluation.

As any yield curve reverts from a negative to a positive slope, the forward rates implied by the curve shift from declining with time to rising. As
long as the realized rates, over the life of the IFRN, are *lower* than those
implied by the initial yield curve, we would earn above market coupons.
Clearly, a note structured in a negatively sloped yield curve environment
would only succeed if rates actually fall *faster* than the implieds. But an
IFRN structured in a flat to positive environment needs only for rates to stay
the same, or even rise but not as fast as the implied forwards, in order to succeed. Combine these general curve observations with the situation in Sweden
and you can appreciate why our fundamental analysis concluded a high probability of success for this particular note. Even an unexpected modest rise in
rates could generate superior results. Our portfolio risk assessment gave further impetus to the decision.

Traditional short portfolios are exposed only to short U.S. interest rates.
These move independently of foreign rates. Exhibit 3 renders powerful evidence for this statement. It shows the pairwise correlations of several European short-term interest rates with respect to each other as well as the U.S.
rate. Note how all the foreign rates essentially exhibit zero correlation with
our own market. Exposure to each of these countries alone creates diversification. But note, also, how independent the various short rates are with respect

EXHIBIT 3 Covariance Matrix of European LIBOR (Three Months) Rates

	France	Germany	Italy	Spain	Sweden	UK	US
France							
Germany	0.28						
Italy	0.17	0.24					
Spain	0.18	0.00	0.11				
Sweden	−0.20	0.15	0.00	−0.03			
UK	0.03	−0.08	0.16	0.00	−0.08		
US	−0.07	0.04	0.14	−0.22	0.00	0.10	

to one another. The highest correlation appears between France and Germany. Yet at 0.28 this correlation itself is very low. This bears some exploration.

Were not European economic policies coordinated? Could we not anticipate that short rates would move in lock-step? We believe that these governments did indeed coordinate their currencies. Evidence abounds that European foreign exchange rates are still highly positively correlated, even post-ERM. But these same policymakers seem to have used *domestic* interest rates to buffer their own economies from currency linkage. Their short-term rates, then, moved in tune with their own diverse conditions. Establishing several smaller positions within one portfolio, then, would produce even more powerful diversification.

In such fashion, our portfolios could withstand some unforeseen reversal in any one country. Our overall strategy for non-dollar IFRNs becomes clear. The economic scenario expounded above for Sweden adequately described the economy Europe-wide. Rates in general could be expected to fall. Anecdotal evidence can be found in our own analysis. When we looked at the same rate correlations in two subperiods, during ERM and post-collapse, the correlation *increased* somewhat in the latter. This counterintuitive result could be explained as an artifact due to the ERM collapse itself. Once the shackles of currency coordination were removed, these governments moved simultaneously to stimulate their domestic economies by lowering rates.

Rather than predicting a particular country's fate, we patiently created exposure to several, waiting for the policy changes and yield curve reshapings to signal the precise timing for each country. From a portfolio standpoint, our success was predicated only on European rates in general remaining lower than the implied forwards at the time of execution. To the extent that rates have already fallen dramatically at the time of writing, our expected returns became quite high relative to traditional U.S. short investments. And the source of these returns varied from the returns generated by other holdings in the existing portfolios. Consequently these investments helped lower aggregate risk.

Not that these notes exhibit zero risk. We avoided credit risk by selecting very high credit quality (mainly U.S. domestic) issuers. We sought to manage liquidity and duration risk by holding these securities to maturity. IFRNs should not ordinarily be viewed as trading instruments. In order to liquidate a holding, one should assume the purchasing dealer would seek to "unwind" the embedded position through hedging. Summing up the bid/ask spread on all the necessary transactions would generate a fairly high combined transaction cost. These notes, moreover, do have residual duration exposure to U.S. rates. To understand this latter point consider Exhibit 2. A non-dollar two-year IFRN essentially means holding both a foreign two-year note (the foreign IRS) and a domestic two-year note (the U.S. IRS). The "duration" of the note, then, depends on the duration of the foreign note combined with the domestic and the correlation between them. The additional diversification, between all the various countries, helped keep the aggregate marginal duration of the portfolio low. Our experience mirrored these observations. These portfolios exhibited high relative yields but low overall variability in value.

The foregoing discussion demonstrates how we combined quantitative evaluation with fundamental assessment and portfolio risk analysis to create an investment with a high expected return and low risk through diversification. In an earlier section, we described an additional goal of using SMTNs as explicit hedges for existing portfolio exposure. This may be considered as a limiting case of diversification. A perfect hedge represents a security whose return has perfect negative correlation with the risk to be hedged, i.e., the correlation coefficient is -1. While such securities may be difficult to create cheaply, one can come quite close when market anomalies allow.

SWAP SPREAD NOTES

Swap spread notes (SSNs) represent our attempt to take advantage of a particular anomaly (historically very low spreads) to create an instrument that would be negatively correlated with other exposures in our portfolios at a very low hedging cost. We will demonstrate using an example from our longer-term fixed income portfolios. The summer of 1992 presented us with a dilemma. Our fixed income style leaves us natural holders of above market weighting to the corporate bond sector. Corporate spreads had contracted to historically low levels. While we benefited from the decline, we were now exposed to spreads widening again. Interest rate swap spreads were also low at the time. While the relationship between swap spreads and corporate bond spreads is somewhat controversial, we believe that there is a link through the use of swaps by corporate issuers.

An issuer can create a fixed rate liability by issuing traditional bonds, or they can fund with floating rate liabilities and fix them by swapping floating for fixed. This linkage has to keep some relationship between IRS spreads and corporate bond spreads. Otherwise one strategy would dominate the other. To the extent that swap spreads historically are lower than corporate bond spreads (about half), we believe that the correlation should deteriorate as swap spreads reach very low absolute levels. We expect that there is some floor to swap spreads at close to zero. While swap spreads may violate this floor temporarily at times, it is hard to conceive that they will turn negative for any long period of time. Conversely, as spreads widen, we could expect the relationship to reestablish. While a detailed examination of these notions is beyond the scope of this chapter, suffice it to say that we obtained some empirical correlation data consistent with these conclusions. How could we benefit?

We created SSNs whereby the coupon would increase with swap spreads. Should spreads have declined further, the coupon could decline subject to a minimum of zero. The note had a final maturity of six years, and the coupon reset once at the end of the first year. This note was created to be a one-year hedge. At reset, the price of the SSN could be expected to increase with spreads and vice versa. To limit the amount of capital devoted to this position we levered the exposure so that a 1–1.5 percent portfolio allocation to the SSN would hedge the entire corporate bond holdings. Our initial coupon was 6.625 percent, which was only 20 basis points lower than a regular fixed rate note by the same issuer—a minimal portfolio cost considering the small amount held. Clearly, as long as swap spreads were somewhat correlated with corporate bond spreads, this note would outperform precisely when the corporates were lagging.

Using the correlation data, we determined an ex-ante hedging matrix summarized in Exhibit 4. Without the note we could expect a typical portfolio to beat our benchmark by 17 basis points for every 10 tightening of corpo-

EXHIBIT 4   Swap Spread Linked Notes—Ex Ante Hedging Analysis

	Swap Spreads Tighten (10 bp)	Swap Spreads Widen (10 bp)
Without Bond	+17 bp	-17 bp
With Bond	+15 bp	+0 bp

rate spreads, and vice versa. With the note we expected to give up two basis points of the upside but fully hedge the downside. This asymmetric pattern derived from the highly asymmetrical nature of the bond's leveraged coupon coupled with the zero minimum. What happened?

Exhibit 5 plots the SSN's price and compares it to the experienced corporate bond spreads. The reader will note that spreads initially rose, as did the price. Corporate bond spreads subsequently declined again, as did the price. In general this note proved to be an accurate hedge, even though the hedge was not really required for this period. This section highlighted the second major use of SMTNs, as hedges for other undesired risk exposures in the portfolio. In the next section, we discuss some structures we have avoided.

SMTNs: REJECTION ANALYSIS

The previous two sections have exemplified the primary uses for SMTNs: yield enhancement, diversification, and explicit risk hedging. We have invested in a large amount of SMTNs structured along these broad principles. There are some structures we have avoided, however. We will discuss three:

EXHIBIT 5 Swap Spread Linked Notes—Actual Price Performance vs. Corporate Bond Spreads

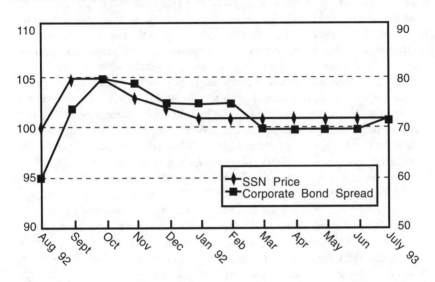

index amortizing notes (IANs); step-up notes (SUNs); and LIBOR/prime differential notes (L/PDNs). In each case these notes failed at least one of our primary criteria.

First, *any* investment can fail the quantitative evaluation test. As we will explain later, this market represents particularly high potential for pricing abuse. Any given structure can be overvalued. Ability to quantify the derivatives leads to successful SMTN security selection. Regardless of the diversification and/or hedging properties, one should only pay the proper price. So much for motherhood and apple pie. We also reject SMTNs when they fail the fundamental analysis and/or the portfolio risk assessment.

IANs and SUNs represent good cases of the latter. IANs are notes that pay a high fixed coupon for an expected maturity of say two years. The maturity schedule can extend, however, if some reference rate (typically U.S. LIBOR) increases. This risk profile is similar to the one inherent in "busted" short CMO PACs. These latter mortgage-related investments extend with lower prepayments. Prepayments typically fall as rates rise. We have invested profitably in this sector and determined that IANs would needlessly add to this risk exposure.

SUNs have an identical risk to old callable industrial notes. Many corporations issued 10-year notes in the mid-1980s that were callable after seven years. Many of these notes have one or two years left to the call. Since rates had declined considerably by the early 1990s, these notes are trading "to the call" and have relatively high coupons. The yield to the call is higher than traditional short-maturity investments. Should rates rise dramatically, these notes risk extending to maturity. Compare this profile with a typical SUN. SUNs are issued with an intermediate maturity (four to five years) and can be called within a shorter period (one to two years). After the call date the coupon steps up to a higher level. The initial coupon equates favorably with traditional short investments. The stepped-up coupon typically is much lower than the regular coupon of old industrials. We were fortunate to invest in the secondary old notes and did not want to increase exposure through SUNs.

The reader will appreciate that total portfolio risk can be a powerful motivation to rejecting a particular SMTN. We will avoid, as well, structures where we do not have a good feel for the underlying fundamentals. L/PDNs represent one good example. In the past two years we have been offered SMTNs that will benefit when the spread between LIBOR and the prime rate contracts. We have also been offered the reverse structure. Try as we might, we do not possess the relevant expertise to assess the prime rate. It used to be the rate banks charged their best corporate customers. In recent years, however, these clients have found direct access to the capital markets. The prime rate instead now drives home equity loan interest charges and other floating *consumer* revolving debt. We consequently believe that past relationships between LIBOR and prime are not particularly useful. As we can see, failure to pass any one of our evaluation criteria constitutes grounds for rejection. The next section will discuss additional pitfalls to avoid.

SMTNs: POTENTIAL PITFALLS

We have already warned of the first pitfall: excess transaction costs. While no one would willingly invest in an overpriced SMTN, be alert for hidden costs. Consider for example our non-dollar IFRNs. Due to our large asset size, we have created a diversified exposure by holding many notes, each exposed to a separate country. Basket structures have also been created whereby the same note is exposed to five or more countries. The diversification benefits were touted as particular advantages to the basket. A basket note is subject, however, to a bid/ask spread in the correlation coefficient of the various underlying markets. To guarantee the zero coupon minimum, one can theoretically embed a cheaper basket cap in this structure. When selling the note, dealers will use a different (higher) correlation assumption in pricing the option than when buying it back. Increasing the correlation assumption increases the price, and vice versa, so a dealer can widen the bid/ask merely by varying the assumption when buying and selling. Practically, however, a basket structure may be the only way to create a diversified IFRN holding in smaller portfolios. One should nevertheless recognize the higher transaction cost relative to separate single country holdings.

Specific issuers can get "greedy." Small banks and thrifts are typical users of SMTNs. These investors, however, are restricted to using the major agencies as issuers. The agencies have learned that they can levy a higher "issuer" cost to these captive users. We consequently restrict our agency SMTNs to those purchased in the secondary market. Let someone else pay the higher issuer cost. Corporate issuers typically require much smaller savings in order to agree to create an SMTN. We typically analyze a given SMTN on its merits, and then seek to negotiate with an issuer who needs funding on that day.

Another common pitfall resides in SMTNs where the structures are flawed. We have seen too many notes that exploit an identifiable anomaly that should correct and that is uncorrelated with other risks. Yet the particular version offered may have very limited upside relative to the downside. This often occurs in highly leveraged SMTNs. We seek to avoid excessive leverage for this reason.

Leverage affects the credit risk of SMTNs. We typically restrict our issuers to very high credit ratings. Yet we have seen, also, BBB-rated issuers in this market. Consider the Swedish IFRN. Should the credit quality of the issuer decline, the expected increase in spreads will propagate through five separate transactions. The bid of this note will fall more dramatically than a typical two-year note of the same corporation.

Last, we cannot overemphasize liquidity risk. While we have argued above that SMTNs make poor trading vehicles, one occasionally needs to liquidate a holding. In such cases we evaluate two theoretical prices. First we determine the "take-out" bid. This price seeks what we would be willing to pay for the note and explicitly hedges it back to a regular floating rate instrument. This should be the lowest price we would be willing to accept. We next evaluate a new issue "replication." If we were to recreate the remaining note today as a new issue, what would it cost? This defines the highest possible price anyone should be willing to pay. The spread between these two extremes defines the potential liquidation expense. Any price within the range is justifiable, though how close to the low "take-out" bid one gets results from negotiation skills.

SUMMARY AND CONCLUSIONS

We have attempted to elaborate in detail our approach to using SMTNs. As can be seen, we believe that these investments can have a far-reaching beneficial impact on portfolio strategy. They provide us with a means to enhance portfolio yield, expand the investment opportunity set, and diversify from the restrictive traditional avenues of managing short-term portfolios. SMTNs offer a very flexible way to create exposure to other markets or to fashion a desired return profile. In this respect they are identical to direct derivative exposure techniques. SMTNs can be risky, however.

Often they are exposed to "hidden" market risk. Our discussion of non-dollar IFRNs, for example, highlighted a residual exposure to short U.S. rates. At first glance this risk is not obvious. We have demonstrated leveraged credit risk because each note represents several transactions. We have also demonstrated the illiquidity of these notes. This cost, too, derives from the fact that each note encompasses several derivative transactions. SMTNs, consequently, *are not* a means to avoid developing derivatives expertise.

They are simply a way to *facilitate* execution of derivative strategies. We could, for example, have created the non-dollar IFRN exposure using the underlying derivatives. But we would have needed to monitor five transactions for each one, together with the associated counterparty risks. Our portfolio management systems and operations personnel would have been that much more taxed. STMNs provided a shortcut to the same result. The issuer cost, then, represents the economic rent we pay for the convenience. Our introduction discussed in detail the perceived risks associated with derivatives. We believe that lack of proper investment expertise is the largest contributor to portfolio mishap. When properly evaluated, assessed, and analyzed, we believe SMTNs represent a powerful addition to an investor's arsenal.

15

Applications of Index Amortization Swaps

Ramine Rouhani
Senior Vice President, CDC Investment Management Company

INTRODUCTION

Structured swaps emerged in early 1990, and since then have exploded in size and variety, providing the capital markets with a wealth of new products for investment, hedging, and speculation. Compared to plain vanilla swaps and swaptions, these new structures are much more flexible and can be more effectively customized to produce desired payoff patterns. With the added flexibility comes the additional complexity. Analytically, these structures are more demanding than the traditional swaps and swaptions. Good intuition and experience in options are essential for understanding these products. However, intuition alone often fails to provide a comprehensive picture of the many risk/reward dimensions of these structures. These swaps are less liquid than their vanilla counterparts, and therefore it is often necessary to engineer hedges to limit their exposures to interest rates and to volatility. To construct such hedges, one needs to evaluate the sensitivities of these instruments to changes in the level of rates, to the steepness of the yield curve and to interest rate volatility.

The purpose of the present paper is to analyze the risk dimensions of Index Amortization Swaps (IAS), known also as "Principal Amortization Swaps" (PAS). There is a fairly large variety of these type of swaps. They are very popular with investors, particularly with banks. In 1992–93, when yields were low and the yield curve was steep, these swaps were extremely effective off-balance sheet vehicles for banks to enhance the yield on their portfolios. As we will see in the following sections, this yield enhancement is not a free lunch, but is accompanied by certain risks that are to be explicitly recognized and dealt with.

INDEX AMORTIZATION SWAPS

An Index Amortization Swap (IAS) is a swap with a notional balance that depends on the random path of another index. The similarities with vanilla swaps are many: The client receives a fixed rate against a floating rate (LIBOR in most cases), there is a fixed maturity, and the two counterparties are exposed to each other's credit. The major difference is that the notional balance of an IAS may decline, and even may converge to zero, before the final maturity date of the swap. Furthermore the decline of the notional balance is non-deterministic, and depends on the path of a short- or a long-term interest rate index, often referred to as "balance index." Three-month and six-month LIBOR have been the dominant balance indexes for index amortization swaps. Seven-year and 10-year Constant Maturity Treasury (CMT) indexes have been also very popular. Index amortization swaps with notional balances linked to long-term rates have been used by portfolio managers as substitutes for mortgage products, or as hedging vehicles for mortgage portfolios.

Here is an example of a 10-year CMT linked index amortization swap (as of 9/17/93):

- Investor receives a fixed rate of 5.12% and pays three-month LIBOR.
- Payments are quarterly.
- The swap starts on 9/17/93 and terminates on 9/17/98.
- The notional balance of the swap is constant for the first year (9/17/93–9/17/94), i.e., there is a "lockout" period of one year.
- After the lockout period, the notional amount changes at each reset time in accordance to the amortization table shown in Exhibit 1.

The most important feature of an IAS is the amortization table. The table relates the amortization rate of the notional balance to the level of the 10-year CMT rates. On 9/17/93 the 10-year yield was 5.38 percent. Exhibit 1

EXHIBIT 1   10-year CMT Linked Index Amortization Swap

10-Year CMT Rate	Average Life	Amortization Rate
–150 bp	1 year	100%
–100 bp	2 years	44.5%
–50 bp	2.5 years	30.5%
Base (5.38%)	3 years	23.6%
+50 bp	3.5 years	17.6%
+100 bp	4 years	11.8%
+150 bp	4.5 years	5.9%
+200 bp	5 years	0%

states that, after the lockout period, at each reset time the notional amount of the swap amortizes at a quarterly rate of 23.6 percent if the 10-year index is equal to 5.38 percent. However, if the 10-year CMT is 4.88 percent (i.e., 50 bp lower than the base rate of 5.38 percent), the amortization rate is 30.5 percent, and, as the index's level drops to 4.38 percent and 3.88 percent respectively, the amortization rate grows to 44.5 percent and 100 percent respectively. Column 3 of Exhibit 1 shows the quarterly amortization rates that will apply to the remaining balances of the swap as a function of the 10-year rate at reset times. The CMT rates are expressed as offsets to the index level at origination (5.38 percent). At reset times, amortization rates are computed by linear interpolation between the two closest levels on the table. If the CMT index falls below 3.88 percent or increases above 7.38 percent, then the closest amortization rate applies (100 percent and 0 percent respectively).

Clearly as the balance index decreases, the amortization of the notional balance accelerates and the swap becomes shorter. On the other hand, as the CMT rate increases the amortization slows down and the swap lengthens. The "Average Life" column of Exhibit 1 shows the average life of the swap for each amortization rate. It is important to comprehend the precise meaning of this column: If at the end of the lockout period, the 10-year CMT index were at 5.38 percent and remained there for the following four years, then the constant amortization rate to be applied every quarter would be 23.6 percent, and the average life of the swap will be three years; similarly, if the CMT rate were to move to 6.38 percent at the end of the lockout period and were to stay there for the ensuing four years, the 11.8 percent constant amortization rate per quarter would result in an average life of four years. Note that this does not suggest that the average life of the swap is three years, nor does it mean that its expected average life is three years. There is no additional information in the Average Life column vis a vis the Amortization Rate column. However, describing the swaps in terms of average life rather than amortization rate is simpler, and investors often believe that they get a better picture of the transaction when it is described in terms of "Average Life," rather than "Amortization Rate." While an average life description seems more intuitive, it also leaves more room for misinterpretation. A common misinterpretation is to tend to believe that the swap has "on average" three years of life, or that the "expected life" is three years. Another misinterpretation is to compare the fixed rate of the index amortization swap to the rate of a vanilla swap with maturity equal to that of the base average life (here three years) in order to assess the relative value of the structure. A simplistic way of assessing the IAS value has been based on comparing the fixed rate of the IAS to the swap rates with maturities corresponding to the shortest and to the longest average life (here one year and three years) to conclude that the swap is "cheap" if its fixed rate exceeds both swaps and "fairly" valued if it falls between the two rates. This type of analysis, while simple and attractive, does not necessarily lead to correct conclusions.

To the naked eye, the average life and the amortization table provide, at best, qualitative information: The buyer of such swaps is short volatility, is short a series of call options (the swap is called as rates move down), and is short a series of put options (the swap extends when rates move up). Everything else being equal (lockout, maturity, base rates, and offsets), the more steep are the change of average life and of amortization rate, the higher is the volatility exposure of the structure. Beyond these, and a few other qualitative assessments, it is very difficult to pursue the examination of the structure without using a model that mimics the behavior of the transaction under different interest rate and volatility scenarios.

PATH DEPENDENCY

At first glance, options embedded in IASs can be approximated by a series of calls and puts. In reality, however, these are more complex options. They differ from traditional fixed-income options in that they are path dependent, and, from this perspective, they are similar to options embedded in mortgage securities and their derivatives. The payoff of a path-dependent structure depends not only on the state variables, here interest rates, but also on the path of these variables. A very common example of a path dependent structure is a cap on the one-year average of three-month LIBOR: The payoff of such a cap depends not only on the final level of LIBOR, but more so on the path of LIBOR in the year preceding the maturity of the cap. To see how the path of the 10-year CMT rate affects the average life and the payoff of the structure, let us consider three scenarios. Exhibit 2 shows the CMT rates for each scenario at the end of the first, second, third, fourth, and fifth year. For example, in scenario 1 (Path 1), the CMT rate moves from 5.38 percent to 4.88 percent at the end of the first year, then it declines to 3.88 percent at the end of the second year, and bounces back to 4.88 percent, 5.88 percent, and 7.38 percent at the end of the third, fourth, and fifth year, respectively. Path 2 and Path 3 of Exhibit 2 show two other scenarios for the balance index. Note that the three paths start from the same level of 5.38 percent and end up at the same level of 7.38 percent at the end of the fifth year. The figures in parenthesis correspond to the notional balance of the swap. Because of the lock period of one year, the notional balance stays at its original level of 100 at the end of the first year in all scenarios. Following Path 1, the notional balance declines to zero at the end of the third year and the resulting average life is 2.5 years. In the case of the second path, the interest rate moves up, comes down, and then increases steadily to 7.38 percent, resulting in a balance profile that declines from 100 to 38.17, and an average life of 3.81 years. Finally, the

EXHIBIT 2   Path Dependency

Time	Path 1 (balance)	Path 2 (balance)	Path 3 (balance)
0	5.38 (100)	5.38 (100)	5.38 (100)
1	4.88 (100)	5.38 (100)	5.88 (100)
2	3.88 (55.6)	6.38 (88.24)	6.38 (88.24)
3	4.88 0	4.38 (49.02)	6.88 (77.85)
4	5.88 0	6.38 (43.26)	7.38 (68.69)
5	7.38 0	7.38 (38.17)	7.38 (68.69)
AVG. LIFE	2.5	3.81	4.35

third path corresponds to a straight increase of the CMT rate from 5.38 percent to 7.38 percent, a slow decline of the notional balance from 100 to 68.69, and an average life of 4.35 years. Although the starting and the ending values of the CMT rates are the same for the three paths, the realized average lives are significantly different, and so are the payoffs.

VALUATION

IASs are interest rate path-dependent options, the analysis of which requires contingent claim technologies similar to those used in pricing and valuation of mortgage backed securities and their derivatives. The shape of the yield curve (the swap curve), the dynamics of the short-term rate (LIBOR) and of the long-term rate (10-year CMT), and their volatilities all affect the valuation of IASs. We use a two-factor arbitrage free model of the yield curve where the state variables are the one-month rate and the 10-year CMT rate. We assume a volatility of 16 percent for the short-term rate and of 12 percent for the long-term rate. Since the optionality of the IASs are linked to the dynamic of the 10-year rate, we expect the volatility of this rate to have a major role in determining the value of these contracts. The valuation and analysis of these structures are based on Monte Carlo simulation. Hundreds of interest rate paths are generated, and for each path the cash flows of the IASs, as well as their present values, are estimated. The statistics of the present-values are then used as the basis of valuation and analysis of the IASs.

EXHIBIT 3   Swap Structure

Fixed Rate	5.12%	5.28%
	Swap 1 Average Life	Swap 2 Average Life
−150	1 year	1 year
−100	2 year	1 year
−50	2.5 year	2 year
BASE (5.38%)	3 year	3 year
+50	3.5 year	4 year
+100	4 year	5 year
+150	4.5 year	5 year
+200	5 year	5 year

Let us consider the IAS of the previous section, which we will refer to as IAS1. For purpose of comparison and discussion we introduce a second IAS (IAS2). The average life schedules of both swaps are shown on Exhibit 3. IAS1 receives a fixed rate of 5.12 percent and pays three-month LIBOR. IAS2 receives a fixed rate of 5.28 percent and pays three-month LIBOR. In the "base case," i.e., when the 10-year CMT rate remains unchanged, both swaps have the same average life of three years. However IAS2 displays more average life variability: It shortens and lengthens more rapidly than IAS1. That is, IAS2 is "more callable" than IAS2, and at the same time it has a higher tendency to extend than IAS1. Compared to IAS1, IAS2 has a greater short position in options. However, IAS2 receives a higher fixed rate than IAS1 (5.28 percent compared to 5.12 percent). Is the rate differential of 16 bp consistent with the excess option position that IAS2 is short?

Static Analysis

As of 9/17/93 the three-year treasury rate was 4.17 percent, and the three-year swap rate was 4.42 percent. The fixed rates of IAS1 and IAS2 were respectively 70 bp and 86 bp greater than the three-year swap rate. To put these two rates in perspective and to be able to compare them, let us first assume that there are no interest rate uncertainties (volatilities are set to zero) and therefore future rates evolve as predicted by forward rates. Applying zero-volatility analysis to these structures we find that their average lives are 3.58 years for IAS1 and 4.08 years for IAS2. Exhibit 4 shows the yield curve and the swap curve as of 9/17/93. The upward sloping yield curve suggests that forward CMT rates are greater than the current CMT rate, and therefore future CMT rates will be above the current CMT rate. The consequences are that both swaps will extend beyond three years, and the second swap extends further than the first one.

In a world with no interest rate uncertainty the holder of IAS1 receives 5.12 percent for an average life of 3.58 years. Interpolating the swap curve between the three-year and the four-year, we get a swap rate of 4.58 percent for a bullet swap with a maturity of 3.58 years. The interpretation of this rate of 4.58 percent is similar to that of the "intrinsic value" of an option. The investor in ISA1 should receive 4.58 percent, since this is approximately[1] the

---

1. Under zero-volatility assumption, the swap becomes an amortizing swap with deterministic notional balances, the average life of which is, for IAS1, equal to 3.58 years. The swap rate corresponding to such a swap is, at first approximation, equal to the swap rate of a bullet swap, with maturity equal to the average life of the amortizing swap.

EXHIBIT 4 Treasury/LIBOR Yield Curve (9/17/93)

Rate	3 mo	6 mo	1 yr	2 yr	3 yr	4 yr	5 yr	7 yr	10 yr	30 yr
Treasury	3.000	3.150	3.390	3.860	4.170	4.455	4.740	4.930	5.380	6.040
LIBOR	3.125	3.313	3.500	4.020	4.420	4.695	4.970	5.290	5.720	6.380

swap rate corresponding to the expected average life under no uncertainty assumption. In reality, however, the volatility is not zero, and the investor should receive the "time value" of the option that is being sold through IAS1. Applying the same analysis to IAS2 we observe that the swap rate corresponding to the zero-volatility average life of 4.08 years is 4.72 percent, which is 14 bp in excess of the 4.58 percent of the first structure. Again this result suggests that the difference in value between the two structures should be at least 14 bp per year, which is the difference between the intrinsic values of the short option positions of the two structures. Note that the absolute difference between the fixed rates of the two structures is 5.28% − 5.12% = 16 bp, of which 14 bp corresponds to the difference of the two intrinsic values.

OPTION ADJUSTED SPREAD

We relax the zero-volatility assumption and examine the value of options that are embedded in these structures. The volatility of the long-term rate plays the dominant role in determining the option value of the structure, since the average life variability is directly linked to the path of the 10-year CMT rate. We choose a volatility of 12 percent for the 10-year CMT rate.

Now let us examine the expected average lives of the above structures and compare them to the zero-volatility case. The expected average lives are shown on Exhibit 5 and are respectively 3.37 and 3.27 years. Note that expected average lives of the swaps are shorter than their zero-volatility average lives. Volatility shortens the average life of IASs. Furthermore we observe that the shortening of expected average life is more pronounced for the second structure than for the first one. The expected average life of the first structure is shortened by .21 years, and the average life of the second structure is .81 years. This result corroborates the intuition that the second structure is more extreme in its average-life variability than the first one.

To determine the value of the option embedded in these swaps we determine their risk neutral rates. An investor is risk-neutral, if he or she is indifferent between bets of different payoffs, as long as the expected value of

EXHIBIT 5

Volatility = 12 %

E (Avg. Life) = 3.37 years	E (Avg. Life) = 3.27 years
Risk Neutral Rate = 4.80%	Risk Neutral Rate = 4.96%
"Time Value" = 4.80 – 4.58 = 22 bp	4.96 – 4.72 = 24 bp

Option Adjusted Spread:

5.12 – 4.80 = 32 bp	5.28 – 4.96 = 32 bp

the payoffs are the same. In the context of the current analysis, the risk-neutral investor is indifferent between a vanilla swap at market (the value of which is zero, abstracting from bid-ask spread) and an index-amortizing swap with a zero expected value. The risk neutral rate is the fixed rate on the index amortizing swap that corresponds to a zero expected value for the swap. For the above two swaps these risk neutral rates are respectively 4.80 percent and 4.96 percent. The difference between these rates and the zero-volatility rates determined previously is the measure of the "time-value" of the options. The values of the options embedded in the swaps, expressed in basis points per year, are as follows:

	IAS1	IAS2
Intrinsic value	458 bp	472 bp
Time value	22 bp	24 bp
Option value	480 bp	496 bp

The time-value of the second swap is marginally greater than the time-value of the first swap. This suggests that compared to the first swap, the short option position of the second swap is larger.

The Option Adjusted Spread (OAS) on each swap is the difference between the fixed rate of the swap and the risk-neutral rate, that is:

OAS on IAS1:	5.12% – 4.80% = 32 bp
OAS on IAS2:	5.28% – 4.96% = 32 bp

A simple interpretation of these OASs is that the investor is expecting to receive 32 bp per year on these swaps net of all option costs. Therefore it would seem that these spreads represent arbitrage opportunities. A more precise interpretation is the following: Assuming the markets are complete in interest rate domain, and volatility is known and constant, then an investor hedging the interest rate exposures of the swap will make about 32 bp per year. Note that in this ideal situation, the OAS is not an expected spread, but an assured arbitrage. In such an idealized world, however, competitive pressure should eliminate this arbitrage opportunity and drive the OASs to zero. Furthermore, in the context of such markets, investors will use OASs as exclusive yardsticks of value, and should, in theory, prefer swaps with higher OASs to the ones with lower OASs. In particular they should be entirely indifferent between the two swaps IAS1 and IAS2, because they produce the same option-adjusted spreads.

In reality, however, markets are not frictionless and complete, and future volatility is not known. Hedging is bound to be imperfect, and the ex-post realized spreads will be different from the ex-ante OASs. OASs are imperfect measures of value, and reducing the analysis of swaps to comparison of OASs may lead to very unpleasant surprises. Nevertheless, we contend that a full and comprehensive option adjusted spread examination should remain an indispensable part, and in most cases the starting point, of the analysis. To see how such an analysis can shed light on different structures, let us again go back to our two examples.

Assume, for the moment, that volatility remains constant as 12 percent forever. Which of the two swaps is more attractive under the constant volatility assumption? Exhibit 6 shows the statistics of the average lives of the swaps. The average life of the second swap has a larger standard deviation and is more skewed than the average life of the first one. Exhibit 7 shows the average-life distributions of the two swaps. While the average life of the first swap has a "bell shape" distribution, the distribution of the average life of the

EXHIBIT 6

	Swap 1	Swap 2
	OAS = 32 bp Avg. Life Statistics	OAS = 32 bp Avg. Life Statistics
E (Avg. Life):	3.37 years	3.27 years
STD:	.82 years	1.38 years
Median:	3.36 years	3.50 years
Skewness:	−.01	−.35
95% Percentile:	4.73 years	5.00 years

EXHIBIT 7 Comparison of Weighted Average Lives

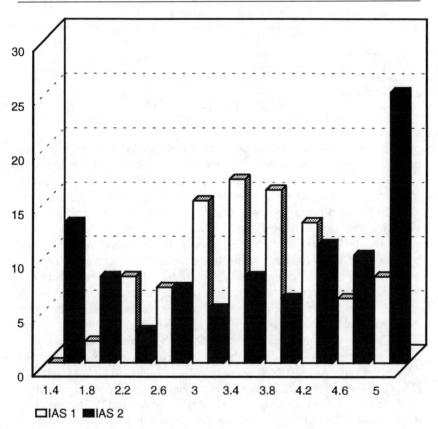

second swap is more weighted on the two extremes. These statistics suggest that hedging the second swap is more difficult than hedging the first swap. To verify this intuition, we estimate the convexity of the swaps. The convexity of the first swap is equal to –1.3, and the convexity of the second swap is –2. The second swap is more negatively convex, and therefore will be more difficult to hedge. In addition, since real-life hedging is not continuous and the swap market is not frictionless, discrete delta hedging will be more costly for the second swap than for the first one. Because of the additional hedging complexity and costs, investors should demand a greater OAS on the second swap than on the first one.

EXHIBIT 8   Sensitivity to Volatility

Volatility	Swap 1	Swap 2
8%	.30	.40
10%	+.15	.22
12%	0	0
14%	−.17	−.20
16%	−.35	−.38

Now consider the effect of volatility uncertainty. As volatility increases, the swaps incur losses, since it becomes more expensive to buy back the option positions that they are short. Hedging volatility exposure is usually more complex than hedging interest rate exposure. In volatility domain, markets are far from being complete, and market frictions are significant. As volatility increases, delta-hedging of interest rate exposure becomes more expensive, both because of increased concavity (negative convexity) and because of the larger bid-ask spreads (liquidity decreases as volatility increases). Therefore everything being equal, investors should demand a higher OAS for structures that are more sensitive to volatility. The premium that investors receive for volatility uncertainty should depend on the sensitivity of the swap to volatility changes. The higher is the sensitivity to volatility, the higher should be the premium. Exhibit 8 shows the effect of volatility changes on the two swap values. The base case volatility is 12 percent. For lower volatilities (10 percent and 8 percent), both swaps increase in value. For higher volatilities (14 percent and 16 percent), the swaps experience losses. Clearly the sensitivity of the second swap to changes in volatility is greater than the sensitivity of the first swap. Therefore the risk premium associated with uncertainty of future volatility should be higher for the second swap than for the first swap, that is, investors should demand a higher OAS on the second swap.

Finally, investors should realize that index amortization swaps are illiquid contracts. Therefore in addition to demanding premiums for market frictions and volatility uncertainty, investors should demand premium for illiquidity.

SENSITIVITY ANALYSIS

Now we turn our attention to sensitivity analysis and hedging. We will examine the sensitivities of the first swap to interest rate shifts and to volatility changes.

Exhibit 9 shows the change of the value of the first swap with respect to a parallel shift of the yield curve. The swap displays negative convexity. A parallel shift of the yield curve modifies the life of the swap, as well as the discount rate of the cash flows. The table associated with Exhibit 9 shows how the duration and the convexity of the swap change as rates move. These duration and convexity numbers are normalized to the notional amount of the swap.

Exhibit 10 shows the value of the same swap with respect to changes in the short-term rate while the 10-year yield remains constant. The yield curve rotates around the 10-year yield, that is, the yield on the 10-year rate remains constant, and the three-month rate is moved by ±50 bp and by ±100 bp. Since

EXHIBIT 9   Sensitivity to Parallel Shift

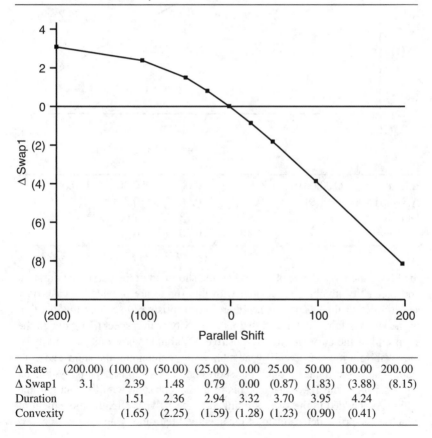

Δ Rate	(200.00)	(100.00)	(50.00)	(25.00)	0.00	25.00	50.00	100.00	200.00
Δ Swap1	3.1	2.39	1.48	0.79	0.00	(0.87)	(1.83)	(3.88)	(8.15)
Duration		1.51	2.36	2.94	3.32	3.70	3.95	4.24	
Convexity		(1.65)	(2.25)	(1.59)	(1.28)	(1.23)	(0.90)	(0.41)	

EXHIBIT 10   Sensitivity to the Short End of the Curve

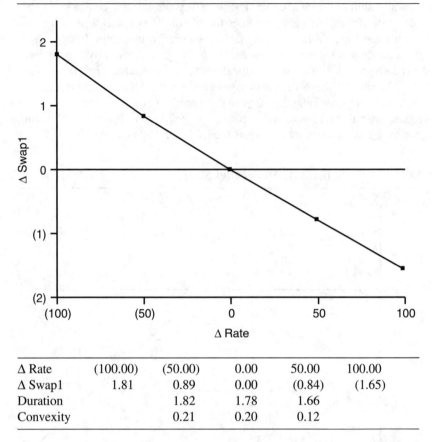

Δ Rate	(100.00)	(50.00)	0.00	50.00	100.00
Δ Swap1	1.81	0.89	0.00	(0.84)	(1.65)
Duration		1.82	1.78	1.66	
Convexity		0.21	0.20	0.12	

the life of the swap does not depend on the short end of the curve, the duration and convexity numbers associated with this figure are proxies for cash-flow sensitivities of the swap. It is not therefore surprising to see that the duration of the swap is fairly stable and that its convexity with respect to a move in the short end of the curve is slightly positive. Exhibit 11 shows the sensitivity of the swap to a move in the 10-year rate, while maintaining the short-end constant. The curve rotates around the short end. The swap is negatively convex with respect to the 10-year rate. This result is consistent with the fact that the options embedded in the swap are linked to the 10-year rate, the movement of which is the prime determinant of the average life of the swap.

EXHIBIT 11   Sensitivity to 10-Year Rate

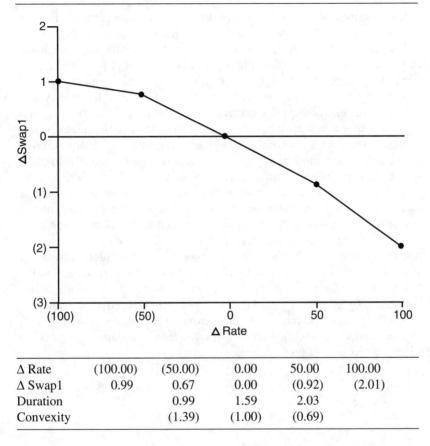

Δ Rate	(100.00)	(50.00)	0.00	50.00	100.00
Δ Swap1	0.99	0.67	0.00	(0.92)	(2.01)
Duration		0.99	1.59	2.03	
Convexity		(1.39)	(1.00)	(0.69)	

Sensitivities to volatility are shown in Exhibit 8. As volatility moves up, the swaps incur losses. Sensitivity to volatility is asymmetric. In the case of the first swap, for the same volatility increment, losses are larger than gains (the swap is negatively convex with respect to volatility). The second swap displays positive convexity with respect to volatility.

To hedge the option components of the above structures, one has to use a combination of 10-year Treasuries (or futures contracts) and options on 10-year Treasuries (or on the associated futures contracts). To hedge the cash-flow exposure, one can use a combination of Eurodollar contracts and short-term Treasury instruments.

COMPARISON WITH MORTGAGES

Index Amortization Swaps, or their cash-market equivalent, Index Amortization Notes, are similar to mortgages: They are negatively convex, they extend as long-term rates increase, and they shorten as long-term rates decline. In the case of mortgages, the average life depends on the level of prepayment. The level of prepayment is strongly linked to the level of the long-term interest rate: As the long-term rate increases, refinancing declines and prepayment falls. But the relationship between prepayment and the level of the long-term rate is not deterministic, and therefore the path of the long-term interest rate is not the only determinant of the average life of a mortgage security. In other terms, prepayment rates have a residual component that is not explained by the variation in the long-term rate. This component, the size of which is not insignificant, induces an additional level of uncertainty in the performance of mortgages. In contrast, index amortization structures are essentially interest rate products. A portfolio of mortgages can be hedged by taking a short position in an index amortization swap with appropriate characteristics. Such a hedging policy is much more effective than the short position in a vanilla swap or in Treasuries. While a significant portion of the duration and of the convexity of a mortgage portfolio can be hedged with such amortizing swaps, the residual prepayment risks of mortgages cannot be covered with such swaps. To mitigate residual prepayment exposures, mortgage portfolios have to use mortgage products. Pure rate products, such as index amortization swaps, are not substitutes for mortgage products.

16

Synthetic Portfolio Management in a U.S. Pension Fund

Matthew R. Smith
Senior Portfolio Manager, Amoco Pension Fund

Beth A. Kostick
Portfolio Manager, Amoco Pension Fund

This chapter presents background information on U.S. pension funds and how they approach investment markets. It also discusses some examples of the use of derivatives in managing portfolios, with specific reference to the Amoco pension fund.

BACKGROUND

The growth of pension fund assets in the United States has been dramatic since the passing of ERISA in 1974. In 1980, the value of these assets was about $600 billion. Today, pension funds have some $3.5 trillion in investments, representing a growth rate of some 13 percent per annum. The size of some corporate and public pension funds is truly staggering. Exhibit 1 shows some of the largest such funds. Even Amoco, with some $2.4 billion in assets, ranks only 75th in size for U.S. pension funds. TIAA-CREF is about the size of the GDP of Norway.

Not only has the absolute level of assets increased rapidly, but the influence on the marketplace by pension funds and other institutional investors, such as mutual funds and insurance companies, has increased as well. Exhibit 2 shows the percent holdings of U.S. equities by market value

EXHIBIT 1   Top U.S. Pension Funds by Asset Size

Top Corporate Funds		*Top Other Funds*	
AT&T	46.3	TIAA-CREF	106.2
General Motors	40.2	California Employees	69.0
General Electric	36.3	New York State	53.2
IBM	30.4	New York City	52.6
Ford Motor	25.5	California State Teachers	42.4

Source: *Pensions & Investments*

EXHIBIT 2   Holdings of U.S. Stocks by Market Value (from Federal Reserve Flow of Funds Account)

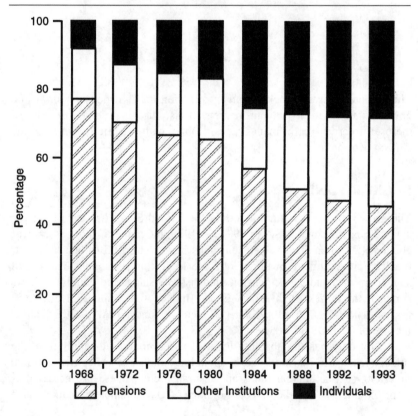

for institutional investors versus individuals. Whereas individuals at one time directly owned over 80 percent of all U.S. stocks, they now own only about 50 percent.

The trend toward institutional dominance of U.S. financial markets is clear. Their power is seen to be so important that the creation of pension funds and pension reform is often cited as a major development in emerging markets such as Latin America.

TYPES OF PENSION FUNDS

There are two main types of corporate pension funds in the United States: "defined contribution" and "defined benefit." The difference relates to the benefits promised employees and hence to the corporate liability.

In a defined contribution plan, employees contribute part of their salary to the fund and the company matches some percentage of this. The money is then invested in a variety of markets, as directed by each employee, perhaps in consultation with a financial advisor. When the employee retires, the value of his or her pension is then the sum of these contributions plus (or minus) the investment returns. The company makes no promise as to the value of the pension at a future date and hence has no liability. The employee assumes all investment risk. This type of pension fund has become increasingly popular due to this risk shifting and relative simplicity. The number of such plans and the participants in them has more than tripled in the past 15 years.

In a defined benefit plan, such as Amoco's, the employer promises each worker an annuity at retirement based, typically, on a formula tied to years of service and average salary level, at no direct cost to the employee. This clearly creates a corporate liability, and so funds are set aside to assure that these promises will be met. In this case, the company assumes all investment risk.

The cost to a company with a defined benefit plan increases as the benefits promised are enhanced and decreases as the investment return rises. The main roles and responsibilities of a pension administration department are, then, to manage this complicated balance between careful investing of the assets and monitoring the long-dated liabilities of the plan's annuitants. These tasks include analyzing and recommending types and mixes of investment strategies, hiring and firing managers, measuring performance, accounting, auditing, regulatory reporting, and coordinating the cash flows of the trust.

To illustrate how complicated the administrative side of a pension fund is, Exhibit 3 shows some data regarding participants in Amoco's plan as of 1992.

EXHIBIT 3   Amoco Plan Participants as of 1992

	Number	Average Age	Annual Compensation
Active Participants	30,192	40	46,900
Retirees and Survivors	18,408	71	6,800
Terminated Vested	5,161	50	3,400

Every month, over 23,000 checks are sent out to Amoco retirees. For the 30,000 workers or "active participants," accounting must be made of the expected annuity promised based on demographics, inflation, salary, and service expectations, and this annuity discounted back to the present using an acceptable discount rate. The ties of an employee to a company may easily last half a century.

INVESTMENT MARKETS AND POLICY PORTFOLIOS

To meet current as well as distant obligations, companies set aside and invest funds with the goal of earning an attractive return. Typically this means purchasing U.S. stocks and bonds. However, Exhibit 4 shows the major investment markets that are available to institutional investors.

While the U.S. equity market receives much attention in the media, it is by no means the largest market. Non-dollar bonds are currently the largest broad asset class available, yet are relatively obscure to most funds. International equities, while larger overall than the U.S. equity market, on average account for only 4 percent of a typical pension fund's equity holdings.

To generate a long-term attractive return on assets with an acceptable level of risk, pension funds ideally invest in and across these broad asset classes. Usually an asset-liability study will be periodically performed to look at characteristics of these asset classes relative to the actuarial and economic projections of the plan's liabilities.

These characteristics are, typically, the risk (usually measured by standard deviation), return, and correlations of these markets. Exhibit 5 shows these performance figures for the main U.S. investment markets since 1925.

Exhibit 5 demonstrates that, at least historically, equities outperform bonds in the long run, although there are periods when this has not been true.

**EXHIBIT 4   Total Investable Capital Markets
as of 12/31/92 ($28.5 Trillion)**

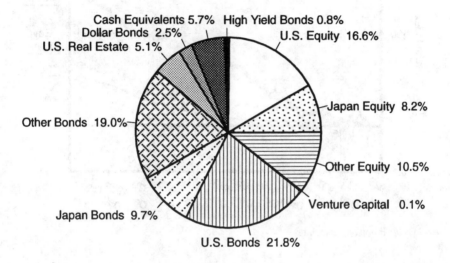

The path taken by stock returns is also much more volatile than that of bonds. However, with the long-term view that a healthy pension fund can afford to take, it should be able to tolerate such uncertain periods.

Such a long history is not generally available for all the markets shown in Exhibit 5, but Exhibit 6 shows their performance from 1977.

The returns and standard deviations of these returns over this period are summarized in Exhibit 7.

Exhibit 8 is a plot of the data in Exhibit 7, with standard deviation on the horizontal axis and return on the vertical axis. It begins to show the inevitable trade-off that must be made between earning more return and taking more risk.

EXHIBIT 5 Long-Term Performance of U.S. Markets

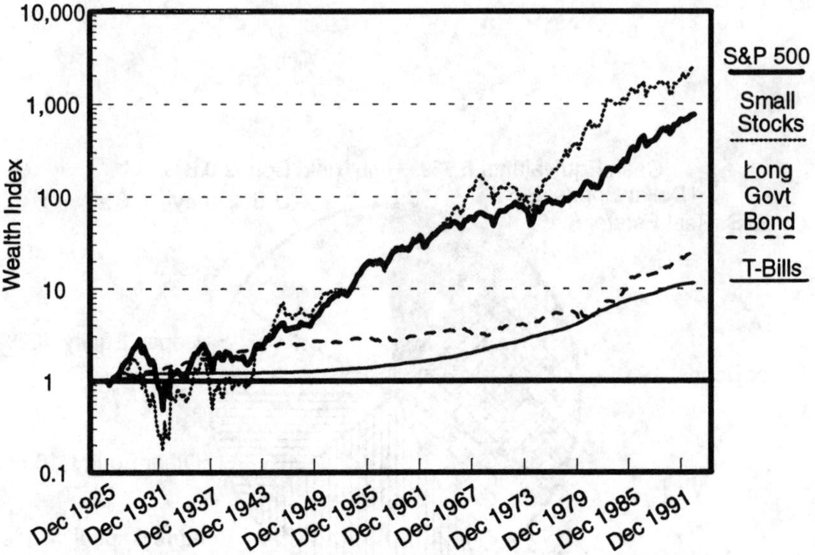

Source: Ibbotson Associates

What it does not show, however, is how risk and return change when the above asset classes are blended together. The change in risk depends on the correlations between these asset classes. Exhibit 9 shows the correlations between all the markets, using the available history.

However, just as risk and return are not constant but change over time, so does correlation. While there are too many correlations to consider here, Exhibit 10 shows how some markets have correlated to the S&P 500 over rolling five-year windows.

To begin to ultimately determine an appropriate blend of all markets, numbers such as expected return, risk, and correlations are usually put into a simple optimizer to derive a so-called "efficient frontier," shown in Exhibit 11. This frontier is meant to represent portfolio combinations with the highest expected return for a chosen level of risk, as measured by standard deviation.

However, the results of this process are highly sensitive to small changes in the inputs and, as we have seen, historically derived estimates are

**EXHIBIT 6 Asset Class Performance
December 1977 to June 1993**

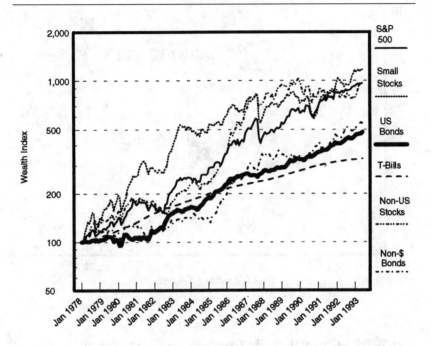

EXHIBIT 7 Returns and Standard Deviations Since 1977

	Return	Standard Deviation
S&P 500	15.84	15.48
Small Stocks	17.29	20.22
Long-Term Treasury	10.98	12.31
T-Bills	8.05	0.84
Non-U.S. Equity	15.87	17.83
Non-Dollar Bonds	11.65	13.06
U.S. Bonds	10.71	7.15

EXHIBIT 8   Risk and Return

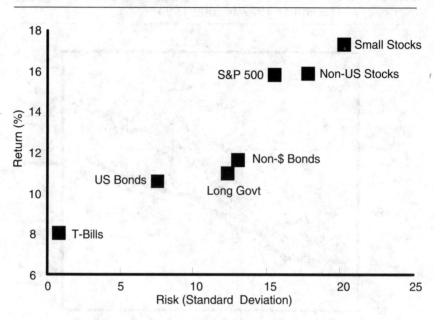

EXHIBIT 9   Correlations Between Major Asset Classes
Monthly Data 2/78–6/93

	S&P 500	T-Bills	Non-U.S. Equities	Non-Dollar Bonds	U.S. Bonds
S&P 500	1.00				
T-Bills	–.10	1.00			
Non-U.S. Equities	.46	–.12	1.00		
Non-Dollar Bonds	.07	–.11	.63	1.00	
U.S. Bonds	.33	.08	.22	.45	1.00

EXHIBIT 10   Rolling 5-Year Correlations with the S&P 500 Monthly Data, 12/74–6/93

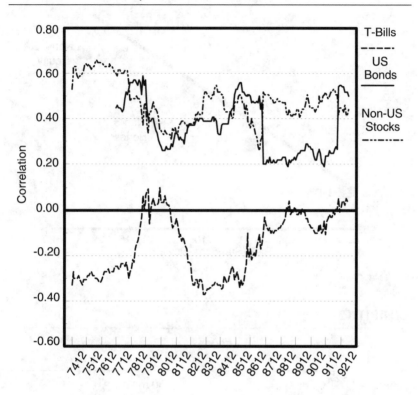

unstable. Therefore, the solution from such an "optimization" is suspect. Thus, the inputs are then tempered with some judgment or preconceived notions of the final result and the optimization process repeated several times. By choosing an acceptable level of risk, usually measured by standard deviation or funding cost levels, a long-term or "policy" asset mix is arrived at. Exhibit 12 shows Amoco's long-term policy asset mix, derived from such an exercise, and its actual mix as of 1992.

EXHIBIT 11 Risk and Return

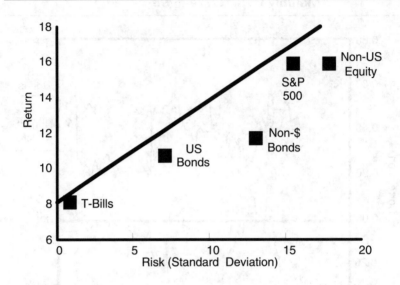

EXHIBIT 12

	Policy Asset Mix	Range	12/31/92 Actual
Equities—U.S. & Foreign	70	50 to 80	73
Fixed Income	15	10 to 30	17
Cash	5	0 to 50	1
Real Estate	5	3 to 10	4
Venture Capital	5	3 to 10	5

Amoco generally subscribes to the belief that equities offer the best long-term return potential, and this is reflected in its policy weighting of 70 percent. This is somewhat more aggressive than most U.S. pension funds, which typically have an equity weighting of about 50 percent. Amoco's foreign equity weighting is about 15 percent, which is also high by U.S. pension standards as noted above.

PORTFOLIO MANAGEMENT

So far, only broad passive market portfolios have been discussed. In order to try to enhance investment returns, many funds employ active strategies to outperform passive market indices. Given the size of pension assets, this goal of beating the market is almost irresistible. Adding just 1 percent of incremental return to Amoco's pension portfolio means an additional $24 million. Of course, this entails some level of additional risk, and the market indices serve as benchmarks for measuring performance.

Traditionally, attempting to beat passive indices has meant using fundamental or quantitative stock-picking tools, adjusting duration, sector or country allocating, currency hedging, market timing, and asset allocation. Exhibit 13 however, shows that this goal of superior investment performance can be very difficult to achieve.

The median equity manager has had a difficult time beating simple passive indices such as the S&P 500. Over the five-year period, even top-quartile managers have underperformed this benchmark, although the longer 10-year record is better. However, this may be due to factors other than skill, such as small stocks outperforming large stocks over time. Even so, one's actual experience could be quite different from this record, because the actual managers in each quartile change and it is not possible to know in advance who will be a top-quartile manager. Given the lower volatility of bonds, the performance of even top-quartile bond managers is even less impressive. Hence pension funds, indeed all investors, constantly seek new ways to achieve "value-added" returns.

EXHIBIT 13   Active vs. Passive Management Returns

	1 Year	2 Years	3 Years	5 Years	10 Years
Equity Only:					
Top Quartile	19.72	17.27	13.96	13.42	16.05
Median Manager	15.26	14.56	11.66	14.52	14.54
Bottom Quartile	10.62	11.68	9.93	11.48	13.23
S&P 500	13.58	13.52	11.44	14.19	14.41
Bonds Only:					
Top Quartile	13.91	14.70	13.44	11.90	12.33
Median Manager	12.22	13.58	12.68	11.30	11.63
Bottom Quartile	10.95	12.63	12.00	10.76	11.11
Lehman Govt/Corp Index	13.15	13.66	12.50	11.37	11.79

THE APPEAL OF DERIVATIVES

The advantages of derivatives lead to several alternative ways to actively manage a portfolio. The primary advantages of derivatives are generally:

- Avoidance of foreign taxes and dividend withholding
- Avoidance of custody costs
- Avoidance of problems with dividend reinvestment and index rebalancing
- Control of the aggregate portfolio using various overlays
- Creation of synthetic securities
- Transfer of expertise from one market to another
- Reduction of "judgmental" risk
- Non-linear payoff patterns

These advantages will be discussed in some detail. There are certainly disadvantages to derivatives, and these will be discussed later.

Costs such as custody, foreign taxes, and dividend withholding can be significant, especially in the international and emerging market arenas. They may amount to 100 basis points or more per year, depending on the country. With suitable counterparties not subject to such taxes or costs and to the extent that these savings are not simply priced into a swap or other derivative structure, this advantage alone makes a simple and compelling argument for the use of derivatives.

Plan sponsors are responsible for managing the aggregate pension portfolio and are uniquely situated to look at the investment portfolio from this point of view. Most external managers see only their small piece of the portfolio. Most derivative contracts, such as options, futures, or swaps, whether exchange-traded or over-the-counter, require little or no initial cash outlay. This feature makes them ideal for such ordinary uses as asset allocation and currency hedging, since the underlying assets need not be disturbed.

The zero-cost feature of futures and swaps allow for the creation of unique hybrid securities and portfolios that result from combining securities, collateral, cash flows, and derivatives. Several such approaches will be discussed in detail below.

If a manager can consistently beat his or her benchmark, this expertise can be transferred from one market to another by swapping one benchmark return for another, say the S&P 500 for the Salomon BIG bond index. To the extent that the cost of the swap is less than the value-added potential of the equity manager, swapping benchmark returns converts an equity portfolio to a bond portfolio, without the manager being aware of this transference. This process is sometimes referred to as "alpha transporting."

We have already seen above how difficult it is to consistently add value over passive indices with active management. A typical performance goal is to beat a passive equity benchmark by 200 basis points per annum. This amounts to less than a basis point a day. One therefore has to wonder about the need to make large portfolio bets based primarily on subjective opinions or limited computer models in this modern age of instantaneous communication and highly efficient markets. The non-linear payoff patterns of options make them ideal for tailoring portfolios and reducing "judgmental" risk.

"Risk" for a portfolio manager is deviation from the benchmark portfolio. Obviously, to add value over a target, some risk or deviation must be made. But derivatives, especially options, create entirely new patterns of returns. For example, to simply over- or under-weight, say, equities relative to cash, without the use of derivatives, means the portfolio manager has only the payoff patterns shown in Exhibit 14.

EXHIBIT 14 Overweighting Stocks: Without Options

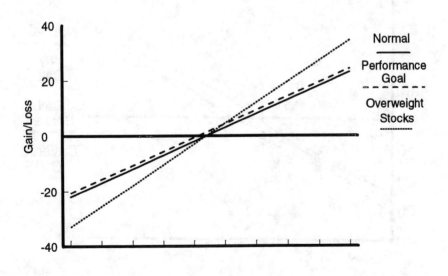

While such a return profile has significant value added if the view that equities will outperform cash over the time frame of the decision is correct, there is significant risk of underperforming if this view is incorrect. The potential return must be weighed against the potential risk and tempered with a realistic view of one's market-timing ability. By employing options, this risk can be reduced substantially. For example, increasing equity exposure through the purchase of a call, a call spread, or selling a covered call against the increased equity position all reduce the risk of underperforming the benchmark. This risk reduction is shown in Exhibit 15. To pay for this protection, one clearly has to give up some upside participation as well. But given the target of adding one basis point a day, one has to weigh the potential value added against the value subtracted as well as the business or career risk of underperforming.

Using options to tailor the distribution of returns is important for risk control. The usual rationales for including bonds in a pension portfolio are to dampen volatility or provide some inflation hedge. However, with options, it may be that the superior long-term performance of equities combined with

EXHIBIT 15   Overweighting Stocks: With Options

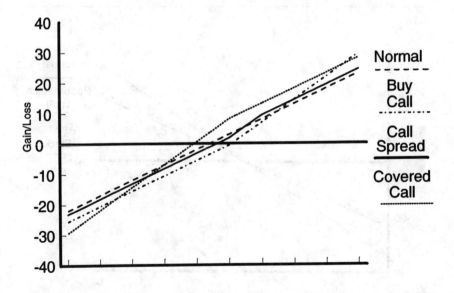

put options can outperform bonds and still dampen volatility. If stocks out-perform bonds by 500 basis points over time and some put protection can be purchased for less than this, then it makes little sense to include bonds in a portfolio. The cost of the puts can also be funded by selling calls, capping the upside potential but still producing a hybrid investment that beats bonds but in general will underperform equities. However, it is known in advance how much upside and downside there is to such an investment. This cannot be said of either stocks or bonds.

Synthetic Portfolios

Where possible, futures or swaps can be priced from a cash-and-carry rela-tionship:

$$\text{Cash instrument} = \text{Future} + \text{Carry cost} - \text{Cash flow}$$

For example, ideally:

$$\text{S\&P 500 index fund} = \text{S\&P 500 index future} \\ + \text{LIBOR-based deposit}$$

The futures price incorporates the carry cost of the underlying. This pricing relationship opens up a whole new way to beat an index by aggres-sively managing the cash collateral for such an investment. Instead of picking stocks to beat the S&P 500, beating the benchmark then becomes a task of finding cash-like investments that beat LIBOR by the desired amount.

One approach is to create a so-called "market neutral" portfolio from a long stock position and a short stock position. Typically this is done using some quantitative ranking scheme, buying, say, the top quartile, shorting an equal or comparable dollar amount of the bottom quartile, and optimizing the mix to minimize volatility. To the extent that the ranking system has information on future returns, this approach allows a manager to extract value from the perceived "winners" as well as "losers." It is, therefore, sometime referred to as a "double alpha" approach.

Another approach suggested by the above equation is to simply manage the cash in a suitably aggressive manner. A simple example of this strategy is to take greater credit risk than is priced in a LIBOR deposit. Short-term debt of emerging market governments, in particular, has been a popular example of increased credit risk taking.

Another strategy is to take duration bets. If one has the view that U.S. rates will be fairly stable or declining, then buying longer-dated Treasuries or corporate bonds will outperform LIBOR. If the yield curve is unusually steep, as was the case in the past few years, then this view is, to some extent, self-hedged since, as time passes, these instruments will "roll down the yield curve." Thus rates could even rise slightly, to a quantifiable extent, and this simple strategy would add value.

The most interesting approach is to use structured notes to incorporate investment views into a cash instrument. We will discuss several such examples now.

Examples

With a view that interest rates will decline, an inverse floating rate note can be created using interest rate put options, or floors. Instead of buying a six-month term deposit that pays, say, 5 percent annually, one can take the 2.5 percent coupon and use it to purchase as many of these options as desired. If each put option costs 60 basis points, one can buy up to four of these and create the payoff patterns shown in Exhibit 16.

EXHIBIT 16   Inverse Floater

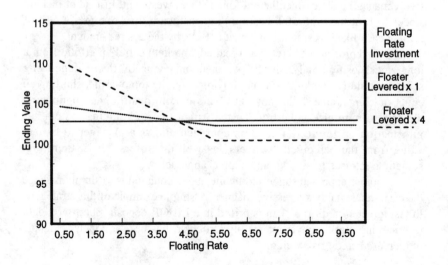

If rates do in fact decline sufficiently to offset the option premium, the put options will create additional payoffs relative to the cash alternative. If rates are stable or rise, then the cost of the puts causes the instrument to underperform. However, this cost and hence the precise amount of possible underperformance is known in advance, unlike picking stocks.

Somewhat more exotic versions of the same idea can be done with baskets of foreign interest rates. For example, a G7 bull note with the following terms:

- Price: Par

- Maturity: 1 year

- Principal redemption: Par + 8 * (6.71 – Average of 2-year swap rates in the G7 countries)

- Minimum redemption: Par

- Currency: U.S. dollars

The formula for principal redemption resembles the payoff from eight put options on the G7 average rate, struck at 6.71 percent, which at the time was at-the-money. While the above expression is simple, the embedded option is actually a complicated swaption on a basket of foreign and domestic rates which, then, has been hedged, or "quantoed" back into dollars. The pricing of such an option depends on the shape of the yield curve, rate volatility, and correlations in and between seven countries as well as hedging six currencies back in dollars on a quanto basis, which in turn depends on rate and currency volatility and correlations. Such a structure would be virtually impossible for most institutional investors to create, yet the note elegantly captures a view that rates in the major world economies will fall.

A slightly different version of this note structure is the so-called "junior/senior" note structure. A recent attractive structure typical of this form has been tied to Mexican T-bill, or Cetes, rates. These rates have recently been around 17 percent per annum. In the junior/senior structure, Cetes are purchased and put into a trust, typically in the Cayman Islands for tax purposes. The trust issues two types of notes: a dollar-denominated senior note (senior in the sense of seniority of claims on the trust assets) that pays, say, LIBOR plus 150 basis points for one year, and a junior note that essentially becomes a highly leveraged play on the Mexican peso. These payoffs are shown in Exhibit 17.

EXHIBIT 17   Junior/Senior Tranches

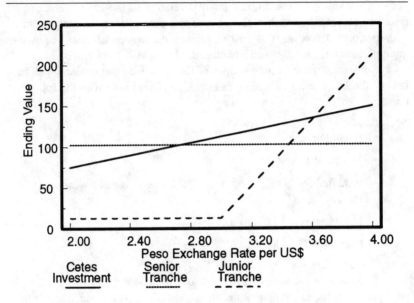

Cetes Investment

Senior Tranche

Junior Tranche

Obviously, the senior note is very attractive as an aggressive cash investment with the potential to be used to beat the S&P 500 by 150 basis points annualized. The main risks of the senior note are the Mexican government defaulting on peso-denominated Cetes (which has never happened) or the risk of the imposition by Mexico of currency controls and hence the inability of the trust to sell the Cetes at maturity and buy dollars to pay off the senior notes. If these risks are seen as minimal or at least acceptable, this type of investment is very attractive. While such a simple structure was once possible, lately the spreads are much narrower, and the senior note may have to accept some small amount of peso currency depreciation risk, say, the risk beyond a 25 percent depreciation.

Another structure that implicitly uses "binary" options is a so-called "daily accrual" note. For example, the following terms:

- Price: Par
- Maturity: 1 Year
- Principal redemption: Par

- Coupon: 6% * (Number of days 5-year Canadian swap rate < 7.40%)/365
- Currency: U.S. dollars

A binary option is an option that pays, say, $1 if the underlying is below the strike price and $0 if it is above the strike. In the above note, the investor uses the amount in excess of the present value of par to purchase a strip of binary options, one for each day of the year, on the five-year Canadian swap rate. These options are struck at 7.40 percent, and each date that this rate is below 7.40 percent the note accrues an above-market coupon of 6 percent. While this coupon is likely somewhat less than the coupon that could be achieved with an inverse floater, it is attractive because a LIBOR rate can be exceeded by a significant margin even if five-year Canadian swap rates are above 7.40 percent at maturity.

DISADVANTAGES OF DERIVATIVES

While, generally, structured notes can cost 20 to 40 basis points in issuance cost, this can be an acceptable cost for several reasons. As mentioned above, some of these structures would be impossible to reconstruct from the embedded pieces to attempt to recover the issuance cost. Additionally, different derivatives have various disadvantages. The main ones are:

- Daily margin flows for futures need to be verified and money transferred
- Tax status of some transactions can be unclear
- Regulatory constraints, especially of international exchange-traded vehicles
- Customized OTC contracts are illiquid
- Counterparty credit risk
- Legal hassles, especially QPAM problems for pension funds
- Lack of pricing sources
- General lack of understanding in the organization

Surveys indicate that only about 35 percent of U.S. pension funds use derivatives, and of those not currently using derivatives, some 75 percent are not considering doing so, citing some of the above reasons.

CONCLUSION

Pension funds in the United States and elsewhere control sizable assets and increasingly dominate markets. They have a constant need for new investment ideas and arenas. Despite their sleepy image, pension funds are inherently large risk-takers. An event like the stock market crash of October 1987 can wipe out the retirement benefits of half a generation of workers in a few days. There is probably not any investment idea or strategy that has not been tried by some pension fund somewhere.

In the pursuit of extra return or risk management, derivatives offer new approaches through combining asset classes in new ways and tailoring returns distributions. A seemingly unrelated skill set such as credit analysis, for example, can be used to beat an equity benchmark through aggressive cash management and equity swaps. This leads to an asset-classless world where the search is for value-added expertise, and then benchmark returns are swapped to the desired portfolio policy mix.

Any investment tool can be abused, and derivatives particularly suffer from this negative image. However, as they have been applied in the Amoco pension fund, derivative strategies have a special feature in that both upside potential and downside risk can, to a large extent, be quantified ex-ante. This is not generally possible with traditional strategies involving stocks, bonds, and other cash market instruments.

Because of the size of their assets and their societal significance, pension funds will continue to grow in importance and be at the forefront of investment ideas.

Financial Risk Management for Developing Countries: IFC's Role

Bernardo Frydman
Director General, Banco Finantia (Lisbon, Portugal)

FINANCIAL RISKS

Financial managers in the industrialized countries have become increasingly concerned with managing their companies' financial risks. For their counterparts in the developing world, financial risks are still largely a force of nature, due to the lack of adequate access to the financial markets providing hedging instruments.

The nature of the financial risks faced by a developing country company (financial and nonfinancial) are not dissimilar to those of companies anywhere else; there are, however, some distinctions that result primarily from local currencies being generally not freely convertible, the lack of financial instruments in local markets with maturities beyond 12 months, and economic environments and policies that distort the relative pricing of financial assets. Thus, when viewing financial risks of companies in a developing country environment (with some growing exceptions, such as the "tiger" countries) it is useful to distinguish between internationally generated risks and purely local currency ones. The focus of this writing is on financial risks belonging to that first category, i.e., that which is derived from companies operating internationally and being exposed to asset-liability mismatches in foreign currencies as well as to commodity price volatility.

What kinds of risks do these companies typically face and what causes them? There is, first, interest rate risk in foreign currencies. A nonfinancial company in a developing country that has accumulated variable rate liabilities in foreign currencies may be exposed to too much interest rate volatility

---

Bernardo Frydman was the Senior Manager, Treasury, International Finance Corporation until September, 1993.

if its foreign and local revenues (the latter, when translated into a foreign currency) cannot be adjusted proportionately to those interest rate movements. Financial companies would need to match the rate bases of their assets and liabilities (or hedge them).

Exposure to different foreign currencies in their assets and liabilities is a common, second source of financial risk to developing country companies. This may manifest itself in a variety of ways. The most widespread cause of asset-liability currency mismatches is, perhaps, the creation of foreign liabilities through the financing of the purchase of capital equipment. Companies in developing countries usually have limited foreign funding alternatives; among such alternatives, export financing may be relatively more accessible. The currency obtained from such financing sources would normally match the origin of the goods and services being purchased, whereas the exports to be produced may be priced and sold in a different currency. Currency mismatch between trade or production cost and revenues is also a common cause of financial risk.

The trading subsidiary of a commodity producer may be exposed to foreign exchange volatility between its foreign revenues (in U.S. dollars) and its international shipping costs (in an EMS currency). An assembly plant may be subject to volatility of exchange rates between its payments for foreign parts and intermediary products (in, let us say, Japanese yen) and its sales revenues from exports to Europe (in an EMS currency). A mining concern may be exposed to commodity price volatility and cross-currency mismatches between the U.S. dollar, in which commodity prices are quoted, and other currencies for payment of liabilities and materials or parts.

Financial institutions may also suffer from asset-liability mismatches in foreign currency. Many developing countries allow local financial assets to be linked to the U.S. dollar (a not uncommon practice in several Latin American countries). Because of limited access to international financing, many financial institutions in developing countries must look beyond the currency of denomination of their assets when borrowing abroad, thus creating a potentially risky exposure.

HEDGING STRATEGIES

Management techniques and financial instruments to hedge the sorts of financial risks afflicting those companies are widely available in the international financial markets. Let us review a few illustrations of common hedging strategies suitable to those situations.

Illustration A: Large-Scale Hedging of Interest Rate Risk

- *Background:* The company, a manufacturing concern, has a large share of its foreign (and total) debt obligations on a floating rate basis.

- *Hedging Objectives:* To take advantage of a steep U.S. dollar yield curve and low floating interest rate (LIBOR) levels, hedge the company simultaneously against rate increases in the longer term and take advantage of the historically low U.S. dollar interest rate levels in general. Interest rate environment prevailing in the spring of 1993.

- The following hedging strategy alternatives could be used depending on management's preferences:

  Alternative 1: A swap from floating rate USD to fixed rate USD for the life of the loans, starting on the next rollover date.

  Alternative 2a: A swap from floating rate USD to fixed rate USD for the life of the loans, starting two years from today, i.e., the company's loan rates would remain floating for the following two years, but would convert into fixed rates on the rollover dates, approximately two years from today, and would remain fixed at the fixed rates set today for the remaining life of the loans. This is called a "forward swap." The forward swap would have the first two years unhedged, i.e., the company's debt would be at the market level floating rates without additional costs.

  Alternative 2b: Another alternative would be to hedge also the two-year portion through a cap or by fixing the rates using future rate agreements (FRAs). The FRA alternative, however, combined with a forward swap would as a hedge be equivalent in terms of results with (and may in fact cost more than Alternative 1) a straight five-year swap, assuming the company would fix the whole two-year floating rate period using FRAs.

  Alternative 3: A cap for the life of the loans.

Illustration B: Long-Term Hedging of Currency Mismatches Between Costs and Revenues

- *Background:* The company, a trading subsidiary of a commodity exporter, incurs international shipping costs, contracted on a long-term basis, in an EMS currency and prices and sells its exports in U.S. dollars.

- *Hedging Objectives:* To ensure that shipping costs, when translated into U.S. dollars, do not exceed certain relative levels in the company's overall cost structure; as the current exchange rate is relatively unfavorable to the company, maintain the company's flexibility to benefit from a potential improvement in rates over a certain time horizon.

- *Hedging Strategy:* Execute a currency swap (or a series of forward currency contracts) to lock in the current foreign exchange rate on *x* percent of future transportation costs over a certain time horizon; purchase a series of put and call currency options to hedge the balance of those costs without completely fixing them. The put and call strike prices could be selected so as to minimize the cost of this hedge.

LIMITED MARKET ACCESS

It would be possible to devise other alternative hedging strategies for the above cases given different situations (such as different market conditions) or management hedging objectives. In fact, a variety of ways exist in which to manage financial risks in each and every one of the situations encountered by the companies described above—*if they had the means to do it.* Their true problem is a general lack of access to the international financial markets, which results primarily from being allotted relatively low country credit risk limits by the international financial institutions. The developing country companies that are aware of the relatively high danger of having unhedged financial risks, even when highly creditworthy in their own right, may have very limited access to the required hedging instruments because of market country risk considerations. Given the 1980s debt crisis and other credit problems prevailing in the international financial markets (as well as domestic problems being faced in some major money centers) that is not surprising.

Country credit risk limits and portfolio credit risk allocations are, of course, not uniformly constraining to all developing country enterprises. As mentioned earlier, companies in the "tiger" countries are enjoying increasingly better market access. On the other hand, new "needy" cases have appeared on the scene, such as the companies being created or reconstructed in Eastern Europe and the former Soviet republics. Another mitigating factor is the availability (at least potentially) of hedging instruments and techniques that do not expose the market to credit risk of the developing country company (e.g., caps).

Overall, however, a limited access to the financial markets for hedging instruments is the norm. To the extent that some derivative instruments are made available to developing country enterprises, they undergo a "natural selection" that favors derivatives that do not generate credit risk to the market. This bias severely constrains the ability of otherwise well-run, creditworthy companies to execute effective hedging strategies. The same factor acts, also, as an important disincentive to the offering of financial risk management consulting services that would help the managers of those companies to develop their know-how in risk management techniques and strategies.

These constraints have serious consequences, as the benefits of hedging financial risks for these companies are not purely financial. The use of hedging instruments, in conjunction with funding strategies and to control financial risks that would otherwise negatively affect the core business of many enterprises, may significantly enhance the competitiveness and long-term financial strength of these companies. They are an important element in their ability to grow and contribute to the development of an efficient private sector in developing countries.

IFC'S ROLE

Recognizing this unmet demand by its developing country clients, the International Finance Corporation (IFC or the Corporation) began, in June 1990, to assist them in developing and executing hedging strategies. Prior to that, in 1987, the Corporation began to make swap-like features available to its clients—private enterprises in the developing world—by providing conversion features of IFC's loans allowing for changes in interest rate bases and currencies.

The wide-ranging and frequent uses IFC makes of swaps and other derivatives, to manage its own asset-liability risks, qualifies it well to provide risk management services to its clients. The Corporation entered the swaps market early in that market's development, having done its first swaps in 1985 in conjunction with its funding transactions. Since then, the use of liability swaps has been an integral part of the Corporation's funding strategy, broadening dramatically its market alternatives and resulting in very attractive funding costs; IFC's management of its funded liquidity within a matched asset-liability policy framework, and the objective of optimizing risk/return investment profiles, also led to the use of derivatives to create synthetic (LIBOR-based) assets and hedge currency positions.

IFC's AAA/Aaa ratings and supranational status as an international issuer of bonds allows for a global market access on the most favorable terms. The combination of IFC's market access with the Corporation's *de facto* preferred creditor status (for transfer risk purposes), with the resulting "umbrella" element, enables the Corporation to attract counterparties that are at the leading edge of the markets to participate in the provision of risk management products and services. In many instances, IFC is able to build on these strengths to promote the execution of hedging transactions directly between an IFC client and market counterparties. Moreover, IFC's excellent and close relations with the leading institutions in the hedging markets allows IFC staff to stay current with market developments and creates the pre-conditions necessary for engaging in financial engineering and the tailoring of efficient technical solutions to clients' specific risk management needs.

IFC's role in assisting private enterprises in developing countries to manage financial risk is, in essence, a natural extension of the role IFC plays when investing in such companies. As it does when engaging in its usual project financing activity, IFC would use its ability to assess country credit risk and evaluate company and project risks in a developing country environment, to determine whether it should intermediate transactions between the derivatives markets and the Corporation's client. Moreover, as it does also when mobilizing market funding to finance projects, the Corporation would act as a catalyst in the financial markets, by providing credit enhancement of its clients to entice market counterparties to enter into hedging transaction with those clients.

The Corporation's readiness to intermediate and enhance the credit of its clients in hedging transactions has the potential to facilitate a greater involvement of the international financial markets in providing these services to companies in developing countries.

The services IFC may provide as part of a risk management facility to its clients would comprise: (a) financial risk management advisory services (to develop hedging strategies, identify and price hedging instruments, etc.); and (b) to execute, to the extent possible jointly with market counterparties, hedging transactions directly for its clients. IFC is also actively seeking to promote the creation of risk management facilities through financial intermediaries in developing country markets (to hedge foreign financial risks).

As of May 31, 1992, IFC had assisted clients in Africa, Europe, and Latin American to hedge financial risks of up to US$743 million of notional/principal amount by intermediating risk management transactions or establishing financial risk management facilities. The following illustrations help demonstrate IFC's role in these transactions, which brings together hedging strategies and credit elements.

ENHANCED SWAP GUARANTEE

The guarantee facility is a credit enhancement mechanism that reduces the amount of the client's credit risk assumed by the market counterparties

(MCPs) on any swap. In fact, the MCPs are trading the credit risk of the client for that of IFC and the guaranteeing banks (GBs). This structure enables large volumes of swaps to be transacted for a single client without IFC needing to take the entire credit risk. Incorporating IFC's umbrella into the structure is expected to provide the same results as in any IFC syndicated loan/guarantee facility. This is how it works (see Exhibit 1):

- IFC brokers swaps for its client. The swaps are executed directly between the client and the market counterparties (MCPs).

- IFC and a group of commercial banks (the guaranteeing banks or GBs) provide a guarantee to the MCPs that covers the mark-to-market value (MTM) of the swap (or losses) in excess of a minimum limiting x percent and up to x percent of the face value of the swaps. This protects the MCPs against defaults by the client up to the amount of the guarantee.

EXHIBIT 1

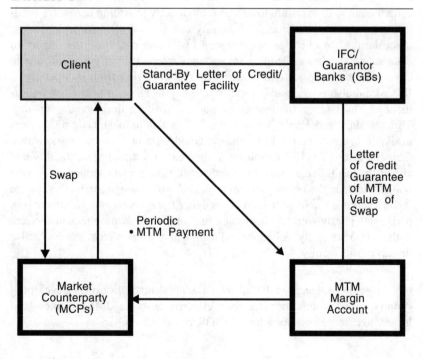

- Periodically, the swaps entered into between the MCPs and the client would be marked-to-market. MTM amounts up to the amount of the guarantee would be covered by IFC and the GBs through a letter of credit (LC) or other mechanism.

- If the client defaults and this default causes the MCPs to incur a cost, then IFC and the GBs would pay the MCPs the amount required to cover such costs up to the amount of the guarantee, whereas the MCPs would share the remaining costs on a pro-rata basis. The amount paid to the MCPs would become a loan from IFC and the GBs to the client.

- The structure of the stand-by guarantee facility would be analogous to a stand-by loan facility and would be priced accordingly. In addition, the facility would have an "A" and "B" component, with the "B" component being syndicated to the pool of GBs.

WHOLESALE RISK MANAGEMENT FACILITY

Hedging Situations: IFC sets up a facility under which it agrees to take on a certain amount of exposure to its client by directly providing derivative products over a period of time. This facility can have several uses, depending upon the type of client: A nonfinancial institution could use the facility to enter into a number of hedging transactions over a certain period of time to cover commodity price and/or currency risks deriving from its operations. IFC would also provide advice on developing hedging strategies, as well as technical assistance for managing and controlling derivative exposure. Through such "wholesale" approaches, IFC is able to make hedging services available to many more clients than it could on a one-by-one basis; with a financial institution, IFC establishes a financial risk management facility that allows the institution to provide financial risk management services to its corporate clients in the developing country. IFC will, through the facility, hedge the institution's financial risk on the hedging transactions and, in some cases, participate jointly with that institution in providing risk management services to the corporate entity. Advisory and technical assistance elements could also be part of this facility.

Hedging Objective: To allow a financial institution in a developing country to raise funds abroad at most effective costs (in DM) and to on-lend locally to corporates as long-term LIBOR-based U.S. dollars.

EXHIBIT 2   Swap with IFC

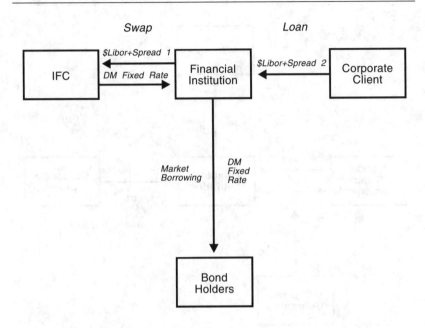

Hedging Strategies: Exhibits 2 and 3 illustrate two intermediation/credit enhancement techniques to achieve this objectives.

Hedging Situation: The company is a manufacturer of steel products that earns revenues in U.S. dollars, while having its foreign debt predominantly in Japanese yen, thus creating a substantial unhedged currency exposure. This has affected the company's profitability and debt service capability.

Hedging Objective: IFC's aim is to help the company eliminate the largest possible amount of currency mismatch risk while seeking to share the credit exposure with market counterparties; IFC would thereby retain some credit limit in order to assist the company with its other financial needs. The company would gain also from entering into a direct transaction with a market counterparty, thus broadening its market access.

EXHIBIT 3   IFC Gives Swap Guarantee

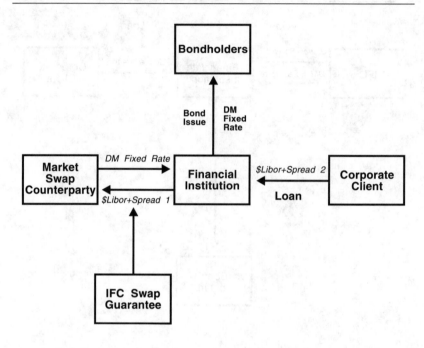

Hedging Strategy: The company would enter into a currency swap transaction directly with a market counterparty. IFC would provide credit enhancement through a partial guarantee of this swap obligation to the market counterparty (MC), who would assume the remaining swap risks in excess of the partial IFC guarantee amount. The share of the swap exposure guaranteed by IFC would be defined through discussions with the market counterparty to reach the required level of comfort that would make the transaction feasible for all three parties to it. See Exhibit 4.

In conclusion, it is clear that companies have a significant economic interest in managing financial risks. The markets have developed a wide range of strategies and instruments to help the concerned financial manager do his job well. However, companies in developing countries, with limited exceptions, have not gained sufficient access to the markets to permit them to adequately manage financial risks. There is a need to bridge that gap in

EXHIBIT 4

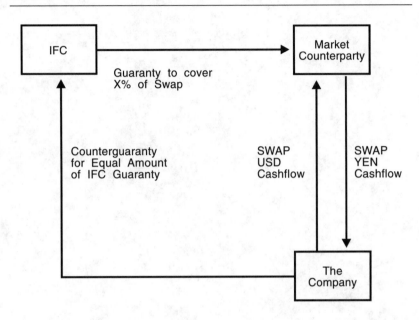

unmet demand, which fits naturally the role and capabilities of the International Finance Corporation. IFC, however, is primarily a catalyst, and, to carry out its mandate, it is seeking to join forces with international financial institutions that have the expertise and capability to provide hedging strategy advice and derivative instruments to developing country private enterprises. IFC would play the roles of intermediation and credit enhancement agent.

18

Derivatives
and the World Bank

Afsaneh Mashayekhi-Beschloss
Senior Manager, Derivatives and Liability Management Division,
Financial Operations Department, World Bank

Arun Muralidhar
Financial Officer, Derivatives and Liability Management Division,
Financial Operations Department, World Bank

The World Bank, which over the years has acquired the reputation of being an innovator by introducing new products like the global bond concept, has on numerous occasions been credited for having transacted the first-ever currency swap with IBM in 1981. While other similar transactions had been attempted, this celebrated public swap transaction paved the way for a new genre and approach to the World Bank's funding operations by reducing its reliance on direct funding operations in any market and opening new vistas for the Bank to acquire liabilities in a particular currency. The World Bank has come a long way from that path-breaking combination of a five-year CHF-USD and DEM-USD transaction for a total of USD 203 million and the swap book today boasts 582 transactions (including currency and interest rate swaps and swaps to hedge structured transactions), with a maturity spectrum ranging from one to 15 years, for a total notional volume of approximately USD 34 billion with 133 counterparties worldwide. The size and diversity of this book, when viewed in the context of the World Bank being an end user, demonstrates the evolution that has taken place, not only in the World Bank's funding operations, but also in the global financial markets.

The World Bank serves in the role of a cooperative pass-through institution, whereby the capital of the Bank, which is provided by the member countries, is used as a base for cost-efficient funding to finance development projects in client countries. Under the Articles of Agreement, the Bank must

The views and opinions expressed in this article represent the views of the authors and not the World Bank.

maintain a gearing ratio of 1:1—which means that the total loans outstanding plus effective guarantees cannot exceed capital plus reserves. Given this premise, the Bank's funding needs are determined by the loan products that are made available to the borrowing countries. At present, the Bank's main loan product has a fixed ratio of three major currencies/currency groups—USD, JPY, and the DEM group (which includes a majority of DEM and some CHF and Dutch guilder [NLG])—so that our clients can, for planning purposes, view the Bank loan as subloans in all three currencies. The Bank is committed to lend in fixed proportions of these three currencies. The lending rate is quite stable since the source of funds is overwhelmingly fixed rate borrowings of five to 10 years maturity. A new product—single currency LIBOR-based loan funding in either USD, DEM, JPY, STG (pound sterling), or FFR—which was approved by the Board in 1993, is now being offered to the Bank's clients. The Bank has continuous and ongoing lending relationships with a substantial volume of loans committed, and on average with new commitments of approximately USD 15 billion per year. Liabilities have been broadly diversified and, with outstanding liabilities of USD 97 billion, USD 94 billion is represented by liabilities of medium- and long-term fixed rate funding in 25 currencies.

Swaps are used in a whole host of ways to support and complement the funding operations. To provide the funds for these loans, the Bank uses its AAA rating to borrow extensively in the world's capital markets and, where necessary, uses currency swaps to transform the borrowed currency into one of the three primary lending currencies—USD, DEM, and JPY, and on occasion into CHF and NLG. For example, the Bank, in yet another path-breaking transaction in March 1994, issued the first-ever Greek drachma (GRD) bond with an associated currency swap. This allowed the Bank to obtain USD funding at an attractive all-in cost and opened the door to other swap-driven GRD issues. The costs of borrowing either directly in these currencies or through a vehicle currency and swapping it into the required target currency are passed to the borrowers on a cost pass-through basis. The Bank, being a non-profit institution, earns a small spread on its loans to defray the costs of its operations. In addition, the Bank uses interest rate swaps to fix floating positions, which allows for the separation of the funding and the rate fixing decisions, thereby enabling the Bank's objectives of borrowing when market conditions are attractive and averaging costs throughout the year. In the last two years, in keeping with its policy of funding on a fully-hedged basis, the Bank has entered into swaps that have converted the cash flows associated with structured notes with plays on interest and exchange rates into plain vanilla funding. Swaps have also been used to allow the Bank to manage existing liabilities efficiently by shifting from one target currency back into a core currency in small volumes. This occurs primarily for cost/risk considerations. An example is moving out of NLG (a target currency) and into DEM (a core currency) because of the relative stability of the DEM/NLG exchange rate and the higher nominal interest rate in NLG.

A perspective on the size of the Bank's annual borrowing operations and the impact of using swaps is provided by examining the Bank's activities in the last fiscal year. During the fiscal year ending June 30, 1993, the Bank borrowed about USD 12.7 billion in 12 currencies. The currency swap program totalled about USD 3.6 billion equivalent, involving nine vehicle currencies into DEM. These swaps were transacted with 19 counterparties, and the average arbitrage savings relative to the notional cost of simultaneous direct market borrowings in the target currencies was 40 basis points. The use of swap transactions has helped the Bank transfer the arbitrage gains and benefits accruing from its special access and fiscal status in certain markets and provide advantageous lending rates to our clients. This trend has continued into this fiscal year with the addition of yet another funding currency (GRD).

While arbitrage gains have declined as markets have developed, and the Bank no longer enjoys special access in countries where it used to, the traditional borrowing program has been complemented by a growing structured note issuance program that allows the Bank to use its strong credit rating to issue notes with embedded derivatives. This increase in structured bond issuance has followed in the wake of the growth and development of the structured bond market worldwide. In addition to providing investors with an avenue to express exchange and interest rate views through the purchase of paper issued by a high-quality borrower, the Bank has gone a step further to design and implement a liquidity facility that provides two facets previously lacking in the secondary market for structured notes: price transparency and liquidity.

The newly implemented Global Multicurrency Note Program (GMNP) has two components to it: flexible issuance and enhancement of secondary market trading in structured bonds. In order to respond to market conditions and investors' needs in a timely fashion, the Bank has set in place a vehicle with streamlined government consent access, which allows for the issuance of individual tranches of structured bonds of maturities ranging from three months to perpetuity, for sizes as small as USD 10 million, in a host of different currencies, and with a choice of (i) clearing and settlement facilities, (ii) listing on exchanges, (iii) governing law, and (iv) form (i.e., registered, book-entry, or bearer). The second component of the GMNP, or the Liquidity Facility as it is called, has the support of seven globally-positioned sponsoring dealers. Under the Liquidity Facility, the Bank guarantees these seven

431

dealers that it will exchange outstanding structured notes (issued under the program) that investors sell to the dealers for a stock of World Bank FRNs at any time. Such a guarantee has, to date, not been offered by other issuers who usually engage in buy-backs on a best-efforts basis or only when there is a positive income implication. In exchange for this guarantee, all seven dealers have made a commitment to post indicative bid-side cash prices that will be updated daily on specially designed Reuters and Bloomberg screens for nearly all notes issued by the Bank under the GMNP, regardless of whether these deals were brought to the market by them or any ad hoc dealer. The exceptions to the secondary market-making activities, which will be very few, will pertain to those transactions that involve an exotic currency or an interest rate that one of these dealers may not be making a market in presently. It is expected that by having recourse to the back-stop facility provided by the World Bank, these seven dealers will be in a position to offer investors regular secondary market prices for outstanding World Bank structured notes that will not only be in competition with one another, but also be favorable to those offered in the asset swap market. (The latter is likely to be true, because in the asset swap market investors usually require LIBOR-plus returns on the synthetic FRNs that are created from the structured note to compensate for the credit risk of the reverse derivative, while World Bank FRNs trade below LIBOR).

The popular press has, in recent weeks, been replete with stories on the impact of derivatives on market volatility and corporate profitability. In addition, regulatory agencies have also been examining whether or not increased supervision is needed in this area. The Bank, as an end-user, uses derivatives on its liabilities to diversify funding sources. It also uses these instruments for risk management purposes as a way of lowering exposure to market risk by converting the market risk of these transactions into credit risk. Since the Bank has designed its business around the overriding concern of high prudential standards, it seeks to substantially limit credit risk. Of course, there is a flip side to this: Using risk-minimizing tools and conservative credit policies limits the types of transactions that can be entered into, as well as the universe of counterparties that the Bank can deal with. This generally reduces the possibilities to maximize arbitrage and creates credit line problems for which innovative solutions need to be found.

Credit has become a scarce resource for the execution of the Bank's derivatives, and this situation is no different from that of other AAA end-users with conservative credit management policies that have a longstanding presence in the market and a large annual swap program. The Bank has a credit risk management system that combines conservative credit line management with a select group of counterparties with regular monitoring of the credit exposure of the entire portfolio. The Bank relies primarily on a high minimum credit rating for counterparties which minimizes expected loss and the need for loss provisioning, and hence the Bank only deals with AA or better-rated institutions and sovereigns. Further, among other policies, the Bank uses three types of credit limits that minimize the variance of loss: (i) first, a USD limit for each counterparty on the sum total of current and potential exposure. This limit is determined as a function of the rating and the financial parameters of each institution; (ii) second, there is a maximum cap on the magnitude of the limit just mentioned, irrespective of credit rating and asset size of the institution; and (iii) third, there is a cap on the total aggregate potential exposure to any given counterparty, measured as a percentage of the total potential exposure of the portfolio.

In addition, the Bank embarked on a major project to revisit potential exposure calculations of plain vanilla swaps to bring them in line with recent developments in the design and modeling of exposure. This was complemented by an initiative to have in-house technology to price and evaluate the credit exposure of the more complex structured transactions. After conducting a survey of market practices, there is confidence that the present methodology being employed to evaluate the credit exposure of swaps is consistent with best market practices in the industry, and that the Bank is very conservative in this area.

In summary, the last 13 years have witnessed a fascinating transition, not only in the size and volume but also in the nature of derivatives transactions entered into by the Bank. On the one hand, the universe of currencies in which the Bank would enter into a swap has expanded gradually and is expected to continue to expand as other countries develop their capital markets to encourage international participation. On the other, the degree of complexity of transactions has increased, especially with the growth of the structured bond market, and the Bank has responded by instituting a prudent and conservative credit risk policy and implementing a sophisticated credit exposure management system. Finally, with ever-evolving global financial markets, the World Bank continues to expect that it will be a major player and innovator and continue to provide value to the participants in the financial markets and its member countries, while at the same time being cognizant of its primary goal of being a provider of cost-efficient funds for development projects in developing countries.

Derivative Financial Instruments: Development and Use at VIAG's Treasury

Hans Gisbert Ulmke
Treasurer, Continental Can Europe

VIAG is a national holding company founded by the German government after the First World War with the aim of combining energy-producing entities with energy-consuming production facilities. It holds major stakes in companies such as Bayernwerk (38.5 percent), Thyssengas (50 percent), Innwerk (100 percent), VAW aluminum AG (100 percent), and SKW (100 percent), achieving a turnover of around DM 10.0 billion. VIAG went public in the period of 1986 to 1988. Since then some important takeovers have doubled this figure, and the group now operates some 500 companies around the world.

Whereas the responsibility of the operational results lies with each individual entity, VIAG, as a holding company, assures a high financial status combined with strategic leadership.

The VIAG Treasury group is now organized as a service center in which the entire spectrum of financial know-how is combined and made available to the group companies. Even though group companies run their own treasuries to take care of the day-to-day business, VIAG is responsible for the major tasks such as capital market issues and asset and liability management.

The treasury consists of a team of twelve, half of whom are involved in assessing financial risks and finding hedging solutions. This is a demanding task considering the wide spectrum of fields the group is engaged in. Rising electricity prices for the aluminum producer and processor VAW have immediate negative P&L effects, whereas the same development positively influences our power-producing entities Bayernwerk, Innwerk, and Thyssengas.

This chapter was written when Mr. Ulmke was Treasurer & Senior Vice President - Finance at VIAG.

EXHIBIT 1   VIAG

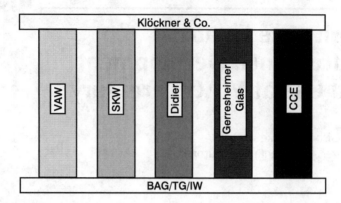

Even though the group's structure seemingly neutralizes this exposure, the time factor on the one side and idiosyncrasies on the other must be taken care of in order to avoid unwanted P&L results at the end of the financial year. The strategy therefore is to find solutions that benefit both the individual companies as well as, more importantly, the holding entity.

The "In-House-Bank" structure of the treasury allows adequate closeness to the financial markets and at the same time fosters an understanding of the needs of operational companies. The prime duty is to assure sufficient funding at minimum cost at all times. As a multinational PLC, VIAG regularly taps the capital market with bonds, warrants, and new shares. Professional investor relations combined with attractive pricing form the basis to this task. Surplus cash is spread—if not used within the group—between bank deposits and corporate paper. Some 90 percent of our corporate investments are in the Euromarket, notably in Euro-Commercial Paper where the pickup in yield is 10 to 20 basis points. The basic criterion is a minimum rating of A1 and no more than 10.0 million U.S. dollars (USD) per issuer. The majority of such assets are swapped into DM.

VIAG's high credit standing also allows better pricing when group companies tap the capital market with their own Euro-commercial paper or commercial paper programs. The treasury not only advises on structure and contract details but also works out interest rate and foreign exchange hedging strategies. Extensive financial reporting by group companies to the holding company form the basis of any proposal put forward by the treasury. The hedge itself may not necessarily be carried out by VIAG but occasionally by the individual companies themselves.

The treasury assesses all cash flows and takes a view on possible interest rate movement. It then decides what amount of risk it is prepared to take and decides on hedging techniques, instruments, and trigger timing. The new position is constantly monitored and new strategies put in place should markets take an adverse turn. For this VIAG calculates daily the duration of the "In-House-Bank" balance sheet and breaks all interest rate transactions down to their present value, allowing the PVBP (Present Value per Basis Point) to evolve. We believe this method to be fairly accurate especially as it avoids mixing apples with pears in regard to derivatives. A set of guidelines sets forth the goals that are to be achieved at given times and, further, the maximum deviation from these goals during the period. They also govern the duration of any hedging product used and stipulate both the method of valuation and the frequency of "what if" analysis. The outcome is reported to the Board of Management and to the Controlling Department. One essential point is, and this goes without saying, that only underlying positions may be hedged. This in our view differentiates "In-House-Banks" or "Service Centers" from "Profit Centers."

Conflicts arise when market views of group companies differ from those of the treasury. For example, a company may wish to fund for a six-month period, while the treasury, also believing in rising interest rates, prefers placing funds for a shorter period, for instance, three months. This conflict of interest may be solved if VIAG sells a three-month Euro-DM future, or more easily, buys a floating rate agreement of three months against six months. In case longer periods need to be hedged, interest swaps form an ideal tool for coverage.

A typical situation for VIAG arises when new funds have been made available after an increase of capital or bond issue. These funds in turn are placed with group companies. The interest rate risk consists of unmatched positions where long-term funds are placed at short term. This risk may be reduced by an interest rate swap where VIAG receives a fixed rate (coupon rate) and pays LIBOR, which it receives from the group company. This works perfectly as long as both positions exist but may become obsolete when either the bond is called or the short-term funds are paid back. In this case, the swaps would need to be reversed, which in today's liquid market is easy to do.

Swap portfolios may, because of consistently changing cash flows, consist of a large number of transactions, which in turn vary in amount, duration, and interest rate. As explained earlier, by present valuing each swap, it is possible to create a macrohedge that equalizes all cash flows to the value required. Markets have developed rapidly within the last two years providing macrohedges for almost all eventualities. Swaps of the second and third generation, some with fancy names, have been developed not only by banks but also by users such as VIAG. If future cash flows can be predicted precisely enough, a "forward swap," "amortizing swap," or "step-up-swap" may well suit the situation, whereby either a single flow or reducing or increasing flows respectively are included in the hedging strategy.

Not all cash flows are exactly predefined; the timing or the amount may vary. At VIAG the turnover of a number of companies depends on yet another variable, namely aluminum prices at the London Mercantile Exchange (LME). The interest rate exposure of future, partly undefined cash flows is hedged by swaptions, which are options on swaps. As with any option they may be but need not be exercised at maturity. Should the expected cash flow not take place, the swaption expires or is sold for cash. The premium paid is normally well spent, especially if the swap period is long.

Again the priority in the use of this tool lies with the uncertainty of the cash flow, where the portfolio manager is hedged should the flow occur.

When we buy interest rate options, we already are aware of the movement of funds and solely wish to reduce the interest rate exposure, or when selling options, taking positions on future developments. Recently when a large export contract became imminent, our sales group was very reluctant to spend any premium up-front for an interest rate hedge. The sale contract itself promised a good return. Instead we bought a contingent swaption where the

EXHIBIT 2   Contingent Swaption

VIAG buys a 1- against 5-years Payer Swaption
at the money spot: DM 8.50%
at the money forward: DM 8.00%

Strike Price (annual bond 30/360)	Normal Swaption Basis Points (1)	Contingent Swaption Basis Points	
		(1)	(2)
7.50%	227	262	287
7.75%	160	221	242
8.00%	107	192	210
8.25%	69	175	192
8.50%	44	174	191

(1) Present value
(2) Future value as normally quoted

premium—even though slightly higher—is due when the option is exercised, which is compulsory when the option is at- or in-the-money. See Exhibit 2.

Many interest rate derivatives have developed on the commodity and foreign exchange floor. The combination of interest rate and foreign exchange products provides yet another hedging possibility. The following example illustrates this.

The buyer of raw material based in USD pays the forward points for future demand reluctantly. Internal regulations require him to buy his USD demand regularly on a six-months basis. In order to reduce the swap premium to zero, we bought a DM/USD interest rate index swap with a lifetime of three years. In this scenario VIAG pays USD LIBOR plus a margin in DM and receives DM LIBOR. Because of the presently contrary interest rate curves, VIAG receives cash up front. This cash amount subsidizes the swap premium the buyer of USD has to pay and reduces the cost of buying USD six-months forward to zero. Whereas the advantages are clear, the risk lies in flattening interest rate curves to a point where forward swap premiums become negative. In this case the buyer of USD could not take advantage of this change. See Exhibits 3, 4, and 5.

EXHIBIT 3   Contingent Payer Swaption

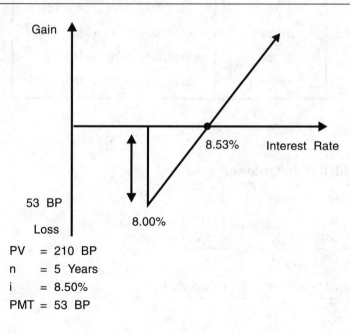

PV   = 210 BP
n   = 5 Years
i   = 8.50%
PMT = 53 BP

EXHIBIT 4   Index Swap

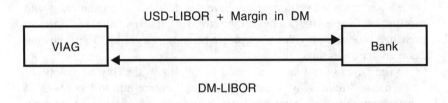

USD-LIBOR + Margin in DM

| VIAG | | Bank |

DM-LIBOR

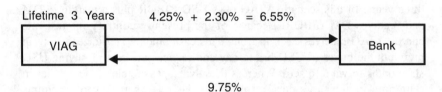

Lifetime 3 Years   4.25% + 2.30% = 6.55%

| VIAG | | Bank |

9.75%

Interest Rate Advantage 3.20%

Period	Margin
2 Years	6M-USD-LIBOR + 325 BP
3 Years	6M-USD-LIBOR + 230 BP
4 Years	6M-USD-LIBOR + 160 BP
5 Years	6M-USD-LIBOR + 130 BP

EXHIBIT 5   Index-Swap

VIAG buys *6 months* forward

Spot 1.6600	+1.60% Gain on Index Swap
Swap 0.0470	−2.83% Forward premium
Forward Fx: 1.7070	1.23%
enhanced forward rate	USD 1.6804

VIAG group companies are using interest rate caps and floors on a regular basis. The combinations of buying one and selling the other at different strike prices, so-called collars, have proven to be good alternatives to straight swaps. Given the high DM interest rates in Germany, the use of this instrument is now small.

Another instrument useful for taking advantage of the inverse DM interest rate curve is the trigger swap. The treasury hedges pension funds' cash with interest rate swaps, thus assuring long-term yields even though the cash may be used within the group.

Because of the inverse interest rate curve, the swap returns are inferior to short-term deposits. A three-year trigger swap allows us to receive three-month DM LIBOR plus a margin, while paying out three-month LIBOR of at least 8 percent. If LIBOR stays above 8 percent (presently 9.75 percent), the bank may cancel the swap after two years, and in return we receive a 40 basis point enhancement. This extra income subsidizes the other swap structures, giving the whole portfolio a better performance. See Exhibit 6.

EXHIBIT 6   Trigger Swap

3-Month-LIBOR versus 3-Month LIBOR Plus Margin
Lifetime: 3-Years

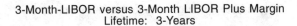
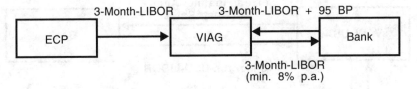

Strike 3-M-LIBOR	Premium Without Trigger	Premium With Trigger
7.75%	+ 40 BP	+ 55 BP
8.00%	+ 75 BP	+ 95 BP
8.25%	+ 120 BP	+ 145 BP

The Bank May Cancel the Swap After 2 Years
(Trigger Effect).

As stated before, risk management has become more important to VIAG. The treasury plays an important role when it comes to creating hedging possibilities for risk positions that before were facts of life. VAW, the aluminum conglomerate, had some important financing to set up for the expansion of an aluminum smelter in Australia.

The cash income of the local company solely depends on the metal price at the LME when the aluminum is sold. The higher the LME, the higher the revenue. Taking this point, VIAG set up two strategies that had one point in common: If the LME price is low, less interest is paid, i.e., below market rate. Should the LME rise to levels where the companies do better, a higher than market rate is affordable. The first structure is an aluminum interest rate swap with presently a lifetime of three years (see Exhibit 7). The underlying loans were arranged separately, the interest rates are LIBOR based, and the cash flows matched with the swap. Exhibit 8 shows the swap structure in comparison to the fixed rate for a standard loan. VAW is thus hedged when

EXHIBIT 7   Interest Rate–Aluminum Swap

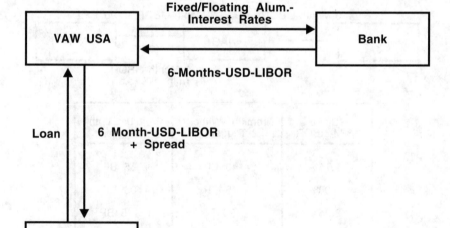

Target: Link funding costs to the Aluminum price

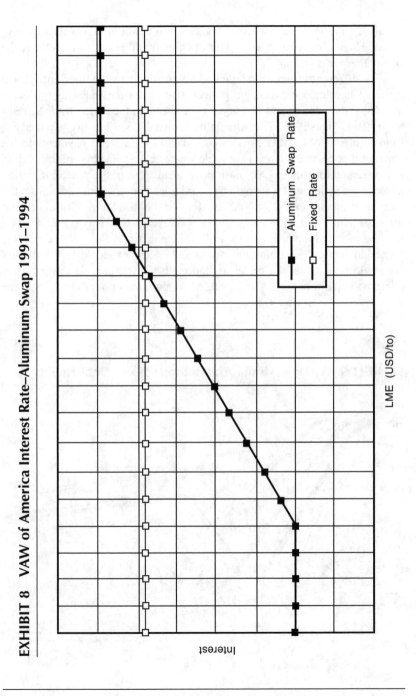

EXHIBIT 8   VAW of America Interest Rate–Aluminum Swap 1991–1994

the aluminum prices fall, whereas higher levels result in higher interest payments. Having wide experience with the aluminum market, we feel that the advantages are dominant.

A different structure needed to be arranged for another entity also involved in the same expansion project. It includes the financing with five individual drawdowns and five equal repayments in the period from November 1991 to June 1996. The Aluminum Indexed Loan Facility was derived from former "Gold Loans"; in our case it links the interest payments to the aluminum price, and interest is payable when the installments are due. Again the average three-month LME cash price is taken from the preceding period in order not to depend on a single day's pricing. The structure varies from the swap as it includes more of VAW's view on the development of aluminum prices. Having sold an aluminum cap at a level that is very unlikely to be reached, we used the premium to subsidize the rest of the curve. The result is higher interest when aluminum prices fall below expected levels, highly favorable rates when the price predictions become true, and again higher interests, but still below a fixed loan, when aluminum prices climb to above those levels (see Exhibit 9).

EXHIBIT 9   VAW Australia Aluminum Indexed Debt Facility

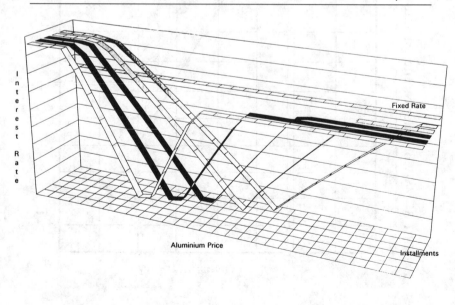

The performance is best when the target prices are reached three months before the different repayment dates, where the savings can be as large as 60 percent compared to a fixed rate loan. Exhibit 9 shows five lines, one for each drawdown and repayment and a sixth line to mark the swap rate for that period.

These two structures show how global risk can be managed and reduced to a chosen level. Markets are beginning to develop a feeling for the corporates' needs. Banks these days are making great efforts to create solutions together with their customers rather than offering standard solutions that often do not fulfill exactly the requirements. One needs to bear in mind that custom solutions need much more time to set up than others. Whereas the developed structure may suit the treasurer's needs fully, the accountant's or tax advisor's views may be different. This is a major drawback when markets are volatile and perfect timing almost impossible.

VIAG is working on structured solutions for other areas of the group, too. One major risk is defining and pricing the risk. Once a price tag is found, we quantify the amount of risk that we wish to take and develop strategies to eliminate the unwanted portion. In our view the markets for hedging numerous commodities are nearly perfect. Our treasury now looks more at opportunities to combine, say, commodities with interest rates or even combining two or more commodities to form one package. We feel that in this area much more development has to be done; but then, looking back to where we were a few years ago, the innovative skills of all market users will most certainly take us to where we wish to go.

20

Asset and Liability Management in Building Societies: Successfully Using Off Balance Sheet Products

Mark Abbott
Head of Corporate Finance, Bristol & West Building Society (UK)

I would like to lay down some general principles about balance sheet management that work for Bristol & West, which has developed to be one of the most product innovative institutions within the financial services arena. I will then explore how we have used derivative products to launch products on both sides of the balance sheet.

ASSET LIABILITY MANAGEMENT IN BUILDING SOCIETIES

Asset and liability management in a building society concerns the following two issues (see Exhibit 1):

1. Managing the spread between mortgages and liquidity, on one hand, and retail and wholesale funding on the other. We always know that if we, as an industry, get greedy and do not manage the mortgage rate versus LIBOR spread the centralized lenders will re-enter the market aggressively as they did in the mid-1980s and steal market share; and

2. Fee income is becoming increasingly important. Structural change in the industry has caused spreads on traditional business to decline,

___

This chapter was first produced in 1991.

EXHIBIT 1   ABC Building Society
The Transformation of Assets by Liabilities Funding

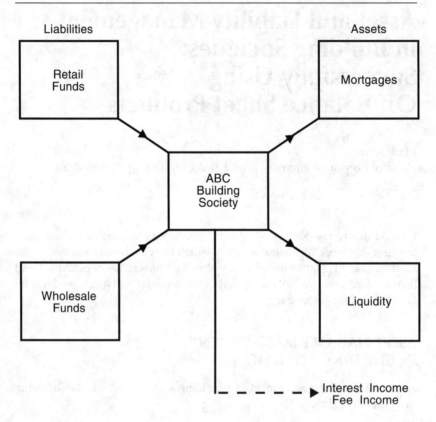

and a greater awareness of the true cost of capital has caused capital to become more scarce. Organizations realize fees don't use much capital.

As a consequence, cross subsidization is taking place, where product profitability is only justified on the basis of the additional fee income earned over and above the interest margin.

Of course there are other major issues, such as managing default risks and business risks from diversification, but these will not be explored in this chapter.

The role of a building society involves managing the interest margin and necessarily involves some transformation in the terms of the funds employed in the business. Thus, any building society's balance sheet inevitably achieves an inexact mismatch of assets and liabilities as to interest rate determination, maturities, and sensitivity to capital value variation. Nevertheless, because building societies offer a relatively small range of products and services, they are exposed to less potential mismatch risks than most commercial banks. The two most important risks are interest mismatches and maturity mismatches.

INTEREST MISMATCH

Relative to most banks, the typical balance sheet structure for a building society is very simple. Stripped to its elements, the composition of an average building society balance sheet in 1991 comprises three categories of rates and is depicted below (see Exhibit 2).

- Variable administered rates
- Variable LIBOR rates
- Fixed rates

Once the building society balance sheet is re-ordered from the consolidated statement to these matched components, one can begin to quantify what the overall effect of a change in interest rates will be on the revenue and capital position of the Society.

Only once this interest rate exposure is measured can one make product or hedging decisions that give true competitive advantage. Product design on nonadministered rate business has to be the responsibility of the treasury, because Societies are effectively cash factories that provide added value to the basic cash products, which are at variable administered rates.

THE FOUR PORTFOLIO APPROACH

Exhibit 3 shows a 1990 consolidated balance sheet for Bristol & West. It is very difficult to determine the extent of the interest mismatch and where Bristol & West makes a margin.

However, Exhibit 4 shows the balance sheet of Bristol & West split by portfolio using the above category of rate, and it is much easier to see the extent of the interest mismatch.

EXHIBIT 2   Composition of a Typical Building Society's Balance Sheet 1991

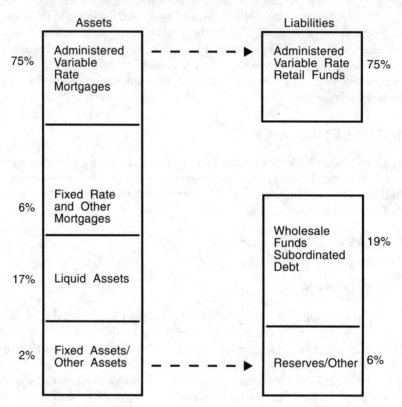

Source: UBS Phillips & Drew.

The four portfolios comprise:

Portfolio (i):

- Variable administered rate mortgages funded by variable administered rate savings.

Typically, in a U.K. Society, 75 percent of a Society's liabilities are administered variable rate retail funds matched by administered rate mortgages. As can be seen in Exhibit 4, in November 1990 Bristol & West

EXHIBIT 3 Bristol & West Building Society, Group Balance Sheet

Assets		Liabilities and Reserves	
	1990	Shares and deposits	
	£000	Retail funds & deposits	3,856,731
Liquid assets	953,674	Non-retail funds	
Commercial assets		and deposits	1,379,205
Advances secured on		Total shares	
residential property	4,321,001	and deposits	5,235,936
Other advances		Other liabilities	
secured on land	180,589	and charges	83,629
Other commercial		Provisions for liabilities	
assets	100	and charges	4,804
		Subordinated liabilities	60,024
Total commercial			
assets	4,501,690	Total liabilities	5,384,393
Fixed assets	170,967	Reserves	
Other assets	20,281	General reserve	186,387
		Revaluation reserve	75,757
		Total reserves	262,144
		Minority interests	75
		TOTAL LIABILITIES	
TOTAL ASSETS	5,646,612	AND RESERVES	5,646,612

showed an administered margin of £1.75 on 65 percent of the balance sheet; this margin is subject to the vagaries of the market and is price led by the Halifax, Abbey National, and Nationwide. However, the key point about this main portion of the balance sheet is that, given that administered rates are set at the discretion of the building society, there is a very high degree of control over this administered spread.

However, as a price follower in the U.K. mortgage market, Bristol & West needs to ensure that this administered margin is managed by our under-

EXHIBIT 4   Interest Rate Mismatch

BALANCE SHEET—NOVEMBER 1990 (BEFORE CASCADE)

	Assets £m.	Return %	Liabilities £m.	Cost %	Spread %
Book 1: Administered Rates	3750	14.5	3750	12.75	1.75
Book 2: Mismatch	600	14.5	600	14.00	0.50
Book 3: Short-term (<1 year) Floating Book	675	14.0	675	14.00	0.00
Book 4: Fixed Rate (>1 year)	600	10.0	600	1.75	8.25
	5635	13.94	5635	11.94	2.00

standing of the average and marginal pricing decisions on savings versus mortgages. This will depend on several issues, including:

- Flows in and out of the business.
- Transfers between accounts.
- The retail/wholesale mix.
- Lag effects between changes in mortgage and savings rates.

Accountability for the administered book must lie with the individual ultimately responsible for the mortgage and savings flows but managed like the other three portfolios by Treasury via the ALCO process.

Portfolio (ii):

- Variable administered rate mortgages funded by variable LIBOR rate wholesale funds (short-term).

The mismatch portfolio arises because of the excess of administered rate mortgages over retail savings in the U.K. The mismatch portfolio in

Exhibit 4 contains significant basis risk. The return to Bristol & West from this portfolio depends on how the mortgage rate LIBOR spread moves over time *and* the size of this portfolio.

There are various actions building societies can take to make this margin more dependable, as follows:

a. Introducing money market linked lending products, for example, on commercial lending. The effect of this is to grow the balance sheet by putting on assets that price off the same basis as wholesale funding.

   These matching assets and liabilities can thus be moved from the mismatch portfolio to the short-term variable (LIBOR linked) portfolio, i.e., portfolio (ii) to portfolio (iii).

b. Marketing fixed rates mortgages to existing administered rate customers at attractive and predetermined margins. The fixed rate assets subsequently put on the balance sheet are matched against the pre-existing fixed liability position or in the interest rate swap market for funding of the same maturity. The effect of this course of action is to move the matching assets and liabilities to the fixed rate portfolio from the mismatch portfolio. I will look at a specific example later on.

c. Engaging in mortgage rate/LIBOR swaps where the building society receives LIBOR plus a margin and pays mortgage rate.

   Broadly, there are agreements to exchange flows of interest on specified dates whereby counterparty A pays LIBOR plus a margin and counterparty B pays the mortgage rate determined by Investment Property Databank (IPD). Under a "quarterly quarterly" arrangement, LIBOR would be fixed at the beginning of each month and the average of the three fixings would be paid at the end of the quarter. IPD determines the mortgage rate by taking the average of the rates quoted by the top 10 building societies for standard variable mortgages after eliminating the top and bottom two rates.

   In order to lock in a profit margin on LIBOR funded administered rate mortgages, a perfect hedge would be achieved if, for example, fixing dates were set to coincide with re-fixes on a bond issue and the mortgage rates fixed by IPD coincided exactly with the Bristol & West mortgage rates (see Exhibit 5).

EXHIBIT 5   LIBOR/Mortgage Rate Swap

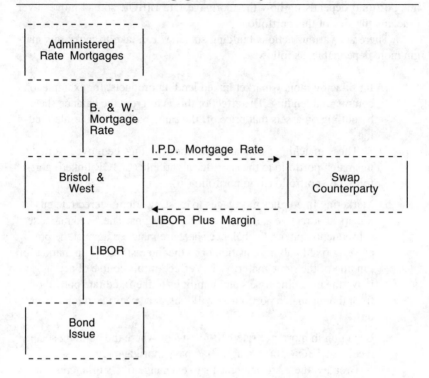

The risks to the margin once this swap has been effected are:

i. The Society's mortgage rate falling below the IPD rate due to:

    a. Commercial decisions.

    b. Timing of a rate change compared with other societies. If the Society engaging in the swap leads and lags more than the average of the top 10, the margin will obviously be enhanced (and vice versa).

ii. If there is no bond issue supporting the swap to match the variable leg, the margin would be affected if the Society failed to raise funds at the level at which LIBOR on the swap fixes. However, this is a risk inherent in any kind of swap, and a standard risk every treasury would expect to manage.

Questions that need to be addressed when considering this type of transaction include:

1. What is an attractive margin?
2. What will the size of the mismatch portfolio be in the future?
3. Over what period should the swap be struck?

If we now turn to the fixed rate portfolio, this gives us an excellent opportunity to market products such as fixed rate and capped rate mortgages to new customers. The fixed rate portfolio contains fixed rate assets such as mortgages, property, etc., and fixed rate liabilities such as free reserves, which are at zero cost because building societies do not pay dividends.

Any new product offering on the asset side can be managed against the existing liability position, resorting to the markets in cash and non-cash instruments to ensure exposure is kept in line with Board limits.

Our two PIBS issues increased our capital base and our average cost of capital but also gave us great opportunities in launching long-term fixed rate mortgages that are securitizable via the normal techniques.

MATURITY MISMATCH RISK

Apart from interest rate mismatch, the other major risk is maturity mismatch. Building societies lend for a period of 25 years, while nearly all retail funding can be withdrawn without notice. As we noted earlier, 75 percent of a Society's balance sheet is mismatched in this regard. However, most mortgages are redeemed within seven years, and they are not typically transferable between properties and/or vendor-purchasers.

Also, as UBS Phillips & Drew point out, in reality retail balances are extremely stable. The consequence of this is that the retail funding base of building societies provides each society with a stock of long-term funds to finance mortgage loans, and the extent of the maturity mismatch is, hence, reduced.

PRODUCT INNOVATION PROCESS

The product innovation process generally requires excellent communication of the yield curve internally and an understanding of the Society's business strategy by banks. Exhibit 6 shows that nonadministered rate innovation

EXHIBIT 6 Product Innovation Process

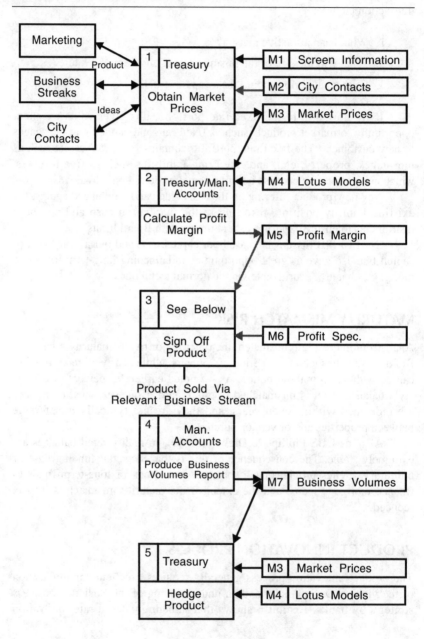

gives treasury a pivotal role both internally with the business streams and externally with the markets.

Discussions take place with representatives of the business streams and marketing daily, and treasury acts as a conduit for information between the city and the Society. All product ideas are evaluated using spreadsheet models, and successful ideas are signed off by relevant parties at the Asset & Liability Committee. Representatives of the business streams, marketing, finance, and treasury attend this forum to ensure all aspects of the product are covered; marketing for this purpose includes administration.

Once launched, the business volumes are monitored by finance, and the decision when and how much to hedge is made by treasury in line with the Board approved policy.

Other prerequisites are flexible systems and good administration. Bristol & West changed its core systems in 1991 to be more responsive to the customer. As the mortgage market continues to fragment and technology becomes more important, the product orientation of the late 1980s is replaced by a service oriented business, and products become a necessary but not sufficient condition for prosperity in the 1990s.

SPECIFIC PRODUCTS HEDGED VIA DERIVATIVE PRODUCTS

(i) Cascade

The first derivatives backed product I want to look at is Cascade, which offered a consumer proposition as follows:

"LENDERS TO REWARD THE FAITHFUL"

"Bristol & West Building Society was one of the first to make a special offer to existing borrowers when it launched its Cascade mortgages in November 1990.

This gave borrowers the chance to guarantee that their loan rate would fall by 3 percent over the next year from the standard (administered) rate prevailing at the time of 14.5 percent. The seven thousand who took the offer had their rates cut to 13.5 percent in February, 12.5 percent in May and to 12 percent in August. The final fall was to 11.5 percent in November.

Now that three months has expired, the borrowers neatly move on to the standard variable rate of 10.99 percent when that comes down next month."

THE TIMES

457

EXHIBIT 7 Cascade, Balance Sheet Effects

BEFORE CASCADE

	Assets £m.	Return %	Liabilities £m.	Cost %	Spread %
Book 2:					
Mismatch	600	14.5	600	14	0.5
Book 4:					
Fixed Rate	600	10.0	600	1.75	8.25

{£500m. moved from mismatch to fixed rate at a return of 14.5% and a cost of 13%. We also received a fee from every customer of £80}.

AFTER CASCADE

	Assets £m.	Return %	Liabilities £m.	Cost %	Spread %
Book 2:					
Mismatch	100	14.5	100	14	0.5
Book 4:					
Fixed Rate	1100	12.5	1100	6.9	5.6

£500m. @ £1.50 p.a. plus fees

Cascade was one of the first products a building society had marketed to its existing customer base. It was a situation where the international money markets were discounting a more aggressive view of mortgage rates than were in the retail market. By buying the international money market forward, using combinations of swaps and forward rate agreements, we were able to lock into a fixed margin in excess of 150 basis points but, more importantly, move several hundred million of administered rate mortgages from the mismatch portfolio to the fixed rate portfolio as Exhibit 7 illustrates. Effectively, by using swaps, we widened our margin and made it more dependable.

Cascade was so successful in moving customers from the mismatch portfolio to the fixed rate portfolio that we made several Cascade offers to new customers as well, using our fixed rate portfolio. In addition, we managed to lock out the product against our high cost wholesale money, our floating rate notes, using a series of forward rate agreements and swaps. To avoid gapping on maturity, we also transacted some basis swaps.

A typical hedging strategy was as follows:

1. Existing administered business switched to Cascade.

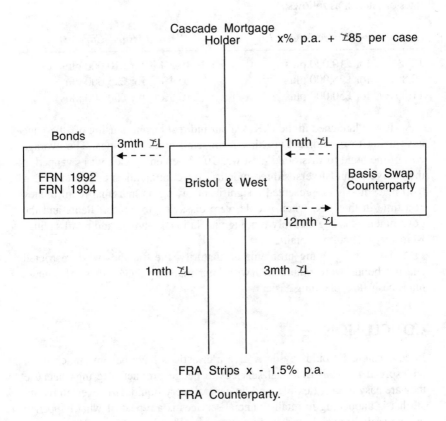

2. Bristol & West received x percent from the Cascade Mortgage holder and paid x – 1.5 percent in the FRA market. To guard against gapping, a basis swap was transacted.

In summary the product gave us a very high profile in the press with spin-off benefits, and many consumers benefited from the rate assurance Cascade gave them. Overall, Cascade improved Bristol & West's retail franchise.

(ii) Balmoral Fixed Rate Bond

The other derivatives backed product I want to look at is the Balmoral Fixed Rate Bond, which was a one-year savings product that offered tiered fixed rates of interest as follows:

(First Issue—Closed August 1992)	*(Second Issue—Current)*
10.6% for £10,000 plus	10.2% for £10,000 plus
10.8% for £25,000 plus	10.4% for £25,000 plus
11.00% for £50,000 plus	10.5% for £50,000 plus

It was launched in the U.K. via our indirect business using off-the-page advertising to minimize switching from retail branch savings. The average cost of the bond to Bristol & West was 10.83 percent, which was swapped in the one-year annual versus three-months market at an all-in cost below £L + 0.40 percent. This represented a significant saving on marginal retail money at a time in the U.K. when people were dissaving to pay off debts and the government was aggressively funding via National Savings and retail savings were very difficult to obtain.

To avoid gapping problems on maturity, the tranches were restricted and the bonds were relaunched with later maturity dates. This, of course, made cash-flow planning easier.

CONCLUSION

In conclusion, I would say derivative transactions have become much more widespread in retail financial services to hedge product offerings because they are easy to use, flexible, and, in general, very liquid. However, in reality all that is happening in retail financial services is a repeat of what happened in wholesale financial markets five years ago. That is, as the markets mature, derivative transactions became more commodity-like. Competitive advantage in retail financial services then accrues to organizations that:

i. Have low cost advantage, e.g., Cheltenham & Gloucester Building Society.

ii. Have the largest retail franchise and therefore price lead the market, e.g., Halifax Building Society and Abbey National.

iii. Best understand distribution systems and segmentation and can rent out distribution to City partners for product exploitation.

In conclusion, I would argue that it is often easier to take on fixed rate exposure in, say, the mortgage market than the treasury market because you start with the mortgage rate vs. LIBOR spread. However, it is then that good systems become important to accurately control mortgage pipeline risk and good communication matters between marketing and treasury departments to assure correct product offerings and pricings. A liquid derivatives market just makes this easier.

INDEX